T0233725

Lecture Notes in Computer Science   9732

Commenced Publication in 1973
Founding and Former Series Editors:
Gerhard Goos, Juris Hartmanis, and Jan van Leeuwen

More information about this series at http://www.springer.com/series/7409

.

Masaaki Kurosu (Ed.)

Human-Computer Interaction

Interaction Platforms and Techniques

18th International Conference, HCI International 2016
Toronto, ON, Canada, July 17–22, 2016
Proceedings, Part II

 Springer

Editor
Masaaki Kurosu
The Open University of Japan
Chiba-shi, Chiba
Japan

ISSN 0302-9743 ISSN 1611-3349 (electronic)
Lecture Notes in Computer Science
ISBN 978-3-319-39515-9 ISBN 978-3-319-39516-6 (eBook)
DOI 10.1007/978-3-319-39516-6

Library of Congress Control Number: 2016940127

LNCS Sublibrary: SL3 – Information Systems and Applications, incl. Internet/Web, and HCI

Printed on acid-free paper

This Springer imprint is published by Springer Nature
The registered company is Springer International Publishing AG Switzerland

Foreword

The 18th International Conference on Human-Computer Interaction, HCI International 2016, was held in Toronto, Canada, during July 17–22, 2016. The event incorporated the 15 conferences/thematic areas listed on the following page.

A total of 4,354 individuals from academia, research institutes, industry, and governmental agencies from 74 countries submitted contributions, and 1,287 papers and 186 posters have been included in the proceedings. These papers address the latest research and development efforts and highlight the human aspects of the design and use of computing systems. The papers thoroughly cover the entire field of human-computer interaction, addressing major advances in knowledge and effective use of computers in a variety of application areas. The volumes constituting the full 27-volume set of the conference proceedings are listed on pages IX and X.

I would like to thank the program board chairs and the members of the program boards of all thematic areas and affiliated conferences for their contribution to the highest scientific quality and the overall success of the HCI International 2016 conference.

This conference would not have been possible without the continuous and unwavering support and advice of the founder, Conference General Chair Emeritus and Conference Scientific Advisor Prof. Gavriel Salvendy. For his outstanding efforts, I would like to express my appreciation to the communications chair and editor of *HCI International News*, Dr. Abbas Moallem.

April 2016   Constantine Stephanidis

HCI International 2016 Thematic Areas and Affiliated Conferences

Thematic areas:

- Human-Computer Interaction (HCI 2016)
- Human Interface and the Management of Information (HIMI 2016)

Affiliated conferences:

- 13th International Conference on Engineering Psychology and Cognitive Ergonomics (EPCE 2016)
- 10th International Conference on Universal Access in Human-Computer Interaction (UAHCI 2016)
- 8th International Conference on Virtual, Augmented and Mixed Reality (VAMR 2016)
- 8th International Conference on Cross-Cultural Design (CCD 2016)
- 8th International Conference on Social Computing and Social Media (SCSM 2016)
- 10th International Conference on Augmented Cognition (AC 2016)
- 7th International Conference on Digital Human Modeling and Applications in Health, Safety, Ergonomics and Risk Management (DHM 2016)
- 5th International Conference on Design, User Experience and Usability (DUXU 2016)
- 4th International Conference on Distributed, Ambient and Pervasive Interactions (DAPI 2016)
- 4th International Conference on Human Aspects of Information Security, Privacy and Trust (HAS 2016)
- Third International Conference on HCI in Business, Government, and Organizations (HCIBGO 2016)
- Third International Conference on Learning and Collaboration Technologies (LCT 2016)
- Second International Conference on Human Aspects of IT for the Aged Population (ITAP 2016)

Conference Proceedings Volumes Full List

1. LNCS 9731, Human-Computer Interaction: Theory, Design, Development and Practice (Part I), edited by Masaaki Kurosu
2. LNCS 9732, Human-Computer Interaction: Interaction Platforms and Techniques (Part II), edited by Masaaki Kurosu
3. LNCS 9733, Human-Computer Interaction: Novel User Experiences (Part III), edited by Masaaki Kurosu
4. LNCS 9734, Human Interface and the Management of Information: Information, Design and Interaction (Part I), edited by Sakae Yamamoto
5. LNCS 9735, Human Interface and the Management of Information: Applications and Services (Part II), edited by Sakae Yamamoto
6. LNAI 9736, Engineering Psychology and Cognitive Ergonomics, edited by Don Harris
7. LNCS 9737, Universal Access in Human-Computer Interaction: Methods, Techniques, and Best Practices (Part I), edited by Margherita Antona and Constantine Stephanidis
8. LNCS 9738, Universal Access in Human-Computer Interaction: Interaction Techniques and Environments (Part II), edited by Margherita Antona and Constantine Stephanidis
9. LNCS 9739, Universal Access in Human-Computer Interaction: Users and Context Diversity (Part III), edited by Margherita Antona and Constantine Stephanidis
10. LNCS 9740, Virtual, Augmented and Mixed Reality, edited by Stephanie Lackey and Randall Shumaker
11. LNCS 9741, Cross-Cultural Design, edited by Pei-Luen Patrick Rau
12. LNCS 9742, Social Computing and Social Media, edited by Gabriele Meiselwitz
13. LNAI 9743, Foundations of Augmented Cognition: Neuroergonomics and Operational Neuroscience (Part I), edited by Dylan D. Schmorrow and Cali M. Fidopiastis
14. LNAI 9744, Foundations of Augmented Cognition: Neuroergonomics and Operational Neuroscience (Part II), edited by Dylan D. Schmorrow and Cali M. Fidopiastis
15. LNCS 9745, Digital Human Modeling and Applications in Health, Safety, Ergonomics and Risk Management, edited by Vincent G. Duffy
16. LNCS 9746, Design, User Experience, and Usability: Design Thinking and Methods (Part I), edited by Aaron Marcus
17. LNCS 9747, Design, User Experience, and Usability: Novel User Experiences (Part II), edited by Aaron Marcus
18. LNCS 9748, Design, User Experience, and Usability: Technological Contexts (Part III), edited by Aaron Marcus
19. LNCS 9749, Distributed, Ambient and Pervasive Interactions, edited by Norbert Streitz and Panos Markopoulos
20. LNCS 9750, Human Aspects of Information Security, Privacy and Trust, edited by Theo Tryfonas

Human-Computer Interaction

Program Board Chair: **Masaaki Kurosu, Japan**

- Jose Abdelnour-Nocera, UK
- Sebastiano Bagnara, Italy
- Simone Barbosa, Brazil
- Kaveh Bazargan, Iran
- Adriana Betiol, Brazil
- Simone Borsci, UK
- Michael Craven, UK
- Henry Duh, Australia
- Achim Ebert, Germany
- Xiaowen Fang, USA
- Stefano Federici, Italy
- Ayako Hashizume, Japan
- Wonil Hwang, Korea
- Yong Gu Ji, Japan
- Mitsuhiko Karashima, Japan
- Heidi Krömker, Germany
- Glyn Lawson, UK
- Tao Ma, USA
- Cristiano Maciel, Brazil
- Naoko Okuizumi, Japan
- Philippe Palanque, France
- Alberto Raposo, Brazil
- Eunice Sari, Indonesia
- Dominique Scapin, France
- Milene Selbach Silveira, Brazil
- Guangfeng Song, USA
- Hiroshi Ujita, Japan
- Fan Zhao, USA

The full list with the program board chairs and the members of the program boards of all thematic areas and affiliated conferences is available online at:

http://www.hci.international/2016/

HCI International 2017

The 19th International Conference on Human-Computer Interaction, HCI International 2017, will be held jointly with the affiliated conferences in Vancouver, Canada, at the Vancouver Convention Centre, July 9–14, 2017. It will cover a broad spectrum of themes related to human-computer interaction, including theoretical issues, methods, tools, processes, and case studies in HCI design, as well as novel interaction techniques, interfaces, and applications. The proceedings will be published by Springer. More information will be available on the conference website: http://2017. hci.international/.

General Chair
Prof. Constantine Stephanidis
University of Crete and ICS-FORTH
Heraklion, Crete, Greece
E-mail: general_chair@hcii2017.org

http://2017.hci.international/

Contents – Part II

Mobile and Wearable Interaction

Multi-platform, Migratory and Distributed Interfaces

Gesture, Motion-Based and Eye-gaze Based Interaction

Combining Low-Cost Eye Trackers for Dual Monitor Eye Tracking

Sebastian Balthasar[1], Manuel Martin[2], Florian van de Camp[2(✉)],
Jutta Hild[2], and Jürgen Beyerer[2]

[1] University of Applied Sciences Karlsruhe, Karlsruhe, Germany
[2] Fraunhofer IOSB, Karlsruhe, Germany
`florian.vandecamp@iosb.fraunhofer.de`

Abstract. The increasing use of multiple screens in everyday use creates a demand for multi-monitor eye tracking. Current solutions are complex and for many use cases prohibitively expensive. By combining two, low-cost single monitor eye trackers, we have created a dual monitor eye tracker requiring only minor software modifications from the single monitor version. The results of a user study, which compares the same eye trackers in a single monitor and a dual monitor setup, show that the combined system can accurately estimate the user's gaze across two screens. The presented approach gives insight into low-cost alternatives for multi-monitor eye tracking and provides a basis for more complex setups, incorporating even more screens.

1 Introduction and Related Work

Today, typical input devices for computer systems are mouse and keyboard. Over the years, several techniques for user-interface enhancement have been investigated. Eye gaze tracking systems are such an enhancement [ZJ04], which provide input based on the current eye gaze of the user. In situations where manual input is challenging, e.g. due to physical limitations, gaze-based interaction provides a powerful alternative [HGB14]. Multi-monitor setups are becoming the norm and double-monitor systems are widespread in professional environments. Hence, it is worth considering gaze-based interaction also for multi-monitor setups. To our best knowledge, there are only sparse contributions on double monitor eye tracking [CXS+12], whether on how to build such a system or even on what performance such a system could provide. The few commercial solutions are prohibitively expensive for most use cases and require a complex setup.

We present an eye tracking system for a horizontal double-monitor setup. The system uses two self-designed remote single-monitor eye tracking devices using the pupil-corneal reflection method to determine the gaze position [QWLY13,GEVC04,HRF14]. We show how the system can be made robust agains depth changes and how the occuring interference between the eyetrackers can be compensated without degrading the performance.

© Springer International Publishing Switzerland 2016
M. Kurosu (Ed.): HCI 2016, Part II, LNCS 9732, pp. 3–12, 2016.
DOI: 10.1007/978-3-319-39516-6_1

Fig. 1. Eye tracker setup with high resolution Flea3 camera, Asus Xtion, IR Led clusters and processing unit.

2   Implementation

The eye tracking device consists of a Point Grey Flea3 camera with an IR band pass filter, one Asus Xtion PRO Live camera system, two IR-LED clusters, and one processing unit (Fig. 1). The detection pipeline consists of modules for face detection, pupil detection, corneal reflection detection, and gaze point determination. The basic approach is as follows: The RGB camera of the Asus Xtion is used to detect the face of the user. The bounding box is transferred to the camera image of the Flea3 by means of coordinate transformation between the two calibrated cameras. The rough areas around the eyes are then extracted from the high-resolution Flea3 image using basic facial geometric assumptions. These eye patches are then used to detect the pupil and the two corneal reflections caused by the IR-LED clusters. Afterwards, the pupil position and the corneal reflections are used to calibrate the system and to estimate the gaze (Fig. 2). The IR band pass filter is necessary because the Asus Xtion projects a pattern of IR dots into the scene (Fig. 3 top) which are hard to discern from the corneal reflections. The IR filter causes a darker image but removes any interference with the Asus Xtion (Fig. 3 bottom). In the following, we describe each of the steps in detail.

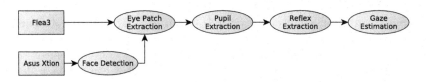

Fig. 2. The eye tracker processing pipeline, using the two image sources in parallel.

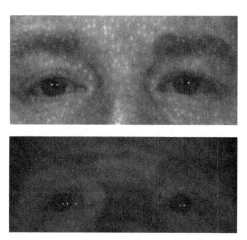

Fig. 3. IR pattern projected by the Asus Xtion (top), image with IR band pass filter (bottom)

2.1 Eye Patch Extraction

The first step in eye tracking is to find the eyes. To do this efficiently, a face detector is used on the color image of Asus Xtion. Based on the face detection the rough positions of the eyes (u_a, v_a) are determined. In addition to the position of the eyes the depth image of the Asus Xtion is used to extract the distance of the eyes (d_a) to the camera. Using this information and a device specific stereo calibration between the two cameras (C: Camera Matrix, T: Extrinsic Transformation) the eye positions in the Flea3 camera Image (u_f, v_f) can be computed by the following formula:

$$\begin{pmatrix} u_f \cdot w \\ v_f \cdot w \\ w \end{pmatrix} = C_f \cdot T \cdot C_a^{-1} \begin{pmatrix} u_a \cdot d_a \\ v_a \cdot d_a \\ d_a \end{pmatrix}, \quad \text{with } C = \begin{pmatrix} f_x & 0 & c_x \\ 0 & f_y & c_y \\ 0 & 0 & 1 \end{pmatrix} \quad (1)$$

The rough positions of the eyes in the Flea's Image are then used to extract the eyepatches shown in Fig. 6.

2.2 Pupil Detection

The detection of the pupil is based on the assumption that it is the darkest part of the image. As we do not work on the whole image at this stage of the processing pipeline, this assumption holds true in all cases we have come across. An implication of this assumption is that the pupil can be extracted from the image using a simple threshold. Depending on the head-pose of the user, height and position as well as eye color the best threshold is not only different from person to person but also changes while using the eye tracker. We therefore use an automatism to constantly adjust the threshold. The basic idea is that a low threshold will cause many foreground blobs while a high threshold will only leave few foreground pixels. Figure 4 shows these two cases. For every frame, the foreground pixels are analysed and if more than one foreground blob exists after basic cleanup using morphological operators, the current threshold is increased. If there is no foreground blob found, the current threshold is decreased. The constraints of what number of connected foreground pixels constitutes a blob can be configured by providing a minimum width and height of the bounding box of such a blob. A typical image for a good threshold can be seen on the very left of Fig. 5. The next image shows the resulting blob after erosion. The area of the resulting foreground blob is then analysed to find the center and minimal enclosing circle which are then used as the current estimate of the pupil position.

Fig. 4. A low threshold will cause many foreground pixels and blobs (left), a high threshold will only leave few foreground pixels (right)

Fig. 5. From left to right: Initial extraction of the pupil, erosion to remove scattered foreground pixels, analysis of blob area, center and minimum enclosing circle

2.3 Corneal Reflection Detection

The detection of the corneal reflections is similar to the detection of the pupil. However in case of the corneal reflections we assume they are the brightest parts of the image. The small size of the reflections cause an additional challenge as there might be additional reflections caused by tear fluid on the eyes (Fig. 3) which are hard to discern as the reflections just consist of a few bright foreground pixels. For this reason, in a first step, all reflections are detected using a threshold, in a second step the relative position of the reflections, as well as the position in relation to the position of the pupil, are taken into account to decide which reflections are the actual, direct corneal reflections. While in the case of the pupil a single blob is desireble, for the corneal reflections we need two for a single eye tracker and expect up to four in a dual monitor setup. The number of reflections is therefore used to adjust the threshold as less reflections than required are an indication for a high threshold and to many reflections are an indication for a low threshold.

2.4   Calibration and Gaze Estimation

For the estimate of the gaze point on the screen a calibration procedure is necessary. There are a wide variety of mapping functions employed by different research groups. We use a second order polynomial and a 9 point calibration pattern to map the vector between the center of the two corneal reflections and the center of the pupil (v_x, v_y) to screen coordinates(s_x, s_y). The polynomial is defined as:

$$s_x = a_0 + a_1 v_x + a_2 v_y + a_3 v_x v_y + a_4 v_x^2 + a_5 v_y^2,$$
$$s_y = a_6 + a_7 v_x + a_8 v_y + a_9 v_x v_y + a_{10} v_x^2 + a_{11} v_y^2,$$
$$(2)$$

The parameters a_0 - a_{11} are unknowns. Each of the 9 calibration points results in two equations resulting in an over-constrained system with 12 unknowns and 18 equations which is solved using least squares. To make the calibration more robust against outliers we collect, for each calibration point, a number of samples and take the pupil corneal reflection vector with the median length of all measures for calibration. As discussed in [MM05] this gaze mapping approach is robust against all rotations and translations in front of the eye tracker except for back and forth movement. This movement causes a length change of the pupil-corneal reflection vector without a real change of the gaze direction. The result is a deviation in the measurement which quickly degrades the performance of the results if the eye tracker is used without some kind of fixation for the head. A way to improve this is to normalize the length of the pupil-corneal reflection vector to a length that is independent of depth changes. The algorithm already has the distance of the head to the eye tracker from the depth image of the depth camera. The following function can be used to normalize the length of the vector v:

$$\hat{v} = (m \cdot d_a + b) \cdot v \qquad (3)$$

where m and b are unknown and need to be calibrated once per device. The calibration procedure is as follows. A test person sits in front of the uncalibrated eye tracker fixates a single point on the screen from different distances and takes some samples at each distance. Solving following equation results in the missing parameters:

$$m \cdot d_a + b = \frac{1}{||v||} \qquad (4)$$

where d_a is the distance of the head to the eye tracker and v is the vector between pupil and corneal reflection. Solving the equation needs, at least, two measurements in different distances. After the calibration, the normalized vector will have a length of 1 at the point used for calibration independent of the distance to the eye tracker.

2.5 Extensions for the Dual Monitor Setup

To extend the single-monitor eye tracker to a dual-monitor setup, two eye trackers one below each monitor are used. The use of two eye trackers causes four corneal reflections instead of just two in the image of each eye tracker. The placement of the eye trackers, however, causes two distinctive pairs of reflections which can be separated and correlated to either eye tracker, by using their relative location to each other: the eye tracker to the right of the user will cause the pair of reflections on the left (looking at the eye) and vice versa. Figure 6 shows the right eye as seen from the left eye tracker (Fig. 6 left image) and from the right eye tracker (Fig. 6 right image). While this setup allows for eye tracking on two screens, an important question is how the additional corneal reflections affect the detection robustness and therefore, the accuracy of the whole system.

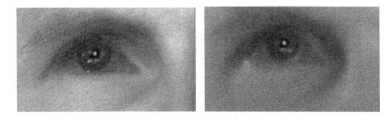

Fig. 6. Detected cornea reflections of the left eye tracker (left image) and the right eye tracker (right image)

3 Evaluation

For evaluation of the eye tracking system, 13 students volunteered in a user study (7 male, 6 female, average age 32.5). None of them wore glasses, one wore contact lenses. The apparatus consisted of two eye tracking devices, each placed in front of a monitor with a resolution of 1920x1200 pixels. The two monitors stood side by side, slightly turned towards the user (Fig. 8). The participants sat in the center. We did not use a chinrest in our evaluation as this would not be accepted by our target users. For evaluation, the participants first calibrated each eye tracker with a 9-point calibration and then had to fixate fifteen points presented on each monitor. The points can be grouped into three sets: two sets followed the design provided by Tobii [Tob11] on their website, one containing points located within 30° of visual angle (main), the other set contained points laying at the upper corners of the monitors (top). The third group consists of two points located at the border where the monitors meet (border) (Fig. 7).

The procedure is as follows: The points are displayed in order from the top left to the bottom right on the left screen and top right to bottom left on the right screen, row by row across screens. The press of a button triggers the collection of evaluation samples and the display of the next point afterwards. This evaluation was done on both screens with both eye trackers running and on the left screen with just the left eye tracker running.

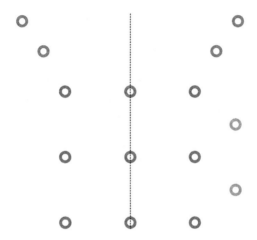

Fig. 7. The pattern used for evaluation with the areas top, main and border. The pattern for the right monitor is mirrored on the dashed line.

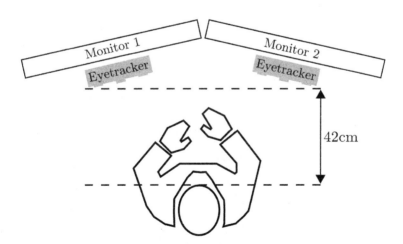

Fig. 8. Setup of two monitors and two eye trackers for dual monitor eye tracking.

3.1 Results

The heatmaps in Fig. 9 give a first impression of the accuracy of the double
monitor system compared to the single monitor system. The hotspots are com-
pareable showing less consistency for the top and bottom targets in both cases.
An important aspect besides accuracy is the extraction quality, which describes
the percentage of frames in which both the pupil and the corneal reflections could
be found. The eye tracker run at an average of 90 frames per second. Figure 10
shows the percentage of frames for the different systems in which a gaze point
could be determined. Here the dual monitor setup slightly outperforms the single
monitor setup. The same is true for the accuracy, which is presented in Table 1.
These results not only show that the additional corneal reflections do not cause
any problems with the detection of reflections, the multi-eye tracker setup even
outperforms the single eye tracker in terms of accuracy as well. Our best guess
for this is the additional IR light sources, which improve the overall image quality
and therefore, aid the accurate detection of the pupil and corneal reflections.

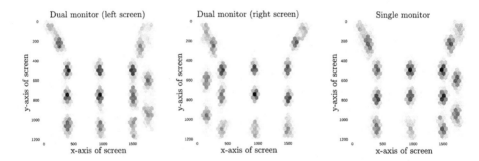

Fig. 9. Heatmaps of the gaze positions over the course of the experiments.

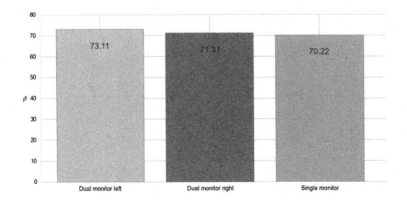

Fig. 10. Extraction quality in percent, with the value representing the percentage of
frames in which a gaze point could be determined.

Table 1. Average error in degree for the different setups and target sets.

Point set	Main	Top	Border
Dual right	$1 : 27°(\sigma = 1 : 61°)$	$1 : 63°(\sigma = 3 : 07°)$	$1 : 68°(\sigma = 1 : 79°)$
Dual left	$1 : 51°(\sigma = 2 : 09°)$	$2 : 09°(\sigma = 3 : 44°)$	$1 : 82°(\sigma = 1 : 77°)$
Single	$1 : 61°(\sigma = 3 : 05°)$	$2 : 23°(\sigma = 4 : 72°)$	$1 : 72°(\sigma = 1 : 41°)$

4 Conclusion and Future Work

We presented a low-cost, remote eye tracker setup capable of accurately detecting the gaze position on a dual monitor setup by using one eye tracker per screen. We have shown how depth information can be used to create a mapping function for estimating screen coordinates robust to distance changes of the user. We have also shown how simple duplication of a single monitor system can lead to a working double monitor system by handling the occurring interferences of the used infrared emitters. Our evaluation shows that the dual monitor setup is equally accurate compared to our single screen system despite the interferences. In the future, we hope to improve this approach to scale to an arbitrary number of screens enabling accurate large scale eye tracking for analysis but also interaction purposes.

Acknowledgement. The underlying projects to this article are funded by the WTD 81 of the German Federal Ministry of Defense as well as by Fraunhofer IOSB in-house funding. The authors are responsible for the content of this article.

References

[CXS+12] Coddington, J., Xu, J., Sridharan, S., Rege, M., Bailey, R.: Gaze-based image retrieval system using dual eye-trackers. In: Proceedings of the IEEE International Conference on Emerging Signal Processing Applications (ESPA), pp. 37–40 (2012)

[GEVC04] Goni, S., Echeto, J., Villanueva, A., Cabeza, R.: Robust algorithm for pupil-glint vector detection in a video-oculography eyetracking system. In: Proceedings of the 17th International Conference on Pattern Recognition (ICPR), vol. 4, pp. 941–944 (2004)

[HGB14] Hild, J., Gill, D., Beyerer, J.: Comparing mouse and magic pointing for moving target acquisition. In: Eye Tracking Research and Applications Symposium (ETRA), pp. 131–134 (2014)

[HRF14] Hansen, D.W., Roholm, L., Ferreiros, I.G.: Robust glint detection through homography normalization. In: Proceedings of the Symposium on Eye Tracking Research and Applications (ETRA), pp. 91–94 (2014)

[MM05] Morimoto, C.H., Mimica, M.R.: Eye gaze tracking techniques for interactive applications. Comput. Vis. Image Underst. **98**(1), 4–24 (2005). special Issue on Eye Detection and Tracking

[QWLY13] Qin, H., Wang, X., Liang, M., Yan, W.: A novel pupil detection algorithm for infrared eye image. In: Proceedings of the IEEE International Conference on Signal Processing, Communication and Computing (ICSPCC), pp. 1–5 (2013)

[Tob11] Tobii Technology AB, "Accuracy and precision test method for remote eye trackers," Tobii, Technical Report, 02 2011

[ZJ04] Zhu, Z., Ji, Q.: Eye and gaze tracking for interactive graphic display. Mach. Vis. Appl. **15**(3), 139–148 (2004)

Exploring the Throughput Potential of In-Air Pointing

Michelle A. Brown[1(✉)] and Wolfgang Stuerzlinger[2]

[1] Akendi, Toronto, Canada
michelle@akendi.com
[2] Simon Fraser University, Burnaby, Canada
http://ws.iat.sfu.ca

Abstract. We present an analysis of how pointing performance in in-air un-instrumented pointing can be improved, towards throughput equal to the mouse. Pointing using a chopstick is found to achieve the highest average throughput, with 3.89 bps. This is a substantial improvement over using the finger to point at the screen. Two potential reasons for the throughput gap between chopstick and finger operation were explored: the natural curvature of human fingers and tracking issues that occurs when fingers bend toward the device. Yet, neither one of these factors seems to significantly affect throughput. Thus other, yet unexplored factors must be the cause. Lastly, the effect of unreliable click detection was also explored, as this also affects un-instrumented performance, and was found to have a linear effect.

Keywords: Human-computer interaction · Fitts' law · Pointing tasks · Leap motion

1   Introduction

Un-instrumented in-air interaction has rapidly gained popularity with the introduction of a number of new interaction devices. Potential applications for un-instrumented in-air pointing include interaction in environments where mouse is inadvisable, such as while cooking, mobile computing, medical scenarios [9], and interaction on large wall displays.

The associated tracking devices for in-air interaction enable new and interesting interaction possibilities, including gestures and multi-finger interaction. Yet, previous work [7] has identified that the raw pointing throughput for in-air pointing is substantially less than for the mouse. Thus, it is unclear whether un-instrumented pointing has the potential to match (much less exceed) mouse throughput levels. It is also unclear what aspects of un-instrumented pointing tracking need to be improved to possibly reach mouse-like levels.

Fitts' Law [17] implies that the further away or the smaller a target is, the harder it will be to select. Building on decades of research, the ISO 9241-9 standard [14] standardizes Fitts' law experimental methodologies. It defines throughput T as the primary measure of performance, calculated as $T = log2(De/We + 1)/MT$, where, De is the effective distance and We the effective width. These effective values measure the task that the user actually performed, not the one that she or he was presented

© Springer International Publishing Switzerland 2016
M. Kurosu (Ed.): HCI 2016, Part II, LNCS 9732, pp. 13–24, 2016.
DOI: 10.1007/978-3-319-39516-6_2

with [17]. This reduces variability in identical conditions, which facilitates comparisons between different Fitts' law studies.

1.1 Related Work

Ray pointing is a method for pointing at objects, where the user moves a tracked arm or finger or a tracked object, such as a pen or laser pointer, and orients it in the direction she or he wishes to point to. The first object along that ray is then highlighted and selected when the user indicates selection, e.g., through a button click. Ray pointing remains a popular selection method for large screen and virtual reality systems. Many studies have investigated this technique in large displays [8, 13, 15, 18, 29, 33], Virtual Reality [11, 14, 24, 27], or tabletop scenarios [5]. All these comparisons used devices.

Ray pointing uses 3D input to afford control over a 2D cursor. Effectively users rotate the wrist (or finger) to move the cursor. Early work on finger-pointing used optical tracking [10]. Balakrishan and MacKenzie [4] identified that a finger affords about 75 % of the bandwidth relative to the wrist. Either moving the finger or the whole hand to control the cursor affords efficient pointing [3]. Yet, tracking very small hand rotations with 3D tracking systems with sufficient accuracy is difficult, as tracking noise is magnified increasingly along the ray. This is the most likely explanation why ray pointing is inferior to other pointing methods in small-scale environments, such as desktops, e.g., [27].

Gallo et al. [9] explored an un-instrumented hand tracking device in a medical context, where sterility is a major concern. Several approaches used various camera systems [14, 19]. In another work [12], the authors look at the requirements of un-instrumented tracking systems and their FingerMouse application used a one-second dwell time for selection. Song et al. [24] used finger pointing to select and move virtual objects. None of the above work evaluates the performance of un-instrumented in-air pointing with the throughput measure as defined by the ISO standard. The exception identified that its throughput was slightly less than 3 bps [7]. This is substantially lower than standard mouse throughput, which is often found to be approximately 4 bps.

1.2 Motivation and Contributions

This paper explores several open explanations for the lower throughput of un-instrumented pointing relative to the mouse [7]. We first evaluated the throughput of a (rigid) chopstick as pointing device, which might have a tracking advantage over a regular finger. It is longer, more cylindrical, and allows for a grip that may offer better directional control. Next, we evaluated pointing throughput of a finger with and without a rigid cast to determine if forcing the finger into a more cylindrical shape would improve tracking. Finally, we investigated the effect of click detection reliability on throughput, as this is another issue that can decrease performance in in-air interaction. Our contributions are:

- An evaluation of the selection performance of a rigid pointing device (chopstick).
- An evaluation of the selection performance of a perfectly cylindrical finger (cast).

- An analysis on the effect unreliable bent finger tracking has on selection performance.
- An evaluation of the effect selection reliability on throughput.

We deliberately chose the Leap Motion for our work, as it is currently one of the best devices for tracking un-instrumented fingers. We considered attaching individual markers to fingers with an optical tracking system. Yet, tracking orientations of fingers requires a large tracking target, which may slow down movements and cause fatigue.

1.3 Pilot Study

Looking at various options to improve tracking robustness, we found that the Leap Motion API supports also long, thin, rigid, cylindrical objects, such as pencils. Based on advice from the Leap Motion forum, we picked a chopstick. We hypothesized that using a chopstick would also increase throughput because it can be held more stably in a pencil grip, i.e., between three fingers.

We recruited 8 participants (mean age 21 years, SD 4.4 years). Two participants were male and all right handed. The Leap Motion sensor was placed directly in front of the display. The Leap Motion software used for this first study was version 1.0.9 + 8410 and the hardware device was LM-010. We used USB3 and Vsync was turned off in all conditions to minimize latency. Both choices increase interaction performance [6], to avoid the potential impact of large differences in latency on pointing performance [22, 24]. End-to-end latency with the Leap Motion was 48 ms, and with the Microsoft IntelliMouse Optical 32 ms. We used the default pointer speed of Windows 7. The software used for this study was FittsStudy [32]. We only added support to read data from the LeapMotion.

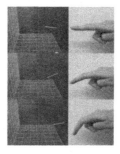

Fig. 1. The setup of the pilot study (left), issues observed with tracking bent fingers (right)

For this experiment there were two input conditions for selecting targets for the participants to use: the Chopstick and the Mouse. The Chopstick method required the user to hold a standard disposable wooden chopstick in her or his dominant hand, held like a pencil. Targets were then selected by aiming the tip of the chopstick toward the target on the screen. The Mouse method required the user to operate a computer mouse as they normally would. After targets had been acquired using one of these two methods, targets were selected using the left click button in the Mouse method and the spacebar on the keyboard in the Chopstick method. The spacebar was operated by the non-dominant hand of the participant and was placed in a comfortable operating position so that the dominant hand used for object acquisition was not obstructed Fig. 1 left illustrates the setup.

First, each participant was given a brief background questionnaire, to record gender, age, and handedness. Then, the participant was introduced to the Chopstick condition and shown how it worked. Participants were required to use a pencil grip for holding the chopstick. After comfortable with basic operation, one of the input conditions was explained to the participant. The order of the input methods was counterbalanced so that each of the possible orders was represented equally. When participants were comfortable with the input method, they completed a series of Fitts' law selection tasks using either the mouse or the chopstick in her or his dominant hand. Ten blocks of 9 Fitts' law conditions with 11 trials were completed with the ISO methodology for a total of 990 trials per condition. Target widths were 32, 64, and 96 pixels and amplitudes 256, 384, and 512 pixels. Then the next input method was presented and the above process repeated. At the end of the experiment, participants were given a brief questionnaire about any discomfort they might have experienced while using un-instrumented tracking and the mouse.

Data was first filtered for obvious participant errors, such as hitting the spacebar twice on the same target or pausing in the middle of a circle (less than .004 % of data collected). For all other analysis and following the ISO standard, we recorded an error whenever the cursor was outside the target upon selection, regardless if this occurred due to human or system, i.e., tracking error. As our data is not normally distributed and fails Levene's test for homogeneity, we conducted ANOVA tests after a Aligned Rank Transform (ART) for nonparametric factorial data analysis, [31].

In terms of throughput there was a significant effect for device used ($F_{1,7} = 19$, $p < .001$) with a power $(1 - \beta)$ of .97 and a large effect size (η^2) of .25. For a graph of average throughput values see Fig. 2 (3.54 bps for the chopstick and 4.13 bps for the mouse). There was a significant effect for device used for movement time ($F_{1,7} = 18$, $p < .01$) with a power $(1 - \beta)$ of 0.95 and a very small effect size (η^2) of .05. See Fig. 2 for average movement times. There was a significant effect for device used on error rate ($F_{1,7} = 8$, $p < .05$) with a power $(1 - \beta)$ of .68 and a negligible effect size (η^2) of .01. The mean error rate was 9.8 % for the chopstick and 3.9 % for the mouse. There was no observed statistically significant learning affect across all blocks ($F_{9,63} = 14$, $p < .001$) with a power $(1 - \beta)$ of .99 or in the learning curve between devices ($F_{9,142} = 0.83$, ns). Figure 2 shows performance over time. Device used (chopstick or mouse) crossed with ID value had no significant effect on throughput ($F_{6,97} = 0.02$, ns). Figure 2 shows average movement times for each ID value. The R^2 values show an excellent fit with Fitts' law.

The throughput for the chopstick still has a .39 bps difference in throughput from the mouse by the last block (3.89 vs. 4.28 bps). Yet, latencies in our conditions were in a region (below 50 ms) where they does not seem have a significant effect [22]. This makes it unlikely that latency alone can explain the result. The potential confound of using the mouse and its button with one hand vs. clicking the space bar with the other hand in the chopstick condition is also an unlikely explanation [7]. The error rate for the chopstick is substantially higher in our current study, either due to limitations in tracking by the Leap Motion or human limits on the ability to point precisely at a distance. Currently we do not have enough information to reliably distinguish between these two causes.

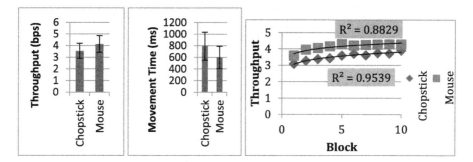

Fig. 2. Graph of average throughput (left) and movement times (middle) for chopstick and mouse. Error bars show standard deviation. Difference is statistically significant. Graph of learning over time (right). Average throughput for each block is displayed. Power curve is fitted to data.

Our results shows that a well-chosen in-air pointing device can achieve high pointing performance: 3.89 bps. That is within the lower end of throughput values observed for the mouse (3.7 bps – 4.9 bps) [25]. With more practice this value may increase further. Interestingly, two participants reached a crossover point where the chopstick achieved a throughput greater than the mouse. An expert user (not a participant), who had been practicing various pointing methods for four months, achieved an average throughput of 4.75 bps with the chopstick and 4.73 bps with the mouse. Yet, while mouse-like levels appear to be attainable with more training, such amounts of training are daunting. Still, we cannot rule out that the chopstick will match the mouse in the long term. In this pilot we did not observe noticeable fatigue effects. The chopstick achieved a throughput of 3.89 bps by the last block, much more than finger operation in prior work [7]. Even accounting for differences in latency (48 ms with our chopstick vs. 63 ms with the finger in [7]), this gap is still substantial. The reason behind this are further explored in the next study.

2   User Study 1

The main objective of this user study was to determine if a perfectly cylindrical, rigid finger would be capable of achieving the same levels of throughput seen with a chopstick in a comparable environment. After all, one possible explanation for the chopstick's superior performance is its rigid cylindrical nature, making it potentially easier to track. In pilot studies we identified that finger direction tracking reliability of the Leap Motion decreased, if the finger was bent too far towards the tracking device. See Fig. 1, right for a depiction of this problem. In this figure, the top two frames show a straight finger and the corresponding finger direction arrow. Subsequent frames show results with increasing finger bend, where the direction deviates more and more. Moreover, we observed that some users had significantly more curved fingers than others. An example for this finger curve is visible in the index finger in Fig. 3, rightmost image.

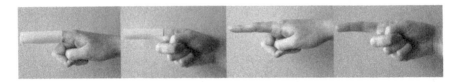

Fig. 3. Pictures of the four input conditions. From top left to bottom right: *Cast Normal*, *Cast Side*, *Normal*, and *Side*

We also speculated that finger tracking might behave differently depending on whether the users held their hands palm facing down or rotated 90° inwards. We included such conditions here as it might be easier for the device to track the position of the finger and determine the pointing direction – if finger curvature plays a significant role.

2.1 Input Conditions

For this user study there were four input conditions for selecting targets for the participants to use. These were the *Cast Normal*, the *Cast Side*, the *Normal*, and the *Side* method, as shown in Fig. 3. The *Cast Normal* method required the user to wear a paper "cast" around her or his dominant pointer finger. This cast was specially designed and adapted to each user's finger. A piece of regular computer paper was cut so that it was wide enough to wrap around the user's finger and long enough to cover the finger to the tip. This piece of paper was then wrapped around the user's finger and taped with clear adhesive tape to form the "cast". The finger was held in the "normal" pointing orientation with the bottom of the user's palm facing down. In the *Cast Side* method, the "cast" was again worn on the user's finger but this time the finger was held in the "side" position with the user's palm perpendicular to the desk. The *Normal* method required the user to hold their hand with the palm facing down, toward the desk, without a cast. In the *Side* condition the user's palm was held perpendicular to the desk, again without a cast. In all conditions, after targets had been acquired through pointing, selection was indicated via the spacebar on the keyboard. The spacebar was operated by the non-dominant hand of the participant and was placed in a comfortable operating position so that the dominant hand used for object acquisition was not obstructed. We hypothesized here that if finger cast performance reaches chopstick levels, then the grip style is likely not the cause of the chopstick's performance. In this case, rigidity would be a more likely explanation.

2.2 Participants and Procedure

We recruited 8 different participants for this study (mean age 20 years, SD 2.3 years). Three participants were male and all but one were right handed. First, participants were given a brief background questionnaire which recorded gender, age, and handedness.

Next, a "cast" was created for each participant as described in the Input Conditions. Then, the participant was introduced to the finger tracking system and the experimenter demonstrated how it worked. After was comfortable with basic operation, one of the input conditions was explained to the participant. The order that participants were exposed to each of the input methods was determined by a Latin Square design. Once comfortable with the current input method, the participant completed a series of Fitts' law selection tasks using one of the four input conditions. Five blocks of 9 Fitts' law conditions with 11 trials per condition for a total of 495 trials were completed, again using the ISO methodology. Target widths of 32, 64, and 96 and target amplitudes of 256, 384, and 512 pixels were used. The participant was then presented with the next input method and so on.

2.3 Results

Data was first filtered for errors, such as hitting the spacebar twice on the same target or unusually long pauses (less than .01 % of total data). The data is not normally distributed and fails Levene's test for homogeneity, and we again used ART before ANOVA.

There was no significant effect for the used interaction method ($F_{3,21} = 1.35, p ; .05$) on throughput, nor for any pair of conditions. See Fig. 4 for average throughput values.

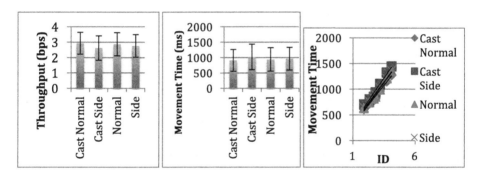

Fig. 4. Graph of average throughput values (left) and movement time (middle) and Fitts' law model (right) for each condition. Error bars show standard deviation.

There was no significance effect for the used interaction method ($F_{3,21} = 2.57$, $p > .05$) on movement time, nor for any pair of conditions. See Fig. 4 for average movement times. The used interaction method had no significant effect on error rate ($F_{3,21} = 0.27$, ns). The four conditions had error rates of 14 %, 12 %, 13 % and 13 % respectively. Across all blocks there was no significant effect on learning ($F_{4,28} = 1.15, p > .05$) and no effect on learning crossed with the used interaction method ($F_{12,145} = 1.64, p > .05$). The used interaction method crossed with ID had no significant effect on throughput ($F_{18,207} = 1.03, p > .05$). See Fig. 4 for the data for all conditions. The equations and fit values for the Fitts' law models are as follows: *Cast Normal*: $y = 310.58\ x - 7.9434$, $R^2 = 0.9857$, *Cast Side*: $y = 356.31\ x - 26.25$,

$R^2 = 0.9743$, *Normal*: $y = 337 x - 49.201$, $R^2 = 0.9826$, *Side*: $y = 329.88 x - 8.9465$, $R^2 = 0.9879$, again all conforming to Fitts' law.

2.4 Discussion

This study indicates that the cast conditions are similar to finger tracking. Therefore, it is unlikely that the natural curvedness and potential flexibility of a human finger cause lower pointing throughput relative to a rigid object. Yet, there is still a 15 + % difference (0.6 bps) between the throughputs of finger operation and chopstick operation that remains unaccounted for. The higher throughput from the pilot study must thus be due to some other factor, such as tracking a longer object or the different grip on the chopstick. Our results largely confirm the results of previous work [4], but also extend it through our use of the ISO methodology, which removes the effect of the speed-accuracy tradeoff.

Moreover, informal observations during this experiment identify fatigue as a potential issue, similar to [7]. This may be due to the duration of the experiment, which lasted about one hour. After all, many people are not used to using their index finger for long periods as a pointing "instrument". Still, performance did not drop noticeably in later trials.

3 User Study 2

To further investigate the potential of in-air interaction, we decided to look at the effect that varying degrees of click detection reliability have on throughput. After all, even a device that affords highly precise pointing may suffer if the selection of targets cannot be indicated reliably. To accurately and *reproducibly* control the level of reliability, we decided to perform this study with a mouse, as its buttons are normally 100 % reliable. The results of such an experiment can then be used to infer the *potential* performance impact of a selection method that is not 100 % reliable, such as in in-air "click".

3.1 Participants, Setup and Procedure

We recruited 10 different participants for this study (mean age 23 years, SD 4.7 years). Four participants were male and all but one were right handed. The left-handed person preferred to operate the mouse with the right hand. The mouse used was a Microsoft IntelliMouse Optical set to the default pointer speed on the Windows 7 operating system. The system used with the mouse had an end-to-end latency of 28 ms (Vsync was off). The software used for conducting the Fitts' law tasks was again FittsStudy [32].

First, the participant was given a brief background questionnaire to record gender, age, and handedness. Then, the participant was informed that the mouse button used for clicking would not always be reliable and that sometimes it might need to be clicked again. We chose to inform participants in advance to avoid potential confounds due to side effects of frustration. We tested five levels of reliability: 100 %, 99 %, 98 %, 95 %, and 90 %, to keep frustration levels at an acceptable level. The order that participants received each of these conditions was counterbalanced so that each of the possible orders was represented equally. Participants then completed 2 blocks of 12 Fitts' law conditions with 11 trials per condition for a total of 264 targets with the ISO methodology. Target widths of 16, 32, 64, and 96 pixels and amplitudes of 256, 384, and 512 pixels were used.

3.2 Results

As our data is not normally distributed and fails Levene's test for homogeneity, all ANOVA tests were again conducted on data transformed using ART.

There was a significant effect for reliability level ($F_{4,36} = 7, p < .001$) on throughput with a power ($1 - \beta$) of .99 and a medium effect size (η^2) of .09. A Tukey-Kramer Multiple-Comparison test identified two statistically different groups. Group one consists of 90 % and 95 % reliability and group two of 98 %, 99 %, and 100 % reliability. See Fig. 5 for average throughput values. There was a significant effect for reliability level ($F_{4,36} = 8, p < .001$) on movement time with a power ($1 - \beta$) of .99 and a very small effect size (η^2) of .01. A Tukey-Kramer Multiple-Comparison test again identified two statistically significant groupings. However, the groupings were different than the throughput groupings. Group one consisted of 90 %, 95 % and 98 % reliability and group two consisted of 98 %, 99 % and 100 % reliability. In other words, 98 % was not statistically different from all other conditions. See Fig. 5 for average movement times.

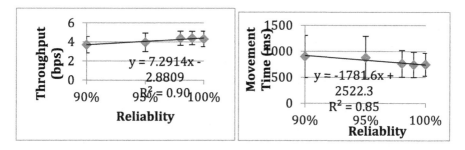

Fig. 5. Average throughput values (left) and movement times (right) for each reliability level. Error bars show standard deviation. A linear trendline and its corresponding equation is also shown.

The used reliability level had no significant effect on error rate ($F_{4,9} = 1.86$, $p > .05$). The mean error rates for the 90 % to 100 % conditions were 4.2 %, 1.4 %, 3.7 %, 4.8 % and 0.8 % respectively. Across all blocks, there was no significant effect on learning ($F_{1,18} = 0.05$, ns) and no effect on learning crossed with level of reliability ($F_{4,85} = 1.08, p > .05$). Reliability level crossed with ID had no significant effect on throughput ($F_{32,428} = 6, p > .05$). See Fig. 5 for the data for all conditions. The equations for the Fitts' law models are as follows: 90 %: $y = 170.82\,x + 155.98, R^2 = 0.988$, 95 %: $y = 148.78\,x + 212.89, R^2 = 0.988$, 98 %: $y = 167.44\,x + 95.258, R^2 = 0.987$, 99 %: $y = 156.39\,x + 103.94, R^2 = 0.996$, 100 %: $y = 141.48\,x + 138.47, R^2 = 0.998$.

3.3   Discussion

These results indicate that there is a roughly linear drop-off in pointing performance as a selection technique becomes more unreliable. The 90 % and 95 % conditions performed significantly worse than 98 % and above in terms of throughput. We see this as an indication (but not as proof) that any click-gesture recognition system that is 95 % reliable or less is going to noticeably and negatively impact interaction performance with a system. While there was no significant difference in performance between 100 %, 99 %, and 98 %, some participants did still notice when they were not at 100 % condition. This indicates that while a system with reliability above 95 % might not suffer much in terms of throughput, failures might still be noticeable to the users. Small amounts of errors might be less notable in systems without force feedback or where users expect it to be unreliable.

From observations during the experiment we also identified a behavioural difference for many in the 90 % condition: most participants would pause after selecting a target before the next one. Thus, it seemed like the participants expected failure rather than success in the 90 % condition. We suspect that as the reliability gets even lower all participants would anticipate a failure, not just most of them.

Perfect reliably in un-instrumented in-air pointing with a single camera is very difficult. Even very recent work does not achieve 100 % reliability [23]. Thus on top of tracking issues one must also factor in a loss in throughput due to click detection unreliability.

4   Overall Discussion

We explored several possibilities for the lower throughput of un-instrumented pointing relative to the mouse, as identified by previous work [7]. First, we identified that pointing with chopsticks can approach the performance traditionally seen with mice. This points to new interesting avenues for future user interfaces. We also evaluated finger pointing with and without a rigid cast. Given that we found no significant difference, it is unlikely that the rigidity of the input device is the primary explanation. This leaves the length of the chopstick or the grip style as possible explanations. Finally, we evaluated the effect of click detection reliability on throughput, another potential issue in in-air interaction. Our results indicate that in-air "click" detection must have between 95 and 98 % reliability, for in-air interaction to have the potential to perform as well as a mouse.

5   Conclusion

In this paper we evaluated several factors that were hypothesized to affect pointing performance: the shape of the finger, finger bend tracking difficulties, and click detection reliability. Moreover, we showed that by using a chopstick, users could reach the lower end of the range of pointing throughputs seen with the mouse. We also identified that finger curvedness or rigidity have no effect on pointing throughput with the Leap Motion.

Finally, we showed that unreliable selection techniques affect performance (approximately) linearly and identified key values between 90 % and 100 % reliability.

References

1. Arif, A.S., Stuerzlinger, W.: Predicting the cost of error correction in character-based text entry technologies. In: ACM CHI 2010, pp. 5–14 (2010)
2. Arif, A.S., Stuerzlinger, W.: User adaptation to a faulty unistroke-based text entry technique by switching to an alternative gesture set. Graphics Interface 2014, pp. 183–192 (2014)
3. Balakrishnan, R., Baude, T., Kurtenbach, G., Fitzmaurice, G.: The Rockin'Mouse: integral 3D manipulation on a plane. In: ACM CHI 1997, pp. 311–318 (1997)
4. Balakrishnan, R., MacKenzie, I.S.: Performance differences in the fingers, wrist, and forearm in computer input control. In: ACM CHI 1997, pp. 303–310 (1997)
5. Banerjee, A., Burstyn, J.: Pointable: an in-air pointing technique to manipulate out-of-reach targets on tabletops. In: ACM ITS 2011, pp. 11–20 (2011)
6. Bedikian, R.: "Understanding Latency," Leap Motion Developer Labs (2013). http://labs.leapmotion.com/post/55354675113/understanding-latency-part-1
7. Brown, M.A., Stuerzlinger, W., Mendonça Filho, E.J.: The performance of un-instrumented in-air pointing. In: Graphics Interface 2014, pp. 59–66 (2014)
8. Das, K., Borst, C.W.: An evaluation of menu properties and pointing techniques in a projection-based VR environment. In: IEEE 3DUI 2010, pp. 47–50 (2010)
9. Gallo, L., Placitelli, A., Ciampi, M.: Controller-free exploration of medical image data: experiencing the kinect. In: Computer-Based Medical Systems 2011, pp. 1–6 (2011)
10. Gokturk, M., Sibert, J.L.: An analysis of the index finger as a pointing device. In: Extended Abstracts ACM CHI 1999, p. 286 (1999)
11. Grossman, T., Balakrishnan, R.: Pointing at trivariate targets in 3D environments. In: ACM CHI 2004, pp. 447–454 (2004)
12. Von Hardenberg, C., Bérard, F.: Bare-hand human-computer interaction. In: Workshop on Perceptive User Interfaces 2001 (2001)
13. Jota, R., Nacenta, M., Jorge, J.: A comparison of ray pointing techniques for very large displays. In: Graphics Interface 2010, pp. 269–276 (2010)
14. Kolaric, S., Raposo, A., Gattass, M.: Direct 3D manipulation using vision-based recognition of uninstrumented hands. In: Symposium on Virtual and Augmented Reality 2008, pp. 212–220 (2008)
15. Kunert, A., Kulik, A., Lux, C., Fröhlich, B.: Facilitating system control in ray-based interaction tasks. In: ACM Symposium VRST 2009, pp. 183–186 (2009)
16. ISO 9241-9 Ergonomic requirements for office work with visual display terminals (VDTs)-Part 9: Requirements for non-keyboard input devices, ISO (2000)
17. MacKenzie, I.S.: Fitts' law as a research and design tool in human-computer interaction. Hum. Comput. Interact. 7(1), 91–139 (1992)
18. MacKenzie, I., Jusoh, S.: An evaluation of two input devices for remote pointing. In: Nigay, L., Little, M. (eds.) EHCI 2001. LNCS, vol. 2254, pp. 235–250. Springer, Heidelberg (2001)
19. Matikainen, P., Pillai, P., Mummert, L., Sukthankar, R., Hebert, M.: Prop-free pointing detection in dynamic cluttered environments. In: Face and Gesture 2011, pp. 374–381 (2011)
20. Oakley, I., Sunwoo, J., Cho, I.-Y.: Pointing with fingers, hands and arms for wearable computing. In: Extended Abstracts ACM CHI 2008, pp. 3255–3260 (2008)
21. Oh, J., Stuerzlinger, W.: Laser pointers as collaborative pointing devices. In: Graphics Interface 2002, pp. 141–149 (2002)

22. Pavlovych, A., Stuerzlinger, W.: The tradeoff between spatial jitter and latency in pointing tasks. In: ACM EICS 2009, pp. 187–196 (2009)
23. Sharp, T., Keskin, C., Robertson, D., Taylor, J., Shotton, J., Kim, D., Rhemann, C., Leichter, I., Vinnikov, A., Wei, Y., Freedman, D., Kohli, P., Krupka, E., Fitzgibbon, A., and Izadi, S.: Accurate, robust, and flexible real-time hand tracking. In: ACM CHI 2015, pp. 3633–3642 (2015)
24. Song, P., Yu, H., Winkler, S.: Vision-based 3D finger interactions for mixed reality games with physics simulation. In: ACM SIGGRAPH International Conference on Virtual-Reality Continuum and Its Applications in Industry 2008, article no. 7 (2008)
25. Soukoreff, R.W., MacKenzie, I.S.: Towards a standard for pointing device evaluation, perspectives on 27 years of Fitts' law research in HCI. IJHCS **61**(6), 751–789 (2004)
26. Teather, R.J., Pavlovych, A., Stuerzlinger, W. MacKenzie, I.S.: Effects of tracking technology, latency, and spatial jitter on object movement. In: IEEE Symposium 3DUI 2009, pp. 43–50 (2009)
27. Teather, R.J., Stuerzlinger, W.: Pointing at 3D targets in a stereo head-tracked virtual environment. In: IEEE Symposium 3DUI 2011, pp. 87–94 (2011)
28. Teather, R.J., Stuerzlinger, W.: Pointing at 3D target projections with one-eyed and stereo cursors. In: ACM CHI 2013, pp. 159–168 (2013)
29. Vogel, D., Balakrishnan, R.: Distant freehand pointing and clicking on very large, high resolution displays. In: ACM UIST 2005, pp. 33–42 (2005)
30. Wingrave, C., Bowman, D.: Baseline factors for raycasting selection. In: HCI International 2005 (2005)
31. Wobbrock, J.O., Findlater, L., Gergle, D., Higgins, J.J.: The aligned rank transform for nonparametric factorial analyses using only ANOVA procedures. In: ACM CHI 2011, pp. 143–146 (2011)
32. Wobbrock, J.O., Shinohara, K., Jansen, A.: The effects of task dimensionality, endpoint deviation, throughput calculation, and experiment design on pointing measures and models. In: ACM CHI 2011, pp. 1639–1648 (2011)
33. Zigelbaum, J., Browning, A., Leithinger, D., Bau, O., Ishii, H.: G-stalt: a chirocentric, spatiotemporal, and telekinetic gestural interface. In: ACM TEI 2010, pp. 261–264 (2010)

A Methodology to Introduce Gesture-Based Interaction into Existing Consumer Product

Lorenzo Cavalieri[✉], Maura Mengoni, Silvia Ceccacci, and Michele Germani

Department of Industrial Engineering and Mathematical Sciences,
Università Politecnica delle Marche, Via Brecce Bianche, 12-60131 Ancona, Italy
{lorenzo.cavalieri,m.mengoni,s.ceccacci,m.germani}@univpm.it

Abstract. The continuous progress of interaction technologies reveals that we are witnessing a revolution that is leading to a redefinition of the concept of "user interface" and to the development of new ways to interact with the electronic devices of all sizes and capabilities. Current trends in research related to the Human-Machine Interaction (HMI) show a considerable interest toward gesture, motion-based and full-body based interactions. In this context, a User-Centered Design (UCD) methodology to implement these novel interaction paradigms into consumer products is proposed with the aim to improve its usability, intuitiveness and experience. A case study is used to validate the methodology and measure the achieved improvements in user performance.

Keywords: Gesture interaction · Design methods · User interfaces · User-Centered design

1 Introduction

The potentiality of Human-Machine Interfaces is progressively increasing to allow users to interact with electronic devices of any dimension and capability with a low cost impact and with an improved usability. Investigations on the effectiveness of natural, brain, gesture-based interfaces and so on and on the effects on the user experience appear to be really significant to drive the design and development of remote controls, electronic devices, game consoles, etc.

The paper focuses on a specific typology of electronic devices that are musical keyboards, where touchless interaction could play a key role to improve learning and use [1].

On the marketplace, there are some examples of musical applications exploiting gesture-based interfaces. One is the MiMu Gloves [2, 3] equipped with a motion tracker, an haptic motor, bend sensors, LEDs and x-OSC. Authors developed a robust posture vocabulary, an artificial neural network-based posture identification module and a state-based system to map the identified postures onto a set of performance processes. Another proposed technology is Titan Reality Pulse, that is a MIDI controller that allows the user to trigger and play software instruments using hands. It is pressure-sensitive and can recognize the number of fingers you're holding up to it. The device combines gesture interaction with the classic touch controller in a single object [4].

© Springer International Publishing Switzerland 2016
M. Kurosu (Ed.): HCI 2016, Part II, LNCS 9732, pp. 25–36, 2016.
DOI: 10.1007/978-3-319-39516-6_3

The above-mentioned applications exploit general-purpose gesture-based applications such as Kinect and Leap Motion that are useful tools for programming music controls. However the achieved results' performance is often left to the capability of developers and to the user's skill. Moreover, it is worth to notice that literature lacks of a design methodology to guarantee a robust and efficient interaction to control music parameters in a live performance or in a recording studio.

These are the main motivations that trigger out the present research work whose aim is both to define a User-Centered methodology to implement the gesture-based interaction paradigm into musical devices and to develop a usable, intuitive and friendly technology for non-expert performers. The paper describes the adopted approach, gives an overview of the implementation results and illustrates some preliminary experimental achievements.

2   Research Background

The main issues in gesture-based interaction in music are as follows: (1) interaction modalities, (2) recognition patterns of interaction, (3) enabling technologies and (4) the role of the music in the human conditions.

In the music world the main adopted interaction mode is touch. However, in the field of electronic music many touchless solutions have been implemented to allow the performer to play sounds.

Several research works are reported in literature. For instance some technologies exploit smartphones with an embedded digital compass [5, 6]. The touchless interaction is implemented by changing the magnetic field around the smartphone by moving a handle tiny magnet. Other works use infrared signals to enable the interaction [7]. Marrin [8] implemented the so-called *Digital Baton*, to allow a real-time gestural control. The hardware system consists of a baton, an external infrared sensor, a tracking unit, and a computer. The sensors on the baton include an infrared LED for positional tracking, five piezoresistive strips for finger and palm pressure, and three orthogonal accelerometers for beat tracking.

In the presented works, some opened issues still remain. They mainly regard the creation of an accurate pattern recognition model and a structured and repetitive method to map the recognized gestures with the functionalities to be enabled.

About the first issue, one aspect deserves the present research interest that is the design of proper recognition models to map the performed interaction with sound.

The major problems actually appear when the mode of interaction is based on gestures; in this case a precise detection system and an accurate process of mapping are required to obtain a usable system [9–11].

First of all, the most important aspect is the definition of gesture meanings in music. Godøy [12] explored the meanings of gestures in the different fields of the music (e.g. instrument-related gestures or director ones) and defined accurate models to recognize and map them with the proper musical event. Ng [13] presents a novel framework to map natural human languages (i.e. gestures) with multimedia event (i.e. audio output).

Gesture recognition and modeling are as accurate and repetitive as the movements are accurately captured. For that purpose, Vigliensoni [14] compared different three-dimensional (3D) position tracking systems (i.e. Vicon, Polhemus, Kinect, and Gametrak) in terms of static accuracy and precision, update rate, and shape of the space they sense. Vicon resulted to be the best one for gesture-based interaction in music. Other works are focus on the recognition of the gesture of a choir/orchestra director for an interactive music system [15–17]. A baseline study is the Morita's work [15]. The proposed gesture recognition system is based on a sensorized baton and a data glove to detect user intentions about the management of musical features (time pattern, velocity, instrument activation). Then an artificial intelligence supports the manipulation of MIDI data in order to properly reproduce the music. The work proposed by Morita represents a key reference for the present research, that is a step forward it as it overcomes the problems of data glove invasiveness and barriers of the baton by integrating an optical tracking system.

In another significant example, Je tries to understanding of four musical time patterns and three tempos that are generated by a human conductor of robot orchestra or an operator of computer-based music play system using the hand gesture recognition [16]. Je's work allows to have a valid reference point to the pattern recognition about tempo performance and its sound modulation due to the gesture decoding.

Finally, Marrin Nakra [17] presented the design and implementation of the Conductor's Jacket. The proposed wearable device is able to measure physiological and gestural signals to analyze, understand and synthesize expressive gesture in a musical context. The identified recognition patterns are exploited to develop a musical software system that analyzes and performs music in real-time based on the performer's gestures and breathing signals.

The second issue regards human conditions in relationship with music. Some works focused on the influence that musical parameters have on human perception [18], others on the monitoring of the brain activity while music plays [19, 20]. However, a more important line of research concerns the study of eye movement of musicians to understand their brain activity [21–23].

Therefore, inspired by works on interaction design in music, a methodology to support the user interface redesign once gesture-based interaction has been introduced is here developed.

3   A Methodology to Improve HMI Design

The integration of the above-described interaction paradigms into existing musical keyboards and electronic devices in general requires an adaptive design process.

It is divided into three stages as follows. In the first one, an *analysis of existing products* is conducted to identify the main usability issues, the usual user behavior, and the enabling technologies suitable to be integrated to the product itself. The second stage regards the *identification of possible design solutions* by starting from the identified critical issues and the technologies to be integrated in. Finally, the third stage consists in the *implementation and evaluation of the elaborated solutions* to fulfill user needs and expectations. Every stage generates functional outputs representing the input data to the next one.

Figure 1 shows the workflow of the Design Methodology to improve the HMI by adapting it to new interaction paradigms. It is called *M.I.I.D.*

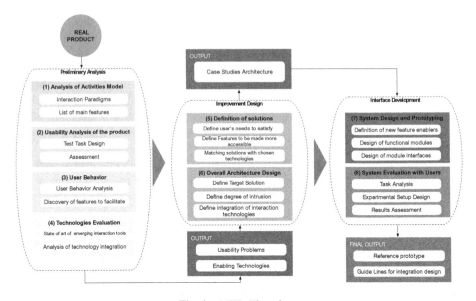

Fig. 1. *MIID Flowchart.*

3.1   Stage 1: Preliminary Analysis

The preliminary analysis represents the first stage of MIID; in this phase an analysis of the key-aspects of the product use scenarios is carried out. It takes care of four main aspects as follows: interaction modalities, performed tasks, user behavior and available technologies to support interaction.

The first aspect is studied by the construction of **an Activities Model** that tries to understand the nature of interactions and the functionalities (activities) activated by the user. It seeks to highlight the main interaction modalities and to define a list of the main features of the product. The *interaction modalities* can be found by directly analyzing the physical interface of the product that means the identification of buttons, touch screens, knobs, infrared sensors, joysticks. The *definition of main product features* is more complex because it also takes into consideration the elements influencing the affordance of the product in relation to the user needs.

The critical issues emerging in user-machine interaction are identified thanks to the **Usability Analysis of the Product.** A set of test tasks is defined to represent the overall range of choices the user has. A predictive evaluation according [24] is adopted to assess the usability performance, such as the number of steps to achieve the goal and the task execution time.

At the same time a **User Behavior Analysis** is carried out. It allows analysts to understand how consumers use the product interface focusing on the identification of primary and secondary behaviors. Direct user observations during usability tests and ethnographic techniques are used for that purpose.

In this case the analysis is aimed at identifying and decoupling a *primary behavior*, bound to actions the user makes to interact with the product and its functionalities, and a *secondary behavior*, made of all those gestures that are not directly connected with the product use but that have to be considered.

Two findings come from decoupling: (1) the strengths of the interface identified by possible uniform behavior of different users, but also (2) the weaknesses identified by an uneven behavior. This allows the identification of which modes of interaction to maintain, which require corrections, and which new types of interactions without interfering with the main ones improve the interface naturalness and intuitiveness.

Finally, **Technologies Evaluation** is used to investigate the tools improving interaction. It passes through the overview of the state-of-art of emerging HMI that can be applied on the target product category.

3.2   Stage 2: Improvement Design

Improvement Design aims to upgrade interaction and solve current interface failures and drawbacks. It follows the well-known adaptive design process.

The first task to be fulfilled is the **Definition of Solutions** at a conceptual and abstract level of detail. The complexity of this stage is directly proportional to the identified usability problems to be solved and the needs to be satisfied. The decomposition of the overall design problem into sub-problems can be useful to conceive targeted solutions and make the process more efficient. After problem framing, a plan of goals to be achieved is defined. This plan contains at first the functionalities not satisfied by the interface and a hypothesis of additional features and/or redesigned ones and the set of design requirements to start with the conceptual and detail design of each solution.

The **Overall Architecture Design** starts with the identification of each solving technology and the iterative evaluation of the changes propagation across the whole product structure in order to minimize the effects of modifications in terms of economic impact and technical feasibility (e.g. manufacturability, sustainability, etc.). Once conceived each solution, the evaluation of all technologies' integration is performed. The result of this stage is represented by the formalization of one or more case studies architecture, with the description of the functional parts of the solution and their own interconnections useful to reach the goal of the improvement design and to satisfy the user's needs.

3.3   Interface Development

The final stage of the MIID Methodology consists of (1) system development and (2) evaluation with end-users to test the reliability and performance of the improved interface solutions. It represents the implementation and validation phases of the overall redesign process: all collected data and taken design decisions are developed in this stage and tested in order to verify the achievement of initial objectives.

System development consists of **System Design and Prototyping**. The first aims at develop the conceived architecture and each constituting modules thanks to the adoption of a Systematic Engineering approach. Each module is characterized by its core functionality, all the attributes and the connections with other modules.

Enabling features and integrating technologies allow the designer to define the requirements for the design of each module. However, it is possible that the product under study does not directly support the selected interface features. In this case it is necessary to choose a platform compatible with the product. This represents a further requirement to add to the design requirements' list.

Each module is able to implement both high-level functionalities (exposed to the user) and low-level ones (exposed to the product). It also has to provide interfaces with other modules to enable data communication and interchange while keeping them independent each other.

Prototyping aims at implement the so-defined modular architecture by exploiting the proper platform and the conceived technologies to reach the fixed goals. It could be both low-fidelity prototype (e.g. paper-sketches) or high-fidelity one (e.g. virtual or physical mock-up). As previously mentioned, the choice of technology strongly influences the possibilities for integration. If the degree of intrusiveness is high, through suggesting a significant change within the current user interface, such choice is crucial thinking about a future integration.

The last and more important phase is the **Evaluation of the implemented solutions with end-users**. Being a methodology based on the user-centered approach, this step is a key point of the methodology. The prototype is tested to understand the degree of reliability, efficiency, effectiveness that the integrated solution proposes.

User tasks analysis is adopted for the evaluation. The assessment is made by separating the interaction of individual tasks in order to avoid interference among different tasks. In this way, it will be possible to evaluate the user's performance in terms of effectiveness (how many times the goal is achieved) and efficiency (in how much time the user reaches the target). In addition, to determine a full usability profile, an evaluation questionnaire is proposed to the user at the end of the performance in order to measure the degree of satisfaction in use.

Moreover the set-up of experimentation is defined. It takes into consideration aspects such as environment, used equipment (invasive or not), data flow management, experimental protocol to ensure repeatability and to define the boundaries of target user actions (what can and cannot he/she do?).

Finally, the results elaboration is carried out to validate improvements of the interaction with the proposed solution.

3.4   Prototype and Integration Guidelines

The final outputs of the overall methodology are a final reference prototype of the improved interface solution and a set of integration guidelines to drive designers into adaptive design processes in case of new interaction paradigms implementation.

The **Reference Prototype** can be either low-fidelity or high-fidelity according to the stage the development has stopped (i.e. conceptual, embodiment or detail design). If the design of the solution arrives at the concept stage, the final application will be developed by exploiting rapid prototyping techniques and paper-sketches without the need to implement the application logics (html wireframe, interactive interface builder). If it arrives at detail design, the prototyping will adopt a development platform compatible with the product and exploit a proper programming language to implement all features.

Design Guidelines contain useful instructions for the integration of the designed solution into a product at different level of detail according to the type of developed reference prototype. Results can be the definition of a format of the integration (library, scripting code, a bridge application, hardware design changes etc.) and the data interchange language to be used to allow the product to interact with the new solution.

4   A Case Study: Control Musical Parameter with Hands

4.1   Analysis of Korg Pa800 Musical Keyboard

The proposed approach is applied to re-design the user interface of an electronic musical keyboard (Fig. 2). Application aims to verify the methodology reliability. The analyzed target task is *"Create New Sound"*. The usability test is composed by two main phases.

Fig. 2. Korg Pa800 musical keyboard

In the first phase, the study focuses on the *number of interactions* the user has to perform to reach the task and on the feedback the keyboard gives in reaction. Every interaction is classified into *three different typologies*, i.e. *wheel rotation, tap&list selection and tap interaction on display*. The goal of this assessment is the analysis of two aspects of interaction as follows: (1) the number of user interactions ($25 < N_i < 40$) and (2) the paths done to reach the target task ($N_p = 3N_i$), which depends from the three detected interaction modalities.

The second phase is focused on the occurrences of a given interaction typology. The analysis is carried out on the sound setting menu exploring the different sound modulation sections. In every tab, the interaction occurrences are monitored observing the different input mode. Results show the *wheel rotation* as the main interaction paradigm used in the performance of the task. The *tap&list selection* is the second one. However, this interaction mode represents a hybrid solution between the *tap interaction* and the *wheel rotation*: so it appears an alternative way to select menu items or combo box options instead the wheel movement. From these considerations, the role of wheel is clearly fundamental to the setting of keyboard functionalities.

The conducted study shows some critical drawbacks of the real product as follows: (1) *too many interaction steps are necessary to reach the task*; (2) *three different paths are vaguely chosen by the user* creating confusion; (3) some *buttons are not easily visible and finally (4)* some selected functions have *too many parameters* to be set. A workflow is used to illustrate the results of the analysis (Fig. 3).

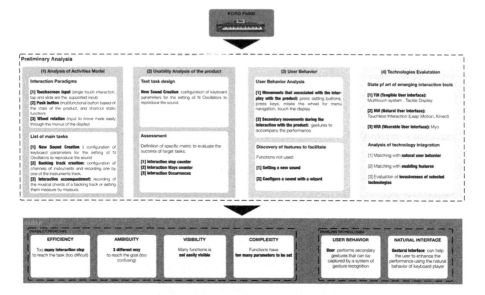

Fig. 3. Pre-analysis workflow

4.2   Design of the Case Study

The detected problems of *efficiency*, *ambiguity*, *complexity* and *visibility* drive the benchmark of natural interfaces and related enabling technologies to overcome them.

Three different solutions have been developed according to the structure of the second stage of the proposed design methodology. One has been evaluated the best and described below. It presents an improvement about the minimization of *visibility* and *complexity* as it avoids the use of a multi-level menu of the keyboard.

The solution comprehends an educational application to support orchestra conductors in performance direction that exploits hand gesture-based interaction modes. The application allows to manage the tempo, velocity and instrument activation in a target performance. The user can control the *volume level*, *tempo beats* and finally the *toggle of the orchestra instruments*.

An independent module is properly developed and prototyped to manage the new technology and implemented functionalities.

4.3   Interface Development

The development phase consists of the (1) *Definition of the architecture* and design requirement of the new module, the (2) *Design of the User Interface with a feedback system* and the (3) *Design of experimental setup.*

In this context, the architecture of the software application is shown in Fig. 4. It is composed by three main parts as follows: (1) a **gesture monitor module** that connects the Motion Controller with the core, (2) a **pattern recognition module** to identify the user gesture, and (3) an **actuator method module** that sends the MIDI commands to a sequencer for the modulation of the target MIDI file.

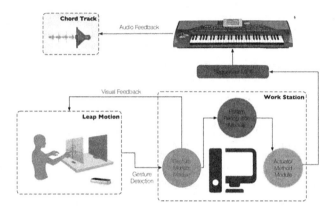

Fig. 4.   Director App Architecture

The interface development phase consists in the design of the interaction modality according to the User Interface Design proposed by Norman [25]. In particular, the focus is on the definition of the necessary feedbacks to ensure a certain degree of user perform-ance (see Fig. 5(a)).

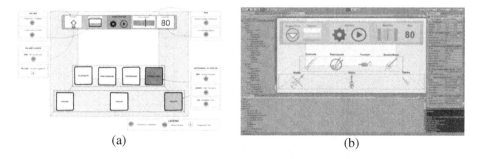

(a)   (b)

Fig. 5.   Interface Design of application

A **prototype application** using Leap Motion SDK and Unity3D Environment connected with an external MIDI sequencer are developed. Furthermore, the core application is developed in C\# language and is able to be integrated with Korg Firmware through a

C-porting process and make a library package of the recognition and activation algorithms. The prototype is shown in Fig. 5(b).

4.4 Experimental Setup and Evaluation

A user-oriented experimental protocol based on task analysis is defined. The chosen tasks the user has to perform by the application are: (1) *tempo control*, (2) *velocity control* and (3) *instruments activation*. For each task usability metrics are measured. They are the following:

1. *Efficiency*, measuring the delay between the performance feedback trigger and the user action. The feedback system provides to suggest the user the action to be performed: once unleashed the feedback is measured how long it took the user to take the proper action.
2. *Effectiveness*, counting the number of failures of the task. If the user doesn't act the right action after the feedback visualization, a counter index increases.
3. *Satisfaction*, through compiling a Likert questionnaire about the sensations felt by the user during the performance. These data are useful to understand the user experience of the new interaction modalities.

Users perform the direction of a classic track in the following experimental environment: a large screen shows the user interface with an iconic representation of the instrument spatially arranged as in real orchestra; the musical keyboard are connected with a gesture controller in front of the user; a stereo audio system with two speakers are connected with the musical keyboard to enhance the audio feedback of the performance. The sample consists of a number of ten elements, with a mean age of 26 years. Users have experience in the music field, but they are not professional users.

Table 1 shows data related to the usability validators of the sample users in the three tasks: looking at the summarized results three considerations can be made:

Table 1. Results of user evaluation

USER	Efficiency (ms)			Effectiveness			Satisfaction
	T1	T2	T3	T1	T2	T3	
1	812	838	938	1	0	3	72,63 %
2	1050	1056	1056	3	0	2	73,68 %
3	857	1010	1046	0	0	2	85,26 %
4	991	833	917	4	2	3	63,16 %
5	999	908	1032	3	1	1	69,47 %
6	832	842	1091	2	1	3	70,53 %
7	1028	928	893	1	0	3	77,89 %
8	825	876	896	2	2	2	68,42 %
9	1070	824	823	1	1	3	74,74 %
10	866	966	846	2	1	3	65,26 %
TOTAL				19	8	25	
AVERAGE	933	908,1	953,8	1,9	0,8	2,5	72,11 %

- Efficiency, considering the update frame offset of 700 ms, turns out to be very low, showing the good responsiveness of the user to the system stimuli;
- In a typical performance session (9 min), the total average errors are 5, 2. The results indicates a good degree of effectiveness, even if the performance has room for improvement;
- Finally, the Likert Questionnaire base on IBM Template [26] show a satisfaction rate greater than 70 %.

5   Conclusion and Future Works

A methodology to introduce gesture-based interfaces into consumers' products as musical keyboards is presented and validated through a real case study. Experimental results demonstrate how the proposed methodology supports the interface re-design with the objective of simplifying and maximize the system usability. Moreover, it allows the definition of innovative applicative functions, which can be obtained through the combination of pre-existing functions and new interaction modalities. Future work will be focused on a deep investigation of user experience and achieved performance. This will lead to extend the technology to other products.

Acknowledgements. This work is carried out with the collaboration of Korg Italy SPA, which has provided the actual product and your skills and knowledge to support the analysis phase.

References

1. O'hara, K., et al.: On the naturalness of touchless: putting the "interaction" back into NUI. ACM Trans. Comput. Hum. Interact. (TOCHI) **20**(1), 5 (2013)
2. Hughes, D.: Technologized and autonomized vocals in contemporary popular musics. J. Music Technol. Educ. **8**(2), 163–182 (2015)
3. Mitchell, T.J.: Soundgrasp: a gestural interface for the performance of live music (2011)
4. Titanrealitycom: Titanrealitycom. Retrieved 11 February, 2016. https://titanreality.com
5. Ketabdar, H., et al.: MagiMusic: using embedded compass (magnetic) sensor for touch-less gesture based interaction with digital music instruments in mobile devices. In: Proceedings of the Fifth International Conference on Tangible, Embedded, and Embodied Interaction. ACM (2011)
6. Yuksel, K.A., Ketabdar, H., Roshandel, M.: Towards digital music performance for mobile devices based on magnetic interaction. In: 2010 IEEE International Symposium on Haptic Audio-Visual Environments and Games (HAVE). IEEE (2010)
7. van Dorp Skogstad, S.A., Jensenius, A.R., Nymoen, K.: Using IR optical marker based motion capture for exploring musical interaction, pp. 407–410 (2010)
8. Marrin, T.: Possibilities for the digital baton as a general-purpose gestural interface. In: CHI 1997 Extended Abstracts on Human Factors in Computing Systems. ACM (1997)
9. Cabral, M.C., Morimoto, C.H., Zuffo, M.K.: On the usability of gesture interfaces in virtual reality environments. In: Proceedings of the 2005 Latin American Conference on Human-Computer Interaction. ACM (2005)
10. Manresa-Yee, C., et al.: Hand tracking and gesture recognition for human-computer interaction. In: Progress in Computer Vision and Image Analysis, pp. 401–412 (2010)

11. Rico, J., Brewster, S.: Usable gestures for mobile interfaces: evaluating social acceptability. In: Proceedings of the SIGCHI Conference on Human Factors in Computing Systems. ACM (2010)

12. Godøy, R.I., Leman, M. (eds.): Musical Gestures: Sound, Movement, and Meaning. Routledge, New york (2010)

13. Ng, K.C.: Music via motion: transdomain mapping of motion and sound for interactive performances. Proc. IEEE **92**(4), 645–655 (2004)

14. Vigliensoni, G., Wanderley, M.M.: A quantitative comparison of position trackers for the development of a touch-less musical interface. In: Proceedings of the 12th International Conference on New Interfaces for Musical Expression (NIME 2012), Vancouver, Canada (2012)

15. Morita, H., Hashimoto, S., Ohteru, S.: A computer music system that follows a human conductor. Computer **24**(7), 44–53 (1991)

16. Je, H., Kim, J., Kim, D.: Hand gesture recognition to understand musical conducting action. In: The 16th IEEE International Symposium on Robot and Human interactive Communication, 2007. RO-MAN 2007. IEEE (2007)

17. Nakra, T.M.: Inside the Conductor's Jacket: Analysis, interpretation and musical synthesis of expressive gesture. Ph.D. thesis Massachusetts Institute of Technology (1999)

18. Finney, S.A.: Auditory feedback and musical keyboard performance. Music Percept. **15**(2), 153–174 (1997)

19. Pfordresher, P.Q., et al.: Brain responses to altered auditory feedback during musical keyboard production: an fMRI study. Brain Res. **1556**, 28–37 (2014)

20. Zamm, A., Pfordresher, P.Q., Palmer, C.: Temporal coordination in joint music performance: effects of endogenous rhythms and auditory feedback. Exp. Brain Res. **233**(2), 607–615 (2015)

21. Bigand, E., et al.: Looking into the eyes of a conductor performing lerdahl's "Time after Time". Musicae Sci. **14**(2), 275–294 (2010)

22. Wurtz, P., Mueri, R.M., Wiesendanger, M.: Sight-reading of violinists: eye movements anticipate the musical flow. Exp. Brain Res. **194**(3), 445–450 (2009)

23. Gilman, E., Underwood, G.: Restricting the field of view to investigate the perceptual spans of pianists. Vis. Cogn. **10**(2), 201–232 (2003)

24. Nielsen, J.: Usability inspection methods. In: Conference Companion on Human Factors in Computing Systems. ACM (1994)

25. Norman, D.A.: The Design of Everyday Things: Revised and Expanded Edition. Basic Books, London (2013)

26. Lewis, J.R.: IBM computer usability satisfaction questionnaires: psychometric evaluation and instructions for use. Int. J. Hum. Comput. Interact. **7**(1), 57–78 (1995)

Walking in Place Through Virtual Worlds

Niels Christian Nilsson[(✉)], Stefania Serafin, and Rolf Nordahl

Aalborg University Copenhagen, Copenhagen, Denmark
{ncn,sts,rn}@create.aau.dk

Abstract. Immersive virtual reality (IVR) is seemingly on the verge of entering the homes of consumers. Enabling users to walk through virtual worlds in a limited physical space presents a challenge. With an outset in a taxonomy of virtual travel techniques, we argue that Walking-in-Place (WIP) techniques constitute a promising approach to virtual walking in relation to consumer IVR. Subsequently we review existing approaches to WIP locomotion and highlight the need for a more explicit focus on the perceived naturalness of WIP techniques; i.e., the degree to which WIP locomotion feels like real walking. Finally, we summarize work we have performed in order to produce more natural WIP locomotion and present unexplored topics which need to be address if WIP techniques are to provide perceptually natural walking experiences.

Keywords: Virtual reality · Locomotion · Walking-in-Place · Perceived naturalness

1 Introduction

Immersive virtual reality (IVR) has existed for decades, but 2016 is likely to become the year where it truly becomes accessible to consumers for the first time. This is an exciting prospect, but also one that involves a series of challenges. One activity which is likely to pose a challenge is virtual travel. Virtual travel, or locomotion, is regarded as one of the most common and universal activities occurring during interaction with three-dimensional (3D) computer-generated environments [3]. Throughout the following we use terms travel and locomotion interchangeably. Generally, travel can be understood as the low level actions performed in order to get from one point to another within a virtual (or real) environment; e.g., controlling the orientation, position and velocity of the virtual viewpoint [3].

In this paper we focus on a specific approach to facilitating virtual travel which appears to be ideally suited for use in relation to consumer IVR; namely Walking-in-Place (WIP) techniques. These techniques enable user's to travel through virtual worlds by performing stepping-like moments on the spot that serve as a proxy for real steps. Particularly, we present a taxonomy of virtual travel tecniques, review past work on WIP locomotion, and summarize our recent work which has sought to increase the perceived naturalness of WIP locomotion [14–20].

© Springer International Publishing Switzerland 2016
M. Kurosu (Ed.): HCI 2016, Part II, LNCS 9732, pp. 37–48, 2016.
DOI: 10.1007/978-3-319-39516-6_4

2   A Taxonomy of Virtual Travel Techniques

A plethora of different virtual travel techniques have been proposed—all uniquely suited for completing particular tasks and useful within specific contexts. Consequently, classification and categorization of interaction techniques has become a common theme within 3D interaction research, and several different, yet complementary, taxonomies classifying and categorizing interaction techniques for virtual travel have been proposed [3]. Our general taxonomy for describing virtual travel techniques [16] is inspired by existing categorisations [3,23,25,30] and organizes virtual travel techniques into three orthogonal classifications: *user mobility*, *virtual movement source*, and *metaphor plausibility*.

Metaphor plausibility: First, virtual travel techniques may qualify as either *mundane* (virtual movement based on a metaphor adopted from real-world travel) or *magical* (virtual movement based on a metaphor that is not limited by real world constraints; e.g., the laws of physics, biological evolution, or the current state of technological development).

Virtual movement source: Second, one may distinguish between travel techniques that simulate *body-centric* travel (virtual movement is generated by directly exerting forces to the environment; e.g., simulation of walking, swimming, or flying) or *vehicular* travel (forces are indirectly produced through interaction a virtual vehicle or interface; e.g., the throttle and steering wheel).

User Mobility: Finally, it is possible to distinguish between travel techniques where the user is *mobile* (physical movement is necessary for virtual travel) or *stationary* (the user remains stationary while moving virtually).

Most of the travel techniques belonging to each of the eight sub-categories of the taxonomy (Fig. 1) have their merits in that they provide the users with a means to navigate virtual environments. Nevertheless, not all are equally viable in relation to consumer IVR, and the nature of the individual techniques makes them useful only to a limited set of applications [16]. In relation to metaphor plausibility there are important difference between techniques that qualify as either magical or mundane. For one, Bowman et al. [4] have suggested that magical techniques in many cases can be designed so as to offer superior task performance compared to mundane techniques. To exemplify, if the user is required to traverse great distances in the VR, then teleportation is likely to be much more efficient than virtual walking. However, the superior task performance can come at the expense of familiarity [4] and the given application may itself call for a technique based on a mundane metaphor; i.e., any scenario taking place in a world adhering to the same rules as physical reality. IVR has been used to simulate a range of different types of mundane forms of vehicular transport, and vehicle simulators have arguably used to provide some of the most compelling IVR experiences [5]. However, we frequently navigating our surroundings on foot and walking is generally regarded as a natural and promising approach to virtual travel [24]. Thus, it seems likely that many applications for consumer IVR will also involve body-centric modes of locomotion, such as walking and running. Turning to the question of user mobility, allowing users to physically walk through virtual environments provides a number of advantages;

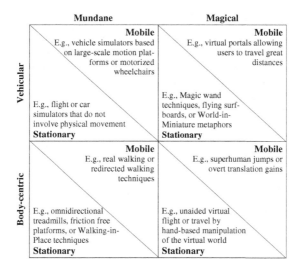

Fig. 1. Illustration of our taxonomy [16] which organizes virtual travel techniques based on virtual movement source (vertical axis), metaphor plausibility (horizontal axis), and user movement (division of each cell).

e.g., the physical translation produces vestibular self-motion information which furthers the walker's spatial understanding [3]. Indeed, real walking has been highlighted as the most obvious and direct technique for virtual travel [3]. However, real walking poses a considerable problem since the virtual environment is likely to be larger than the physical interaction space. A number of mobile travel techniques have sought so minimize this issue. Most notably, redirection techniques that makes it possible to discretely or continuously, reorient or reposition the user through overt or subtle manipulation of the stimuli used to represent the virtual world (for an overview of redirection techniques see [25]). While such solutions seem very promising they do require the user to physically move and therefore do not seem feasible for consumer IVR where the spatial constraints are prominent. Several stationary approaches to virtual walking have been proposed, including but not limited to, omnidirectional treadmills [8], human-sized hamster balls [13] and friction-free platforms, [26]. In principle such systems could be deployed in the homes of consumers, but most current solutions require a considerable amount of space and even the cheaper alternatives [7] come at a relatively high price. Walking-in-Place techniques, constitute a practical and inexpensive alternative which can implemented using off-the-shelf hardware. The advantages of WIP locomotion include, cost-effectiveness and convenience [9], good performance on simple spatial orienting tasks [33], proprioceptive feedback similar, though not identical, real walking [22], and the ability to elicit a stronger sense of presence than more traditional peripherals [29]. Combined, these potential benefits suggest the need for finding the best possible WIP technique.

3   Walking-in-Place Techniques

It is possible to break down the process of producing virtual walking from steps in place into three steps: (1) proxy step detection, (2) speed estimation, and (3) steering [32]. The following review focuses on different approaches to these three steps (for a more comprehensive review of proposed WIP techniques and the evaluations of these please refer to [16]).

3.1   Proxy Step Detection

Proxy step detection can be performed using a variety of different hardware based on tracking of different body parts and varying properties of the performed movement. Generally it is possible to distinguish between systems that detect discrete gait events (e.g., foot-ground contact) and systems that track continuous movement (e.g., foot position and velocity) [14].

Physical walking platforms fall into the former category. Bouguila et al. [2] describe such an interface which is able to detect the user's stepping speed based on four load sensors embedded in the platform. Moreover, this platform is able to reorient the user towards the visual display, and it is able to simulate surface inclines and declines via three air cylinders mounted underneath the platform. Similarly, the *Walking Pad* is a physical platform that is able to detect the user's step frequency based on 60 iron switch sensors embedded on a 45 cm × 45 cm plexiglass surface [1]. This high number of sensors also makes it possible to detect the user's orientation when both feet are grounded. Notably, this type of interaction has also been accomplished using commercially available hardware. Specifically, Wii Balance Boards, which are embedded with four pressure sensors, have been used to detect user's steps during virtual locomotion [33]. The technique dubbed *Shadow Walking* [35] takes a very different approach to proxy step detection; i.e., a camera is used to track the shadows cast by the users' feet onto the floor of an under-floor projection system within a six-sided CAVE, and based on this information the stepping speed is derived.

Interestingly, one of the earliest WIP techniques—the *Virtual Treadmill* [22]—did not involve tracking of the lower limbs. Instead, this technique relied on electromagnetic tracking of the user's head movements and used a neural network to determine if the user was walking in place. The technique *Low-Latency, Continuous-Motion Walking-in-Place* (LLCM-WIP) relied on magnetic tracking to determine the vertical velocity of the user's heels [9]. The successor of the LLCM-WIP—called *Gait-Understanding-Driven Walking-In-Place* (GUD-WIP)—similarly derived walking speeds from the velocity of the user's vertical heel movement, but did so using an optical motion capture system [31]. One of the most recent WIP techniques—*Speed-Amplitude-Supported Walking-in-Place* (SAS-WIP)— also used optical motion tracking but relied on the footstep amplitude rather than heel-motion velocity [6]. Continuous tracking of the user's movement can also be achieved using commercially available hardware. Particularly, the technique *Sensor-Fusion Walking-in-Place* (SF-WIP) is based on the acceleration and magnetic sensors embedded within two smart phones in combination with a magnet [10], and the skeletal data provided by Microsoft's Kinect has also been used to facilitating WIP locomotion [12].

Finally, a combination of discrete and continuous tracking has also been used to facilitate WIP locomotion; e.g., the *Gaiter* WIP technique, allowed users to control virtual movement through a combination of force sensors embedded in shoe insoles and magnetic [27] or optical motion tracking [28].

3.2   Speed Estimation

Much of the literature on WIP techniques do not provide detailed accounts of how virtual speeds are produced from the user's input [9]. Perhaps as a consequence, there is no generally accepted way of doing so. Based on a personal correspondence with one of the creators of the Virtual Treadmill, Feasel et al. [9] describe that this early WIP technique produced discrete viewpoint displacement; i.e., when the neural network registered a step, the viewpoint abruptly jumped a full step length forward. Moreover, this technique suffered from noticeable starting and stopping latency because movement was not instigated until four steps in place were detected, and movement would not be terminated unless no steps were detected for two full gait cycles. The LLCM-WIP, developed by Feasel et al. [9], was designed in order to provide low starting and stopping latency, continuous motion between steps, control of the speed during steps, and minimize erroneous movement during turns on the spot. LLCM-WIP does as mentioned take the velocity of the user's heel movement as input (derived from the positional tracking through numerical differentiation). In very general terms the algorithm produces the virtual speed by smoothing the heel velocities of each foot (low-pass filtering), summing the resulting signals, and scaling this sum so that the output speed on average matches the users' real walking speeds. The GUD-WIP algorithm reportedly outperforms the LLCM-WIP and differs from its predecessors in that it is informed by human biomechanics and produce walking speeds that better correspond with those of real walking. Moreover, it determines the virtual speed based on a biomechanics-inspired state machine that can estimate the step frequency several times per step. Since real walking speeds can be estimated from the height of an individual and a given step frequency, this permits the algorithm to produce realistic walking speeds (for implementation details see [31]). SAS-WIP does as mentioned rely on footstep amplitudes, rather than step frequencies, for producing virtual speeds. This approach was chosen since steps in place, unlike real walking, predominantly involve vertical motions and each step may also take less time to complete. Specifically, the virtual velocity is calculated through multiplication of the foot speed and a scale factor based on the foot amplitude, and movement is stopped when both feet are grounded for more than an amount of time which is varied based on the foot speed [6]. Finally, Langbehn et al. [12] have proposed *Leaning-Amplified-Speed Walking-in-Place* (LAS-WIP). This technique is not interesting because of the way virtual speeds are derived from steps in place. Instead, it involves a novel way of scaling the speed derived from the steps in place; i.e., the user is able to increase the speed by leaning the torso forward.

3.3   Steering

In relation to virtual travel steering amount to the continuous manipulation of the direction of heading [3]. The direction of heading can either be derived from the data used for proxy step detection, as was the case in relation to the physical platforms described in subsection 3.1, or it can be obtained from additional trackers mounted on the user. At least five different approaches to steering during WIP locomotion have been used: joystick-controlled steering, gaze-directed steering, torso-directed steering, hip-directed steering, and feet-directed steering [9,14,33,34]. A potential limitation of using joysticks or similar peripherals for steering is that this will deprive the user of the proprioceptive and kinesthetic feedback produced by whole body turns [28]. An advantage of gaze-directed steering, which translates the virtual position in the viewing direction, is that one does not need sensors besides from the ones used for head tracking. A limitation of this approach is that it limits the user's ability to look around the environment while walking [33]. Nevertheless, it has been documented that gaze-directed steering may be experinced as preferable and perform better than torso-directed steering in regards to certain spatial orienting tasks [34]. Notably, in relation to torso-directed steering, trackers are often placed on the chest [9]. However, it has been suggested that placement of the tracker near the waist may be preferable [3] (i.e., something akin to hip-directed steering).

4   A Question of Naturalness

The novelty of proposed WIP techniques often derives from the particular hardware or algorithms used to enable virtual movement, and the evaluations usually involve comparisons with existing WIP techniques or other approaches to virtual locomotion (for a more detailed account of common measures please refer to [16]). Improvements to hardware and algorithms are undoubtedly crucial. However, considering that the general aim of WIP techniques is to provide an alternative to real walking, it seems meaningful for research on WIP locomotion to focus more explicitly on how we increase the *perceived naturalness* of the walking experience; i.e., how we can make the experience of navigating through virtual worlds using WIP techniques feel more like the real thing. Specifically, we have argued that when striving to increase the perceived naturalness of WIP locomotion, it is meaningful to take as the point of departure, the degree of correspondence between the sensorimotor loop of real walking and walking in place [15]. This view has led us to focus on two distinct, albeit interconnected questions: (1) How can we increase the perceived naturalness of the actions perform by the user during WIP locomotion? (2) How can we increase the perceived naturalness of the perception of the virtual environment resulting from said actions? In what follows we address each of these two general research questions and present the work we have performed thus far in order to address them.

5 Perceptually Natural Actions

The question of how to facilitate natural actions may be subdivided into at least two different, albeit interconnected, challenges; namely, the challenge of finding the gestural input which is perceived as the most natural by the user, and the challenge of how to provide the user with the most natural method for steering.

5.1 Gestural Input for WIP Locomotion

While a few exceptions exist [27], it would seem that most WIP techniques generally take the same gesture as input; i.e., a stepping gesture where the user alternately lifts each leg as if marching on the spot. However, it was the belief that this gesture might be less than optimal for two reasons: (1) It appeared to be more physically straining than real walking which may decrease perceived naturalness. (2) When used in combination with a head-mounted display (HMD), the user tends to physically drift in the direction of heading [32]. This motivated us to perform two within-subjects studies exploring alternative gestural input for WIP locomotion. The first study ($n=27$) [14] compared three gestures: the common WIP gesture, *Wiping* (alternately bending each knee as if wiping the feet on a doormat), and *Tapping* (alternately tapping each heel against the ground). The second study [15] ($n=20$) was focused on gestures devoid of explicit leg motion and compared four gestures: the common WIP gesture, *Hip Movement* (alternately swinging the hips to the left and right), *Arm Swinging* (alternately swinging each arm back and forth), and keyboard input (while standing the user pressed a button to move). In both studies the participants performed a simple walking task requiring them to walk along a predefined path within a scenic virtual environment. The visuals were presented using a HMD and the users' movements tracked using an optical motion capture system. The different types of gestural input were among other things compared based on self-reported measures of how natural they were (to what extent did they feel like real walking) and how physically straining they were compared to real walking. The amount of physical drift was logged during all walks. The results of the first study revealed that Tapping was perceived to be as natural as the traditional gesture and corresponded best with real walking in terms of perceived exertion. Also, Tapping led to significantly less drift than Wiping and the traditional gesture. The second study revealed that Arm Swining and the traditional gesture were perceived to be the most natural, and Arm Swinging provided the best match with real walking in terms of physical strain. The fact that Arm Swinging prevents walkers from interacting with their hands while walking combined with the ratings of naturalness across the two studies led us to believe that Tapping probably would be preferable for most applications. Even though Tapping, or a variation of this gesture, seems promising, it does not solve the problem of how to enable backwards and lateral movement. While a few exceptions exist [27, 35], most work on WIP locomotion has focused on forwards movement. Thus, it is necessary for future research to explore the gestural input and algorithms, that can produce perceptually natural movement in other directions.

5.2   Perceptually Natural Steering

The question of what body part to rely on when deriving the user's orientation is still an open question. While gaze-directed steering may be superior on certain spatial orienting tasks, this steering method will presumably be perceived as less natural since it differs notably from how steering is performed during real walking. At first glance, the difference between torso-directed and hip-directed steering seems negligible. However we have informally observed that torso-directed steering using a tracker on the chest may be less natural compared to feet-based or hip-based steering since users may slightly turn their upper bodies while looking around the environment and thereby veer off course. Future studies should compare these steering methods in order to determine which ones are the most natural and how they affect performance and spatial perception.

6   Perceptually Natural Self-Motion and Limb-Movement

The question of how to facilitate natural perception, may also be subdivided into at least two challenges; i.e., the challenge of facilitating natural self-motion perception and natural movement of virtual limbs.

6.1   Motion Perception During WIP Locomotion

Existing WIP techniques have aspired to produce realistic walking speeds [9,31], and intuitively one might expect realistic speeds to be preferable. However, studies have shown that individuals tend to underestimate visually presented speeds when walking on a linear treadmill; i.e., visual speeds mathcing the treadmill speed feel too slow (for examples see references in [17]). If the same is true of WIP locomotion, then it is necessary to establish what speeds are perceived as natural during this form of locomotion. We performed seven studies and two meta-analyses in order to determine if speeds are indeed misperceived during WIP locomotion, and explore what factors that influence this misperception [17–20]. Common to all seven studies was that the participants would walk in place and walk on a treadmill down a virtual corridor at a fixed step frequency (1.8 steps per second) while a HMD displayed a range of visual gains; i.e., scalar multiples of their normal walking speed (1.0 would correspond to their normal walking speed). They were then asked to determine at what gains the speed was natural; i.e., it matched the movement they were performing. Across the studies three different gain presentation methods (GPMs) were used, implying that there were differences in terms of how the gains were presented and how the participants provided their judgements. (1) *Randomized Order* (RO): Each gain was repeated twice and they were presented in randomized order, and the participants judged if each gain was 'too slow', 'natural', or 'too fast'. (2) *Reversed Staircases* (RS): Each gain was repeated twice, but either in an ascending or descending series, and judgements were made as in relation to RO. (3) *User Adjustment* (UA): the speed would either start at the lowest or the highest gain, the participants controlled the visual speed using a scroll wheel and had to identify the upper and lower limits of the speeds they found natural. The three methods were adapted from existing psychophysical methods (the method of constant stimuli, the method of limits and the method of adjustment) All seven studies (S1-S7) relied on within-subjects designs and compared WIP and treadmill locomotion. S1 involved two additional movement types (Tapping and no leg movement), S2 compared four different display field of view (FOV), S3 compared three different geometric FOV, S4 compared three different degrees of peripheral occlusion, S5 compared two different HMD weights, S6 compared three different step frequencies, and S7 compared the three different gain presentation methods outlined above. Table 1 presents the number of participants, gain presentation method, range of gains and conditions used in S1 to S7.

Table 1. No. of participants, GPMs, range of gains and conditions of S1 to S7.

Study	n	GPM	Gain range	Conditions[a]
S1 [17]	20	RO	1.0-3.0	4 movement types
S2 [17]	20	RS	1.0-3.0	4 display FOV
S3 [20]	20	UA	0.1-4.0	3 geometric FOV
S4 [20]	20	UA	0.1-4.0	3 deg. of periperal occlusion
S5 [19]	19	UA	0.1-4.0	2 HMD weights
S6 [18]	19	UA	0.1-4.0	3 step frequencies
S7 [20]	20	RO, RS, UA	1.0-4.0	3 gain presentation methods

[a] All studies compared WIP and treadmill locomotion

S1 did not reveal significant differences between the traditional WIP gesture, Tapping, treadmill walking and no leg movement. However, we were able to demonstrate that underestimation of visually presented walking speeds may indeed occur during WIP locomotion, and there appear to exist a range of gains that are perceived as natural. S2 revealed significant differences between the different display FOV across both WIP and treadmill locomotion, suggesting that the size of the FOV may be inversely proportional to the degree of underestimation. In other words, the misperception appear to decrease as the FOV of the display becomes larger. In relation to S3, a similar effect was observed with respect to the geometric field of view. S4 and S5 found no significant effects in relation to varying degrees of peripheral occlusion and increased HMD weight. S6 provided some indication that high step frequencies may be accompanied by an increased underestimation of the visually presented speeds. Finally, S7 revealed that the choice of gain presentation method may affect the upper and lower bounds of the gains which participants find natural. While S1 did not suggest that the underestimation of speeds varies across WIP and treadmill locomotion, we were able to provide evidence that there may be a difference through meta-analyses of the data from all seven studies [16]. Particularly, the meta-analyses suggested that individuals tend to find slightly higher speeds natural when walking on a treadmill compared to when they are walking in place.

6.2 Self-Perception During WIP Locomotion

The sensation of virtual body-ownership may be crucial to compelling IVR experiences [21]. However, it may prove difficult to sustain this illusion during WIP locomotion if the virtual legs exhibit normal gait behaviour in response to the user's steps in place. This would produce visuomotor asynchrony which is believed to break the illusion of ownership of the virtual body [11]. Thus, it will be necessary for future work to investigate if there are ways to produce a sense of virtual body-ownership during WIP locomotion.

7 Conclusions

Throughout this paper we presented arguments suggesting that WIP locomotion may prove to be a meaningful way of facilitating virtual walking in relation to consumer IVR. However, there are still challenges that needs to be met. While, WIP techniques have improved greatly since Slater et al. [22] proposed the Virtual Treadmill, it remains important to try and improve techniques with respect to the virtual-locomotion speed-control goals introduced by Feasel et al. [9]: smooth between-step locomotion speed, continuous within-step speed control, real-world turning and manoeuvring, and low starting and stopping latency. With respect to perceptually natural actions, future work should try to determine what gestures that provide the most natural experience of walking forward, backward and laterally, and what steering methods will be perceived as the most natural. With respect to natural perception, we still do not know exactly what causes underestimations of visually presented walking speeds, or if this perceptual distortion will be eliminated once we get HMDs of even higher fidelity. As a consequence it may be necessary to establish HMD specific guidelines describing what gains to apply in order to produce perceptually natural motion perception. Moreover, it has yet to be documented whether virtual body-ownership can be sustained during WIP locomotion. Obviously, the limitations of the available tracking and display systems will constrain the degree of naturalness developers can opt for. To exemplify, systems such as the HTC Vive currently do do not support full body tracking, making it impossible generate self-motion and virtual leg movement from tracking of the lower extremities, and it precludes torso or hip-directed steering. Fortunately, tracking solutions such as Microsoft's Kinect or Sixsense's STEM System could resolve this issue.

The experience of WIP locomotion will probably never become truly mistakable for real walking. Nevertheless, if the challenges outlined in the current paper are addressed, it seems possible that this type of virtual travel may serve as meaningful substitute in relation to consumer IVR. Our hope is that the findings outlined in the current paper will help bring WIP locomotion one step closer to this goal.

References

1. Bouguila, L., Florian, E., Courant, M., Hirsbrunner, B.: Active walking interface for human-scale virtual environment. In: 11th International Conference on Human-Computer Interaction, HCII. vol. 5, pp. 22–27. Citeseer (2005)
2. Bouguila, L., Iwashita, M., Hirsbrunner, B., Sato, M.: Virtual locomotion interface with ground surface simulation. In: Proceedings of the International Conference on Artificial Reality and Telexistence, Tokyo (2003)
3. Bowman, D.A., Kruijff, E., LaViola Jr., J.J., Poupyrev, I.: 3D User Interfaces: Theory and Practice. Addison-Wesley Professional, Reading (2004)
4. Bowman, D.A., McMahan, R.P., Ragan, E.D.: Questioning naturalism in 3D user interfaces. Commun. ACM **55**(9), 78–88 (2012)
5. Brooks Jr., F.P.: What's real about virtual reality? IEEE Comput. Graph. Appl. **19**(6), 16–27 (1999)
6. Bruno, L., Pereira, J., Jorge, J.: A new approach to walking in place. In: Kotzé, P., Marsden, G., Lindgaard, G., Wesson, J., Winckler, M. (eds.) INTERACT 2013, Part III. LNCS, vol. 8119, pp. 370–387. Springer, Heidelberg (2013)
7. Cakmak, T., Hager, H.: Cyberith virtualizer: A locomotion device for virtual reality. In: ACM SIGGRAPH 2014 Emerging Technologies. p. 6. ACM (2014)
8. Darken, R., Cockayne, W., Carmein, D.: The omni-directional treadmill: A locomotion device for virtual worlds. In: Proceedings of the 10th annual ACM symposium on user interface software and technology. pp. 213–221. ACM (1997)
9. Feasel, J., Whitton, M., Wendt, J.: Llcm-wip: Low-latency, continuous-motion walking-in-place. In: Proceedings of the 2008 IEEE Symposium on 3D User Interfaces. pp. 97–104. IEEE (2008)
10. Kim, J., Gracanin, D., Quek, F.: Sensor-fusion walking-in-place interaction technique using mobile devices. In: 2012 IEEE Virtual Reality Short Papers and Posters. pp. 39–42. IEEE (2012)
11. Kokkinara, E., Slater, M.: Measuring the effects through time of the influence of visuomotor and visuotactile synchronous stimulation on a virtual body ownership illusion. Perception **43**(1), 43–58 (2014)
12. Langbehn, E., Eichler, T., Ghose, S., von Luck, K., Bruder, G., Steinicke, F.: Evaluation of an omnidirectional walking-in-place user interface with virtual locomotion speed scaled by forward leaning angle. In: Proceedings of the GI Workshop on Virtual and Augmented Reality (GI VR/AR). pp. 149–160 (2015)
13. Medina, E., Fruland, R., Weghorst, S.: Virtusphere: Walking in a human size VR hamster ball. In: Proceedings of the Human Factors and Ergonomics Society AnnualMeeting. vol. 52, pp. 2102–2106. SAGE Publications (2008)
14. Nilsson, N., Serafin, S., Laursen, M.H., Pedersen, K.S., Sikström, E., Nordahl, R.: Tapping-in-place: Increasing the naturalness of immersive walking-in-place locomotion through novel gestural input. In: Proceedings of the 2013 IEEE Symposium on 3D User Interfaces. IEEE (2013)
15. Nilsson, N., Serafin, S., Nordahl, R.: The perceived naturalness of virtual locomotion methods devoid of explicit leg movements. In: Proceedings of Motion in Games. ACM (2013)
16. Nilsson, N.C.: Walking Without Moving: An exploration of factors influencing the perceived naturalness of Walking-in-Place techniques for locomotion in virtual environments. Ph.D. thesis, Aalborg University Copenhagen (2016)
17. Nilsson, N.C., Serafin, S., Nordahl, R.: Establishing the range of perceptually natural visual walking speeds for virtual walking-in-place locomotion. vol. 20, pp. 569–578. IEEE (2014)

18. Nilsson, N.C., Serafin, S., Nordahl, R.: The influence of step frequency on the range of perceptually natural visual walking speeds during walking-in-place and treadmill locomotion. In: Proceedings of the 20th ACM Symposium on Virtual Reality Software and Technology. pp. 187–190. ACM (2014)

19. Nilsson, N.C., Serafin, S., Nordahl, R.: The effect of head mounted display weight and locomotion method on the perceived naturalness of virtual walking speeds. In: Virtual Reality (VR), pp. 249–250, IEEE (2015)

20. Nilsson, N.C., Serafin, S., Nordahl, R.: The effect of visual display properties and gain presentation mode on the perceived naturalness of virtual walking speeds. In: Virtual Reality (VR), IEEE 2015, pp. 81–88. IEEE (2015)

21. Slater, M.: Place illusion and plausibility can lead to realistic behaviour in immersive virtual environments. Philosophical Transactions of the Royal Society B: Biological Sciences 364(1535), 3549–3557 (2009)

22. Slater, M., Usoh, M., Steed, A.: Taking steps: the influence of a walking technique on presence in virtual reality. ACM Trans. Comput.-Hum. Interact. 2(3), 201–219 (1995)

23. Slater, M., Usoh, M.: Body centred interaction in immersive virtual environments. Artif. Life Virtual Reality 1, 125–148 (1994)

24. Steinicke, F., Visell, Y., Campos, J., Lécuyer, A.: Human Walking in Virtual Environments: Perception, Technology, and Applications. Springer, Heidelberg (2013)

25. Suma, E., Bruder, G., Steinicke, F., Krum, D., Bolas, M.: A taxonomy for deploying redirection techniques in immersive virtual environments. In: 2012 IEEE Virtual Reality Short Papers and Posters. pp. 43–46. IEEE (2012)

26. Swapp, D., Williams, J., Steed, A.: The implementation of a novel walking interface within an immersive display. In: Proceedings of the 2010 IEEE Symposium on 3D User Interfaces. pp. 71–74. IEEE (2010)

27. Templeman, J., Denbrook, P., Sibert, L.: Virtual locomotion: Walking in place through virtual environments. Presence 8(6), 598–617 (1999)

28. Templeman, J.N., Sibert, L.E., Page, R.C., Denbrook, P.S.: Immersive simulation to train urban infantry combat. Technical report, DTIC Document (2006)

29. Usoh, M., Arthur, K., Whitton, M., Bastos, R., Steed, A., Slater, M., Brooks Jr., F.: Walking > walking-in-place > flying, in virtual environments. In: Proceedings of the 26th annual conference on Computer Graphics and Interactive Techniques. pp. 359–364. ACM Press/Addison-Wesley Publishing Co. (1999)

30. Wendt, J.: Real-walking models improve walking-in-place systems. Ph.D. thesis, University of North Carolina at Chapel Hill (2010)

31. Wendt, J., Whitton, M., Brooks, F.: Gud wip: Gait-understanding-driven walking-in-place. In: Proceedings of the 2010 IEEE Virtual Reality Conference. pp. 51–58. IEEE (2010)

32. Whitton, M.C., Razzaque, S.: Locomotion interfaces case study (2008)

33. Williams, B., Bailey, S., Narasimham, G., Li, M., Bodenheimer, B.: Evaluation of walking in place on a wii balance board to explore a virtual environment. Proc. ACM Trans. Appl. Percept. 8(3), 19 (2011)

34. Williams, B., McCaleb, M., Strachan, C., Zheng, Y.: Torso versus gaze direction to navigate a ve by walking in place. In: Proceedings of the ACM Symposium on Applied Perception, 67–70. ACM (2013)

35. Zielinski, D., McMahan, R., Brady, R.: Shadow walking: An unencumbered locomotion technique for systems with under-floor projection. In: Proceedings of the 2011 IEEE Virtual Reality Conference, pp. 167–170. IEEE (2011)

Body Editing: Dance Biofeedback Experiments in Apperception

Paula Gardner[✉], Hart Sturgeon, Lee Jones, and Stephen Surlin

Mobile Lab, OCAD University, Toronto, Canada
gardnerp@mcmaster.ca

Abstract. Body Editing is a dual gesture-based and EEG platform that transforms movement, gesture and brain wave data into visual and audio feedback with which dancers engage improvisationally. The platform, uniquely, offers a creature that responds in emergent fashion to the dancer's movement, allowing for improvisation. The emergent algorithm directing the creature's response is informed by Karen Barad's understanding that intra-action in emergent systems is a form of performativity. The wireless EEG monitor provides intuitive musical sounds corresponding to brain wave data that signal to the dancer moments when she is dancing in an unthought or apperceptive manner, in contrast to moments when she is thinking the interface and thus learning, but not improvising. Dancers describe this experience as performing duets with the emergent creature.

Keywords: Gesture based experience · Dance improvisation · EEG monitor · Interactive media · Human computer interaction · Emergent behaviour · Biometric feedback

1 Introduction

Body Editing is a gesture and biofeedback installation that asks critical human computer action questions regarding how we understand our movement and biodata data when it is presented in various forms—both as 2D graphic output and as aesthetic (sound, music visual or other) feedback in a digital installation format. In this research, conducted at the Mobile Experience Lab at OCAD University (Toronto), we investigate user experiences with movement and biometric data feedback, asking at what stage and with what technological assistance users might engage in embodied interaction or unthought dance.

1.1 Body Editing Platform and Experiments

The platform uses a depth sensing 3D camera for gesture and movement capture, and a wireless EEG sensing headset to capture brain wave and heart rate data. Our agile software interface enables us to code aesthetic feedback including real-time generated graphics and music or sound effects that respond to biofeedback, gesture and movement in the installation space.

Our research experiments with the platform inquires into whether participants must "learn" the machine-feedback programming (how the algorithm translates their data

© Springer International Publishing Switzerland 2016
M. Kurosu (Ed.): HCI 2016, Part II, LNCS 9732, pp. 49–60, 2016.
DOI: 10.1007/978-3-319-39516-6_5

into feedback) in order to engage in apperceptive or "unthought" movement with their own data feedback. This paper will examine our research experiments with improvisational dancers to: query the role of the graphic markings of bodies in space; make transparent the complex algorithm to determine whether it helps dancers to learn the system or perhaps frustrates dancers; and in either case whether these learnings release dancers into apperceptive performance.

We experiment with relaying visual and audio feedback in frequencies that are similar symbolically, conceptually and metaphorically to users' biodata. The study addresses whether certain biodata is assumed to be more readily identifiable in particular graphic or audio feedback forms. We query whether mimicking exact bio-frequencies in the audio or visual feedback help dancers to move apperceptively or in "unthought" manners.

Finally, we will discuss our experiments delivering visual elements using procedural generation that produces animated mandalas that respond to dancers' movement and biodata. We query whether dancers' ongoing random interaction with the mandala creates an experience that is phenomenologically different from one where the programmer has written and can teach the algorithm to the dancers. In other words, if dancers are continually interacting with newly generated mandala patterns, does it qualitatively change the dance experience? In this case, does the dance become a duet rather than a dancerly response to data?

2   Background

2.1   Theory Meets Practice

Art practice provides the distinct opportunity to probe these interfaces through experiments that ask how participants perceive and mediate space, machinic logic, and aesthetic feedback in manners that are embodied, or perhaps intermittently embodied. Where theory can trace what appears to be experiences of presence, apperception, embodiment, or interaction, art practice invites us, as participants, to reflect by engaging in material experience and importantly, to do so via creative and aesthetic experience. In our art based research creation practices, then, we specifically inquire into how art practice interacts with perception and apperception. More, we ask how dancer's interactions with gesture and movement data might differ or intersect with interactions with their brain wave data.

2.2   HCI Concerns Regarding Embodiment, Perception and Apperception

Researchers are concerned that in our contemporary practices with biometric machines, we are losing an understanding of the complex network of mind-body relations. Researchers show that scientific research in neural networks, the human genome, and genetic sequencing digest the human mind and body into computational, biological entities. (Galloway 2004; Kember and Zylinska 2012). This so-called reductionist view has far reaching effects; Nikolas Rose laments that the "recoding of everyday affects and conducts in terms of their neurochemistry is only one element of a more widespread mutation in which we in the West... have come to understand our minds and selves in terms of our brains and bodies." (2003, 46). Specifically, researchers have argued that data visualisations often succumb to the Cartesian grid, missing other spatial actions beyond 3D environments. The invisibility of the algorithm results in common cultural practices of data fetishization, where we unduly trust that data as objective, and coherently reference it a discernible thing. For Chun (2009), the separation of algorithm from interface or software from hardware makes it a powerful metaphor for everything we believe is invisible, and yet generates visible effects. This separation creates an understanding of code as a thing rather than a process, fetishizing and reducing the complexity of code processing, and generating the sense in participants that seeing (the output) is knowing (the complexity of the instructions).

Researchers have called for HCI research and art practices to open up algorithms and interfaces to transparency, encouraging users to understand the complex cognitive, perceptive and aesthetic interactions between humans and computers (Hayles 1999; Braidotti 2013; Suchman 1987). Suchman (1987) charges that interaction is not information exchange or operationalized intention; rather, it is the ongoing, contingent, coproduction of diverse matter, things, output, and selves. Marc Andrejevic (2013) charges that we view physical data, such as that produced by sensors, as outside of symbolism or cognition– as 'automatic, immediate, and unreflexive.' To counter our disembodied and unproblematic readings of data, Chun (2009) suggests we should engage in play with code, thus cracking open subject-object relations. Recognizing that the digital environment frames the user's affective experience, Munster (2006) calls for exploiting the exaggerated aesthetics of digital/material interfaces in sensual engagements; in so doing, we can, she argues, embody users in spaces of difference, enabling an acute querying of subjectivity and the body. Similarly, Suchman (1987) calls on us to engage the creative and aesthetically performative human.

Our premise, then, is that as makers, we need to craft human machine interactions, meaning both machining and aesthetic practices, allowing for transparent, process-based, and multisensorial experiences, in order to more fully engage participants in interactivity, immersion and embodiment. Our team's research interventions assume that how users perceive and interpret algorithms and biodata visuals is linked to their ability to maintain agency and critical engagement with machines. That is, participants trust the data visualization/output produced by the algorithm only in so far as it resonates with their embodied experience. As such, this project undertakes experiments that engage the problem of interactivity and queries the nature of how participants sense very different types of data – gesture and movement data, as well as brain wave data.

3 Background- Art Experiments

3.1 Biofeedback Interactions

Artists have engaged in movement and meditation experiments to query how participants engage via aesthetics to understand spatialisation, and how mindfulness, or control of brain wave function, might create engaging aesthetic experiments.

Australian artist George Khut has experimented in biofeedback and embodiment, for example, in Res'onance-Body [box] (2003). In these experiences, participants sat in a dark space, in reclined chairs facing a projection screen with circular pulsating visualizations of their breath and heart rhythm biofeedback. Khut's research aims to understand how arts practice can represent subjectivity as a physiologically embodied phenomenon. (2006) Notably Khut's team concludes that elements of the research apparatus (e.g. lighting) caused unstable periods of "mindfulness" that signaled failed embodiment.

David Rokeby's Very Nervous System (1986–1990) is an interactive sound installation that responds to participants' movements with responsive music. The computer observes, through video camera, the physical gestures of bodies, and responds with improvised music to the action. Rokeby here is trying to counter the computer's "tiny playing field of integrated circuits" that disembodies, by making the human experience take place in human-scaled physical space. Rokeby notes that the interface is invisible and diffuse; the interaction is unclear at first but becomes clearer as the user engages. He describes the interaction as a feedback loop where human and computer elements change in response to each other—the two "interpenetrate until the notion of control is lost and the relationship becomes encounter and involvement. (Rokeby 2016, p. 1) After an hour in the responsive system, Rokeby described feeling strongly connected to his surrounding environment; he notes that continued use of the interface can become a type of 'belief system'—that the interfaces we use leave imprints on us, and the longer we use them the stronger the imprint (2016).

Char Davies's performance work, Osmose (2009) engages with users' biometric (heart rhythm) data to explore their spatial natures, with careful attention to the role of aesthetic experience. Uniquely, Davies is an artist, programmer, and a reader of quantum theory. Davie's work is thus deeply informed by the theoretical problematics of rendering virtual and digital space into a Cartesian grid that is often anything but immersive. Davies finds that the realist, visual aesthetic common to Virtual Reality and computer graphics recreates a false (Cartesian) dichotomy of subject/object. Her success in thwarting that separation comes from her unique, informed, critical attention to the sensual and aesthetic experience of the time/space of the digital. Davie's work queries the human-object and human-human interface with technology by probing our relationships to our own data – of motion, and biodata. She presses questions regarding the phenomenological experience of this interface, asking how much the interface can meld with experience so that the technology becomes one, with and alongside our own, well known and deeply felt, experiences of breath, and of movement.

The work of Kutz addresses user's sense of spatialization made possible through mindfulness or biometric experiences that are aestheticized with attention to the experience, but not necessarily the role of the aesthetic. As well, we understand mindfulness differently as an incoherent, unstable experience wherein one migrates in and out of the "mindfulness"; this is evidenced in our own research experiences capturing "mindfulness" periods using brain wave monitors (Gardner and Wray 2013) Rokeby's feedback loop experience notes a decidedly "apperceptive" type of experience; we are interested in the types of engagement that become possible in both "responsive" and other types of environments that are less responsive, and more random. Our experiments, as we shall present, query whether instead of Rokeby's "belief system" formed in response to anticipating the feedback, one can engage in apperception in response to an inability to anticipate the rules structure. Davies' work inspires our project in its probing of both the scales of human to human and human to computer interactions, querying the role of the interfaces in the experience—in our experiment, that of apperception.

3.2 Apperception, Embodied Theory and Improvisational Dance

Apperception, according to Emmanuel Kant, is where the world and experience come together—it is internal experience uniting with conscious experience. (1781/1996) Gilles Deleuze (1968) provided a more digestible understanding of apperception as the "unthought," or what is yet to be thought. For Deleuze, the unthought is automatic and autonomous – it is not a response to a thing, as in representation, but rather it is a process–a becoming. It is not a performance, but rather "something in the world forces us to think." (Deleuze 1968, p. 139). Digital theorists have, as noted above, suggested that embodiment is an undertheorized experience of the digital interface. We suggest that the embodied and apperceptive nature of dance improvisation presents an opportunity to query potentials for apperceptive interaction in human-machine interfaces. Notably, dancers employ techniques that heighten or challenge possibilities to engage in improvisational moment.

One standard technique of improvisation uses a technique of "Yes, and...," where dancers or performers accept and work with whatever aesthetic, movement or intervention is offered to them by another performer. A second technique can be described as "mini challenges," where, while the improvisational dancer works in a interface, she attempts to engage a certain action in response to a certain probe (e.g. a particular dancerly response (e.g. "juicy") when a particular sound or musical event occurs. In this way, the dancer adds additional aesthetic challenges to the already unpredictable nature of improvisational dance, heightening the tension between incoming stimuli and dancerly response, or instigating the mind/body to respond in an "unthought" dancerly manner. Our challenge was to create a human-computer interface that manifest these potentials for improvisational or unthought movement between dancer and her data feedback.

4 Prototypes Toward Apperceptive and Embodied Movement

4.1 Introduction to Prototypes

To meet this challenge, we sought to engage with both the concept of interface transparency, and lack of transparency, as well as multisensorial feedback opportunities. We developed multiple platform prototypes that sought to, iteratively: (a) engage users in apperceptive response to gesture-and movement-based data is visual form; (b) engage users in apperceptive brain wave-based data in audio form; and (c) to analyse the relationship between these two coinciding experiences of responding to gesture and brain wave data.

4.2   Experiments with Responsive Visuals

The Body Editing platform seeks to create a responsive audiovisual environment, which reacts to the motions and mental activity of the dancer. The responsive visuals take the form of a procedurally generated 'mandala' created out of many overlapping components with different kinds of symmetry.

The mandala mimics a life form in some ways. Each mandala has a 'genotype' of random numbers, which is then 'transcribed' into the visual representation (the 'phenotype'). In this way, it contains both elements of randomness and curation. The mandala is a fractal image; first, a set of small symbols is randomly generated, along with a palette of colors. Then those symbols are combined into radially symmetric rings and layered. Slight random animations are also created to give the mandala some life and organic motion. (See Fig. 1) Each time a user is detected by the Kinect, a new set of linked animations is created for the mandala. Sixteen to thirty-two links are created, with each link taking one property from the Kinect skeleton tracking, for example the position of the left hand, and attaching that to a property of the mandala.

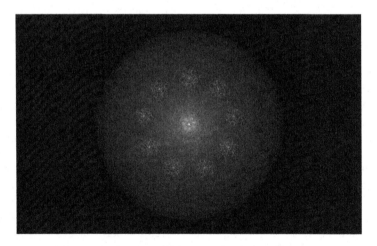

Fig. 1. Emergent mandala visualisation

Parameters tracked include position, distance, depth, normalized distance, and angle of hands, head, torso, and knees. These can be linked to the offset, rotation, position, transparency, speed of animation, or scale of elements in the mandala. This creates a wide range of possible ways for the dancer to affect the movement of the mandala. Some random aspects of animation will remain, even as linked animations are added, giving the dancer something to respond to in the mandala even when they are totally still.

During the Body Editing research process, the team has moved from the Kinect V1 to the Kinect V2. In our research we confronted various limitations with the Kinect V1; for example, dancers disappeared entirely from the system if limbs went outside the sensor area, the sensor did not recognize participants sitting in wheelchairs, and lacked accurate detection of the dancer's position in the performance space. The Kinect V2, which we programmed using Processing, has solved these problems. If a participant's body is slightly out of frame, the Kinect V2 still recognizes the parts that are within, and fixes for those that are outside. Most importantly, the Kinect V2 can pick up on subtle movements such as hand gestures, as well as more joints and body points for increased accuracy.

The Body Editing platform uses a web server running the Meteor framework to synchronize all of the different components. Messages are sent through OSC (open sound control, a network protocol) to and from the web server, allowing the system to synchronize events between audio and visuals and adapt to input from the Kinect and Muse headbands. One computer is used to process the data from the Kinect, a second is used to generate the audio component and read the EEG data, and a third is able to be dedicated solely to running the visual elements. This modular architecture allows for a wide range of possible setups and can accommodate many different kinds of input or applications. (See Fig. 2).

Fig. 2. The Installation Space: Putting on the InterAxon EEG Monitor and testing the gesture interaction with the mandala.

As our series of prototypes developed, we moved away from mapping the input from the Kinect in one-to-one or easily predictable ways. We found that even when the associations between the dancers' actions and the systems' response were complicated and not easily expressible, the dancer still feels that they were generating the interaction and were unable to intuitively sense the unthought response to the feedback. Ultimately, our final prototype produced for the dancer the sense of a 'duet' in which the system both produces content for the dancer to react to and responds gracefully to their actions; this is examined below.

In addition to responding within the structure of the dance itself, the genomic structure of the algorithm permits an element of intuitive composition or choreography, as well. Before beginning a session, the dancer can choose between many randomly constructed mandalas and animations, even mutating and evolving patterns that they like, to collaboratively guide the system toward an audio-visual response that the dancer feels appropriate to their movement. In future prototypes we hope to further explore the possibilities of building an entire dynamic backdrop for a longer form production in which the visuals can change and shift as the show moves between sections blending pre-planned choreography and responsive interaction.

4.3   Experiments in Sound Responses to Data

A second piece of the experiment is to determine how audio feedback in response to brainwave monitors might bring users into apperceptive experiences of dance. Might it be possible that users, when they are able to sense their brain function, (e.g. thinking hard about the how the interaction is programmed; thinking in a relaxed and meditative fashion, other types of thought,) they might be brought more readily into an apperceptive state? How does this experience intersect with the experience of visual feedback in response to participants' gestures and movements in the space? How does audio feedback relate to spatial and movement feedback?

Our information aesthetics experiments query whether dancers respond to particular tones or tensions in music to help them understand different frequencies of brain waves, with attention to Alpha and Beta waves. We tested charts of colours and conceptual sounds that aligned conceptually with the Hz frequencies of these brain waves, to ask whether conceptual affinities helped dancers to either comprehend or intuit (and apperceptively move,) to this data feedback.

The data sonication process uses several stages of hardware and software to translate the users' movement and brainwaves into sound and music. The audio is generated using the visual coding environment Max/MSP 7, to translate numerical data from sensors into musical notation. This musical notation, communicated digitally as MIDI, is turned into music and/or abstract sound by the DAW (Digital Audio Workstation) Ableton Live 8. Within Ableton, notes generated by the users' data are processed into several categories based on the type of brain wave and movement data received from the Muse EEG headset worn by the user. Max and Ableton also processes the notes using a system of filters that nudge the data into musical modes or scales, e.g. C Major, or D Minor and etc. By doing this, the data can be made more musical in a traditional sense, allowing for varying emotional resonances, and brain patterns, depending on the scale chosen.

4.4   Brain Wave Feedback

We conceptualized brain waves detected by the Muse headset, with the following associations, and programmed the system to provide the following corresponding feedback:

Delta waves – .5–.3 Hz: Low frequency and deeply penetrating, like a drumbeat; associated with deep, dreamless sleep (NREM). The amplitude of these waves was used to trigger percussive instruments like real and synthesized drums.

Theta waves – 3–8 Hz: Frequency range associated with dreaming and the intention for movement. The amplitude of this range was tuned to create notes on a droning abstract synthesizer that has a meditative long decay.

Alpha waves – 8–12 Hz: Frequency range associated with being calm and alert. The amplitude of this range was scaled to create chords on a digital grand piano. The intensity of movement along with the amplitude of this range could generate calm relaxing chords or quick and percussive phrases of a piano.

Beta waves – 12–38 Hz: Frequency range associated with being alert and excited at a continually high frequency. This range controlled a bright and fluttering synthesized arpeggio sound, reminiscent of vintage synthesizers.

Gamma waves – 38–42 Hz: Frequency range associated with conscious integration of sensory and mental data and working memory. This range controlled an abstract synth based on pitched noise. The intensity of movement could cause this sound to be a soothing wash of sound, similar to the calm crashing of waves, or to become a full and nearly overwhelming wash of sound.

4.5   Accelerometer Feedback

The accelerometer (3-axis movement sensor) data collected by the Muse headset was programmed to provide the following responses in the system:

X-axis – The left and right lateral movement of the user was used to adjust the length of the user's generated notes. A more abrupt movement to a users' left would create a note held for over 1 s, where a slow movement creates a shorter note.

Y-axis – The up and down movement of a user controlled the rhythm of the generated notes. Fast vertical movements like a high jump or quick crouch would generate fast (1/32 note or 1/16) notes, while slow movements may produce ¼ or whole notes.

Z-axis – The forward and back motion of the user changed the sets the volume or velocity of the notes generated. A fast forward motion would create a loud sound with a MIDI velocity value of 127, while a slow movement may cause a value of 60. For certain synthesis, this value greatly changes the sounds characteristics, including level of filter cutoff frequency or distortion.

This system was designed to allow the user to decipher trends in their brainwave patterns, to facilitate more apperceptive experiences, by creating a correspondence between the conceptual aesthetic readings of the output and their embodied dancing— their dual conceptualization of the system and dancer with it. For example, dancers' fast and large movements/gestures create loud and fast sounds, including movement along the Z-axis, which, if initiated toward an audience, would make the sounds louder. The dancer is also able to mute and unmute individual tracks/brain waves in order to isolate the effects of movement or thought on their mental state, i.e. soloing Theta and Gamma waves to increase the ability to meditate, creating a symbiotic loop.

Using these methods, dancers appeared to struggle with the lack of direct control of audio response that one might be used to, with traditional instruments. However, once a certain amount of control was released by the dancers, they were able to work with the interface and enter a less conscious process of music generation, and by their reflections, a less controlled and more apperceptive experience of movement. Occasionally the interface would create a particularly unexpected sound, based on a spike in certain brain activity, along with a certain movement, this might cause the users' brain pattern to drastically shift, which affected the music, and in turn, broke the dancer out of the apperceptive or embodied dance.

4.6   Discussion: Body Editing Research Experiments

Our series of research experiments with dancers progressively tested their experiences dancing without knowledge of the programmed, platform; with knowledge of the algorithm and with informational graphics that help them to locate their movement and data in the space; in a space where the feedback is programmed by the dancers; and finally, with the generative genomic algorithm producing the changing mandala figure.

In the early iterations, when no instruction is given to the dancer, one can see that she is "sleuthing" the algorithm—she is thinking hard while she moves, trying to remember how to reach for a certain sound, and try to figure out how to remember how to effect a particular sound or image. The feedback seems neither metaphorical nor intuitive to her; instead, she is trying to remember to dance improvisationally. She looks like she is trying to learn and that she is not dancing or "in the zone.'

We found that over time, dancers became more comfortable with "intuitive" algorithmic feedback. One might, for example, reach high for high notes, and move forward to increase musical feedback pace, or move left to right to play a piano keyboard. In such instances, dancers begin to move more fluidly dance with the data, but they weren't dancing in an unthought manner– because they were trying to "work" the interface. The dancing folded toward learning rather than unthinking. In these cases, the machine still led the experience, and the dancers didn't engaged in apperception or embodied interaction.

Our mistake was to assume that apperceptive unthinking or improvisation could be created by relieving the memory of its work. We guessed that training – with visuals in the space that showed for example a gesture into the Y-axis producing a certain sound —could eventually become embodied knowledge. This never happened. So we next recreated the interface to include a brain wave monitor to try to understand how adding brain wave data to the dancer's movement and motion experience might induce 'unthought' dance. Here, the mandala was programmed to intuitively respond to the dancer. The dancers were more engaged in the second iteration, but were entranced by the possibility to anticipate the algorithm, which was clearly based on a rules structure.

The third iteration created a dance most closely resembling apperception. In this version, recall that musical sounds responded to brainwave data, and the animated mandala responded movement and acceleration in the space. It was here that the interaction became one that the dancer described as a "duet." There were two key reasons for this. Foremost, the animated mandala responses, because they based on emergent programming, could not be anticipated. The emergent figure was so lively that we began to refer to it as the organism. Secondly, the brain wave data suggested to the dancer moments when she was spiking cognition (or was in the Beta zone, "thinking the interface") or when, differently she was instead in an Alpha zone, and dancing with the organism. The gentle reminder of brainwave activity worked itself as a form of biofeedback that prodded the dancer to let go and dance, while the organism, with its constantly shifting response to the dancer's movement impelled the dancer to improvisationally respond in duet.

5 Summary

Our experiments in conjoining biofeedback and emergent algorithmic structures to induce unthought movement taught us some key things. First, the dancer's attempt to learn the algorithm in fact disrupts improvisational, unthought dance and instead creates in the dancer the desire to constantly think the dance interface. Second, the brain wave monitors worked in a manner we didn't anticipate, serving as a biofeedback that helped dancers remember to dance improvisationally and to be attuned to the improvisational opportunities offered by the emergent behavior of the visual organism. Notably, the digital interface affords the possibility of employing emergent (rather than responsive) algorithms that invite emergent behaviors or "unthought" dance. It is crucial to note that the aesthetic nature of the organism and the aesthetic qualities of the music feedback afforded this interaction as an art experience for dancers—one that is replete with textural and multi-sensorial qualities that evoke experimental and creative response. The interface allowed the coincidence of these many features—to result in moments of poetic duets between the dancer and the organism.

References

Andrejevic, M.: Infoglut: How Too Much Information Is Changing the Way We Think and Know. Routledge, New York (2013)

Braidotti, R.: The Posthuman. Polity, Cambridge (2013)

Buzsáki, G.: Rhythms of the Brain. Oxford University Press, Oxford (2006)

Chun, W.: Programmed Visions: Software and Memory. MIT Press, Cambridge (2011)

Cohen, A.J.: Film music and unfolding narrative. In: Arbib, M.A. (ed.) Language, Music and the Brain. Strüngmann Forum Reports, J. Lupp, series ed., vol. 10, pp. 173 – 201. MIT Press, Cambridge, MA (2013). ISBN: 978-0-262-01810-4

Cohen, A.J.: How music influences the interpretation of film and video: Approaches from experimental psychology. In: Kendall, R.A., Savage, R.W. (eds.) Selected Reports in Ethnomusicology: Special Issue in Systematic Musicology, vol. 12, pp. 15–36 (2005)

Davies, C.: Osmose. [Art Installation and Video] (1995). http://www.immersence.com/osmose/

Deleuze, G.: Difference and Repetition (1968). Trans. Paul Patton. New York, Colombia University Press (1994)

Galloway, A.R.: Protocol: How Control Exists After Decentralization. MIT press, Cambridge (2004)

Gardner, P., Wray, B.: From Lab to Living Room: Transhumanist Imaginaries of Consumer Brain Wave Monitors. Ada: A Journal of Gender, New Media, and Technology, No. 3 (2013). doi:10.7264/N3GQ6VP4

Hagendoorn, I.G.: Cognitive dance improvisation. How study of the motor system can inspire dance (and vice versa). Leonardo **36**(3), 221–227 (2003)

Hagendoorn, I.: Emergent patterns in dance improvisation and choreography. In: Minai, A.A., Bar-Yam, Y. (eds.) Unifying Themes in Complex Systems IV, pp. 183–195. Springer, Heidelberg (2008)

Hayles, N.K.: How We Became Posthuman: Virtual Bodies in Cybernetics, Literature and Information. University of Chicago Press, Chicago (1999)

Kant, E.: Critique of Pure Reason. Hackett, Indianapolis (1781/1996). Pluhar, W. (Trans.)

Kember, S., Zylinska, J.: Life After New Media: Mediation as a Vital Process. MIT Press, Cambridge (2012)

Khut, G.: Development and Evaluation of Participant-Centred Biofeedback Artworks [Doctoral Exegesis]. University of Wester Sydney, School of Communication Arts, Sydney, Australia (2006). http://georgekhut.com/research/exegesis/

Jung, D., Jensen, M.H., Laing, S., Mayall, J. (2012) Cyclic: an interactive performance combining dance, graphics, music and kinect-technology. In: Proceedings of the 13th International Conference of the NZ Chapter of the ACM's Special Interest Group on Human-Computer Interaction, pp. 36–43. ACM, July 2012

McRobert, L.: Char Davies' Immersive Virtual Art and The Essence of Spatiality. University of Toronto Press, Toronto (2007)

Popper, F.: From Technological to Virtual Art. MIT Press, Cambridge (2007)

Rokeby, D.: Transforming mirrors. Leonardo Electron. Almanac **3**(4), 12 (1995)

Rokeby, D.: The construction of experience: Interface as content. In: Digital Illusion: Entertaining the future with high technology, pp. 27–48 (1998)

Rokeby, D.: Home Webpage (2016). URL: http://www.davidrokeby.com/vns.html

Rodrigues, D.G., Grenader, E., Nos, F.D.S., Dall'Agnol, M.D.S., Hansen, T.E., Weibel, N.: MotionDraw: a tool for enhancing art and performance using kinect. In: CHI 2013 Extended Abstracts on Human Factors in Computing Systems, pp. 1197–1202. ACM, April 2013

Rose, N.: Neurochemical Selves. Society **41**(1), 46–49 (2003)

Spadoni, R.: Uncanny Bodies: The Coming of Sound Film and the Origins of the Horror Genre. University of California Press, Berkeley (2007)

Suchman, L.: Plans and Situated Actions: The Problem of Human-Machine Communication. Cambridge University Press, Cambridge (1987)

Real-Time Gaze Estimation
Using Monocular Vision

Zhizhi Guo[1(✉)], Qianxiang Zhou[1], Zhongqi Liu[1],
Xin Zhang[2], Zhaofang Xu[1], and Yan Lv[1]

[1] School of Biological Science and Medical Engineering,
Beihang University, Beijing 100191, China
1016759797@qq.com
[2] China National Institute of Standardization, Beijing 100191, China
zhangx@cnis.gov.cn

Abstract. Improving the accuracy of gaze estimation and the tolerance of head motion is a common task in the field of gaze estimation. The core problem of gaze estimation is how to accurately build up the mapping relationship between image features and gaze position. To this end, we propose a method to reconstruct input features in the optimized subset as the key to our solution. The HOG feature is considered as the input feature. First, we found the closest calibration point to gaze position and constituted the optimized subset. Then, we get a set of weights that can linear reconstruct test samples in the optimized subset. And this set of weights is used to express the mapping relationship. At last, a linear equation is fitted to solve head motion problem. In this paper, the experiment results demonstrate that our system can achieve high accuracy gaze estimation with one camera.

Keywords: Gaze estimation · Feature reconstruction · Head move compensation · Optimized subset

1 Introduction

Eyes as one of the most important organs, is regarded as an important information input source in the human-interactive, and gaze estimation is considered as an important new type of human-interactive method. Because of its convenience and rapidity, the gaze estimation has been widely researched in recent years. And with the development of image and video processing technology, the high precision gaze estimation on monocular data has been achieved.

In general, gaze estimation method can be roughly divided into model-based method and interpolation-based method. The former method uses the eyeball geometric model, image features and hardware parameters to calculate the gaze position. Although this kind of method has been achieved in the literature [1–7], these systems tend to take at least 2 cameras and some hardware parameters. Even if the hardware cost and the complexity of calibration do not be considered, the deviation of the gaze direction calculated through the model is above 4 degrees.

© Springer International Publishing Switzerland 2016
M. Kurosu (Ed.): HCI 2016, Part II, LNCS 9732, pp. 61–70, 2016.
DOI: 10.1007/978-3-319-39516-6_6

Unlike the model-based method which needs accurate mathematical model as the input information, the interpolation-based methods do not require a calibrated hardware setup or extensive information about the user. This kind of method using the calibration process to construct the mapping relationship between the high-dimensional image features and the low-dimensional gazing space, and the mapping relationship is used to calculate the gaze position of test image. Sugano et al. [8] introduced a method that through Gaussian process regression establishes the mapping relationship between the eye image and the gaze point. They use visual saliency map as the input feature and achieve the accuracy of 3.5 degrees. Villanueva et al. [9] established the mapping relationship using the vector from pupil center to two corneal reflection centers, and the system accuracy reached less than 4 degrees. Cerrolaza et al. [10], Ramanauskas et al. [11] used a similar method to establish the different types of mapping relationship, which reached a similar gaze estimation accuracy.

On the other hand, the interpolation-based method also has its own disadvantages. The accuracy of gaze estimation is closely related to the number of training samples. Xu et al. [12] and Tan et al. [13] used more than 200 training samples to build the mapping relationship between input features and gaze points. Obviously, such a long time calibration process makes the user feels fatigue and disgust, so it can't be spread to commercial use or other applications.

In this paper, we propose a novel interpolation-based gaze estimation method. It utilizes the PCA + HOG feature as input feature. The core idea of the method is to found the optimized subset among all the training samples and used the ℓ^1-minimize to reconstruct test feature vector in optimized subset. The linear combination of the optimized subset is the initial gaze estimation result. Then we construct a gaze compensation equation to compensate the initial gaze estimation result, it can compensate the effect of head movement on initial gaze estimation. Eventually, the gaze estimation result gains good accuracy in the case of only using 33 calibration points.

2   Gaze Estimation Method

This paper obtains the mapping relationship between input feature and gaze position based on the input features reconstruction. The selection of input features is very important, it has decisive effect on the accuracy of features reconstruction. HOG feature has strong robustness to illumination changes and image geometric deformation. Therefore this paper uses the HOG feature as the system input feature.

2.1   Feature Extraction

When gaze position changes, the most intuitive feeling from the 2-D image is that the pupil position in the eye changed. We use the face alignment method proposed by Ren et al. [14] to find the left eye region and the right eye region as the interest area Fig. 1. In the process of HOG feature extraction, the whole eyes image is regarded as a block, and each block is divided into 3*6 cells Fig. 1. In this way, in each eye image, we get a 162-D (3*6*9) feature vector.

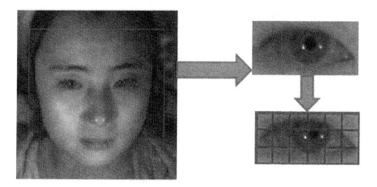

Fig. 1. Feature vector extraction.

Such a big feature vector not only affects the speed of feature reconstruction but also contains a lot of useless feature dimension which will become noise in the process of reconstruction. The main factor that reflects the essence of image changes can be analyzed from high dimensional feature vectors by PCA. It can be seen from Fig. 2, the former 10-D features contains 90 % information of the feature space. Therefore, we use PCA to reduce feature vector dimensions from 162 to 10, and make it to be the system input feature.

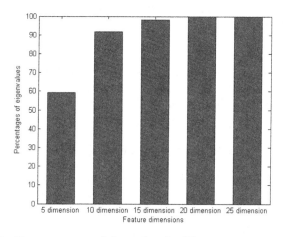

Fig. 2. The percentages of eigenvalues in different feature dimensions

The proposed gaze tracking system is a real-time system, the sizes of two consecutive frames of eye image do not appear a big change. To each test frame, we use the former frame to judge if the interest area is right or not. If the height or weight of interest area has a large change, we skip the frame to test next frame.

2.2   Initial Gaze Estimation

The feature vector reflects the changes of 2-D eye image when gazing at different positions. Assuming a training set of eye images consist of all the eye features matrices $E = [e_1, e_2, \ldots, e_n] \in \mathbb{R}^{m*n}$ and corresponding gaze position matrices $P = [p_1, p_2, \ldots, p_n] \in \mathbb{R}^{1*n}$. We hope to find a mapping from E to P:

$$P = AE \tag{1}$$

where $A \in \mathbb{R}^{1*m}$ is the projection matrix. Obviously, if n > m, the system of equation is overdetermined. We cannot find a mapping matrix that is accurate for all the training samples. However, if n < m, the certain A can be found. So we need to choose the optimized subset $E' = [e'_1, e'_2, \ldots, e'_{n'}]$ and $P' = [p'_1, p'_2, \ldots, p'_{n'}]$ in all training sets. The new mapping can be found:

$$P' = A'E' \tag{2}$$

where A' is the new projection matrix. We hope any test sample $(\hat{e}, \hat{p})$ can find the corresponding A'. So in the process of the mapping relationship constructing, only a few e'_i weights is allowed to be different than zero. We can make the problem of solving the mapping matrix A transformed into selecting the fewest e_i to construct optimized subset in all image training samples. The optimized subset E' should be closely to the test image feature $\hat{e}$, so that they can have a same mapping relationship, and a existed set of reconstruction weight $\{w_i\}$ can linear reconstruct $\hat{e}$.

$$\hat{e} = \sum_i w_i e'_i \tag{3}$$

Ideally optimized subset would contain the samples which are close to the test image in the gaze space. A training feature vector which has the minimum Euclidean distance to test feature vector can be found by Eq. 4. The calibration point corresponding to this vector is marked for the main point, which is the closest to the real gaze position.

$$\min_i d_i = argmin \parallel \hat{e} - c * e_i \parallel_1 \tag{4}$$

where $\hat{e}$ is the feature vector of test image, e_i is the ith feature vector of training samples, c is a coefficient, d_i is the minimum Euclidean distance. The feature vectors, corresponding to the main point and six other calibration points around it, constitute the optimized subset $\hat{E} = [e_{main}, e^1_{main}, \ldots, e^6_{main}]$. If the main point is on the edge, it is used to constitute the optimized subset with the existed calibration points around it.

Reconstructing the weight w in optimized subset is formulated as a sparse reconstruction problem, which can be solved by minimizing the ℓ^1 norm of w [15, 16]. Due to the existence of real noise, it may not be possible to represent the test sample exactly as a linear combination of the optimized subset. A small constant ε was introduced to express the maximum allowed Euclidean distance from $\hat{E}w$ to the ground true $\hat{e}$. The reconstruction weight w can be get by:

$$\hat{w} = \text{argmin} \ || \ w \ ||_1 \quad s.t. \ || \ \hat{E}w - \hat{e} \ ||_1 < \varepsilon \tag{5}$$

Lu et al. [17] has demonstrated that use of the same weights to estimate the gaze parameters is justified by locality, as the linear combinations in the subspaces spanned by $\{e'_j\}$ and $\{p'_j\}$ are equal. Finally, the test gaze position $\hat{p}$ can be calculated by:

$$\hat{p} = \sum_i w_i p_i \tag{6}$$

2.3 Gaze Position Compensation

The vertical height changes of the ground truth gaze point on the influence of the initial gaze results are shown in Fig. 3. In Fig. 3, the vertical direction of gaze estimation result has the trend to close the center of the screen. The vertical error of test points in the screen edge are bigger than in the screen central (point height between 300 and 800). In addition, the error of gaze estimation results in vertical direction is larger than in horizontal direction (Sect. 4). The main reasons for the above phenomenon are: 1. Due to the people vision area on horizontal is wider than it on vertical, people move head largely when changing the gazing point on vertical. 2. When the gaze point changes in the horizontal direction, the eye image has significant changes; when the gaze point changes in the vertical direction, the eye image has little changes.

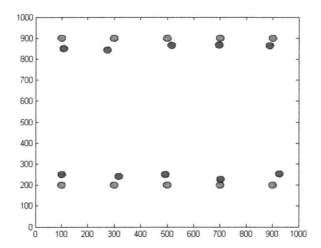

Fig. 3. Initial gaze estimation result under different gaze positon.

The curves of mean errors and eye open sizes have almost the same linear relation. Therefore, after the initial gaze position is got, a linear equation is used to compensate the vertical deviation. The final gaze estimation result in vertical direction is calculated by:

$$p_{yf} = \hat{p}_y + (S_h - S_l)/(H_h - H_l) * (H/2 - \hat{p}_y) \tag{7}$$

where $\hat{p}_y$ is the estimated value of initial gaze estimation in vertical direction, H is the total pixels in the screen vertical direction, S_h is the eye open size when gazing the highest training point on the screen, S_l is the eye open size when gazing the lowest training point on the screen, H_l is the vertical coordinate of the lowest training point on the screen, H_h is the vertical coordinate of the highest training point on the screen.

3 Experiments

In this section, the experiments performed to evaluate the proposed gaze estimation system. 6 male and 4 female subjects are chosen to do the experiment under a condition of one camera with a resolution of 1280*720 and 2 infrared light sources with 850 nm wavelength. We implemented our system with a 24-inch computer screen, and the resolution is 1920*1080 pixels. The subject was asked to sit at a distance of 600 mm from the computer screen. In the experimental process, subject's head tries to aim at the screen center as much as possible, and the subject is allowed to have slight head motion.

The whole experiment process is divided into calibration stage and test stage. In the process of calibration, the subject focused on each calibration point shown on the screen and allowed the camera to capture frontal appearance. In the process of test, the subject watched the test points shown on screen. There are 30 test points distributed in each position of the screen, and were shown in random order.

3.1 Evaluation and Comparison

For each input image, the gaze positions of the left eye and the right eye are calculated respectively, the average value of the two gaze positions is regard as the double-eye gazing position. In order to show the experimental result directly and compare with other state-of-the-art methods, the angular of estimation error will be calculated by:

$$\text{error} \approx \arctan(||\hat{p} - p_0||_2/D) \tag{8}$$

where $||\hat{p} - p_0||_2$ denotes the Euclidean distance between a real 2D gaze position p_0 and the estimated 2D gaze position $\hat{p}$, D indicates the distance between the subject's eye and screen.

Table 1 shows the mean errors of the gaze estimation system for each subject. It shows the highest estimation accuracy in all subjects. In general, the gaze estimator of one eye achieves a mean error of 83 pixels, corresponding to an angle error of 2.15°; while the gaze estimator of double eyes has a mean error of 69 pixels, corresponding to an angle error of 1.79°. In some subjects, the left eye's gaze estimation accuracy is higher than the right eye's, while other subjects are opposite. The left and right eye's overall average gaze estimation precisions are basically the same. It demonstrates that which eye's gaze estimation result is more accurate depends on the subjects' own individual differences, and every double eye gazing estimation accuracy is higher than one eye gazing estimation accuracy.

Table 1. Mean pixel error and mean angel error

Subject	Left eye		Right eye		Double eye	
	Pixels	Angle	Pixels	Angle	Pixels	Angle
1	75	1.94°	86	2.23°	68	1.76°
2	85	2.20°	98	2.54°	76	1.97°
3	98	2.54°	86	2.23°	83	2.15°
4	64	1.66°	80	2.07°	52	1.35°
5	73	1.89°	87	2.25°	65	1.68°
6	77	1.99°	73	1.89°	61	1.58°
7	79	2.05°	94	2.44°	73	1.89°
8	92	2.38°	84	2.18°	76	1.97°
9	81	2.10°	88	2.28°	70	1.81°
10	80	2.07°	85	2.20°	69	1.79°
All avg	**80**	**2.07°**	**86**	**2.23°**	**69**	**1.79°**

In addition, we compare our system with other gaze estimation systems which without head fixed device. Comparison results are shown in Table 2, compared with other excellent methods in recent years, our method has better positioning accuracy no matter in one eye or double eye gazing estimation.

Table 2. Comparison with the state-of-the-art method

Method	Error
Our Method(Double eye)	**1.79°**
Our Method(One eye)	**2.15°**
Feng et al. [17]	2.3°
Valenti et al. [18]	(1.9°, 2.2°)
Sugano et al. [8]	3.5°

3.2 Compensation Equation Evaluation

To compensate the error caused by slight head motion during gaze estimation, a gaze compensation algorithm is proposed in Sect. 2.3. This section is mainly to evaluate the effect of the compensation algorithm for the final result of gaze estimation.

It can be seen from the Fig. 4, the mean pixel error of initial double-eye gazing estimation on the y direction (mean error 61) is obviously larger than it on the x direction (mean error 37), and the reason has been explained in Sect. 2.3. After the use of gaze compensation method, the mean pixel error on y direction is descended from 61 to 45, decreased by 35 %.

3.3   Distance Change

In the above experiment, the distance between subjects and screen is set to be 600 mm. This section evaluates the robustness of the proposed method in test with distance changes between subjects and screen. We choose three subjects to do the experiment, the test distances were respectively set as 500 mm, 600 mm, 700 mm and 800 mm. The experiment processes are exactly as described in Sect. 3.1.

It can be seen from the experimental results in Table 3, the overall gaze accuracy under different distances are basically equal. This proves the gaze estimation method mentioned in this paper has a good robustness to distance changes.

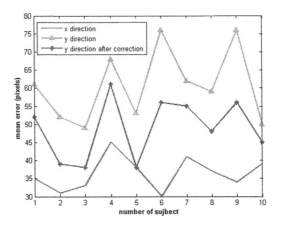

Fig. 4. Mean error at x direction and y direction

Table 3. The mean error of gaze estimation under different distance

Subject	500 mm		600 mm		700 mm		800 mm	
	Pixel	Angle	Pixel	Angle	Pixel	Angle	Pixel	Angle
1	61	1.90°	76	1.97°	84	1.86°	100	1.26°
2	60	1.87°	70	1.81°	77	1.71°	94	1.14°
3	58	1.81°	69	1.79°	79	1.75°	89	1.05°
avg	**59**	**1.84°**	**72**	**1.86°**	**80**	**1.78°**	**94**	**1.14°**

4   Conclusion and Future Work

In this paper, we have proposed an accurate gaze estimation method under a little calibration points. First, the main point is found by using the minimum Euclidean distance among the all calibration feature vectors. The main point and the calibration points around it constitute the optimized subset. In the optimized subset, a set of sparse reconstruction weights is solved by using the ℓ^1-minimum and utilized to linear express the initial gaze estimation result. Based on the result of initial gaze estimation, we use gazing compensation equation to get the final gaze estimation result. Experiment shows that our method can achieve an accuracy of 1.79° under monocular vision.

However, limitations still exist. First, although our method can achieve high precision gaze estimation with slight head motion, it is still powerless with free head motion. Second, the calibration process is necessary to each subject. The mapping relationship between input feature and gaze position cannot be found without calibration. Overall, handling large head motion and completely removing training stage are currently impossible in this work. For further research, the method could be improved on basis of this paper, 3D head pose estimation can be added, in the meanwhile, reconstructing the head motion compensation equation, and then the free head motion gaze estimator would be achieved.

Acknowledgement. This research was funded by National science and technology support plan "User evaluation technology and standard research of display and control interface ergonomics"(2014BAK01B04).

References

1. Valenti, R., Gevers, T.: Accurate eye center location through invariant isocentric patterns. IEEE Trans. Pattern Anal. Mach. Intell. **34**(9), 1785–1798 (2012)
2. Markuš, N., Frljak, M., Pandžić, I.S., et al.: Eye pupil localization with an ensemble of randomized trees. Pattern Recogn. **47**(2), 578–587 (2014)
3. Morimoto, C.H., Mimica, M.R.M.: Eye gaze tracking techniques for interactive applications. Comput. Vis. Image Underst. **98**(1), 4–24 (2005)
4. Zhu, Z., Ji, Q.: Novel eye gaze tracking techniques under natural head movement. IEEE Trans. Biomed. Eng. **54**(12), 2246–2260 (2007)
5. Villanueva, A., Cabeza, R.: A novel gaze estimation system with one calibration point. IEEE Trans. Syst. Man Cybern. Part B Cybern. **38**(4), 1123–1138 (2008)
6. Timm, F., Barth, E.: Accurate eye centre localisation by means of gradients. In: VISAPP, pp. 125–130 (2011)
7. Coutinho, F.L., Morimoto, C.H.: Improving head movement tolerance of cross-ratio based eye trackers. Int. J. Comput. Vis. **101**(3), 1–23 (2012)
8. Sugano, Y., Matsushita, Y., Sato, Y.: Appearance-based gaze estimation using visual saliency. IEEE Trans. Pattern Anal. Mach. Intell. **PP**(99), 1 (2012)
9. Sesma-Sanchez, L., Villanueva, A., et al.: Gaze estimation interpolation methods based on binocular data. IEEE Trans. Biomed. Eng. **59**(8), 2235–2243 (2012)
10. Cerrolaza, J., Villanueva, A., Cabeza, R.: Taxonomic study of polynomial regressions applied to the calibration of video-oculographic systems. In: Proceedings of the Symposium on Eye Tracking Research & Applications, pp. 259–266. ACM (2008)
11. Ramanauskas, N., Daunys, G., Dervinis, D.: Investigation of calibration techniques in video based eye tracking system. In: Miesenberger, K., Klaus, J., Zagler, W.L., Karshmer, A.I. (eds.) ICCHP 2008. LNCS, vol. 5105, pp. 1208–1215. Springer, Heidelberg (2008)
12. Xu, L.Q., Machin, D., Sheppard, P.: A novel approach to realtime non-intrusive gaze finding. In: BMVC, pp. 428–437 (1998)
13. Tan, K., Kriegman, D., Ahuja, N.: Appearance-based eye gaze estimation. In: WACV, pp. 191–195 (2002)

14. Ren, S., Cao, X., Wei, Y., et al.: Face alignment at 3000 FPS via regressing local binary features. In: 2014 IEEE Conference on Computer Vision and Pattern Recognition (CVPR), 1685–1692. IEEE (2014)
15. Wright, J., Ganesh, A., Zhou, Z., et al.: Demo: Robust face recognition via sparse representation. In: IEEE International Conference on Automatic Face and Gesture Recognition, Fg 08, pp. 1–2 (2008)
16. Donoho, D.L., Tsaig, Y.: Fast solution of l1-norm minimization problems when the solution may be sparse. IEEE Trans. Inf. Theory 54(11), 4789–4812 (2008)
17. Lu, F., Sugano, Y., Okabe, T., et al.: Adaptive linear regression for appearance-based gaze estimation. IEEE Trans. Pattern Anal. Mach. Intell. 36(10), 2033–2046 (2014)
18. Valenti, R., Sebe, N., Gevers, T.: Combining head pose and eye location information for gaze estimation. IEEE Trans. Image Process. 21(2), 802–815 (2012)

Acceptable Dwell Time Range for Densely Arranged Object Selection Using Video Mirror Interfaces

Kazuyoshi Murata[1(✉)] and Yu Shibuya[2]

[1] Aoyama Gakuin University, Kanagawa, Japan
kmurata@si.aoyama.ac.jp
[2] Kyoto Institute of Technology, Kyoto, Japan
shibuya@kit.ac.jp

Abstract. We evaluated an acceptable dwell time range to decrease erroneous selections using a video mirror interface. In this interface, users select a target object by moving his/her palm and dwelling on the object. We focused on a situation wherein objects are densely arranged and users must select a target object from these objects. The effects of dwell time, object size, and distance between objects on the object selection task were experimentally evaluated. The results indicated that a dwell time of 0.3 s is the most appropriate to decrease both erroneous selections and unpleasant experiences. The results of this study can contribute to defining an effective basis for dwell time for selection operations in gesture-based interaction systems.

Keywords: Dwell time · Object selection · Gesture interaction system · Video mirror interface

1 Introduction

Non-touch interfaces using body gestures are becoming increasing popular. For example, popular body gesture sensing devices allow users to play games using body gestures. Body gestures are also used as an input method for public displays or large displays. Furthermore, gesture-based interaction has several advantages for interactive public displays [22]. Touch-based interaction is still common for interactive public displays; however, it may be inappropriate for reasons such as hygiene [22].

A video mirror interface is a type of non-touch interface. Figure 1 shows a user selecting an object using a video mirror interface. As shown in Fig. 1, a mirrored video image is displayed on a screen in front of the user, and some objects are superimposed on the video image. Users can select these objects by moving his/her palm over the desired object and dwelling on it. This type of interaction is intuitive and commonly used for selecting actions in gesture-based interaction systems [5, 23].

Objects such as file icons are often densely or closely located in common interfaces. The required dwell time for object selection affects the usability of video mirror interfaces. If the required dwell time is short and objects are densely arranged or are close to the target object, then erroneous selections occur frequently. This is because of the "Midas Touch" problem [7], i.e., users cannot select an object without touching other

© Springer International Publishing Switzerland 2016
M. Kurosu (Ed.): HCI 2016, Part II, LNCS 9732, pp. 71–81, 2016.
DOI: 10.1007/978-3-319-39516-6_7

objects. An easy way to avoid the "Midas Touch" problem is to increase the required dwell time; however, long dwell time slows down interactions, causing unpleasant experiences for users.

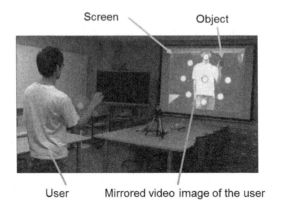

Fig. 1. Object selection using a video mirror interface.

Our study evaluates an acceptable dwell time range using a video mirror interface for users in order to decrease erroneous selections. In particular, we focus on a situation wherein objects are densely arranged and users must select a target object from these objects. This study can contribute to the definition of appropriate dwell time for target selection in gesture-based interaction systems such as video mirror interfaces.

2 Related Work

Many studies related to defining an appropriate dwell time for target selection have been conducted in various human-computer interaction fields. For example, in eye gaze interaction systems, the dwell time, i.e., the time for looking at objects to be selected, is commonly used as an alternative to mouse clicking. Jacob reported that the minimum dwell time for a simple object selection task was 0.15–0.25 s, while a dwell time over 0.75 s is not beneficial and causes the user to suspect that the system has crashed [7]. However, Stampe reported no difficulty for dwell times as long as 1 s [18]. Penkar et al. conducted experiments to confirm the relation between dwell time and button size [16]. In their case, a 0.2 s dwell time was appropriate for easy and accurate selection of a circle button with a 150-pixel diameter.

The use of a laser pointer as an interaction device for large displays has also been studied. Dwelling is also a popular selection method for laser pointer interaction systems, and several studies have reported that a 1–2 s dwell time is required to perform accurate object selection [14, 15].

Pen-based or touch-based interactions have become increasingly popular with the development of touch screen devices. In such interactions, when an object is touched for a period with a stylus or a user's finger, a context-aware popup menu or help menu is displayed. Bau et al. applied a dwell time of 0.25 s to their pen-based interaction system to display its dynamic guidance function [1]. Freeman et al. proposed Shadow-Guides, which is a system for learning multi-touch and whole-hand gestures using an interactive surface that requires a dwell time of 1 s [4].

The dwelling technique for item selection is also used in cascading menu selection. Some menu selection implementations such as Java Swing and several commercial products require a certain dwell time after a mouse cursor enters a parent cascade menu item before displaying its associated menu [3].

There are alternatives to mouse clicking for gesture-based object selection other than dwelling, such as pushing, drawing, grabbing, and enclosing [5]. Vogel et al. used finger air-tapping [21], and Bolt proposed combinations of gestures and user speech, such as "put that there." [2] However, these alternatives require that users learn how to use the system. Users who pass by a public display can interact with the display inadvertently. In this case, dwelling is more appropriate than the above alternatives because dwelling is more intuitive and provides greater availability without requiring help or guidance. However, there are few clear guidelines for selection operation dwell time with gesture-based interaction systems such as video mirror interfaces. We expect that our research will contribute to defining an appropriate dwell time for such systems.

Various interaction systems with a mirrored user image have been studied. In ALIVE [10], users can interact with a virtual 3D environment wherein the user's mirrored video image is integrated. The Mirror Metaphor Interaction system [6] lets users interact with CG objects and real world objects in a projected video image. Yolcu et al. proposed a virtual mirror system to select clothes in an online shopping system [25]. Taylor et al. proposed a posture training system [19]. Rather than a live video image of the user, several other systems have used computer graphics images such as a silhouette [8, 13, 22] or a virtual character [11, 20]. However, object selection operations are still required for such systems, and our work can contribute to improving the usability of such systems.

3   Experiment

The effects of dwell time, object size, and distance between objects in an object selection task were experimentally evaluated. Figure 2 shows the object arrangement in the experiment. Densely arranged objects often appear in a typical window system, e.g., items on a menu bar and file icons in a folder window. In this experiment, the selection of a target object that is surrounded by distracter objects was performed to mimic the abovementioned object selection tasks.

3.1   Dwell Time

Our pilot study [12] showed that dwell time > 0.5 s caused participant fatigue. Therefore, the dwell time conditions in this experiment were set to 0.0, 0.1, 0.2, 0.3, 0.4, and 0.5 s.

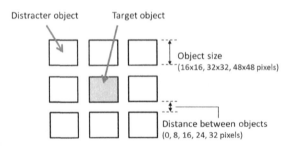

Fig. 2. Experimental object arrangement

3.2 Object Size

A user's palm often passes over a distracter object while selecting a target object. In this case, the dwell time must be longer than the time elapsed when passing over a distracter object. In this experiment, both the target and distracter objects are squares. The object sizes were 16×16, 32×32, and 48×48 pixels[1]. These sizes are in accordance with standard Windows application icon sizes[2].

3.3 Distance Between Objects

Selecting a target object without touching distracter objects is difficult when the distracter objects are in closely proximity with the target object. In this case, a certain amount of dwell time is needed to avoid erroneous selection. In this experiment, the distances between objects were 0, 8, 16, 24, and 32 pixels. The 0-pixel condition means that the target object adjoins a distracter object.

3.4 Experimental Settings

Our experimental system comprised a web camera, PC, projector, and screen. A video image of a participant was captured by the web camera, which was positioned in front of the participant. The captured video image was sent to the PC, which trans-formed the video to a mirrored video image. Square objects were generated by the PC, which were then superimposed over the mirrored video image. Finally, the processed video image was projected on the screen. The distance between the screen and participant was 5 m. As shown in Fig. 3, nine objects were arranged on the screen to the right of the participant, and one object was arranged to the left of the participant. The object at the center of the nine objects was considered the target object. The other objects were considered distracter objects. The object on the left side of the participant was a home object. The distance between the target object and home object was 320 pixels. All objects were arranged within reach of the participant's right hand.

---

[1] In this experiment, the real object size on the screen was 95×95 mm when the object size was 48×48 pixels.

[2] http://msdn.microsoft.com/en-us/library/dn742485.aspx.

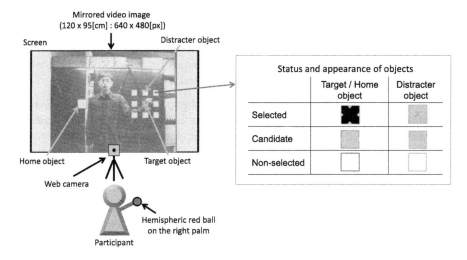

Fig. 3. Experimental settings (object size: 32 pixels; distance between objects: 24 pixels)

When the participants selected the home object with his/her right palm, they were required to twist his/her body and stretch his/her right arm to the left side of his/her body. In this case, it was possible for these postures to cause detection errors with gesture input devices such as Kinect. Therefore, a red hemispheric ball placed on his/her palm was used to detect the palm position using image recognition. The diameter of the ball was 70 mm, and the size of the ball on the screen was 32 pixels. The experimental system recognized that the user's palm was over an object when the red ball overlapped the object.

Figure 3 also shows the status and appearance of the objects. Note that the appearance of the target/home objects and the distracter objects differ.

- Selected object: an object currently selected by the participant.
- Candidate object: an object on which the participant's palm is located within the dwell time. When this status is maintained and the dwell time passes, the status of the object changes to the "Selected object."
- Non-selected object: an object that is not selected. This is the initial status of all objects.

3.5   Procedure

A simple target selection task was used in this experiment.

1. The participant stood in front of the screen. Only the home object was displayed on the screen. The participant was asked to select the home object. After the participant selected the home object, the target object and distracter objects were displayed.
2. The participant selected the target object. The participant was asked to perform the task as quickly as possible while avoiding erroneous selections. The participant

continued attempting to select the target object even if a distracter object was selected.

3. The participant selected the home object after selecting the target object.
4. The participant repeated steps 2 and 3 fifteen times because 15 combinations of object size and distance between objects were used in the experiment.

The participants were asked to perform five sets of the above tasks for each dwell time condition. The results of the first set were not used for analysis because this was considered a practice set. The order of the combinations of object size and distance between objects was counterbalanced. The order of dwell time was also counterbalanced. The experiment was video recorded to confirm participant behavior after the experiment.

3.6 Design

Ten volunteers (age 22–25) were recruited from the Kyoto Institute of Technology to participate in this experiment. All participants were right hand dominant, who had limited or no experience with gesture input systems such as video mirror interface systems.

A within-subject design was used with the dwell time, object size, and distance between objects factors. The dependent variables were erroneous selection rate and selection time. Furthermore, participants were asked to answer a questionnaire to facilitate a subjective evaluation.

Erroneous Selection Rate. When a participant selected a distracter object rather than the target object, the selection was defined as erroneous. The erroneous selection rate was defined as the rate of erroneous selection to the number of times a distracter object was passed over. It is assumed that the erroneous selection rate would be approximately 0 if there was a certain amount of dwell time.

Selection Time. The selection time was defined as the total time required to execute steps 2 and 3, i.e., the total time required for selecting the target object and then selecting the home object. The participant must move his/her palm carefully to avoid touching distracter objects if the distance between objects is short. Therefore, it is assumed that the time required for selection increases as the distance between objects reduces.

Subjective Evaluation. The participants were asked to answer a question after they completed the task for each dwell time condition. The question was "Did you feel unpleasant during the task?"

4   Result and Discussion

Data from this experiment were analyzed in a three-way repeated measures analysis of variance for the following factors: dwell time, object size, and distance between objects. Furthermore, a post hoc test with the Bonferroni procedure was performed after significant primary effects were determined.

4.1 Erroneous Selection Rate

The results of the erroneous selection rate are shown in Fig. 4. Passing over a distracter object always resulted in erroneous selection when the dwell time was 0.0 s. Approximately one-half of the times a distracter object was passed over resulted in erroneous selection even when dwell time was 0.1 s.

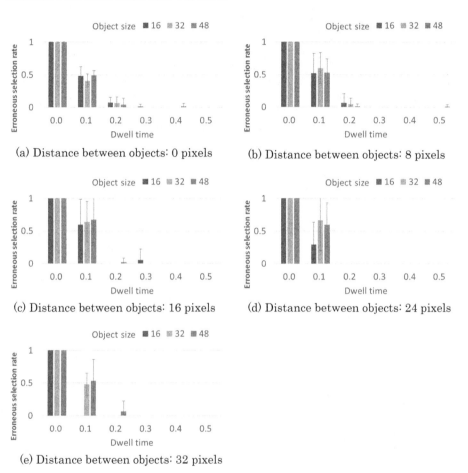

(a) Distance between objects: 0 pixels

(b) Distance between objects: 8 pixels

(c) Distance between objects: 16 pixels

(d) Distance between objects: 24 pixels

(e) Distance between objects: 32 pixels

Fig. 4. Erroneous selection rate results

However, the erroneous selection rate decreased precipitously to approximate 0 when the dwell time was greater than 0.2 s. When the dwell time ≥ 0.3 s, the erroneous selection rate was 0.04 or less for all combinations of object size and distance between objects, except one. Studies of Fitts' law [9, 17, 24] indicate that a 4 % error rate can be predicted in a simple pointing task if the participant is instructed to perform as quickly and accurately as possible. Therefore, in this experiment, it was assumed that the erroneous selection was acceptable when it was less than 0.04. Consequently, these results indicate that a dwell time of at least 0.3 s is necessary for selecting a target object without erroneous selection.

Furthermore, the highest erroneous selection rate was 0.07 when the dwell time was 0.2 s. Therefore, it seems that a dwell time of 0.2 s is acceptable if the user can tolerate a few errors, e.g., in a situation wherein the user can perform an undo action easily.

4.2   Selection Time

The results for selection time are shown in Fig. 5. Significant effects on the dwell time $(F(5, 45) = 22.395, p < .01)$ and object size $(F(2, 18) = 192.670, p < .01)$ were observed. The time for selection increased gradually with dwell time. A post hoc test revealed that selection times for dwell times of 0.4 and 0.5 s were longer than those of 0.0, 0.1, and 0.2 s dwell time. Furthermore, the selection times for 0.5 s dwell time were longer than that for 0.3 s dwell time. A certain amount of dwell time was required to decrease

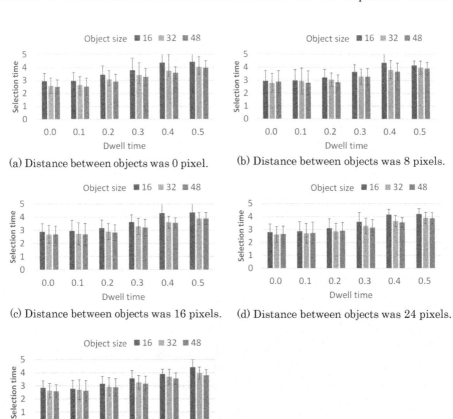

(a) Distance between objects was 0 pixel.

(b) Distance between objects was 8 pixels.

(c) Distance between objects was 16 pixels.

(d) Distance between objects was 24 pixels.

(e) Distance between objects was 32 pixels.

Fig. 5.   Selection time results

erroneous selection. However, overly long dwell time, e.g., 0.4 or 0.5 s, increased selection time. From the video of the experiment, it was observed that participants moved his/her palms from the target object region before the dwell time passed, i.e., participants could not wait until the dwell time expired, when the dwell time was 0.4 or 0.5 s. This was also one of the reasons why the selection time increased.

The distance between objects was also observed to have significant effect. How-ever, a post hoc test revealed that there was no difference among each object distance condition. Therefore, it appears that the effect of object distance was small in this experiment.

4.3   Questionnaire

Figure 6 shows the results of the questionnaire. Participants felt unpleasant if dwell time was too short or too long. When the dwell time ≤ 0.1 s, frequent erroneous selection caused unpleasant experiences. Similarly, unpleasant experiences increased with the dwell time because maintaining the palm in the air proved to be troublesome for the participants. Unpleasant experiences were felt least often with a dwell time of 0.2 s. However, there was no significant effect on dwell time.

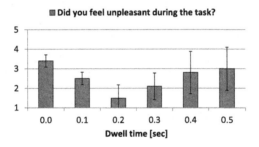

Fig. 6. Questionnaire results (1–5: "No," "a little unpleasant," "unpleasant," "strongly unpleasant," and "very strongly unpleasant")

4.4   Recommendation

Our experimental results indicate that dwell time should be 0.3–0.5 s to decrease both erroneous selections and unpleasant experiences. Erroneous selection does not occur when dwell time is within this range even if objects adjoin each other. However, when the dwell time ≥ 0.4 s, the selection time increases. This can increase the total time for a selection operation if repeated selection operations are required, e.g., selecting files in deep hierarchical folders. Therefore, under our experimental conditions, a dwell time of 0.3 s was most appropriate. A dwell time of 0.2 s was acceptable if the user could tolerate a few errors, e.g., if the user could easily perform an undo operation.

It is possible that the acceptable dwell time range is affected by the given application or environment. Nonetheless, our experimental results can be considered as an effective basis for finding an appropriate dwell time for selection operations in gesture-based interaction systems.

5 Conclusion

Dwelling is commonly used to select an object in gesture-based interaction systems. In this study, an experiment was conducted to evaluate an appropriate dwell time for a selection gesture using a video mirror interface. The experimental results suggested that a dwell time of 0.3 s was the most appropriate to decrease both erroneous selections and unpleasant experiences. Furthermore, a dwell time of 0.2 s was acceptable if users could tolerate a few errors, e.g., if the user could easily perform an undo operation. We expect that the results of this study will contribute to defining an effective basis for dwell time for selection operations in gesture-based interaction systems.

References

1. Bau, O., Mackay, W.E.: OctoPocus: a dynamic guide for learning gesture-based command sets. In: UIST 2008 Proceedings of the 21st Annual ACM Symposium on User Interface Software and Technology, pp. 37–46 (2008)
2. Bolt, R.A.: Put-That-There: voice and gesture at the graphics interface. In: SIGGRAPH 1980 Proceedings of the 7th Annual Conference on Computer Graphics and Interactive Techniques, pp. 262–270 (1980)
3. Cockburn, A., Gin, A.: Faster cascading menu selections with enlarged activation areas. In: GI 2006 Proceedings of Graphics Interface 2006, pp. 65–71 (2006)
4. Freeman, D., Benko, H., Morris, M.R., Wigdor, D.: ShadowGuides: visualizations for in-situ learning of multi-touch and whole-hand gestures. In: ITS 2009 Proceedings of the ACM International Conference on Interactive Tabletops and Surfaces, pp. 165–172 (2009)
5. Hespanhol, L., Tomitsch, M., Grace, K., Collins1, A., Kay, J.: Investigating intuitiveness and effectiveness of gestures for free spatial interaction with large displays. In: PerDis 2012 Proceedings of the 2012 International Symposium on Pervasive Displays, Article No. 6 (2012)
6. Hosoya, E., Kitabata, M., Sato, H., Harada, I., Nojima, H., Morisawa, F., Mutoh, S., Onozawa, A.: A mirror metaphor interaction system: touching remote real objects in an augmented reality environment. In: Proceedings of the 2nd IEEE/ACM International Symposium on Mixed and Augmented Reality, p. 350 (2003)
7. Jacob, R.J.K.: What you look at is what you get: eye movement-based interaction techniques. In: CHI 1990 Proceedings of the SIGCHI Conference on Human Factors in Computing Systems, pp. 11–18 (1990)
8. Krueger, M.W., Gionfriddo, T., Hinrichsen, K.: VIDEOPLACE—an artificial reality. In: CHI 1985 Proceedings of the SIGCHI Conference on Human Factors in Computing Systems, pp. 35–40 (1985)
9. MacKenzie, I.S.: Fitts' law as a research and design tool in human-computer interaction. Hum. Comput. Interact. 7(1), 91–139 (1992)
10. Maes, P., Darrell, T., Blumberg, B., Pentland, A.: The ALIVE system: wireless, full-body interaction with autonomous agents. Multimedia Syst. Spec. Issue Multimedia Multisensory Virtual Worlds 5(2), 105–112 (1997)
11. Marquardt, Z., Beira, J., Em, N., Paiva, I., Kox, S.: Super mirror: a kinect interface for ballet dancers. In: CHI 2012 Extended Abstracts on Human Factors in Computing Systems, pp. 1619–1624 (2012)

12. Murata, K., Hattori, M., Shibuya, Yu.: Effect of Unresponsive Time for User's Touch Action of Selecting an Icon on the Video Mirror Interface. In: Kurosu, M. (ed.) HCII/HCI 2013, Part IV. LNCS, vol. 8007, pp. 462–468. Springer, Heidelberg (2013)

13. Müller, J., Walter, R., Bailly, G., Nischt, M., Alt, F.: Looking glass: a field study on noticing interactivity of a shop wind. In: Proceedings of the SIGCHI Conference on Human Factors in Computing Systems, pp. 297–306 (2012)

14. Myers, B.A., Bhatnagar, R., Nichols, J., Peck, C.H., Kong, D., Miller, R., Long, A. C.: Interacting at a distance: measuring the performance of laser pointers and other devices. CHI 2002 Proceedings of the SIGCHI Conference on Human Factors in Computing Systems, pp. 33–40 (2002)

15. Olsen Jr., D.R., Nielsen, T.: Laser pointer interaction. In: CHI 2001 Proceedings of the SIGCHI Conference on Human Factors in Computing Systems, pp. 17–22 (2001)

16. Penkar, A.M., Lutteroth, C., Weber, G.: Designing for the eye–design parameters for dwell in gaze interaction. In: OzCHI 2012 Proceedings of the 24th Australian Computer-Human Interaction Conference, pp. 479–488 (2012)

17. Soukoreff, R.W., Mackenzie, I.S.: Towards a standard for pointing device evaluation, perspectives on 27 years of fitts' law research in HCI. Int. J. Hum Comput Stud. **61**, 751–789 (2004)

18. Stampe, D.M., Reingold, E.M.: Selection by looking: a novel computer interface and its application to psychological research. Stud. Vis. Inf. Proc. **6**, 467–478 (1995)

19. Taylor, B., Birk, M., Mandryk, R. L., Ivkovic, Z.: Posture training with real-time visual feedback. In: CHI 2013 Extended Abstracts on Human Factors in Computing Systems, pp. 3135–3138 (2013)

20. Vera, L., Gimeno, J., Coma, I., Fernández, M.: Augmented mirror: interactive augmented reality system based on kinect. In: Campos, P., Graham, N., Jorge, J., Nunes, N., Palanque, P., Winckler, M. (eds.) INTERACT 2011, Part IV. LNCS, vol. 6949, pp. 483–486. Springer, Heidelberg (2011)

21. Vogel, D., Balakrishnan, R.: Distant freehand pointing and clicking on very large, high resolution displays. In: UIST 2005 Proceedings of the 18th Annual ACM Symposium on User Interface Software and Technology, pp. 33–42 (2005)

22. Walter, R., Bailly, G., Müller, J.: StrikeAPose: revealing mid-air gestures on public dis-plays. In: CHI 2013 Proceedings of the SIGCHI Conference on Human Factors in Computing Systems, pp. 841–850 (2013)

23. Walter, R., Bailly, G., Valkanova, N., Müller, J.: Cuenesics: using mid-air gestures to select items on interactive public displays. In: MobileHCI 2014 Proceedings of the 16th International Conference on Human-Computer Interaction with Mobile Devices and Services, pp. 299–308 (2014)

24. Wobbrock, J.O., Cutrell, E., Harada, S., MacKenzie, I.S.: An error model for pointing based on fitts' law. In: CHI 2008 Proceedings of the SIGCHI Conference on Human Factors in Computing Systems, pp. 1613–1622 (2008)

25. Yolcu, G., Kazan, S., Oz, C.: Real time virtual mirror using kinect. Balkan J. Electr. Comput. Eng. **2**(2), 75–78 (2014)

Analysis of Choreographed Human Movements Using Depth Cameras: A Systematic Review

Danilo Ribeiro[1]([⊠]), João Bernardes[1], Norton Roman[1], Marcelo Antunes[2],
Enrique Ortega[2], Antonio Sousa[3], Luciano Digiampietri[1], Luis Cura[4],
Valdinei Silva[1], and Clodoaldo Lima[1]

[1] University of São Paulo, São Paulo, Brazil
`danilo.luque@usp.br`
[2] Central Kung Fu Academy, Campinas, Brazil
[3] São Paulo Faculty of Technology, São Paulo, Brazil
[4] Campo Limpo Paulista Faculty, Campo Limpo Paulista, Brazil

Abstract. The use of computer vision to analyze human movement
has been growing considerably, facilitated by the increased availability of depth cameras This paper describes the results of a systematic
review about the techniques used for movement tracking and recognition, focusing on metrics to compare choreographed movements using
Microsoft Kinect as a sensor. Several techniques for data analysis and
pattern recognition are explored for this task, particularly Dynamic Time
Warping and Hidden Markov Models. Most papers we discuss used a single sensor instead of more complex setups and most took advantage of
the Kinect SDK instead of alternatives. Rhythm is rarely considered in
these systems due to the temporal alignment strategies used. While most
systems that use the sensors for some form of interaction instead claim
that this interaction is natural, very few actually perform any sort of
usability or user experience analysis.

1 Introduction

With the increased availability of depth camera technology and movement analysis tools, the use of these tools, such as Microsoft's Kinect sensor and SDK that
track body movements and allow their reproduction in videogames and other
applications, has been more and more explored, including to aid in learning and
practicing activities for which movement is essential and may even be seen as a
mark of quality, personality and individuality [1]. During learning and training,
it is important to have some measure of quality of performance that is as precise
as possible as a form of feedback, particularly if it can detect and show where
the mistakes happened and even suggest how to correct them.

The development of systems using depth sensors to aid in sports, dancing and
martial arts has been gaining prominence and examples of this are the work of
Chye, Connsynn and Nakajima [2], which uses Kinect to complement the training
of martial arts beginners, and that of Hachaj, Ogiela and Piekarczyk [3], which
uses a gesture description language to practice combat and Shorin-Ryu Karate

© Springer International Publishing Switzerland 2016
M. Kurosu (Ed.): HCI 2016, Part II, LNCS 9732, pp. 82–92, 2016.
DOI: 10.1007/978-3-319-39516-6_8

techniques with a reduced risk of trauma. Another application of this technology in this context is distance training for dance and martial arts practitioners using virtual avatars [4].

This paper presents a Systematic Review of the use of depth cameras for the analysis of choreographed human movements in the past years, discussing aspects such as the techniques used for analysis, equipment and setup, applications and interaction.

Kinect is a sensor developed by Microsoft, initially for its Xbox 360 videogame console and later for computers and is composed of two cameras, one RGB and a depth camera that uses an infrared projector which can measure from 0.8 to 3.5 m[5]. The widespread use of this sensor today happens mainly for two reasons, its relatively low cost and high availability and this review focuses on its use.

The paper is organized in a simple manner, as follows: Sect. 1 this introduction and the Sect. 2 describes in detail the methodology adopted for the systematic review. One problem that is often considered in the development of most of these systems is the temporal alignment of movements to facilitate the comparison of those performed by the user with those of another person or some known dataset. Two techniques used for this task are prominent in the literature, Dynamic Time Warping and Hidden Markov Models, both share similarities [6], will be discussed more frequently and, thus, are briefly introduced in the Sect. 3, along with a couple other techniques. The Sect. 4 presents and discusses the work's results and Sect. 5 one brings it to a conclusion.

2   Methodology

Systematic Review (SR) is a form of research in the literature performed in a standardized way, often performed to collect and classify the work done in a specific area or regarding a specific question and to show the state of the art in that area, providing a synthesis of the research regarding that question and its main results up to that point in time [7]. SR follows strict criteria so that its results are trustworthy, reproducible and validatable. Before the review is performed, several of its aspects must be decided and recorded, such as the research questions it must answer, control papers that it should find, databases to be searched, search strings, inclusion and exclusion criteria, what information will be extracted from each work and how it will be summarized. Below we summarize the most important of these aspects.

2.1   Research Questions

Every SR has, as a starting point, research questions that delimit the problem and act as an initial filter for the works found and that must be answered by the end of the process. The questions used in this work are:

1. What methods are used to analyze and compare choreographed human movements (mostly martial arts and dance, but not restricted to them) captured with depth cameras, particularly Microsoft's Kinect?

2. What are the techniques, if any, for temporal alignment of the movements and to analyze their rhythm?
3. What are the main applications of these systems?
4. Is the quality of interaction in these systems, if it exists, analyzed? How?

2.2 Sources and Search Strings

The papers for this review were searched in the databases of the Institute of Electric and Electronic Engineers (IEEE), the Association for Computing Machinery (ACM) and Springer, all of which bring together much of the most important work in this area and have a friendly user interface to facilitate the search process. In each of these databases, six customized searches were performed. Table 1 summarizes the strings used for these searches (which were adapted as needed for each particular engine) and the total number of papers found in each search, followed by the number of papers that were selected or rejected after the application of inclusion and exclusion criteria, the number of duplicated papers and the final number of papers that were used to extract information for this review.

Table 1. Search strings and number of papers found

Order	String	Paper				
		Total	S	R	D	E
1	(((Kinect) OR (depth camera)) AND (martial arts))	529	16	511	2	6
2	((Kinect) AND (dancing)) AND (martial arts))	18	11	5	2	9
3	((Kinect) AND (gesture description language))	3	1	2	0	1
4	"gesture description language"	6	2	3	1	0
5	"gesture recognition" AND "depth camera"	43	1	28	14	0
6	((("rhythm") OR ("choreography")) and(("kinect")OR("depth camera")))	309	0	2	307	0
7	(("choreography")and(("kinect")OR("depth camera")))	500	4	174	3221	4
	TOTAL	1402	34	726	648	20

S – Selected; R – Rejected; D – Duplicated; E – Extracted

Observing this table we verify that 1402 scientific papers were returned using these keywords and search strings but only 20 were finally extracted for the SR. It is interesting to notice that, due to the option for doing independent searches instead of a single search with a complex and long string, many papers, almost half of them (648) were duplicated.

2.3 Inclusion and Exclusion Criteria

Many of the works found in the initial search were excluded for, ultimately, being outside the narrow scope we selected for this review. This process of inclusion or exclusion happened through the following criteria, predetermined in the research protocol:

- Inclusion
  - Work that analyzes sequences of multiple gesture (movement) with metrics to qualify the movements and using depth cameras;
  - Work with metrics for temporal analysis of the movement sequences.
- Exclusion
  - Work analyzing independent gestures;
  - Work analyzing semi random (not predetermined or choreographed) movement patterns;
  - Work that does not use depth cameras.

2.4 Support System

A free software system called "State of the Art through Systematic Review" (Start) was used in this work to store and organize the papers found in this review. It is a rather interactive tool with features such as duplicate filtering and .bib support developed by LAPES (Research Laboratory in Software Engineering) at Federal University of So Carlos, in Brazil, and we would like to extend our thanks to its creators.

3 Brief Description of Techniques

In this section we explain in a very succinct form the main algorithms used in the works included in this review to analyze movements: Hidden Markov Models (HMM), Dynamic Time Warping (DTW), Spherical Self-Organizing Maps (SSOM) and Gesture Description Languages (GDL).

- HMM: stochastic model of temporal data series that represent the probability of the data occurring. The idea is that the process is unknown (hidden) but its results can be known. It is derived from Markovian chains and widely used in pattern recognition (including movement analysis), artificial intelligence and molecular biology [8,9].
- DTW: like HMMs, this algorithm is also based on temporal series, but it solves the problem of finding a common path between two series of different sizes but otherwise similar, without requiring initial or final points to be the same, creating a warping between the two paths and generally using euclidian distance [10].
- SSOM: clusterization techinque that creates a spherical mapping to indicate tridimensional positions, searching for the neighbour that better fits the movement and creating a link to it [11].
- GDL: used both for dynamic movements or static gestures, a script describes a movement or pose and, if recognized correctly by any other means, it is added to a heap, which may contain a chain of scripts or a single one [3,12].

4   Results and Discussion

In this section, we will begin by characterizing the set of papers analyzed in our review. Figure 1 illustrates the year of publication of the papers found in this review and shows that this body of work is quite recent, with most of it (60 %) from 2013. Because we focus on Kinect and how it is making this sort of research and application more easily available, this was expected, since it was released for the Xbox only in November 2010 and for Windows only in February 2012 (although even before the Kinect for Windows release there were several alternatives explored to work with the sensor on personal computers).

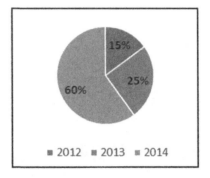

Fig. 1. Years of publication

From a geographic point of view, Fig. 2 illustrates which countries are publishing research in this particular area, showing that none of the countries is too far ahead, with each being responsible for 5 to 15 % of published papers.

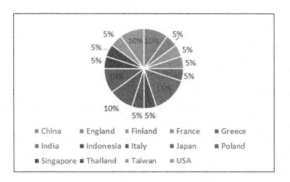

Fig. 2. Countries

If grouped by continent, however, as shown in Fig. 3, Asia pulls ahead significant (and the interest in both martial arts and computer vision in that continent is no surprise), followed respectively by Europe and America.

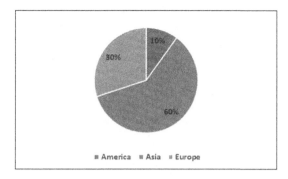

Fig. 3. Continents

Now we present the main results, according to the research questions listed previously. All studies made use of Kinect as a depth camera. Out of all of them, only two used more than one device in the experiment. Hachaj and Ogiela [13] used three sensors around a karate practitioner to aid in the learning process for martial arts techniques. It is interesting to note that the authors tested two distinct spatial configurations for the sensors. The first, less efficient, separated by an angle of $\pi/2$ and the second, more efficient, using an angle of $\pi/4$. Another work by the same group of Hachaj et al. [3] to verify the execution of karate moves compared the use of three sensors versus a single sensors, reporting an error of 13 % in movement capture with three cameras and 39 % with only one. For static poses or gestures, however, the difference between the two setups was not significant.

Different tools were used for image capture and skeleton fitting with the Kinect. Chye and Nakajima [2] use the OpenNI/NITE framework and draw a silhouette of the captured body to develop a game to aid karate practitioners in training. Other systems [14–16] also use this framework to analyze movements to give dancers a post-exercise evaluation [14], compare dance movements to the Bashir method [15] and score karate moves [16]. Microsoft's Kinect SDK was used in all other works (sometimes via a Unity wrapper), apparently being the most widely used alternative in this context. Table 2 briefly summarizes these papers.

In many cases the goal of the analysis was to compare movements between two performers (such as a novice and a master, or to measure the synchronicity of movement in a joint performance), or between one person and a pre-recorded video, using several distinct metrics. Other strategies involved recognizing specific and basic postures or gestures, for instance six basic ballet poses (as in the work of Sun et al. [11] using SSOM without much success to recognize poses or movements beyond those), or tracking user movements and mapping them to an avatar in a virtual world with virtual obstacles and such. Rhythm was often discarded in these metrics (possibly due to the temporal alignment strategies used), even in choreographed performances in which rhythm should indeed have some importance.

Table 2. Work with Kinect SDK

Author	Year	Goals
Alexiadis e Daras	2014	Compare performance of dance practicioner and expert and give feedback
Anbarsanti e Prihatmanto	2014	Analyze and score a Likok Pulo dancer
Gupta e Goel	2014	Aid in the practice of Kathak dance
Kaewplee et al	2014	Eliminate ghosting from captured images
Dancs et al	2013	Recognize ballet movements and compare with performance
Hachaj e Orgiela	2013	Identify karate moves
Holsti et al	2013	Analyze usability of a guidance system for trampoline jumps
Hachaj et al	2013	Increase movement tracking capability
Ho et al	2013	Extract and align music beat with best dance
Lin et al	2012	Synchronize dance videos from different sources
Pisharady e Saerbeck	2013	Recognize fast hand movements
Saha, Ghosh, Konar e Janarthanan	2013	Recognize Indian dance gestures
Saha, Ghosh, Konar e Nagar	2013	Recognize Indian dance gestures
Wada et al	2013	Analyze positions in a specific Kata
Keerthy	2012	Aid distance kung fu practice

Merely using euclidian distance between feature vectors of positions often did not yield very conclusive results but including velocity as a feature and still using euclidian distance showed better performance. Kaewplee et al. [17] use only Euclidian distance without temporal alignment (but using posterior movements to aid in the calculation of articulation angles) to analyze 24 basic Muay Thay movements. Chye e Nakajima [2] also use Euclidian distance and, like the previous work, also faced some difficulty to compare movements because of that, due to even slight temporal variations. Saha et al. [18] attempt to minimize the problem by defining an ideal speed for each movement and only comparing movements that did not deviate much from that speed. The same group used this approach again to recognize Indian dance moves [18]. Translating movements into a common description, such as using the Gesture Description Language [13] to create movement scripts and them comparing them showed good results, with 90 % accuracy in recognizing karate movements and comparing them to those executed by a black belt expert, using a setup with three sensors [3]. Lin et al. [19] developed an algorithm, using 103 videos from a database, that only showed significant synchronization errors when the dancer stepped outside Kinect's range.

More sophisticate algorithms for tracking and comparing temporal series were also explored, such as DTW, SSOM and HMMs. Using SSOM with articulation angles and captured body part lengths, Dancs et al. [20] mostly ignored rhythm while during training and obtained success rates of almost 90 % in leave-one-out and nearest neighbour validation and cross validation. Gupta and Goel [21] use DTW with Euclidian distance and Earth Mover's Distance of finger positions to compare the performance of a subject and a master in Kathak. Zhu and Pun [14] used DTW to score dance practitioners comparing to the Taiji dataset and reached success rates above 80 %. Bianco and Tisato [16] also use DTW and report 96 % precision in recognizing and scoring the execution of karate movements, a similar value to that obtained by Pisharady and Saerbeck [22] using DTW to identify dynamic hand movements. Alexiadis and Daras [23] performed an experiment with and without the use of DTW, with showed a difference of over 20 % in favor of its use when comparing movements to the Huawei 3DLife/EMC Grand Challenge dataset. Keerthy [24] uses DTW in his Master's dissertation to create a Kung Fu training assistant that compares student and master movements. HMM was another technique widely explored. Anbarsanti and Prihatmanto [25] obtained promising preliminary results in modeling the Likok Pulo dance using HMMs and classifying six individual basic dance movements and one undefined movement with almost 95 % accuracy. Masurelle et al. [15] also used HMMs to classify dance movements from a salsa database called 3DLife, comparing the results with the Bashir technique and obtaining 74 % positive matches. Figure 4 summarizes the frequency of use of these approaches to compare and classify human movements.

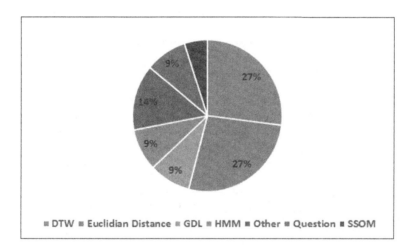

Fig. 4. Comparison approaches

Only two papers described some form of analysis of quality of interaction, Holsti et al. [26], in an application to aid in trampoline jumping, used questionnaires to evaluate their system's usability, with 90 % of users giving positive feedback despite complaining about the delay when showing the movement. Wada et al. [27] also analyzed the usability of their system to analyze kata positions with 89 % positive feedback.

5   Conclusion

The use of computer vision in several day to day applications is becoming more and more frequent, particularly with the popularization of smartphone cameras and depth cameras such as Microsoft Kinect's, which was one focus of this systematic review when applied to analyzing choreographed human movements. In this context, most papers we found take advantage of the Kinect SDK instead of alternatives, euclidian distance between feature vectors containing joint positions or angles was often used but showed poor results, often due to differences in temporal alignment of the movements being compared, but could be improved limiting the range of performance speed to be analyzed or adding speed to the feature vectors. Comparing standardized descriptions for gestures, movements and performances instead of the raw data from the sensors was another approach found. Out of the set of more sophisticate techniques to classify temporal series, DTW was the most commonly used in this context and showed good results, followed by the use of SSOM and HMMs. The quality of interaction with these systems was seldom analyzed in the papers included in this revision.

References

1. Zhang, Z.: Microsoft kinect sensor and its effect. IEEE MultiMedia **19**(2), 4–10 (2012)
2. Chye, C., Nakajima, T.: Game based approach to learn martial arts for beginners. In Embedded and Real-Time Computing Systems and Applications (RTCSA), 2012 IEEE 18th International Conference on, pp. 482–485, August 2012. doi:10.1109/RTCSA.2012.37
3. Hachaj, T., Ogiela, M.R., Piekarczyk, M.: Dependence of kinect sensors number and position on gestures recognition with gesture description language semantic classifier. In: 2013 Federated Conference on Computer Science and Information Systems (FedCSIS), pp. 571–575, September 2013
4. Ogawa, T., Kambayashi, Y.: Physical instructional support system using virtual avatars. In: Proceedings of the 2012 International Conference on Advances in Computer-Human Interactions, pp. 262–265 (2012)
5. Ganganath, N., Leung, H.: Mobile robot localization using odometry and kinect sensor. In: 2012 IEEE International Conference on Emerging Signal Processing Applications (ESPA), pp. 91–94, January 2012. doi:10.1109/ESPA.2012.6152453
6. Fang, C.: From dynamic time warping (DTW) to hidden markov model (HMM). Univ. Cincinnati **3**, 19 (2009)
7. Rosana Ferreira Sampaio and Marisa Cotta Mancini: Estudos de revisão sistemática: um guia para síntese criteriosa da evidência científica. Braz. J. Phys. Ther. (Impr.) **11**(1), 83–89 (2007)
8. Zoubin Ghahramani. Hidden markov models. chapter An Introduction to Hidden Markov Models and Bayesian Networks, pp. 9–42. World Scientific Publishing Co., Inc, River Edge (2002). ISBN: 981-02-4564-5, URL http://dl.acm.org/citation.cfm?id=505741.505743
9. Rabiner, L.R.: A tutorial on hidden markov models, selected applications in speech recognition. Proc. IEEE **77**(2), 257–286 (1989). doi:10.1109/5.18626. ISSN: 0018-9219

10. Li, S.Z., Jain, A. (eds.): Encyclopedia of Biometrics, chapter Dynamic Time Warping (DTW), pp. 231–231. Springer, Boston (2009). ISBN: 978-0-387-73003-5, doi:10.1007/978-0-387-73003-5768
11. Sun, G., Muneesawang, P., Kyan, M., Li, H., Zhong, L., Dong, N., Elder, B., Guan, L.: An advanced computational intelligence system for training of ballet dance in a cave virtual reality environment. In: 2014 IEEE International Symposium on Multimedia (ISM), pp. 159–166, December 2014. doi:10.1109/ISM.2014.55
12. Hachaj, T., Ogiela, M.R.: Semantic description and recognition of human body poses and movement sequences with gesture description language. In: Kim, T., Kang, J.-J., Grosky, W.I., Arslan, T., Pissinou, N. (eds.) MulGraB, BSBT and IUrC 2012. CCIS, vol. 353, pp. 1–8. Springer, Heidelberg (2012). doi:10.1007/978-3-642-35521-91
13. Hachaj, T., Ogiela, M.R.: Qualitative evaluation of full body movements with gesture description language. In: 2014 2nd International Conference on Artificial Intelligence, Modelling and Simulation (AIMS), pp. 176–181, November 2014. doi:10.1109/AIMS.2014.32
14. Zhu, H.-M., Pun, C.-M.: Human action recognition with skeletal information from depth camera. In: 2013 IEEE International Conference on Information and Automation (ICIA), pp. 1082–1085, August 2013. doi:10.1109/ICInfA.2013.6720456
15. Masurelle, A., Essid, S., Richard, G.: Multimodal classification of dance movements using body joint trajectories and step sounds. In: 2013 14th International Workshop on Image Analysis for Multimedia Interactive Services (WIAMIS), pp. 1–4, July 2013. doi:10.1109/WIAMIS.2013.6616151
16. Bianco, S., Tisato, F.: Karate moves recognition from skeletal motion (2013). URL http://dx.doi.org/10.1117/12.2006229
17. Kaewplee, K., Khamsemanan, N., Nattee, C.: A rule-based approach for improving kinect skeletal tracking system with an application on standard muay thai maneuvers. In: 2014 Joint 7th International Conference on and Advanced Intelligent Systems (ISIS). 15th International Symposium on Soft Computing and Intelligent Systems (SCIS), pp. 281–285, December 2014. doi:10.1109/SCIS-ISIS.2014.7044763
18. Saha, S. Ghosh, S., Konar, A., Nagar, A.K.: Gesture recognition from indian classical dance using kinect sensor. In: 2013 Fifth International Conference on Computational Intelligence, Communication Systems and Networks (CICSyN), pp. 3–8, June 2013. doi:10.1109/CICSYN.2013.11
19. Lin, X., Kitanovski, V., Zhang, Q., Izquierdo, E.: Enhanced multi-view dancing videos synchronisation. In: 2012 13th International Workshop on Image Analysis for Multimedia Interactive Services (WIAMIS), pp. 1–4, May 2012. doi:10.1109/WIAMIS.2012.6226773
20. Dancs, J., Sivalingam, R., Somasundaram, G., Morellas, V., Papanikolopoulos, N.: Recognition of ballet micro-movements for use in choreography. In: 2013 IEEE/RSJ International Conference on Intelligent Robots and Systems (IROS), pp. 1162–1167, November 2013. doi:10.1109/IROS.2013.6696497
21. Gupta, S., Goel, S.: Pogest: A vision based tool for facilitating kathak learning. In: 2014 Seventh International Conference on Contemporary Computing (IC3), pp. 24–29, August 2014. doi:10.1109/IC3.2014.6897142
22. Pisharady, P.K., Saerbeck, M.: Robust gesture detection and recognition using dynamic time warping and multi-class probability estimates. In: 2013 IEEE Symposium on Computational Intelligence for Multimedia, Signal and Vision Processing (CIMSIVP), pp. 30–36, April 2013. doi:10.1109/CIMSIVP.2013.6583844.

23. Alexiadis, D.S., Daras, P.: Quaternionic signal processing techniques for automatic evaluation of dance performances from MoCap data. IEEE Trans. Multimed. **16**(5), 1391–1406 (2014). doi:10.1109/TMM.2014.2317311. ISSN: 1520-9210
24. Keerthy, N.K.: Virtual kung fu sifu with kinect (2012)
25. Anbarsanti, N., Prihatmanto, A.S.: Dance modelling, learning and recognition system of aceh traditional dance based on hidden markov model. In: 2014 International Conference on Information Technology Systems and Innovation (ICITSI), pp. 86–92, November 2014. doi:10.1109/ICITSI.2014.7048243
26. Holsti, L., Takala, T., Martikainen, A., Kajastila, R., Hämäläinen, P.: Body-controlled trampoline training games based on computer vision. In: CHI 2013 Extended Abstracts on Human Factors in Computing Systems, CHI EA 2013, pp. 1143–1148. ACM, New York (2013). doi:10.1145/2468356.2468560 ISBN 978-1-4503-1952-2 http://doi.acm.org/10.1145/2468356.2468560
27. Wada, S., Fukase, M., Nakanishi, Y., Tatsuta, L.: In search of a usability of kinect in the training of traditional japanese. In: 2013 Second International Conference on e-Learning and e-Technologies in Education (ICEEE) (2014)

Finding an Efficient Threshold for Fixation Detection in Eye Gaze Tracking

Sudarat Tangnimitchok[1](✉), Nonnarit O-larnnithipong[1], Armando Barreto[1],
Francisco R. Ortega[2], and Naphtali D. Rishe[2]

[1] Electrical and Computer Engineering Department, Florida International University,
Miami, FL, USA
{stang018,nolar002,barretoa}@fiu.edu
[2] School of Computer and Information Sciences, Florida International University,
Miami, FL, USA
fortega@cs.fiu.edu, ndr@acm.org

Abstract. We propose a combined analytical/statistical method to determine an efficient threshold on the dispersion of estimates of the point of gaze (POG) to indicate a user fixation. The experimental data for this study was obtained with an EyeTech TM3 eye gaze tracker (EGT). The experimental protocol to make the user fixate on pre-determined visual targets was implemented using the C language and OpenCV. Subjects first used the system in a training mode, from which an individualized dispersion threshold was obtained. Our approach was verified by applying the individualized threshold to POG data from a second run, in testing mode, with encouraging results.

Keywords: Fixation identification · Eye gaze tracking · Data analysis algorithm

1 Introduction

Eye Gaze Tracking has been used for many years in the Human-Computer Interaction field. As the eyes are another gateway to express human emotions and thoughts, one can identify a person's object of interest by determining where the person is directing his/her gaze. Trying to assign meaning to a person's gaze patterns is not an easy task. Nonetheless, one specific gesture of eye movement that we can extract from eye tracking is fixation. Our point of gaze (POG) tends to stop at a screen location when we are interested in something since our brain needs time to analyze and make sense of what we are looking at. We call this gesture 'fixation', and the method to identify the gesture 'fixation identification' or 'fixation detection'.

The key to identify the fixation gesture is to observe the dispersion of POGs (Points of Gaze), i.e., the distribution of spatial coordinates indicating the gazing point in the display. In an ideal case, the POGs during a fixation should stop at one point for a time interval (i.e., X- and Y- coordinates of the POGs should remain constant for a period of time). In practice, however, even when a person fixes his/her eyes at one point, there will be slight movements from the eye balls. This phenomenon ("microsaccades")

© Springer International Publishing Switzerland 2016
M. Kurosu (Ed.): HCI 2016, Part II, LNCS 9732, pp. 93–103, 2016.
DOI: 10.1007/978-3-319-39516-6_9

has an important role in our visual perception but it prevents us from obtaining the ideal POG constant coordinates we would expect during a fixation.

Several algorithms have been introduced to detect an EGT fixation despite the microsaccades, with most of them detecting a reduction in the spatial dispersion of consecutive POGs. These algorithms have been described in the EGT analysis general literature, e.g., [2–4], and in papers specifically devoted to the investigation of EGT fixation detection algorithms, e.g., [8–10]. Some other researchers have proposed modifications to the basic method [5, 11] aimed at improving the fixation detection performance. A few algorithms also use some temporal constraints in deciding whether or not a fixation has occurred.

However, many of the algorithms use thresholds for dispersion that have been developed as custom, ad hoc solutions to specific implementations and may be expressed in a variety of units (pixels, mm, etc.). This work aims at identifying a recommendable threshold for the POG dispersion that is likely to be effective, and that is not dependent on the specific units of spatial displacement used. Thus the resulting threshold obtained from the study can be applied to any system regardless of the devices and units it may use. We also propose that each EGT system user should have his/her own efficient individualized threshold determined because the specific behavior of the eye gaze during fixations may vary from person to person. So, each user should go through the process of finding his/her best individualized threshold (during a training stage) and apply it for system use afterwards (testing).

2   Methodology

2.1   EyeTech TM3 Eye Gaze Tracker (EGT)

The EyeTech TM3 is a compact and portable eye tracker from EyeTech Digital Systems, Inc. The system consists of a high definition camera, infrared sources, and its software environment. It is capable of tracking with one or both eyes in real time (providing POG estimates every 26 ms, in our experiment) and it can be used with any Windows-based communication software. In this study, we used their provided libraries (OpenCV) [1, 7] to build the visual-based interactive software in the designed experiment. The model specifications are listed in Table 1.

Table 1. Technical specification of EyeTech TM3

Methods	Video, dark pupil, infrared illumination
Spatial resolution	1 degree (approximate)
Temporal resolution	Adjustable, 15–55 samples per second
Freedom of head movements	25 X 16 X19 cm
Temporal resolution	Adjustable, 15-55 samples per second

2.2 Experimental Design

For the purpose of finding an efficient threshold that does not depend on any specific units, we created an interactive program based on the EyeTech TM3 eye gaze tracker (EGT) to record the POGs continuously throughout the experimental session.

We involved 22 participants in the implementation of our approach. After performing the calibration suggested by the eye gaze tracker manufacturer, each subject was instructed to complete 2 experimental stages: Training and Testing. The X- and Y- screen coordinates of the POG were recorded throughout both complete stages. In each stage the protocol presents 5 visual targets (pink circles), located randomly in sequence as shown in Fig. 1. Prior to the beginning of the experiment, the subject is instructed to fixate his/her gaze only on those visual targets, when they appear. To prevent unintended fixations in the intervals between target presentations, a yellow circle, completely different in appearance from the targets, is shown moving around the screen, as a distractor.

Our approach continuously stores the current X coordinate and the previous 49 X coordinates recorded in a 50-point First-In-First-Out (FIFO) buffer and uses them to calculate a standard deviation of the X coordinates every sampling instant. The same process is followed for the Y coordinates of the point of gaze. The standard deviations for both the X and Y axes will be calculated iteratively. Therefore, in our approach we have current estimates ($N = 50$) of the standard deviation of the POG coordinates (i.e., σ_x and σ_y), at every sampling instant.

Fig. 1. Interactive program used in the experiment with the EyeTech TM3system. The pink circle at the lower bottom of the screen is a fixation target.

2.3 Statistical Approach for Fixation Identification

We propose to use the statistical dispersion of the X and Y POG coordinates as the criteria to determine when a fixation has occurred. In particular, we seek to identify a constant threshold, K, for the standard deviations of the POG coordinates in X and in Y

(σ_x and σ_y) to determine the occurrence of EGT fixations, as we expect marked and simultaneous decreases in σ_x and σ_y during fixations (as shown in Fig. 2). Note that our proposed threshold K will, therefore, be unaffected by the type of units in which the EGT system reports coordinates or distances.

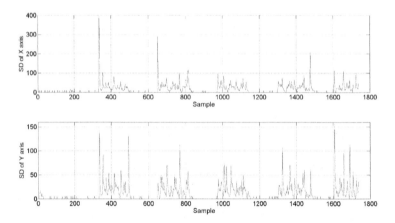

Fig. 2. Plots of the standard deviations of the POG coordinate in X and in Y

Smoothing the Standard Deviation Signals using a one-pole Filter. Due to the abrupt, short-term drops that occur in σ_x and σ_y when a fixation is not taking place (Fig. 2), the system may report brief erroneous fixation detections. To circumvent this problem we apply a one-pole filter of the type used in Gamma memories [6] to σ_x and σ_y. The filter will give the current output sample based on the input sample and the previous output sample. We can adjust the μ parameter ($0 < \mu < 1$) to set whether the output should depend more on the current input or on the previous output. As a result, the filter will smooth the signal that it processes, while retaining the envelope shape of the original signal. Its purpose is similar to that of a running average filter, except that it has faster performance and is much easier to implement, compared to the normal average filter. Figure 4 shows the signal before and after applying the filter (Fig. 3).

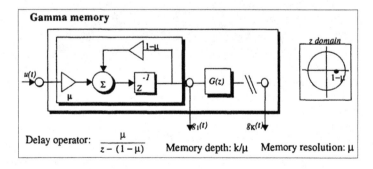

Fig. 3. One-pole filter as used in a Gamma Memory (From [6])

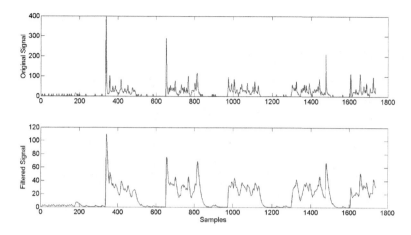

Fig. 4. Standard Deviation of X signal, (σ_x), before and after applying a one-pole filter

Sweeping Threshold and ROC Curve. To identify the most effective K value, the pre-recorded POG files from the training stage of each participant was processed by an algorithm that indicates a fixation only if $\sigma_x < K$ AND $\sigma_y < K$, where the standard deviations are calculated on the basis of the present POG and the immediately previous 49 POGs (i.e., N = 50). The result (Fixation OR No-Fixation) is assigned to the present temporal sample and the analysis is repeated throughout the complete POG file. Since the timing of appearance and disappearance of the 5 actual targets through the experiment is known and recorded, we are able to assess how many of the fixation indications from the system are correct ("True positives") and how many are incorrect ("False Positives"). This process is repeated for increasing values of K (starting at 0), until every

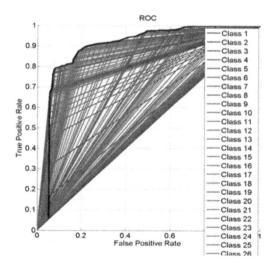

Fig. 5. Receiver Operating Characteristic (ROC) curve of 100 thresholds

POG is reported as a fixation by the system. For each threshold, K, tried the "True positive rate" and "False Positive rate" enables us to calculate and draw one point of the Receiver Operating Characteristic (ROC) curve for the fixation detection process (Fig. 5) and, from the whole curve, we are able to select the best K value (the K value that defines the closest point in the ROC curve to the coordinates "False Positive Rate" = 0 and "True Positive Rate" = 1, located on the top-left corner of the graph). This will be considered the best individualized K value for that specific participant.

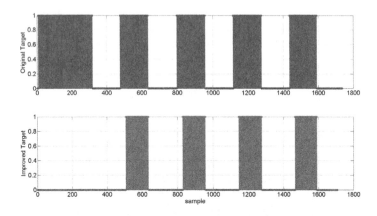

Fig. 6. Original target indications and the adjusted target indications (including only 4 targets)

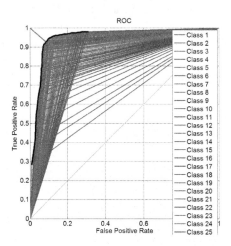

Fig. 7. Improved ROC curve after disregarding the first target presentation

Improved Result from ROC Curve. In processing the POG data from the training stage from all participants we noticed that the evolutions of σ_x and σ_y prior and during the presentation of the first target were extremely inconsistent, seemingly due to the lack of familiarity of the test subjects with the system at the beginning experiment. This confounding effect does not persist after the second target presentation. Accordingly, we decided to perform our analysis only considering the POG evolution during and after the second target presentation ("adjusted target indications", Fig. 6). As expected, this resulted in higher, more consistent levels of accuracy in fixation detection (e.g., Fig. 7).

3   Results

3.1   Diversity of Individualized Thresholds Found

After the individualized thresholds for all the participants were found, in the way described above, the histogram of these thresholds was constructed, as shown in Fig. 8. We observe that the thresholds found to provide the best performance for each of the participants are not all equal, and, in fact are significantly dispersed around their mean value. This provides some level of verification of our expectations and further confirms that an individualized threshold should be obtained for each EGT user through training for efficient operation of the fixation detection process.

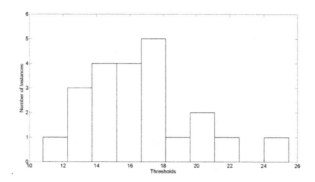

Fig. 8. Histogram of individualized best thresholds found for the participants

3.2   Testing the Individualized Thresholds

For the purpose of testing the performance of the individualized thresholds, we asked the test subjects to go through the experiment a second time, in the testing stage, and recorded the POG data (sequence of X- and Y-coordinates) for the second time. In this second stage, however, the individualized threshold found for the specific participant is applied in real-time to the σ_x and σ_y calculated continuously as the experiment takes place. Therefore, this time there will be a small red dot that appears in the display to indicate the test subject's POGs. The dot's color will remain red if the system detects no fixation, and turn to yellow when a fixation is detected.

The instructions to the subject in the testing stage are the same as during the training stage: Whenever the visual target appears (Target = 1), we ask the subject to fix his/her gaze on it so the algorithm is supposed to indicate a fixation (Result = 1). On the contrary, whenever the target disappears (Target = 0), we ask the subject to follow the distractor (moving yellow circle) in the display to prevent the occurrence of an unintended fixation.

Thus the result is presumed to be non-fixation (Result = 0). This setup allows us to also calculate the correct and incorrect results provided by the system and, therefore, evaluate the system error rate (1 – accuracy).

After we apply the individualized best threshold obtained from the training stage to the testing stage recorded data, we obtained the error rate results as shown in Fig. 9 (bottom trace). Please note that it takes some time after the target appears before the test subjects can actually locate it and move their gaze to the visual target. As a result of that, we set the value in the target vector in those transition intervals to zero and call the resulting target indicators 'Improved target' indicators (middle trace of Fig. 9). This adjustment allows the calculation of a more realistic error rate, which we obtained for all subjects, for both their training POG data and their testing POG data. These error rates are shown and compared Fig. 10. The graph in the continuous line is the error rate from the training stage, while the graph in the dashed line is the error rate from the testing stage. We can appreciate that, for the vast majority of subjects, the testing and training performances are not significantly different.

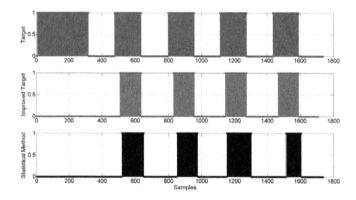

Fig. 9. Target indicators and resulting vector calculated by the system (example). On the top shows the original target vector. In the middle shows the improved target vector after trimming the first target and on the bottom shows the resulting vector from our approach.

To verify the hypothesis that there are no statistically significant differences in mean between the two error rates (from the training stage and the testing stage) of each participant, we ran a Paired T-test [12] using the R-software as shown in Fig. 11. We set the null hypothesis to be that the difference between the mean of two data sets is zero and set the level of significance at 0.05. The p-value resulting from the test was 0.098 which is greater than 0.05, so we do not reject the null hypothesis and conclude that the means are not different at 5 % level of significance. This further supports our observation on the similarity of both traces in Fig. 10.

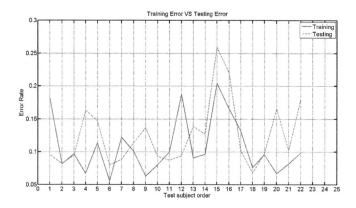

Fig. 10. Plots of error rate from the training and testing stages

```
> # Input Data
> Train = c(0.18,0.08,0.09,0.06,0.11,0.05,0.12,0.10,0.06,0.07,0.09
+ ,0.18,0.09,0.09,0.20,0.16,0.13,0.07,0.09,0.06,0.081,0.09);
> Test = c(0.09,0.08,0.09,0.16,0.14,0.08,0.09,0.11,0.13
+ ,0.09,0.08,0.09,0.14,0.12,0.25,0.22,0.10,0.068,0.10,0.16,0.10,0.18);
> # Test the equality of variance
> var.test(Train,Test);

        F test to compare two variances

data:  Train and Test
F = 0.79683, num df = 21, denom df = 21, p-value = 0.6075
alternative hypothesis: true ratio of variances is not equal to 1
95 percent confidence interval:
 0.330827 1.919228
sample estimates:
ratio of variances
         0.7968263

> # T-test of the difference in means (pair-Testing)
> t.test(Train,Test,var.equal=T,paired=T);

        Paired t-test

data:  Train and Test
t = -1.73, df = 21, p-value = 0.09831
alternative hypothesis: true difference in means is not equal to 0
95 percent confidence interval:
 -0.041739879  0.003830788
sample estimates:
mean of the differences
           -0.01895455
```

Fig. 11. Paired T-test result of the difference in mean of the error rate between training and testing stages using R software

This means that the benefit of having found the best individualized threshold for each participant through the ROC analysis of training stage POG data is kept even in subsequent uses of the EGT system. In our experiment, for example, the system was almost as accurate in detecting fixations in the testing stage as it was during the training stage.

3.3   Adjustable Characteristics of the Algorithm Proposed

Another important aspect of the proposed algorithm is that by adjusting the μ parameter used in the one-pole filter employed for the smoothing of the standard deviation sequences the performance characteristics of the algorithm can be altered. μ has a range from 0 to 1; a small μ value will increase the detection accuracy while a large μ may cause more false fixation detections. Conversely, a small μ tends to promote a slower response, compared to a large μ. The reason behind this is that a smoother standard deviation sequence will have slower level changes and, therefore, may take additional time to drop below the K threshold to indicate a fixation. On the other hand, if the strength of the smoothing effect is lessened, the filtered standard deviation signal is more like the unfiltered version of the signal, still displaying fast transitions, but also containing spurious drops, even when no fixation is taking place.

4   Conclusion

In this work, we aimed at identifying a recommendable threshold for the POG dispersion that is likely to be effective, and that is not directly affected by the specific units of spatial displacement (pixels, mm, etc.) used in any particular device. Further, we proposed that each EGT system user may need a different threshold in the fixation detection algorithm. We showed that such individualized threshold can be obtained from the data gathered during a short training stage, by means of ROC curve analysis.

The histogram of individualized best thresholds found does show diversity for the different participants, indicated by a noticeable dispersion around the mean. Using the individualized threshold in the analysis of a subsequently recorded testing stage proved that the high performance shown in the training stage is kept. Both these observations seem to confirm that it is useful to determine an efficient threshold for the fixation algorithm for each user during the brief training stage.

Moreover, we can adjust the performance balance between accuracy and response time using the μ parameter of the smoothing filter to fit the demands of a specific fixation detection application. By adjusting this parameter, the response time of the fixation detector could be shortened, at the expense of detection accuracy. Conversely, a higher accuracy may require a μ value that might make the detector somewhat slower to respond.

Acknowledgements. This material is based in part upon work supported by the National Science Foundation under Grant Nos. I/UCRC IIP-1338922, AIR IIP-1237818, SBIR IIP-1330943, III-Large IIS-1213026, MRI CNS-1532061, OISE 1541472, MRI CNS-1532061, MRI CNS-1429345, MRI CNS-0821345, MRI CNS-1126619, CREST HRD-0833093, I/UCRC IIP-0829576, MRI CNS-0959985, RAPID CNS-1507611.

References

1. Bradski, G., Kaehler, A.: Learning OpenCV: Computer vision with the OpenCV library. O'Reilly, Sebastopol, CA (2008)
2. Duchowski, A.: Eye tracking methodology: Theory and practice, 2nd edn. Springer, Heidelberg (2009)
3. Jacob, R.J.K.: What you look at is what you get: Eye movement based interaction techniques. Proceedings ACMCHI'90 Human Factors in Computing Systems, pp. 11–18. ACM Press, New York (1990)
4. Jacob, R.J.K.: Eye movement–based human–computer interaction techniques: Toward noncommand interfaces. In: Hartson, H.R., Hix, D. (eds.) Advances in human–computer interaction, vol. 4, pp. 151–190. Ablex, Norwood, NJ (1993)
5. Kumar, M., Klingner, J., Puranik, R., Winograd, T., Paepcke, A.: Improving the accuracy of gaze input for interaction. Proceedings of the 2008 Symposium on Eye Tracking Research and Applications, pp. 65–68. ACM Press, New York (2008)
6. Principe, J.C., Hsu, H.H., Kuo, J.M.: Analysis of short term memories for neural networks. In: NIPS, pp. 1011–1018 (1993)
7. Quicklink2 Library. (n.d.). Retrieved November 5, 2015. https://gitlab.eyetechds.com/windows_public/ql2matlabwrapper/raw/2608b0c438382b32a2d063e89aa42632f806be8b/QL2MatlabWrapper/QL2MatlabWrapper.cpp
8. Salvucci, D.D., Goldberg, J.H.: Identifying fixations and saccades in eye-tracking protocols. Proceedings of the 2000 Symposium on Eye Tracking Research and Applications, pp. 71–78. ACM Press, New York (2000)
9. Shic, F., Chawarska, K., Scassellati, B.: The incomplete fixation measure. Proceedings of the 2008 Symposium on Eye Tracking Research and Applications, pp. 111–114. ACM Press, New York (2008)
10. Spakov, O., Miniotas, D.: Application of clustering algorithms in eye gaze visualizations. Inf. Technol. Control **36**, 213–216 (2007)
11. Urruty, T., Lew, S., Ihadaddene, N., Simovici, D.A.: Detecting eye fixations by projection clustering. ACM Trans. Multimedia Comput. Commun. Appl. **3**, 23:1–23:20 (2007)
12. Yates, R., Goodman, D.: Probability and stochastic processes: A friendly introduction for electrical & computer engineers. John Wiley, New York (1999)

Hover Detection Using Active Acoustic Sensing

Masaya Tsuruta[✉], Shuhei Aoyama, Arika Yoshida,
Buntarou Shizuki, and Jiro Tanaka

University of Tsukuba, Tsukuba, Japan
{tsuruta,aoyama,yoshida,shizuki,jiro}@iplab.cs.tsukuba.ac.jp

Abstract. In this paper, we present a technique for hover and touch detection using Active Acoustic Sensing. This sensing technique analyzes the resonant property of the target object and the air around it. To verify whether the detection technique works, we conduct an experiment to discriminate between hovering the hand over the piezoelectric elements placed on a target object and touching the same object. As a result of our experiment, hovering was detected with 96.7 % accuracy and touching was detected with 100 % accuracy.

Keywords: Prototyping · Everyday surfaces · Touch activities · Acoustic classification · Machine learning · Frequency analysis · Ultrasonic · Piezoelectric sensor · Proximity sensing

1 Introduction

Hover is the gesture that is placing a hand or a finger closely above an object. It can be detected easily by simply adding proximity sensors to the object. This method is useful for improving usability since it can add another interaction modality (i.e., hover) to the object. For example, a hover-sensitive device can automatically wake up from standby mode for an instant interaction.

In this paper, rather than adding proximity sensors to an object, we show a lightweight technique that can detect hover over an object by attaching a pair of piezoelectric elements to the object: a vibration speaker and a contact microphone. This technique is based on our Active Acoustic Sensing [1], which is a technique to make existing objects touch-sensitive using ultrasonic waves and frequency analysis. The Active Acoustic Sensing utilizes the fact that the resonant property of a solid object is sensitive to how they are touched. In other words, the resonant property of an object changes with respect to the manner in which the object is touched. Since these changes can be observed as different resonant frequency spectra, we can estimate how the object is touched by analyzing the spectra.

The contribution of this paper, in addition to determining how an object is touched, is identifying that hover can also be observed as different resonant frequency spectra. Thereby, this technique will further enrich the vocabulary of interaction for prototyping objects.

© Springer International Publishing Switzerland 2016
M. Kurosu (Ed.): HCI 2016, Part II, LNCS 9732, pp. 104–114, 2016.
DOI: 10.1007/978-3-319-39516-6_10

2   Related Work

2.1   Passive Sensing

Some studies detect tactile gestures by passively capturing the sound or vibrations created by these gestures using microphones [2–4]. For example, Toffee [3] detects around-device taps by capturing mechanical vibrations generated by a finger tap; it uses four microphones attached to each corner at the bottom of a device and uses time differences between the arrivals of acoustic vibrations to estimate the tapped position. Braun et al. [4] sense interaction on everyday surfaces with some microphones attached to these surfaces. Their system detects taps and swipe gestures using machine learning. In contrast to these studies which need a user-activated interaction that emits sounds, our study does not require users to emit any sound as our device emits the sounds actively.

2.2   Active Sensing

In addition to the aforementioned techniques, there are others that can detect user interaction using active acoustic signals [5–8]. For example, Acoustruments [5] is a sensing technique used for tangible interaction on a smartphone. This technique connects the speaker and the microphone of the smartphone by a plastic tube. The sensing system detects changes of acoustic waves in or around the plastic tube to recognize a variety of interaction. While this study uses changes of acoustic waves in or around the tube with a smartphone, our study focuses on using changes of acoustic waves diffused in the air to detect hover over arbitrary solid objects. SoundWave [6] measures Doppler shifts with the speakers and microphones already embedded in commodity devices to detect in-air gestures. In contrast, our study is a lightweight technique, which uses a pair of piezoelectric elements attached to an existing object to detect hover over the object, in addition to touch gestures that can be detected by [1]. EchoTag [7] enables a smartphone to tag and remember indoor locations by transmitting an acoustic signal with the smartphone's speaker and sensing its environmental reflection with the smartphone's microphone. This study makes use of reflection of acoustic signals around the device. On the other hand, our study uses acoustic signals to sense hover. Wang et al. [9] use a swept frequency audio signal to detect tapped positions on a paper keyboard placed on a desk. Our study can detect hover in addition to how the object is touched.

2.3   Hover Detection

Various methods to detect hover have been researched. Wilson et al. [10] use a depth camera. Withana et al. [11] use IR sensors. Rekimoto [12] uses capacitive sensing. By contrast, our study uses Active Acoustic Sensing [1] to detect hover over an existing object.

3   Detection Mechanism

We will now present our mechanism to detect hover and touch using ultrasonic waves and their frequency analysis.

3.1   Principles of Touch and Hover Detection

The principle of our Active Acoustic Sensing [1], which is a technique to detect how an existing solid object is touched using its acoustic property and also serves as a basis of our hover detection, is simple. Every object has a resonant property. This causes a vibrational reaction, which is unique to that object. When the object is touched, its resonant property changes with respect to the nature of the touch. As a result, the vibrational reaction also changes. Our technique uses this phenomenon to estimate how the object is touched (i.e., touch gestures) in accordance with the following procedure. Initially, an actuator attached to the object causes the object to vibrate at a wide range of frequency. Next, the frequency response from the object is acquired using a sensor attached to the object. Finally, our technique uses machine learning with frequency response labeled as touch gestures.

In this work, to realize hover detection, we focus on the waves leaked into the air. If there is nothing in the air around the sensor, the waves observed by the sensor mainly consist of the waves emitted from the actuator and propagated through the body of the object where the sensor is attached. In contrast, if a hand or a finger is above the sensor (i.e., hovering), the waves emitted from the actuator into the air are reflected by the hand or finger and propagated to the sensor (Fig. 1). Consequently, the waves observed by the sensor change (i.e., now contain such waves) before hovering. This change can also be detected as hover using machine learning with frequency response. As described above, our technique is a lightweight method to detect hover over an object, in addition to the manner in which the object is touched, by attaching a pair of actuator and sensor to the object.

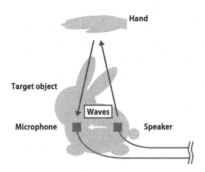

Fig. 1. Principle of hover detection.

3.2   System

The overview of our system is shown in Fig. 2. This system consists of the following: software to generate waves and analyze the frequency response, a pair of actuator and sensor that are attached to the object, and an amplifier.

The actuator and sensor used in this system are our own piezoelectric vibration speaker and microphone respectively. The two have the same composition, which consists of a piezoelectric film and an acrylic plate (Fig. 3). This acrylic plate is pasted to the piezoelectric film by an adhesive to enhance durability of elements and stability of the wave propagation. The piezoelectric vibration speaker and microphone should be attached near the location where we want to detect hover. In our system, we used a double-sided tape to attach these elements to the surface. Note that these elements should be exposed to air to make the ultrasonic waves propagate adequately into the air.

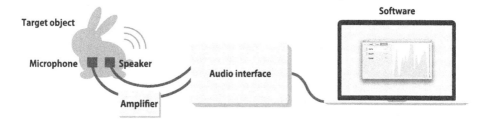

Fig. 2. System overview.

Fig. 3. Microphone/speaker.

The software generates a sinusoidal sweep signal from 20 kHz to 40 kHz as the wave emitted from the speaker. To detect touch and hover, the software uses Fast Fourier Transform (FFT) to obtain the spectrum of the wave acquired by the microphone and a Support Vector Machine (SVM) as the classifier similar to that used in [1]. The user interface of the software is shown in Fig. 4. On the left side of the window is an area for labels representing the different types of interaction. In the "Label" tab, the user initializes the different types of interaction he wants to detect. In the "Train" tab, he iterates the actions to train and build an SVM model. In the "Predict" tab, each label shows its likelihood correspondence with an action. The right side of the window is an area for visualized sound spectrum of the frequency response, which is the result of FFT. It is used to understand how our system works and to confirm whether the system is runs normally. When user interactions such as hover or touch induce changes, the shape of the spectrum change as well, and the corresponding label in the "Predict" tab is highlighted.

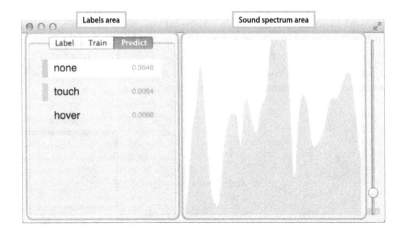

Fig. 4. Software.

4   Experiment

To verify whether the detection technique works, we conducted an experiment to discriminate hover and touch. For this purpose, we attached a piezoelectric vibration speaker/microphone pair to an acrylic table as shown in Fig. 5. We also used a doorknob and a portable safe as target objects. We call the three scenes of experiment "Table", "Doorknob", and "Safe" according to the target objects. The distance between the two piezoelectric elements was 20 mm.

A participant covered the piezoelectric elements with his hand over 5 mm above them (Hover). He touched the point that was 11.18 mm away from the elements (Touch). To measure the accuracy of our technique, the participant first touched the target object 10 times and then performed hover 10 times. We counted the number of times that the gesture were detected correctly under both conditions.

Following are the results. For "Table", Hover was correctly detected 9 times implying an accuracy of 90 % (The failed trial was detected as Touch); Touch was correctly detected 10 times implying an accuracy of 100 %. For "Doorknob", Hover was correctly detected 10 times implying an accuracy of 100 %; Touch was correctly detected 10 times implying an accuracy of 100 %. For "Safe", Hover was correctly detected 10 times implying an accuracy of 100 %; Touch was correctly

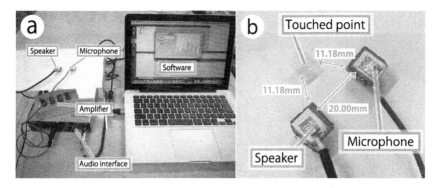

Fig. 5. Setup of the experiment: (a) Overview, (b) the attached piezoelectric vibration speaker and piezoelectric microphone.

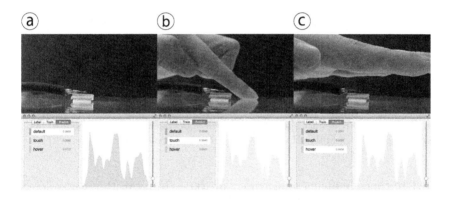

Fig. 6. Observed sound spectra of "Table": (a) Default, (b) Touch, and (c) Hover.

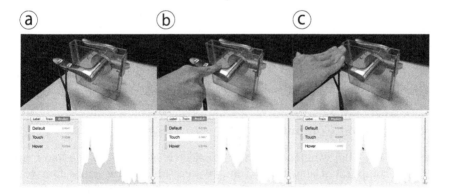

Fig. 7. Observed sound spectra of "Doorknob": (a) Default, (b) Touch, and (c) Hover.

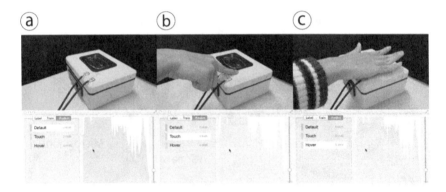

Fig. 8. Observed sound spectra of "Safe": (a) Default, (b) Touch, and (c) Hover.

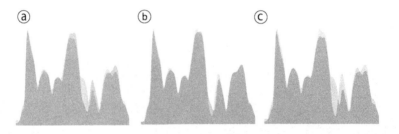

Fig. 9. Differences of sound spectra of "Table" between the three conditions: (a) Default – Touch, (b) Default – Hover, and (c) Touch – Hover.

detected 10 times implying an accuracy of 100 %. In total, Hover was detected with 96.7 % accuracy; Touch was detected with 100 % accuracy. The observed sound spectra supported these results. Figures 6, 7 and 8 show examples of sound spectra observed in the following three conditions: Default, Touch, and Hover. These sound spectra are different from each other as shown in Fig. 9 for example. Thus, our system could detect hover and touch accurately.

5   Applications

We present three applications as examples of our hover detection technique.

5.1   Shortcuts on Computers

As shown in Fig. 10a, we attached the piezoelectric elements to the lower right corner of a computer. Using this setup, we were able to recognize four touch gestures and a hover gesture on the computer (Fig. 11). We assigned a shortcut to each of them. For example, we assigned the finger top gesture to Ctrl+z, which is a widely used shortcut for undoing, and the hover gesture to Ctrl+s, which is a frequently used shortcut for saving.

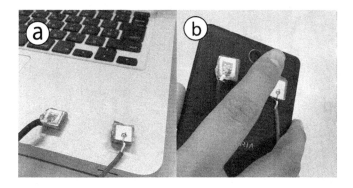

Fig. 10. Applications: (a) Shortcuts on computers and (b) back-of-device interaction on smartphones.

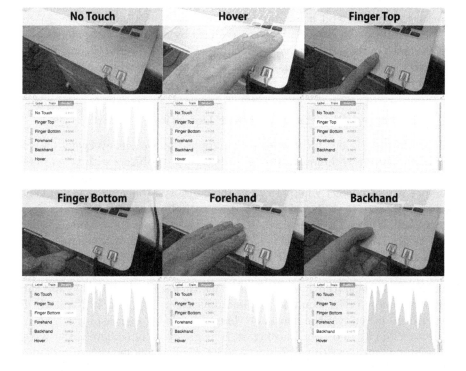

Fig. 11. Four touch gestures and hover on the computer.

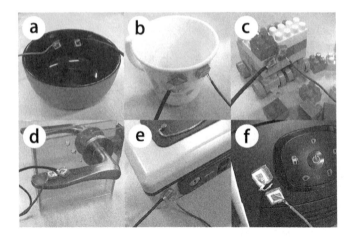

Fig. 12. Prototyping objects with hover detection.

5.2 Around-Device Interaction on Smartphones

By using our technique, hover can be made available even outside of the screen area without using dedicated smartphones. As shown in Fig. 10b, we pasted a piezoelectric speaker and a microphone at the back of a smartphone. In this case, back-of-device interaction [13] was realized by assigning the undo shortcut to it. As shown in this application, our technique is useful for prototyping around-device interaction including back-of-device interaction and will possibly promote researchers to conduct such research as [14,15].

5.3 Prototyping Objects with Hover Detection

As shown in Fig. 12, our technique can be applied to various everyday objects. This shows that our technique is useful for prototyping objects with hover detection. Figure 12a and b are prototypes of crockery sensitive to grasp/hover. Our technique can also detect whether or not the crockery is filled with water. When there are contents in it, hover triggers a voice indication such as "The vessel has content". Figure 12c is a touch/stack/hover sensitive toy car model made out of blocks. When hover is detected, it emits the sound of an engine, which the user has applied in advance. Figure 12d and e are proximity sensitive objects with locking mechanisms. When these devices are approached by the hands of an unwelcome person, they automatically lock themselves even if they are carelessly left unlocked. For example, in the application described in Fig. 12d, if a user performs hover over the doorknob three seconds before grasping it, the system detects him as an owner. In contrast, if he grasps it immediately, the system detects him as an unwelcome person. As this application shows, our technique is also useful to detect whether the person is the owner or not. Figure 12f is an example of adding function to a ready-made product. While conducting an iterative development of a prototype, it is possible to add another function quickly even though it does not exist as a button.

6   Discussion

Our experiments show that, our technique can detect hover near the piezoelectric speaker and microphone. Moreover, we tested the detectable height of hover; the height was 13.8 mm in our current implementation. This implies that it is only possible to detect whether a hand or a finger hovers or not. However, this also implies that a high-output speaker with an amplifier and a more sensitive microphone will increase the detectable height, thus making it possible for more complex gestures to be detected.

Further experiments can also be conducted. In this paper, we discriminated between a single type of hover and touch gesture. While this experiment shows a possibility of application of our sensing technique, we should investigate the discrimination accuracy of various types of hover and touch gestures in our next experiment.

7   Conclusions and Future Work

In this paper, we presented a technique to detect hover by our Active Acoustic Sensing and acquiring ultrasonic waves leaked into and reflected from the air. As a result of our experiment, hovering was detected with 96.7 % accuracy and touching was detected with 100 % accuracy. However, the detectable height limits the detection to a hover gesture made by a hand or a finger and at present more complex gestures are not detectable. We believe dedicated implementation may accomplish detection of more complex gestures. For example, we already confirmed that when we use an ultrasonic speaker designed for emitting waves into the air, the detection height is extended to around 15 cm, and multiple steps of hover can be detected. Moreover, this also can be used with touch gestures. We are now dedicated to implement a new method with Support Vector Regression (SVR), which can detect hover gestures as continuous values and we plan to complete it as a part of our immediate future work.

References

1. Ono, M., Shizuki, B., Tanaka, J.: Touch & activate: adding interactivity to existing objects using active acoustic sensing. In: Proceedings of the 26th Annual ACM Symposium on User Interface Software and Technology, UIST 2013, pp. 31–40. ACM, New York (2013)
2. Murray-Smith, R., Williamson, J., Hughes, S., Quaade, T.: Stane: synthesized surfaces for tactile input. In: Proceedings of the SIGCHI Conference on Human Factors in Computing Systems, CHI 2008, pp. 1299–1302. ACM, New York (2008)
3. Xiao, R., Lew, G., Marsanico, J., Hariharan, D., Hudson, S., Harrison, C.: Toffee: enabling ad hoc, around-device interaction with acoustic time-of-arrival correlation. In: Proceedings of the 16th International Conference on Human-computer Interaction with Mobile Devices & Services, MobileHCI 2014, pp. 67–76. ACM, New York (2014)

4. Braun, A., Krepp, S., Kuijper, A.: Acoustic tracking of hand activities on surfaces. In: Proceedings of the 2nd International Workshop on Sensor-Based Activity Recognition and Interaction, WOAR 2015, pp. 9:1–9:5. ACM, New York (2015)
5. Laput, G., Brockmeyer, E., Hudson, S.E., Harrison, C.: Acoustruments: passive, acoustically-driven, interactive controls for handheld devices. In: Proceedings of the 33rd Annual ACM Conference on Human Factors in Computing Systems, CHI 2015, pp. 2161–2170. ACM, New York (2015)
6. Gupta, S., Morris, D., Patel, S., Tan, D.: SoundWave: using the doppler effect to sense gestures. In: Proceedings of the SIGCHI Conference on Human Factors in Computing Systems, CHI 2012, pp. 1911–1914. ACM, New York (2012)
7. Tung, Y.C., Shin, K.G.: EchoTag: accurate infrastructure-free indoor location tagging with smartphones. In: Proceedings of the 21st Annual International Conference on Mobile Computing and Networking, MobiCom 2015, pp. 525–536. ACM, New York (2015)
8. Harrison, C., Schwarz, J., Hudson, S.E.: TapSense: enhancing finger interaction on touch surfaces. In: Proceedings of the 24th Annual ACM Symposium on User Interface Software and Technology, UIST 2011, pp. 627–636. ACM, New York (2011)
9. Wang, J., Zhao, K., Zhang, X., Peng, C.: Ubiquitous keyboard for small mobile devices: harnessing multipath fading for fine-grained keystroke localization. In: Proceedings of the 12th Annual International Conference on Mobile Systems, Applications, and Services, MobiSys 2014, pp. 14–27. ACM, New York (2014)
10. Wilson, A.D.: Using a depth camera as a touch sensor. In: ACM International Conference on Interactive Tabletops and Surfaces, ITS 2010, pp. 69–72. ACM, New York (2010)
11. Withana, A., Peiris, R., Samarasekara, N., Nanayakkara, S.: zSense: enabling shallow depth gesture recognition for greater input expressivity on smart wearables. In: Proceedings of the 33rd Annual ACM Conference on Human Factors in Computing Systems, CHI 2015, pp. 3661–3670. ACM, New York (2015)
12. Rekimoto, J.: SmartSkin: an infrastructure for freehand manipulation on interactive surfaces. In: Proceedings of the SIGCHI Conference on Human Factors in Computing Systems, CHI 2002, pp. 113–120. ACM, New York (2002)
13. Fukatsu, Y., Hiroyuki, H., Shizuki, B., Tanaka, J.: Back-of-device interaction using halls on mobile devices. In: Proceedings of Interaction 2015, Information Processing Society of Japan, pp. 412–415 (2015). (In Japanese)
14. Kratz, S., Rohs, M.: Hoverflow: expanding the design space of around-device interaction. In: Proceedings of the 11th International Conference on Human-Computer Interaction with Mobile Devices and Services, MobileHCI 2009, pp. 4:1–4:8. ACM, New York (2009)
15. Hakoda, H., Kuribara, T., Shima, K., Shizuki, B., Tanaka, J.: AirFlip: a double crossing in-air gesture using boundary surfaces of hover zone for mobile devices. In: Kurosu, M. (ed.) HCI 2015. LNCS, vol. 9170, pp. 44–53. Springer, Heidelberg (2015)

Identification of Gracefulness Feature Parameters for Hand-Over Motion

Etsuko Ueda[1]([✉]), Kenichi Iida[2], Kentaro Takemura[3],
Takayuki Nakamura[4], and Masanao Koeda[5]

[1] Osaka Institute of Technology, Osaka, Japan
etsuko.ueda@oit.ac.jp
[2] National Institute of Technology, Nara College, Nara, Japan
[3] Tokai University, Kanagawa, Japan
[4] Wakayama University, Wakayama, Japan
[5] Osaka Electro-Communication University, Osaka, Japan

Abstract. As robots in the welfare and service industries must come into contact with humans, they are required to make favorable impressions on human sensibilities. Our research focuses on the concept of "graceful motion," as defined by Hogarth. In order to implement graceful motion in robots, we analyze the hand trajectories which highly skilled servers generate in the task of passing a wine glass to extract graceful and ungraceful curve features. We propose to model the hand trajectory by a polynomial of the fourth degree and to adjust the S-shaped curvature of the hand trajectory. An impression evaluation is then conducted, which indicates that a $20\% - 60\%$ S-shaped curvature correspond to gracefulness in a hand-over motion; this parameter corresponds to Hogarth's definition.

Keywords: Graceful motion · Motion capture · Human-robot interaction

1 Introduction

Robot applications are entering fields that require close contact with humans, for example, the welfare and service industries. In these fields, the impressions made by robots during human-robot interactions are more important than efficiency. In an environment where humans and robots coexist, the exhibition of human-like behavior by robots makes a favorable impression on human sensibilities, because such behavior generates a sense of safety. Although there are many factors involved in the expression of humanity by robots, we focus on robot motion.

Many researchers have investigated methods to develop human-like motion in robots. For example, Zhang [1] has focused on cooperative motion between two humans in order to identify the characteristics of human-like motion, with a view to application in robots. Kanda [2,3] has analyzed human impressions of human-robot interactions. Yokoi [4] has investigated the manner in which robot motions

M. Kurosu (Ed.): HCI 2016, Part II, LNCS 9732, pp. 115–124, 2016.
DOI: 10.1007/978-3-319-39516-6_11

can positively reassure a human observer. Important studies focusing on human hand motion and its trajectories have also been conducted. For example, Atkeson and Hollerbach [5] have determined that the hand tip trajectory is approximately linear, and that the velocity trend for human multi-joint movement exhibits a bell shape. Hence, Flash and Hogan [6] have proposed the minimum-jerk model as a means of reproducing these features. Further, Uno [7] has proposed the minimum-torque-change model, which considers the body kinematics. Unfortunately, as far as we know, a precise model of human-like motion has not yet been developed.

Schiller [8] has stated that "grace is the beauty of action and can be applied to unbeautiful appearances." This statement suggests that the appearance of any motion can be made graceful through refinement of that motion. Moreover, "gracefulness" is a characteristic inherent in human motion. Therefore, we can assume that robot motions can be made to appear more human-like through improved gracefulness.

In this study, we identify the gracefulness feature parameters in a hand-over motion and develop a model for generation of graceful trajectories. We first quantify William Hogarth's definition of graceful motion, which will be discussed below. Then, the graceful hand trajectories (S-curves) involved in the passing of a wine glass are analyzed to determine whether or not they conform to the "line of beauty" defined by Hogarth. Hence, we model graceful hand trajectories and identify their parameters, so as to achieve a model that facilitates automatic graceful trajectory generation.

2   The "Line of Beauty" and Modeling of Grace Hand Trajectory Using Quartic Equation

Graceful motion has been defined qualitatively by both William Hogarth and Frederik Jacobus Johannes Buytendijk [9], and this study focuses on Hogarth's definition in particular. Figure 1(a) shows the "line of beauty" presented in the cover art of Hogarth's book, "The Analysis of Beauty [10]." Hogarth suggested that S-shaped lines (serpentine lines) appear beautiful and graceful. Discussing examples of various S-shaped curves (Fig. 1(b)), he stated that: "Strictly speaking, there is but one precise line, properly to be called the line of beauty, which in the scale of them Fig. 1(b) is number 4: the lines 5, 6, 7, by their bulging too much in their curvature becoming gross and clumsy; and, on the contrary, 3, 2, 1, as they straighten, becoming mean and poor." Therefore, according to Hogarth, line number 4 in Fig. 1(b) can be considered to be a "line of beauty."

In this study, we focus on the task of "passing a wine glass," considering the gracefulness of the hand trajectory. The S-shaped curvature of the hand trajectory determined the gracefulness, in accordance with Hogarth's "line of beauty." We consider that skilled servers working at a hotel constantly exhibit graceful motion, because these individuals are very conscious of their mannerisms and are trained to make a favorable impression on hotel clients. In our experiment, four people who had been educated at a particular school for hotel staff (Subjects 1–3: male, Subject 4: female) were taken as subjects. These individuals performed the

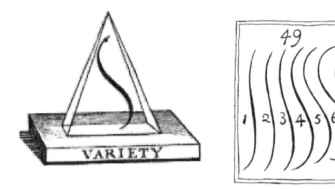

(a) "The Analysis of Beauty" cover art   (b) Various S-curve shapes

Fig. 1. Line of beauty defined by William Hogarth

motion of "passing a wine glass" three times. Their motions were measured via motion capture, using the MVN BIOMECH full-body human measurement system (Xsens Co. USA), which incorporates inertial sensors, biomechanical models, and sensor fusion algorithms. The sampling rate was 120 Hz.

Figure 2 shows a sample "passing a glass" motion. The real trajectory of one such motion is a three-dimensional (3D) curve. In order to analyze these movements simply, we focused on the plane in which each subject performed, and then converted the 3D trajectory into a two-dimensional (2D) curve. This plane was extracted by conducting a principal component analysis of the real hand

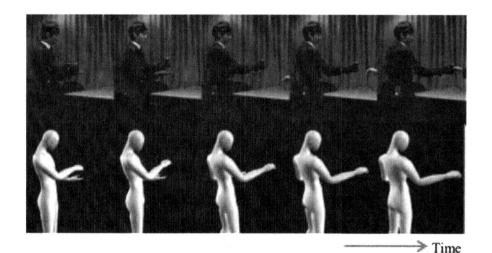

Time

Fig. 2. Example of wine-glass passing motion

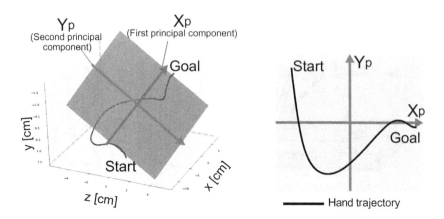

Fig. 3. Motion characteristics plane and projected hand trajectory

trajectory. The plane was comprised of the first (x-axis) and second (y-axis) principal components, and was defined as the "motion characteristics plane." The 2D curve was then obtained by projecting the 3D trajectory onto the motion characteristics plane, as shown in Fig. 3. We approximated this projected trajectory using a polynomial of the fourth degree. These coefficients are obtained by the least squares method. The right-hand trajectory was thus expressed as

$$y = a_4 x^4 + a_3 x^3 + a_2 x^2 + a_1 x + a_0, \tag{1}$$

where the $a_{0 \sim 4}$ terms are coefficients.

Our previous research [11] has shown that graceful motions have an inflection point, where the shape of the trajectory changes from concave down to concave up. Therefore, these trajectories are considered to be S-shaped. Furthermore, our previous findings indicate that motions performed in crosswise directions are superior to those in vertical directions, as regards perception of gracefulness. The simulation results obtained in that study indicate that motion in a 45° oriented plane produce the most favorable impression on human observers.

This paper aims to identify the shape parameters of the S-curve corresponding to graceful hand trajectories. It is difficult to control the shape of the S-curve by simultaneously adjusting the $a_0 \sim a_4$ coefficients of the quartic equation (Eq. (1)). Therefore, we propose the use of the local extremum value to control the S-shaped curve. By differentiating Eq. (1), we obtain

$$y' = A(x - M_1)(x - M_2)(x - M_3), \tag{2}$$

where A is an arbitrary constant and $M_1, M_2,$ and M_3 are the x-values at which the y-value is a local extremum. Note that $M_1 < M_2 < M_3$.

Figure 4 shows examples of 2D hand trajectories with graceful S-curve features and their $M_1, M_2,$ and M_3 values. By integrating Eq. (2), we obtain

$$y = A(Bx^4 + Cx^3 + Dx^2 + Ex) + F, \tag{3}$$

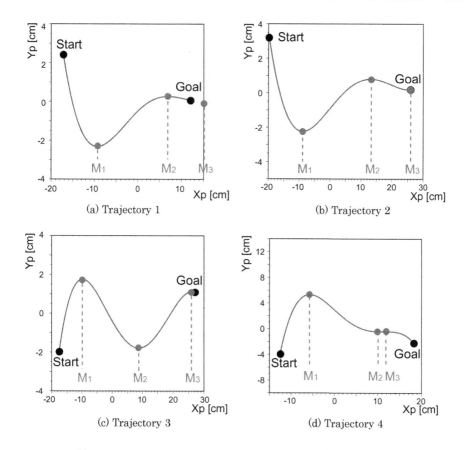

(a) Trajectory 1

(b) Trajectory 2

(c) Trajectory 3

(d) Trajectory 4

Fig. 4. Two-dimensional trajectories with S-shaped features

where, $B = 1/4$, $C = (M_1 + M_2 + M_3)/3$, $D = (M_1M_2 + M_2M_3 + M_1M_3)/2$, and $E = -M_1M_2M_3$. However, the A and F coefficients are undefined. As the start (x_s, y_s) and goal (x_g, y_g) points are fixed, A and F can be determined by utilizing these points as constraints. Thus, we obtain our proposed S-curve model, where

$$A = \frac{y_s - y_g}{B(x_s{}^4 - x_g{}^4) + C(x_s{}^3 - x_g{}^3) + D(x_s{}^2 - x_g{}^2) + E(x_s - x_g)}, \quad (4)$$

$$F = y_s - A(Bx_s{}^4 + Cx_s{}^3 + Dx_s{}^2 + Ex_s). \quad (5)$$

3   S-Curve Shape Control

In Eq. (2), the S-shaped curvature of the hand trajectory can be changed by fixing M_1 and M_3 and adjusting M_2. Thus, the y-value of M_1 (or M_3) can be controlled by M_2 alone. Figure 5 shows S-shape deformation results obtained by

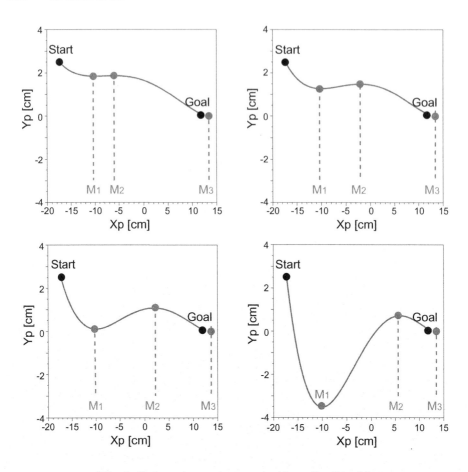

Fig. 5. S-shaped curvature control by adjusting M_2

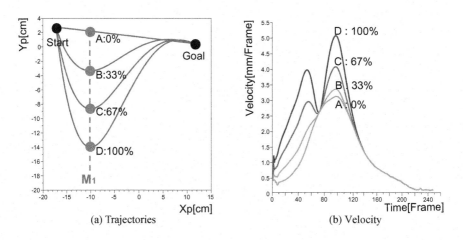

(a) Trajectories   (b) Velocity

Fig. 6. Generated curves and corresponding velocities

adjusting M_2 for the trajectory in Fig. 4(a). Note that the S-shaped curvature is one of the parameters of gracefulness, as defined by Hogarth in terms of the curves shown in Fig. 1. By adjusting M_2 with fixed M_1 and M_3, the S-shaped curvature of the hand trajectory can be changed.

Figure 6(a) shows sample generated trajectories, while Fig. 6(b) shows the change in velocity of each trajectory in Fig. 6(a). The "0 %" point" is the intersection of the line between (x_s, y_s) and (x_g, y_g) with the line $x = M_1$ (or M_3). The "100 %" point" is the greatest y-value extension the hand trajectory can achieve when the x-value is M_1 (or M_3). As indicated by Fig. 6, each trajectory has a different length. Thus, the peak movement velocities differ if the movement duration is constant, which would affect the observer impressions of the motion. To avoid this effect, we adjusted the movement duration to conform to the obtained motion's peak velocity. Figure 7 illustrates the adjusted results.

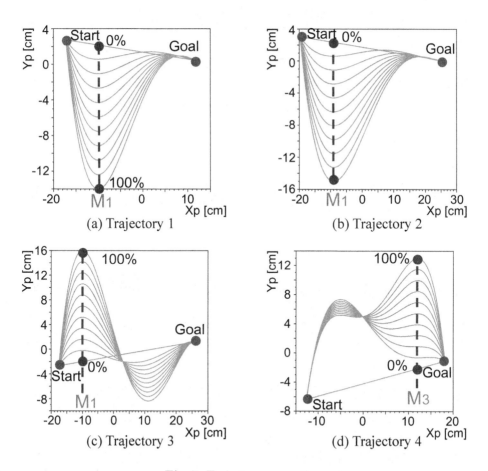

(a) Trajectory 1

(b) Trajectory 2

(c) Trajectory 3

(d) Trajectory 4

Fig. 7. Trajectory generation

4   Impression Evaluation

In total, 11 trajectories (with different S-shaped curvature) were generated for each trajectory in Fig. 4, using the proposed S-curve model. Figure 7 shows the generated trajectories. The "0 % point" and "100 % point" were defined as in the previous section. Various curvatures were calculated, in 10 % increments between the 0 % and 100 % points. In this paper, we refer to each trajectory as "$n\%$ curvature trajectory." An impression evaluation of the two trajectories (Fig. 7(a) and (c)) was then conducted using the Thurstone's paired comparison method [12]. The number of observers was seven. To evaluate the observers' impressions of the trajectories, 3DCG was used to recreate the motion of a waiter "passing a glass," employing the 11 obtained trajectories. Figures 8 and 9

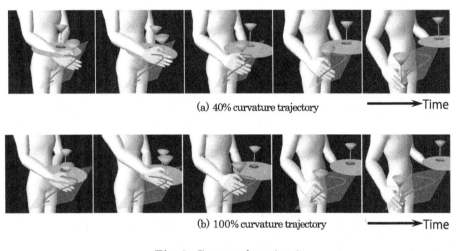

Fig. 8. Generated motion 1

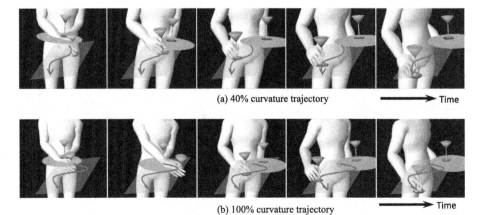

Fig. 9. Generated motion 3

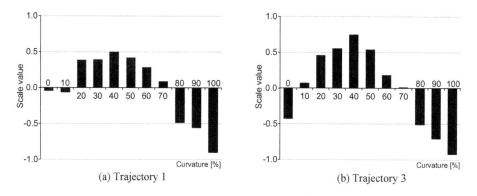

Fig. 10. Impression evaluation results (Thurstone's scale values)

show examples for the motions with 40 % and 100 % curvature trajectory in Fig. 7(a) and (c), respectively, while Fig. 10 shows the impression evaluation results for these motions. The vertical scale in Fig. 10 represents the Thurstone's scale values. These values indicate the gracefulness.

As Fig. 10 indicates, the 40 % curvature trajectory yields the best impression, and this impression decreases with curvatures further from 40 %. Hence, it was determined that a 20 % ∼ 60 % curvature trajectory corresponds to perceived gracefulness in hand-over motions. Through these experiments, we confirm that this parameter corresponds to Hogarth's definition of the "line of beauty," and the validity of our modeling method of the graceful hand trajectory.

5   Conclusions

This paper attempted to identify the parameters of gracefulness through analysis of the motion involved in passing a wine glass, and proposed a method for adjusting the S-shaped curvature of a hand trajectory by controlling the extremum. Our research results (both from this study and a previous report) suggest that the trajectory that satisfies the following conditions can produce an impression of gracefulness for observers of a serving task:

1. The motion characteristics plane should be oriented at 45°.
2. The S-shaped curvature is 20 % to 60 %.

In the next stage of our research, we will confirm the validity of the proposed modeling method through application to other tasks. The effective modeling of graceful movements will allow robots to replicate this behavior, thereby increasing human acceptance of their presence.

Acknowledgment. This work was supported by JSPS KAKENHI Grant Number 26330322.

References

1. Zhang, N., Ikeura, R., Wang, Y., Mizutani, K., Sawai, H.: Characteristics of the human arm based on a musculoskeletal model of cooperative motion between two humans. J. Biomech. Sci. Eng. **3**(1), 50–61 (2008)
2. Kanda, T., Ishiguro, H., Imai, M., Ono, T.: Body movement analysis of human-robot interaction. In: Proceedings of the 18th international joint conference on Artificial intelligence, pp. 177–182 (2003)
3. Kanda, T., Miyashita, T., Osada, T., Haikawa, Y., Ishiguro, H.: Analysis of humanoid appearances in human-robot interaction. IEEE Trans. Robot. **24**(3), 725–735 (2008)
4. Yokoi, K., Arisumi, H., Komoriya, K.: Gentle motion of robot manipulator - how does human feel hand-over motion of a robot? J. Mech. Eng. Lab. **52**(4), 149–155 (1998)
5. Atkeson, C.G., Hollerbach, J.M.: Kinematic features of unrestrained vertical arm movements. J. Neurosci. **5**(9), 2318–2330 (1985)
6. Flash, T., Hogan, N.: The coordination of arm movements: An experimentally confirmed mathematical model. J. Neurosci. **5**(7), 1688–1703 (1985)
7. Uno, Y., Kawato, M., Suzuki, R.: Formation and control of optimal trajectory in human multijoint arm movement. Biol. Cybern. **61**(2), 89–101 (1989)
8. Schiller, J.C.F., Über Anmut und Würde. Neue Thalia, vol. 2 (1793)
9. Buytendijk, F.J.J.: Allgemeine Theorie der Menschlichen Haltung und Bewegumg. Springer, Heidelberg (1972)
10. Hogarth, W.: The Analysis of Beauty: Written With a View of Fixing the Fluctuating Ideas of Taste. Georg Olms Verlag, New York (1974). https://books.google.co.uk/books?id=szQGAAAAQAAJ
11. Tanaka, T., Tsuduki, T., Ueda, E., Takemura, K., Nakamura, T.: Modeling of graceful motions: determining characteristics of graceful motions from hand-over motion. In: Computational Methods and Experimental Measurements XVI, vol. 55, pp. 453–463. WIT Transactions on Modeling and Simulation (2013)
12. Thurstone, L.L.: Psychophysical analysis. Am. J. Psychol. **38**(3), 368–389 (1927)

Multimodal, Multisensory and Natural Interaction

Virtual Reality Interaction Techniques for Individuals with Autism Spectrum Disorder: Design Considerations and Preliminary Results

Evren Bozgeyikli[1(✉)], Lal Bozgeyikli[1], Andrew Raij[2], Srinivas Katkoori[1], Redwan Alqasemi[3], and Rajiv Dubey[3]

[1] Department of Computer Science and Engineering, University of South Florida, Tampa, USA
{evren,gamze,katkoori}@mail.usf.edu
[2] Institute for Simulation and Training, University of Central Florida, Orlando, USA
raij@ucf.edu
[3] Department of Mechanical Engineering, University of South Florida, Tampa, USA
{alqasemi,dubey}@usf.edu

Abstract. Virtual reality systems are seeing growing use for training individuals with Autism Spectrum Disorder (ASD). Although the tested systems indicate effective use of virtual reality for training, there is little work in the literature evaluating different virtual reality interaction techniques for this specific group of audience. Individuals with ASD are stated to have different characteristics and perceptions. This requires careful exploration of good design principles in interaction. This paper presents design and preliminary evaluation of interaction techniques for individuals with ASD to be used in a highly immersive virtual reality vocational training system VR4VR [1]. The system includes motion tracking cameras, a head mounted display, real time tracked objects, and several interaction tools such as haptic device and touchscreen. In this system, tangible object manipulation, haptic device interaction, touch and snap technique and touchscreen interaction were implemented for object selection and manipulation; real walking and walk in place techniques were implemented for locomotion. A user study was performed with five individuals with ASD who had no prior VR experience. The preliminary testing results and observations that show the preference of the users with ASD on the implemented interaction techniques are shared in this paper with the aim of contributing to the future studies that utilize VR for individuals with ASD.

Keywords: Virtual reality · Interaction techniques · Vocational rehabilitation · Autism spectrum disorder

1 Introduction

Autism Spectrum Disorder (ASD) is a lifelong developmental disability that may impact people's understanding of their environment. It can result in difficulties with social relationships, communication and behavior [2, 3]. The latest studies show that today, about 1 in 68 children is identified with ASD [4]. Because of the limiting properties of ASD, it is usually harder for individuals with autism to find jobs and succeed in them without

© Springer International Publishing Switzerland 2016
M. Kurosu (Ed.): HCI 2016, Part II, LNCS 9732, pp. 127–137, 2016.
DOI: 10.1007/978-3-319-39516-6_12

proper training. There are many scientific studies for job training of individuals with ASD and many of them are using virtual reality. However, there is little work to understand which virtual reality interaction techniques are acceptable and useful for individuals with ASD.

Virtual reality training applications for individuals with ASD usually reported to have positive effects [5, 6] but they show different results in terms of effectiveness and acceptance by the users. One of the main reasons for these differences could be the interaction techniques that are used in these systems. The literature has not yet extensively examined different virtual reality interaction techniques for individuals with ASD. Although there are many possible advantages of using virtual reality systems for job training, effective interaction techniques must be implemented for the users to truly benefit from these advantages of virtual reality. Since perception and behaviors of the individuals with ASD are different from neuro typical individuals, using the same interaction techniques that work well for neuro typical individuals may not be a good practice for individuals with ASD.

In our VR4VR system, individuals with ASD are trained on six vocational skills in highly immersive virtual environments. These skills are: cleaning, shelving, environmental awareness, loading the back of a truck, money management and social skills. Several different interaction techniques for object selection and manipulation and locomotion were implemented in these skills of our VR4VR system. These skills and interaction techniques were selected based on discussions with the job coaches who are experts in vocational training of individuals with ASD. We have worked with six different professional job coaches who currently provide vocational training services to individuals with ASD. In selection of tasks, prevalence in employment of individuals with ASD played an important role. For interaction techniques, the most appropriate methods that allow for acclimatization to tasks were identified. These interaction techniques were designed following both research and discussions with the job coaches. For object selection and manipulation; tangible object manipulation, haptic device interaction, touch and snap technique and touchscreen interaction techniques were designed and implemented. For locomotion; real walking and walk in place techniques were designed and implemented. In this paper, we present our design considerations for the virtual reality interaction techniques for individuals with ASD in our VR4VR system with our preliminary user testing results and indications.

2   Related Work

Advances in technology have been used for assisting individuals with ASD recently. Current applications usually use touchscreen devices since they are easy to use, affordable and available. Furthermore, one of the recent studies showed that tablet applications with multi touch interactions can make children with ASD more verbally and physically engaged as compared to the traditionally performed similar activities [7]. In a study conducted by Madsen et al., researchers developed touch screen applications for teaching children with ASD to recognize facial expressions [8]. In this study, lessons learned about the software and hardware design of touch screen applications for this specific population were shared very briefly. In a study on developing an expression recognition game for individuals with ASD using touch enabled mobile devices, the authors explored available ASD games and tried to consolidate guidelines for designing user interfaces for children with autism [9].

Another popular approach in designing applications for individuals with ASD is using touchless interactions. The availability of depth sensors, such as Microsoft Kinect and their use for skeleton tracking made this technique easily implemented and popular. Moreover, some researchers suggest not using wearable sensors since some individuals with ASD may not prefer to wear any sensors on them [10]. A study by Bartoli et al. showed that games with touchless interaction helped in improving the attention skills for children with autism [11]. Another recent study for individuals with ASD was aiming at improving their motor skills [12]. With this goal, Garzotto et al. developed and evaluated a motion based touchless application.

There are also some applications that use more than one interaction technique. One study focused on full body interaction techniques for low functioning children with ASD [13]. An environment similar to a virtual reality cave was developed with projectors, cameras and sensors. Some touchless interaction techniques as well as touch based interaction techniques were implemented, and the children's acceptance of the system was discussed. Most of the children accepted the system and used it effectively.

With the emerging technology of virtual reality, some researchers are integrating virtual reality interaction techniques into training applications for people with ASD. In a study, researchers used a virtual reality system to teach street-crossing skills to children with ASD [5]. The results showed that training in virtual reality improved these skills. In another study, a virtual reality driving training system was developed [6].

Another study that aims at increasing social engagement of children with ASD used two different games with two different interaction techniques [14]. One used multiple mice while the other used a Diamond touch surface. Another recent study showed observations on the usability of basic 3D interactions such as translation and rotation for the adolescents with ASD [15]. The authors tried to find the differences in use of 3D user interaction techniques between neuro typical individuals and individuals with autism. The results showed that the deficits in hand-eye coordination in individuals with ASD caused some difficulties in using these 3D interaction techniques. The authors suggest that developers should add some assistive cues to aid individuals with ASD with the hand-eye coordination.

Although different interaction techniques and their effects on user experience have been thoroughly examined for neuro typical individuals so far, only limited research in this area has been explored for individuals with ASD. It must also be noted that most of these studies were designed for children. Previous studies that utilize some interaction techniques for virtual reality applications for individuals with ASD do not examine user experience or provide insight on suitable interaction techniques for this specific group of audience.

3   Interaction Techniques

In our VR4VR system, there are six modules that were developed for the vocational training of individuals with ASD. The most convenient interaction technique for each skill was decided by research and discussions with the job coaches. The job coaches who gave input in designing the system currently give professional vocational training services for individuals with ASD. These job coaches are experts in vocational training of individuals with ASD. In this study, the interaction techniques that were tested within the VR4VR system are categorized into two as selection/manipulation and locomotion.

3.1   Object Selection and Manipulation

For object selection and manipulation, four different interaction techniques were implemented and tested. These are used in different skill modules to interact with the virtual world. These four interaction techniques are presented in the following subsections.

Tangible Object Manipulation. In this interaction technique, two types of real tangible objects are tracked and represented in the virtual world: (1) identical looking real boxes that are shown in the virtual world with different textures or labels, and (2) a broomstick handle that is represented in the virtual world as a vacuum cleaner or a mop that the user uses to clean the virtual environments.

The users tested these interaction techniques while training on some shelving and cleaning tasks. There were three different shelving tasks: the first task was to rotate the boxes on the shelves such that the front sides faced the user. In the second task, the users were asked to put the required boxes on the table and then place the boxes on the correct levels of the correct shelves according to their projected label textures. In the third task, instead of the label textures, labels with different code numbers were projected on the boxes. These code numbers indicated the shelf/level the boxes belonged to.

An immersive tangible object manipulation technique was implemented and tested with the shelving tasks. With this technique, the users could move and rotate the real

Fig. 1. Tangible object manipulation. Left: the user rotates a real box in shelving tasks. Right: the user uses a broomstick as a virtual mop in cleaning tasks.

tangible boxes in the tracked area (Fig. 1 Left). Head mounted display (HMD) was used along with hand bands with reflective markers on them. This enabled real time head and hand tracking.

Two different cleaning tasks were implemented: vacuuming and mopping in the virtual world. The objectives of these tasks were to clean the virtual warehouse by using the real broomstick handle to vacuum clean the dry dirt piles and to mop the wet dirt piles. The users used a tangible broomstick handle to interact with the virtual world. The real broomstick handle was replaced with a virtual vacuum cleaner or a virtual mop in different tasks (Fig. 1 Right). To be able to track the real stick with the cameras in real-time, we attached three pieces of reflector marker tape around the cylinder. Since the cylinder was symmetric along its longitudinal axis, we used software calculations to visualize the cleaning head (nozzle or mop) according to the angle between the cylinder and the ground. This time, in addition to HMD and hand bands, feet bands with reflective markers were also worn by the user. This enabled real time head, hand and feet tracking.

Haptic Device. Haptic device interaction was also tested by individuals with ASD in our VR4VR system. Haptic devices utilize force feedback to create a sense of touch. In this module, Phantom Omni® haptic device [16] was used to interact with the virtual world. Phantom Omni® creates a sense of weight for the users so that they can feel if they are interacting with a light or heavy object. This was suggested to help in increasing immersion by the job coaches. Although they were hesitant about the 3D nature of this interaction device, job coaches found it very promising for comfortable use of individuals with ASD with the provided force feedback. As an alternative, mouse interaction was also implemented in case users had difficulty with the haptic device interaction.

In the loading back of a truck task which used this interaction technique, the users were expected to fill up an empty truck with different sized 2D boxes in a virtual environment. The boxes had different properties such as weight, fragility and directional arrows. The aim of this module was to fit all of the boxes into a limited area by moving and rotating the boxes. The working area of the haptic device was restricted to a planar surface that was parallel to the display area. This helped the users to relate the haptic device input to the visual output easily and also removed the ambiguity coming from the extra degree of freedom for the sake of this task. The buttons on the haptic device handle were assigned for specific commands (Fig. 2). One of the buttons was used to hold the boxes similar to the vastly used mouse gesture for drag and drop. The other button was used to rotate the boxes by 90 degrees counterclockwise.

Touch and Snap. Touch and snap interaction technique is often used in virtual reality applications. In this technique, a virtual object is snapped to a moving object which usually is selected to be the virtual hand of the user. To trigger the release of the snapped object, different techniques can be used such as time triggering, position triggering or gesture triggering.

Fig. 2. Haptic device interaction technique. Left: the user holds boxes with the haptic device. Right: the haptic device.

This interaction technique was used in the litter collection task of our VR4VR system. In this task, the users were asked to collect randomly distributed litter objects from the ground and throw them into virtual trash bins that were located around. User's hands were equipped with reflective markers to be tracked in real time by the optical tracking system cameras. Virtual litter object was snapped to the user's virtual hands when the user bended and hands came close to the litter. Users carried the litter objects in the virtual world and once litter arrived in the vicinity of a trash bin, it disengaged from the hand and fell into the trash bin. Required actions in this task were moving the hands close to the litter in the virtual world by bending and reaching out in the real word and then bringing the held litter close to a virtual trash bin to release it by extending the arm in the real world (Fig. 3).

Fig. 3. Touch and snap interaction technique. Left: the user tries to take the litter object from the ground with their right hand. Right: the user carries a litter object.

Touchscreen. With the increasing number of mobile devices such as cell phones and tablet computers, touch interaction became one of the most popular and prevalent interaction techniques. In our project, touchscreen interaction was used in a module related to the cash register skills. Three tasks were used for testing: (1) recognizing money, (2) counting money, and (3) giving change. Currently, most of the digital cash registers use touchscreens to get input from the cashier, so this interaction technique was selected for this module to increase the realism and immersion.

In this module, only the single touch static touching technique was used instead of the more complicated dynamic or multi touch interactions. The tasks required the user: (1) to identify the given bill or coin amounts by touching on the corresponding value among the given options, (2) to type the sum of the presented bill and coin amounts by touching the numbers on the touchscreen keypad, and (3) touching the bill and coin visuals on the cash register to fetch the required change to be given to a customer based on the shopping simulation. A touchscreen keypad similar to the real cash register keypads was presented to the user. The only possible interaction technique in this module was the touch interaction.

3.2   Locomotion

Locomotion techniques are used to move the viewpoint (and the avatar, if used) of the user in the virtual world. There are many different locomotion techniques in virtual reality. In our study, we used two of those locomotion techniques; real walking and walk in place.

Real Walking. To move the virtual avatar in the virtual world in this locomotion technique, the user really walks in the tracked area as they would do in real life. Although this is a very intuitive method, there is the significant restriction of the limited tracked area. The user is equipped with reflective markers on their hands and head so that the real position of the user is approximated by these tracked position values and transferred into the virtual world. The virtual world is viewed inside from a virtual camera that is attached to the position of the virtual head and this view is rendered to the HMD. The movement and the rotation of the real head affect the virtual camera's position and rotation so that a realistic view of the virtual world can be displayed in the HMD.

In our project, real walking interaction technique was evaluated in a virtual warehouse environment. Since this technique is restricted by a limited tracking area, the user was surrounded by two physical shelves and one desk. All the tasks were designed so that they could be performed inside that limited area.

Walk in Place. If the real tracked area is smaller than the virtual world, then real walking technique becomes hard to use due to this restriction. To overcome this limitation, walk in place technique is commonly used in virtual reality implementations. In this technique, the user marches in the same place while the virtual avatar walks in the virtual world in the direction the user faces. This way, the limitation of the tracked region can easily be overcome. But this comes with the additional gesture of walking in place instead of intuitive real walking motion. Our implementation of this technique included different walking speeds, depending on the speed of the walking in place gesture, so that the user could adjust the virtual speed of the avatar by modifying their real marching speed. The walking direction of the virtual avatar was controlled by the head direction of the user.

This technique was used in two modules. The first one was the cleaning module in which the users were required to go near the dirty areas to clean them or go near litter objects to collect them. The other module was the environmental awareness module. In this module, the users were required to walk to the specified check points in the parking lot of a virtual shopping mall environment. Both of these modules used only the "walk in place" technique for locomotion.

4   Preliminary Results

A user study is currently ongoing with individuals with ASD. So far, five individuals with ASD participated with ages ranging from 20 to 27. The participants had no secondary disabilities. All five participants were on the high functioning side of the autism spectrum. None of the participants had prior experience of virtual reality. These participants went through each module task of our VR4VR system. It took approximately four hours (two sessions of two hours on different days) for each participant to go through all six modules. Three job coaches accompanied the users during the testing sessions. Here, we present the preliminary results that were obtained during these testing sessions. Since the user study has not been finished yet, instead of providing statistical results, we provide our initial findings based on the statements of users with ASD and the job coaches. Our testing with individuals with ASD yield to the following results:

- Our participants with ASD liked touchscreen interaction the most as compared to the other interaction techniques they tested in our VR4VR system.
- Our participants with ASD stated that they found the haptic device difficult to use.
- The users interacted with the tangible boxes and the broomstick very easily and stated that they enjoyed interacting with those.
- Our participants with ASD liked real walking better than the walk in place. It took time for the users to learn the walk in place technique and even when learned, some of our participants were frustrated when using the walk in place technique for locomotion.
- Our participants with ASD stated more problems with motion sickness in tasks that used walk in place locomotion technique as compared to the tasks that used real walking locomotion technique.
- We did not encounter any problems with the acceptance of HMD by our participants with ASD.

5   Discussion

Interaction techniques constitute a crucial part of the user experience in virtual reality. Individuals with autism have their own characteristics and preferences related to their cognitive information processing. This makes the effectiveness of the previously proven virtual reality interaction techniques for neuro typical individuals speculative when it comes to individuals with autism.

In our preliminary testing sessions, individuals with ASD stated preference for touchscreen interaction. This may be caused by the users' previous experiences since touchscreens are commonly found in everyday lives. The job coaches stated that the reason behind the haptic device's creating confusion for some individuals with ASD might have been the third dimension as compared with the commonly used mouse interaction. Even though mouse interaction was implemented as an alternative to haptic device interaction, the job coaches observed positive effects of force feedback provided by the haptic device and suggested continuing using haptic device interaction.

Our participants with ASD stated preference for real walking. Again, this may be caused by the users' previous everyday experiences. Some users got frustrated while they were using the walk in place technique for locomotion. It was hard for the users with ASD to comprehend the walk in place and keep doing that locomotion gesture without really walking forward. After their observations in the testing sessions, the job coaches stated negative comments about the suitability of the walk in place technique for individuals with autism and asked us to look for alternative techniques that might work better for individuals with autism. Hence, we interpret these views of the users and the job coaches as walk in place being a questionable locomotion technique to be used for individuals with ASD. On the other hand, real walking locomotion technique was found very comfortable by the users and the job coaches, hence it might be utilized into virtual reality implementations for individuals with autism. Of course this is not easy to achieve due to the limitation imposed by the motion tracking cameras but the tasks would be designed such that the users do not need to go outside the tracking area naturally. To sum up, our participants with ASD found the interaction techniques that are familiar to them from real life more comfortable to use in virtual reality.

6   Conclusion

This study aims at exploring suitability of the interaction techniques in our immersive virtual reality vocational training system for individuals with ASD. Several interaction techniques were implemented after discussions with the job coaches and testing sessions with five individuals with ASD were performed. Although preliminary testing results do not provide statistical results, opinions of the users with ASD and the job coaches state preference over touchscreen and tangible interaction techniques, and real walking locomotion technique. These techniques were the ones that had the most resemblance to everyday real life interaction. Participants with ASD had more difficulty in gesture based and more abstract interaction techniques.

Our future work will consist of finishing the ongoing user study and sharing the statistically valid results. After that, we will be implementing several isolated modules for evaluation of different virtual reality locomotion techniques for individuals with autism that will also be evaluated with a user study.

Acknowledgments. The authors would like to thank the Florida Department of Education, Division of Vocational Rehabilitation for funding the VR4VR project.

References

1. Bozgeyikli, L., Bozgeyikli, E., Clevenger, M., Raij, A., Alqasemi, R., Sundarrao, S., Dubey, R.: VR4VR: vocational rehabilitation of individuals with disabilities in immersive virtual reality environments. In: Proceedings of the 8th ACM International Conference on Pervasive Technologies Related to Assistive Environments (PETRA 2015), Article 54 (2015)
2. Alberta Learning: Teaching Students with Autism Spectrum Disorders. Book 9 in the Programming for Students with Special Needs series, Edmonton, Alberta, Canada (2003)
3. Heldrich, J., Bloustein, E.: Employment Guide for Adults with Autism Spectrum Disorders. Autism New Jersey, Robbinsville (2009)
4. MMWR Surveillance Summaries: Prevalence of autism spectrum disorder among children aged 8 years-autism and developmental disabilities monitoring network, 11 sites, United States, 2010. Morbidity and mortality weekly report. Surveillance summaries 63, no. 2 (2014)
5. Josman, N., Ben-Chaim, H., Friedrich, S., Weiss, P.: Effectiveness of virtual reality for teaching street-crossing skills to children and adolescents with autism. Int. J. Disabil. Hum. Develop. 7(1), 49–56 (2007)
6. Wade, J., Bian, D., Fan, J., Zhang, L., Swanson, A., Sarkar, M., Weitlauf, A., Warren, Z., Sarkar, N.: A virtual reality driving environment for training safe gaze patterns: application in individuals with ASD. In: Antona, M., Stephanidis, C. (eds.) UAHCI 2015. LNCS, vol. 9177, pp. 689–697. Springer, Heidelberg (2015)
7. Hourcade, J., Williams, S., Miller, E., Huebner, K., Liang, L.: Evaluation of tablet apps to encourage social interaction in children with autism spectrum disorders. In: Proceedings of the SIGCHI Conference on Human Factors in Computing Systems (CHI 2013), pp. 3197–3206 (2013)
8. Madsen, M., Kaliouby, R., Eckhardt, M., Hoque, M., Goodwin, M., Picard, R.: Lessons from participatory design with adolescents on the autism spectrum. In: CHI 2009 Extended Abstracts on Human Factors in Computing Systems (CHI EA 2009), pp. 3835–3840 (2009)
9. Harrold, N., Tan, C., Rosser, D.: Towards an expression recognition game to assist the emotional development of children with autism spectrum disorders. In: Proceedings of the Workshop at SIGGRAPH Asia (WASA 2012), pp. 33–37 (2012)
10. Kientz, J., Hayes, G., Westeyn, T., Starner, T., Abowd, G.: Pervasive computing and autism: assisting caregivers of children with special needs. IEEE Pervasive Comput. 6(1), 28–35 (2007)
11. Bartoli, L., Corradi, C., Garzotto, F., Valoriani, M.: Exploring motion-based touchless games for autistic children's learning. In: Proceedings of the 12th International Conference on Interaction Design and Children (IDC 2013), pp. 102–111 (2013)
12. Garzotto, F., Gelsomini, M., Oliveto, L., Valoriani, M.: Motion-based touchless interaction for ASD children: a case study. In: Proceedings of the 2014 International Working Conference on Advanced Visual Interfaces (AVI 2014), pp. 117–120 (2014)
13. Parés, N., Carreras, A., Durany, J., Ferrer, J., Freixa, P., Gómez, D., Kruglanski, O., Parés, R., Ribas, J., Soler, M., Sanjurjo, A.: Starting research in interaction design with visuals for low-functioning children in the autistic spectrum: a protocol. CyberPsychology Behav. 9(2), 218–223 (2006)

14. Bauminger-Zviely, N., Eden, S., Zancanaro, M., Weiss, P., Gal, E.: Increasing social engagement in children with high-functioning autism spectrum disorder using collaborative technologies in the school environment. Autism **17**(3), 317–339 (2013)

15. Mei, C., Mason, L., Quarles, J.: Usability issues with 3D user interfaces for adolescents with high functioning autism. In: Proceedings of the 16th International ACM SIGACCESS Conference on Computers & Accessibility (ASSETS 2014), pp. 99–106 (2014)

16. Phantom Omni – Sensable. http://www.dentsable.com/haptic-phantom-omni.htm. Accessed Feb 2016

Transition Times for Manipulation Tasks in Hybrid Interfaces

Allan Christensen[1]([✉]), Simon A. Pedersen[1], Per Bjerre[1],
Andreas K. Pedersen[1], and Wolfgang Stuerzlinger[2]

[1] Aalborg University, Aalborg, Denmark
allanchr@hotmail.com
[2] Simon Fraser University, Burnaby, Canada

Abstract. Compared to the mouse, uninstrumented in-air interaction has been shown to be slower and less precise for pointing. Yet, in-air input is preferable or advantageous in some interaction scenarios. Thus, we examine a three-device hybrid setup involving the mouse, keyboard, and a Leap Motion. We performed a user study to quantify the costs associated with transitioning between these interaction devices, while performing simple 2D manipulation tasks using the mouse and Leap Motion. We found that transitioning to and from the Leap Motion takes on average 0.87 s longer than those between the mouse and keyboard.

Keywords: In-air interfaces · Device transitions · Hybrid user interfaces

1 Introduction

In 3D modeling systems, such as Autodesk Maya, users often use 2D input devices, typically mouse and keyboard, to manipulate objects in virtual environments. While it seems more appropriate to use 3D input devices, current technologies are not yet competitive for such applications. According to Hodson, the Leap Motion represents a huge step in the development of 3D input technologies, and enables the creation of 3D user interfaces that might eventually surpass the mouse [10].

Previous research on in-air interaction has pointed out several weaknesses, such as fatigue, lower accuracy, and in some cases slower interaction speed [16,18]. Fatigue may also cause users to relax the poses needed for gestures, increasing the chances of interpretation errors [16] and decreasing pointing precision [3].

One way to address this is to build hybrid user interfaces that combine the freedom of in-air interaction with the precision of 2D devices. We draw upon the concept of casual and focused interaction. Casual interaction targets a different level of engagement, at which users want to or are able to interact with the system [14,15], which is well suited for the Leap Motion. A hybrid solution might then enable users to perform operations with in-air interaction that are potentially inefficient with 2D input devices, such as coarse-scale 3D rotations,

© Springer International Publishing Switzerland 2016
M. Kurosu (Ed.): HCI 2016, Part II, LNCS 9732, pp. 138–150, 2016.
DOI: 10.1007/978-3-319-39516-6_13

followed by fine-adjustments with a 2D input device. This will also address the fatigue associated with prolonged use of in-air interaction.

Here, we investigate the Leap Motion in comparison to a keyboard and mouse setup for 2D manipulation tasks. We examine related work on in-air interaction, previous approaches for handling 3D and 2D input, and lastly models for determining the efficiency of in-air interaction and transitions between input devices. The goal is to investigate if a hybrid interface is a viable and efficient solution.

1.1   Related Work

Leap Motion. The Leap Motion controller is a 3D interaction device that allows users to interact with a system through free-hand motions and gestures. The device detects a user's hands, and is able to detect and distinguish between unimanual and bimanual interaction, including the orientation of the hands and individual fingers. Previous research examined the accuracy and reliability of the Leap Motion during interaction [8,19] and also identified fatigue issues. Other work compared it to touch or mouse interaction and found it to be less effective, in terms of accuracy and selection speed [16,18] as well as pointing throughput [3]. In a direct comparison with the mouse and with the mouse wheel for (discrete) depth control, the Leap Motion was about half as fast for multiple 3D selection tasks [6]. Han and Gold found that the "normal" upright orientation of the controller seems to deliver the most consistent results in terms of tracking capabilities, followed by placing the controller at an ~45° angle [9].

Un-Instrumented In-Air Interaction. To determine appropriate control schemes for un-instrumented (free-hand) in-air interactions, this section examines research on six degrees of freedom (6 DOF) input devices. We examine three main approaches for six DOF devices. The first approach focuses on absolute control, i.e., a one-to-one mapping between motions [1]. The second approach uses relative control, i.e., an indirect mapping. In one exemplar scheme, hand tilt controls the *velocity* of object tilt [5]. Schlattmann et al. used the direction of the index finger and also found that rotational mappings were preferred and bimanual interaction generated more fatigue than unimanual interaction [17]. The third approach uses more abstract mappings, involving gestures or keyboard clutches. Pareek and Sharma's work for 3D CAD still required switching gestures, which made it more time consuming to go through several stages of manipulation [13].

Interaction with Two Degrees of Freedom Devices. The most common two DOF interaction device is the mouse. While it is often used to perform two DOF tasks, a combination of modifier keys and movements enables work in multiple DOF. This section examines how 2D devices can interact and control environments with more than two DOF. Applications that support full 3D interaction, such as Autodesk Maya and Unity 3D, have all adapted similar control schemes for scaling, rotating and translating of objects in six DOF.

Different combinations of keyboard modifier keys (also known as clutches) together with various mouse actions enable manipulation of different DOFs. Zhao et al. used the (discrete) mouse wheel to control a third DOF for rotation [20].

Fitts' Law. Fitts' law models human movement and predicts the time required for performing a movement to a target area, such as moving a finger or cursor to a target and selecting it. The model is a function of the distance to the target and the target size. Fitts' law uses an index of difficulty (ID) to describe the difficulty of the motor task. The equation for ID is given in Eq. 1 [7,12].

$$Index\ of\ Difficulty\ (ID) = log_2(\frac{amplitude}{width} + 1) \tag{1}$$

The movement time (MT) is then a linear expression of the ID, i.e., MT = a + b * ID. Fitts' law has been used to compare a variety of different input techniques. Bérard et al. [2] presented another application of Fitts' model. They developed a measure of device human resolution (DHR) for three input devices to determine the smallest possible target a user of a given input device can select with reasonable effort.

The Keystroke-Level Model. One of the main models used to predict the performance of keyboard and mouse interfaces is the Keystroke-Level Model (KLM) [4]. This model predicts the completion time of error free tasks. For this, the interaction is split into a sequence of simple operators, each with a time estimate. The total predicted time for a task is then the sum of operators. KLM has been adapted for many interfaces through new time estimates and adding new operators that describe interaction parts for that specific system. Holleis et al. identified that the homing operator, for transitions between keyboard and mouse, is irrelevant for mobile phones [11]. The homing operator is relevant for hybrid interfaces, as adding a device to a system that necessitates additional transitions can impact performance. Here, we are examining transitions between mouse, keyboard and in-air interaction to determine the transition costs.

2   Methods and Materials

Here we explore in-air interaction through three user studies. The initial two pretests collect information about the users and the device, which then informed the design of our main study. The first pretest focuses on uni- and bimanual gestural interaction when interacting with the Leap Motion, as well as the preferred *position* of the Leap Motion, extending the work by Han and Gold, who investigated only orientation [9]. The second pretest measures the DHR for the Leap Motion to identify a reasonable minimum object size for interaction. The findings from these pilots inform the main user study in terms of the best physical position of the Leap Motion, gestures for the manipulation of objects, and reasonable target deviation thresholds for the main user study.

2.1   First Pretest

First, we focused on uni- and bimanual interactions with Leap Motion. This pretest had two phases. In the first one users have to pluck petals, with the device placed at four different positions (in front, behind, left, and right of the keyboard), to identify the most efficient position for the Leap Motion. The second phase was an elicitation study where we prompted users to use gestures for object manipulation (rotate, scale, translate, and select) with the device. The pretest had six right-handed participants, one female, with ages from 21 to 28 years old ($M = 25.7$, $SD = 2.49$), who all had experience with 3D interaction devices.

We did not compare unimanual and bi-manual operation directly. Completion times were significantly different for both unimanual ($F_{3,15} = 3.38$, $p < 0.05$, $\eta^2 = 0.33$) and bimanual ($F_{3,15} = 3.28$, $p < 0.05$, $\eta^2 = 0.33$) interaction. There was also a significant difference between the behind and the left position. There was a significant interaction between the in front and right positions for unimanual and the front position and both the left and right positions for bimanual. The participants rated both the front and behind positions higher than the left and right positions. These differences were statistically significant ($\chi^2(3) = 10.50$, $p < 0.05$). Both in front and behind positions were significantly better than the left, but not compared to the right.

Overall, for both uni- and bimanual interactions the smallest interaction times occurred when the device was placed in front or behind the keyboard. In addition, these positions were preferred and observations confirmed that interaction poses were also more relaxed for these conditions.

For the second phase we elicited gestures for various 3D manipulations. Illustrative examples of the resulting gestures are shown in Fig. 1. In general, users

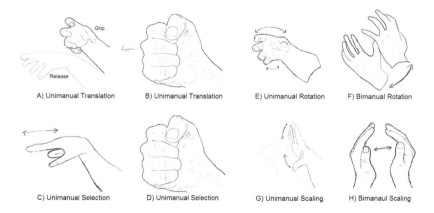

Fig. 1. Exemplary hand gestures proposed by users: (A, B) Unimanual translation. (C, D) Unimanual selection. (A, B, C, D) Users mirror unimanual gestures for bimanual. (E) Unimanual rotation. (F) Bimanual rotation. (G) Unimanual scale. (H) Bimanual scale.

preferred unimanual interaction for tasks involving selection, rotation, and translation, while scaling had equal preference for uni- and bimanual interaction.

The findings of this pretest informed our main study as follows. (1) We position the Leap Motion in front of the keyboard. (2) We use the following gestures for the manipulation of targets in the main user study: For translation tasks, we use the position of the hand to move the targets, as in Fig. 1(A) and (B). For rotation, we orient objects with the rotation of the users' hand and wrist, as in gesture E. For scaling, we use the distance between the fingers and thumb and scale targets proportionally, as in G. No bimanual gestures were used. This also enables us to use the keyboard as a clutch for the Leap Motion in the main study, which lets users control when the Leap Motion should detect interactions.

2.2 Second Pretest - Device Human Resolution

The purpose of this pretest is to determine the DHR [2] of the Leap Motion controller. This determines the minimum usable target size and enables comparisons to the DHR of other devices. We replicated the setup used by Bérard et al. [2]. Participants had to align a pointer within a one-dimensional target area, which decreased in size.

Six male volunteers, with ages 21 to 26 years ($M = 23.33$, $SD = 1.63$) participated. There was a sequence of seven target sizes in decreasing order, with a width of 32, 24, 16, 8, 4, 2, and 1 ticks, each repeated 20 times and with 250 ticks distance from the starting point. The interface was displayed on a 1920×1080 monitor, and a single tick corresponded to moving *four* pixels on screen.

The results of the experiment are summarized in Table 1. We calculated a linear regression for the data to analyze the deviation from Fitts' model, for each subset of three successive IDs each (except for the first and last). Following Fitts' law, we would expect the slope to remain close to constant. A significant increase would indicates a DHR threshold, but no subset slope deviated significantly from the overall one (0.66). Yet, higher ID's show higher amounts of variability, with a great increase for the last ID (where no other comparison point exists).

Table 1. Results of the second pretest

Target size (ticks)	Fitts' ID	Mean time (sec)	Failure rate (%)	Mean slope
32	3.14	1.69	5.5	
24	3.51	1.48	9.8	0.10
16	4.06	1.59	3.2	0.35
8	5.01	1.99	4.0	0.47
4	5.99	2.52	15.5	0.68
2	6.98	3.34	34.4	1.31
1	7.97	5.13	52.6	

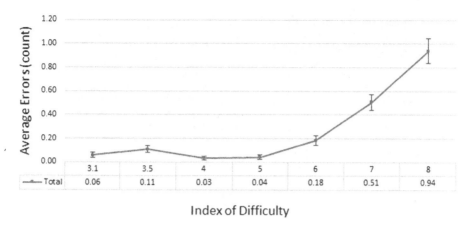

Fig. 2. Average error distance for each ID with standard error bars.

This is similar to the free-space device results in Bérard et al.'s work [2]. For the average error rate per task, shown in Fig. 2, we see a growth between ID 6 and 7, followed by a larger increase. Thus we can expect a reasonable failure rate up to ~2 mm target size. We performed a Friedman ranked sum test on both the error and time data. The two smallest targets have significantly higher errors than the rest $(\chi^2(6) = 28.32, p \ll 0.001)$. This is followed by 4 and 24 ticks target size, followed by the remaining three. In terms of timings, there are significant differences between all pairs $(\chi^2(6) = 35.43, p \ll 0.001)$, except for 32 and 16 tick widths.

We conclude from this pretest that with the Leap Motion target sizes should not go below 1.2 mm (ID of 6). A reasonably low error rate can be achieved for target sizes of 2.4 mm (ID of 5) and above. Thus and to ensure comparable difficulties, we set the task thresholds in our main study to 0.036 mm for the mouse and 2.4 mm for the Leap Motion.

2.3 Main User Study

The purpose of this study is to determine the cost of transitions between the Leap Motion and a keyboard and mouse setup. We also aim to develop a model of transition times for a three device setup, illustrated in Fig. 3. Further, we examine two-dimensional interaction to identify the differences between devices.

Participants. 31 volunteers were recruited from the local university. Ages ranged from 21 to 36 years $(M = 24.6, SD = 3.56)$. Five were female. All participants were right-handed, regular users of computers, and experienced with pointing devices and uninstrumented interactions.

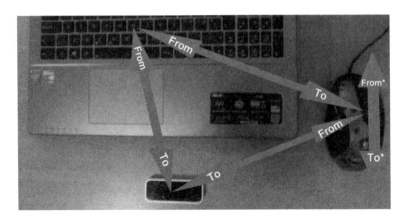

Fig. 3. Illustration of hybrid interface with Leap Motion, keyboard, and mouse. The arrows indicate transitions between center points of individual devices. * Indicates the special mouse to mouse transition, see text.

Apparatus and Materials. The experiment was conducted on laptops with 15.6"screens at 1366×768. We used a Leap Motion controller in the standard configuration and a mouse at 1800 DPI with acceleration disabled. Participants were allowed to relocate the mouse and Leap Motion for a comfortable working posture. Figure 3 shows the setup. Distances between the centers of the devices were measured after each participant had completed the test. The average distances were: keyboard and mouse ($M = 36.4$ cm, $SD = 3.8$ cm), keyboard and Leap Motion ($M = 22.6$ cm, $SD = 2.8$ cm), and finally Leap Motion and mouse ($M = 33.4$ cm, $SD = 5.9$ cm).

Procedure. Before the experiment, each participant was given a short demographics questionnaire and an introduction to the Leap Motion. The following training session used tasks similar to those in the experiment and familiarized users with all control schemes and tasks. Training was repeated at least twice or until participants felt confident in the tasks. Each task involved rotating,

Fig. 4. Illustration of the three main tasks. The rotation task matches the target orientation, assisted by the transparent overlay. In the translation task user drag the green box to the red one. The rightmost image shows the scaling task, where participants had to scale the green box to match the dimensions of the red one.

scaling or translating an object, as shown in Fig. 4. In order to perform each task, the user used a key on the keyboard with one hand (typically the non-dominant one) to "clutch" the tool, and then depending on the task, used the mouse or the Leap Motion with the other (dominant) hand. To complete a task, the user-controlled object needed to match the target within a certain threshold, as determined by the pretest. As previous research indicated that larger numbers of DOF reduce both accuracy and selection time [6] for the Leap Motion, we deliberately restricted manipulation to two DOF. We measured the completion time of each task, the transition time between keyboard, Leap Motion, and mouse in each direction, how precisely the participant matched the target, and finally the amount of times the clutch was engaged during each individual task. The whole test took approximately 10 min.

Design. The experiment was a $3 \times 2 \times 2$ within-subject design, with the main task type (scale, rotation, translation), primary interaction device (mouse and Leap Motion), and alternate tasks (involving either the keyboard or mouse) as independent variables. The three primary tasks are shown in Fig. 4. The main dependent variables were the task completion time, the transition times between the different devices, and the amount of times that the clutch was activated. A timeline illustrating the transitions is shown in Fig. 5.

Fig. 5. A timeline illustrating the different transitions in the main study.

We used alternate tasks to create situations where participants *had* to transition between input devices; this ensured that we measured times consistently. We measured only single hand transitions and enforced this by having the users activate a keyboard clutch with the other hand while interacting. There were two types of alternate tasks. One required a transition to the mouse, the other to the keyboard. For the mouse alternate task, the users had to press an on-screen soft key with the mouse (always with the same movement distance). The keyboard alternate task prompted the users to press *both* control keys on the keyboard to continue. Transition times from the main task devices (Leap Motion and mouse) to the alternate task devices (keyboard and mouse), were measured from the time the participant had completed the main task until they had completed the alternate one. Transitions in the opposite direction, from the alternate task device to the main devices, were measured from when the participant had completed an alternate task until they started a main task. To reduce the potential influence of mental preparation, we deliberately designed the tasks to be simple and effectively routine by the time participants had completed training.

The gestures for manipulating targets for a given task type were based on absolute and relative mappings, see Sect. 1.1. The translation tasks manipulated the x- and y- coordinates, i.e., needed only 2D input, with a relative mapping. The keyboard clutch (the control key) enabled participant to reposition their hand, e.g., when moving outside of the Leap Motion's tracking area. The scaling tasks were visually 2D, but the scaling was uniform, effectively making this a 1D task, with an absolute mapping of the distance between fingertips. The rotation tasks are visually a rotation of a 3D target, inspired by Zhao et al. [20]. Yet, in our study the object rotates only around two axes and the interaction used a relative mapping with the keyboard clutch to avoid over-rotation of the wrist.

Participants received all tasks with the same device in a block, with the device order being counterbalanced across participants. The order of tasks within the two device blocks was randomized. Each of the 31 participants performed a total of 18 trials (2 input devices × 3 tasks × 3 difficulty levels).

Results. Through a repeated measures ANOVA test, we found that the device significantly affected task completion time ($F_{1,30} = 196.72, p \ll 0.001, \eta^2 = 0.15$). The Leap Motion device used significantly more time ($M = 8.75, SD = 0.72$) than the mouse ($M = 4.8, SD = 2.97$), see Table 2. The task type did not significantly affect the data.

Table 2. The first entry in each box is the mean completion time in seconds and the one in brackets is the standard deviation.

Completion time	Rotation	Scale	Translate
Leap motion	8.66 (6.22)	9.06 (6.37)	8.54 (5.18)
Mouse	5.34 (3.60)	4.40 (2.95)	4.67 (2.11)

Looking at the transition times from the main interaction device (Leap Motion or mouse) to the secondary one (keyboard or mouse), we identify a significant effect of the main device ($F_{1,30} = 258.26, p \ll 0.001, \eta^2 = 0.19$). A small effect of the target device is present ($F_{1,30} = 21.52, p \ll 0.001, \eta^2 = 0.02$). There is also an interaction between the two factors ($F_{1,30} = 142.79, p \ll 0.001, \eta^2 = 0.11$). This is likely due to the lack of transitions for the mouse-to-mouse case, which thus measures only mouse travel and reaction times. See Table 3 for the mean transition times. In the transitions from the secondary interaction device to the main one, we found that the transition time was affected to a lesser degree by the main interaction device ($F_{1,30} = 62.11, p \ll 0.001, \eta^2 = 0.06$).

Comparing both transition types, we see that the main interaction device has a small effect ($F_{1,30} = 236.89, p \ll 0.001, \eta^2 = 0.10$). The direction of the transition has also a small effect ($F_{1,30} = 98.26, p \ll 0.001, \eta^2 = 0.05$).

Table 3. The first entry in each box shows the mean transition time in seconds and the one in brackets the standard deviation. The transitions are from the Main Device (MD), either the Leap Motion or the Mouse, to one of the two alternative tasks, or in the opposite direction.

Transition time	Leap	Mouse	Time difference
From MD to mouse	2.30 (0.60)	1.38 (0.47)	0.92 (=66.67%)
From mouse to MD	1.63 (0.70)	1.29 (0.67)	0.34 (=26.36%)
From MD to keyboard	1.76 (0.58)	1.62 (0.53)	0.14 (= 8.64%)
From keyboard to MD	1.65 (0.75)	1.31 (0.62)	0.34 (=25.95%)

A Friedman rank sum test found that the interaction device significantly affects the amount of clutch actions ($\chi^2(1) = 25.14$, $p \ll 0.001$). The Leap Motion needed significantly more clutching. The main task type did not have a significant effect on clutching. See Table 4 for the mean number of clutch actions.

Table 4. First entry in each box is the average amount of clutch activations for each combination of task type and device, and in brackets the standard deviation thereof. The minimum amount of clutch actions needed to complete any task with the Leap Motion was one, and zero with the mouse.

Clutch activations	Rotation	Scale	Translate
Leap motion	1.92 (1.65)	1.37 (0.78)	1.83 (1.09)
Mouse	1.29 (0.75)	1.38 (0.79)	1.10 (0.30)

After completing the study, we gave participants a short questionnaire, which asked about fatigue (on a five-point Likert scale) for interacting with the Leap Motion, as well as their preferred interaction device. Twelve participants (39%) stated that they experienced no fatigue and the rest experienced a moderate amount. Users stated that fatigue was not an issue for short sessions, but might become an issue for longer ones. Several participants placed their elbow on the table to reduce fatigue. 25 participants (80%) expressed a strong preference towards the mouse, three chose the Leap Motion (10%), and the remaining three had no preference (10%). This difference is significant ($\chi^2(2) = 35.68$, $p \ll 0.01$). When asked to elaborate, participants mentioned previous experience and precision for the mouse. Others mentioned lack of fatigue as a factor for their preference towards the mouse. Many mentioned that further experience with the Leap Motion might improve their performance and preference. Several identified the Leap Motion as being fun, engaging, and a new experience.

3   Discussion

The results of our user study showed that the mouse input significantly outperformed in-air interaction in terms of completion time. The high variance for Leap Motion suggests that further training could reduce times. Further exploration is necessary to identify tasks that are better performed with in-air input.

In the current study, we examined the transition times between mouse and keyboard input and the Leap Motion. There was a significantly higher transition cost for the in-air device. However, these differences are not very large. Using the transitions between mouse and keyboard as a baseline, the transitions between the keyboard and the Leap Motion were only 0.48 s (16 % increase) longer, see Table 3. Transitions between the Leap Motion and the mouse took 1.26 s longer (47 % increase). Thus the average extra transition cost to and from the Leap Motion was only 0.87 s (32 % increase), relative to a mouse-keyboard transition. Subtracting the reaction time and mouse travel time (identified from the mouse-to-mouse case) we get an average mouse-keyboard transition of 0.37 s. This is comparable with the 0.4 s homing time from Card et al. [4], which partially validates our methodology.

In the direct comparison with the mouse, the Leap Motion was slower. As transition times are not that long, it is still worthwhile to investigate the role an in-air device could play in a hybrid setup. One suggestion is to use the Leap Motion only for coarse adjustments. This way fewer transitions would be needed and the impact of transition times would be lessened. The tasks in our experiment involved only two DOF, which favors the mouse over the Leap Motion. Tasks that require more DOF could balance this out as the Leap Motion can provide (at least) six DOF for the hand or a single finger and potentially more when multiple fingers are used.

We identified that the amount of clutch activations was higher for in-air interaction. For the translation tasks users had to translate objects from one side of the screen to the other, which required clutching at least once. Also, the tracking of the Leap Motion was worse in the outer reaches of the interaction area. This may have affected precision and encouraged clutching. Yet we also can see that coarse interaction, e.g., putting an object into an approximate position or a "general" orientation, is easier with the Leap Motion. Conversely, in hybrid interfaces, precise fine-tuning is better performed with the mouse. Such a hybrid approach also implicitly limits the amount of time that users spend interacting with the Leap Motion, thereby reducing fatigue.

The second pretest revealed that the Leap Motion could be used to select targets as small as eight ticks without a significant increase in effort. This is consistent with Bérard's findings [2], which partially validates our methodology. Yet, for the Leap Motion the increase in both movement time and error rates happened between one and two target sizes less than the free-space device used by Bérard. Thus the Leap Motion was more precise and could select targets of a smaller size.

4 Conclusion

We evaluated transition times within a three-device hybrid setup, which included a keyboard, a mouse and the Leap Motion. As expected, the Leap Motion was slower to complete 2D tasks than the mouse. Yet, we found that transition times were only slightly affected by the input device, which is a positive result as the Leap Motion could be used together with the mouse without introducing an overly large transition cost between devices. This implies that it is feasible to design hybrid interaction setups, where coarse-scale manipulation tasks are done with the Leap Motion and the mouse is then used for precision work.

References

1. Bassily, D., Georgoulas, C., Guettler, J., Linner, T., Bock, T.: Intuitive and adaptive robotic arm anipulation using the leap motion controller. In: International Symposium on Robotics, pp. 1–7 (2014)
2. Bérard, F., Wang, G., Cooperstock, J.R.: On the limits of the human motor control precision: the search for a device's human resolution. In: Campos, P., Graham, N., Jorge, J., Nunes, N., Palanque, P., Winckler, M. (eds.) INTERACT 2011, Part II. LNCS, vol. 6947, pp. 107–122. Springer, Heidelberg (2011)
3. Brown, M.A., Stuerzlinger, W.: The performance of un-instrumented in-air pointing. In: Graphics Interface 2014, pp. 59–66 (2014)
4. Card, S.K., Moran, T.P., Newell, A.: The keystroke-level model for user performance time with interactive systems. CACM **23**, 396–410 (1980)
5. Codd-Downey, R., Stuerzlinger, W.: LeapLook: A free-hand gestural travel technique using the leap motion finger tracker. In: Spatial User Interaction Symposium, p. 153 (2014)
6. Coelho, J.C., Verbeek, F.J.: Pointing task evaluation of leap motion controller in 3D virtual environment. In: Chi Sparks 2014 Conference, pp. 78–85 (2014)
7. Fitts, P.M.: The information capacity of the human motor system in controlling the amplitude of movement. Exp. Psychol. **47**, 381–391 (1954)
8. Guna, J., Jakus, G., Pogačnik, M., Tomažič, S., Sodnik, J.: An analysis of the precision and reliability of the leap motion sensor and its suitability for static and dynamic tracking. Sensors **14**(2), 3702–3720 (2014)
9. Han, J., Gold, N.: Lessons learned in exploring the leap motion TM sensor for gesture-based instrument design. In: New Interfaces for Musical Expression, pp. 371–374 (2014)
10. Hodson, H.: Leap motion hacks show potential of new gesture tech. New Sci. **218**(2911), 21 (2013)
11. Holleis, P., Otto, F., Hussmann, H., Schmidt, A.: A keystroke-level model for advanced mobile phone interaction. In: CHI 2007, pp. 1505-1514 (2007)
12. MacKenzie, I.S.: Fitts' law as a research and design tool in human-computer interaction. Hum.-Comput. Interact. **7**, 91–139 (1992)
13. Pareek, S., Sharma, V.: Development of CAD Interface Using Leap Motion. http://vaibhav-sharma.com/resources/development_of_a_cad_interface_using_leapmotion.pdf. Accessed 27 October 2014
14. Pohl, H., Murray-Smith, R.: Focused and casual interactions: Allowing users to vary their level of engagement. In: CHI 2013, pp. 2223–2232 (2013)

15. Pohl, H., Rohs, M., Murray-Smith, R.: Casual interaction: Scaling fidelity for low-engagement interactions. In: Workshop on Peripheral Interaction: Shaping the Research and Design Space (2014)
16. Sambrooks, L., Wilkinson, B.: Comparison of gestural, touch, and mouse interaction with Fitts' law. In: Australian Computer-Human Interaction, pp. 119-122 (2012)
17. Schlattmann, M., Zheng, T., Broekelschen, J., Klein, R.: An investigation of Bare-Hands-Interaction in traditional 3D game genres. IADIS Int. J. WWW/Internet **8**(2), 1–16 (2010)
18. Seixas, M., Cardoso, J.C.S., Dias, M.T.G.: The Leap motion movement for 2D pointing tasks: Characterisation and comparison to other devices. In: Proceedings of the 5th International Conference on Pervasive and Embedded Computing and Communication Systems (2015)
19. Weichert, F., Bachmann, D., Rudak, B., Fisseler, D.: Analysis of the accuracy and robustness of the leap motion controller. Sensors **13**(5), 6380–6393 (2013)
20. Zhao, Y.J., Shuralyov, D., Stuerzlinger, W.: Comparison of multiple 3D rotation methods. In: IEEE Virtual Environment Human-Computer Interfaces and Measurement Systems (VECIMS), pp. 1–5 (2011)

BCI-Related Research Focus at HCI International Conference

Gencay Deniz[1,2(⊠)] and Pınar Onay Durdu[2]

[1] Department of Computer Engineering, Graduate School of Natural and
Applied Sciences, Kocaeli University, Izmit, Kocaeli, Turkey
zinedyacneg@gmail.com
[2] Human Computer Interaction Research Laboratory, Department of Computer
Engineering, Kocaeli University, Izmit, Kocaeli, Turkey
pinar.onaydurdu@kocaeli.edu.tr

Abstract. Brain Computer Interface (BCI) is an emerging research area which has been studied over thirty years extensively in the fields of clinical neuro-physiology and neuroscience however it is now recognized as an interdisci-plinary field involving neurobiology, psychology, engineering, mathematics and computer science. HCI community has begun to deal with BCI and substantial publications have been made in HCI related journals and conferences in recent years. In the scope of this research we conducted a systematic mapping study with the articles published in proceedings of HCI International Conferences to reveal the trends, general aims of the articles, which signal recording modality were used, for what kind of practical applications were developed, which feature types and classification algorithms were used and what are the nationalities and institutes of contributing authors in the scope of HCI International conference. The aim was to give insight to the researchers who were studying or would like to study in the area of BCI. According to the results of the mapping, research type of BCI articles were mainly in the category of emerging applications not related to communication and control. General aim of the articles was deter-mined as practical applications of BCI technologies first and then development or improvement of methodologies for signal processing issues. Visual P300 was the mostly applied BCI paradigms and SSVEP and motor imagery followed next. Most of the articles had reported EEG as a signal acquisition method, ICA or bandpass filter as a preprocessing or filtering method, ERP as a feature type and LDA and LR as a classification algorithm method.

Keywords: Systematic mapping study · Brain - computer interface · BCI · BCI research trends · HCI International

1 Introduction

Brain Computer Interface (BCI) is an emerging research area, which has been studied over thirty years extensively although its roots can be taken back to 1929 when Berger [1] first recorded electroencephalographic activity (EEG) from the scalp. BCI can be defined as a system that make people interact with outside world by translating their brain signals into commands rather than using their motor movements to control

M. Kurosu (Ed.): HCI 2016, Part II, LNCS 9732, pp. 151–161, 2016.
DOI: 10.1007/978-3-319-39516-6_14

computers or use communication devices [1]. BCI systems are primarily studied with the goal of helping severely disabled people as an assistive technologies. In addition, these systems have the potential of providing a more natural and intuitive interface that understands human intentions [2].

Despite early BCI studies were conducted mainly in the field of clinical neurophysiology and neuroscience, it is now recognized as an interdisciplinary field involving neurobiology, psychology, engineering, mathematics and computer science [1]. In addition, as the field enhanced its scope from clinical value and practicality of BCI systems to BCI technology for the needs of people, Human Computer Interaction (HCI) related issues such as meeting the needs of specific user groups have been emerged [3]. Therefore HCI community has begun to deal with BCI and substantial publications have been made in HCI related journals and conferences in recent years.

Previously considerable number of research dealing with BCIs have been published in various fields such as biomedical engineering, clinical neurology, neuroscience and neurorehabilitation [4]. Some literature reviews or survey studies that tried to determine the research trends in the BCI field have been conducted based on these. Mason and colleagues [5] have conducted a comprehensive survey of brain interface technologies prior to year 2006 and they have created a meta-analysis of brain interface designs, targeted application areas and possible opportunities for new research or technological advances in the field. They classified the publications according to functional model and taxonomy of the brain interface design framework [6]. Lin et al. [7] conducted a mini-review focusing especially on wireless and wearable EEG systems and brain-computer interfaces. They have also adapted Mason et al. [5]'s taxonomy for the classification of 32 BCI system related papers. Another review summarized the trends in hardware and software for BCI applications [8]. They categorized BCI applications into basic research, clinical/translational research, consumer products, and emerging applications and they summarized technical aspects for these categories for the development of better integrated and more robust BCI hardware and software. Gürkök and Nijholt [2] conducted a survey covering BCI survey specifically focusing on multimodal interaction, while Bi, Fan and Liu [9] focuses on especially EEG-based brain-controlled mobile robots in their survey. Another recent detailed literature survey was again conducted on EEG-based BCIs covering the publications between 2007 and 2011 [4]. This study reported the number of published BCI articles for a five-year period, BCI paradigms, and aims of the articles, target applications, feature types, classification algorithms, BCI system types, and nationalities of the author.

As it is mentioned above, BCI and HCI fields become closely related in the recent years, in this research we mainly tried to deal with what HCI community was interested in BCI research. Therefore we have conducted a systematic mapping study that covers the articles presented during the last decade of HCI International conference [10] to reveal the trends, general aims of the articles, which signal recording modality were used, for what kind of practical applications were developed, which feature types and classification algorithms were used and what are the nationalities and institutes of authors.

2 Method

In this study, a systematic mapping was conducted with the articles published in proceedings of HCI International Conferences since 2005 covering the last decade to determine the BCI research trends in HCI community. In the study, steps of evidence-based software engineering approach proposed by Kitchenham et al. [11] was adopted. Evidence based software development approach was a method to gather best practices and results of the research studies and the approach had its roots in evidence based medicine. There are two main types of studies which are systematic literature review and systematic mapping studies in evidence-based software development approach. These two study methods had similarities but they had significant differences regarding the research question, search process, requirements of search strategy, quality evaluation of studies and their results. These differences can be seen Table 1 below. Petersen et al. [12] summarized the aim of systematic mapping studies as presenting a general idea about a research area and giving information about the number, type and results of the studies conducted. These studies were conducted to determine the trends based on time.

Table 1. Differences between systematic mapping studies and conventional SLR [13]

Process	Mapping Study	SLR
Research Question	General – related to research trends. Which researchers, how much activity, what type of studies etc.	Specific - related to outcomes of empirical studies. Of the form: Is technology/method A better or not than B?
Search process	Defined by topic area	Defined by research question
Search strategy requirements	Less stringent if only research trends are of interest	Extremely stringent – all relevant studies must be found
Quality evaluation	Not essential	Important to ensure that results are based on best quality evidence
Results	Set of papers related to a topic area and counts of the number of papers in various categories	Answer to specific research question, possible with qualifiers (e.g. results apply to novices only).

The research steps proposed by Kitchenham et al. [11] was modified according to the requirements of this study. Since the articles published in the scope of one conference, some steps of Kitchenham's processes were removed. In this scope, study was conducted in three-phases which were planning, investigation and reporting [14]. Research process can be seen in Fig. 1.

The research questions of this study were determined as follows for determining the general trends in the scope of HCI International Conference;

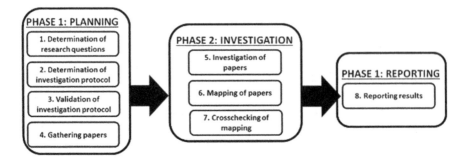

Fig. 1. Research process

- What are the number of BCI-related articles?
- What are the research types studied?
- What are the aims of BCI related articles?
- Which BCI paradigm are used in the articles?
- What are the practical applications of BCI technologies?
- What is used for BCI signal acquisition and signal processing?
- What are the research institutions and authors of the studies?

2.1 Development of the Systematic Mapping Protocol

A systematic mapping protocol was formed based on the research questions to classify the published articles. The protocol was formed of nine sections. These were article general record, research type, aim of the article, BCI paradigm, practical application of BCI technology defined in the article, applied BCI signal acquisition, applied BCI signal processing including filtering, feature extraction and classification methods and finally the subjects. These sections were briefly explained below.

1. *Article general record*: This section involved information related to the year, authors, author's affiliation, proceeding information (volume, issue, etc.), the number of references and the keywords defined for the article.
2. *Research type*: Brunner and colleagues [8] had determined four classification types for the BCI applications as basic research, clinical/translational research, consumer products and emerging applications and their classification scheme was adopted.
3. *Aims of article*: This section was mainly adopted form Hwang et al.'s [4] study to classify the aims of the articles. These were development/improvement of new BCI paradigms, practical applications of BCI technologies, investigation of factors influencing the performance of BCI systems and review studies. In addition to this list, one more item was added as "usability-related BCI studies" since the list did not cover all the studies.

4. *BCI paradigm*: Articles were classified according to the BCI paradigms that were used for gathering brain activities. These were listed as motor imagery, visual P300, SSVEP (steady-state visual evoked potential), non-motor mental imagery, auditory, hybrid and other [4].

5. *Practical application of BCI technologies*: In this section articles were analyzed according to which purpose the BCI system was developed for. The target applications of BCI systems were listed as mental speller, mouse control, robot arm control, game applications, navigation and others.

6. *Applied BCI signal acquisition*: In this section the methods used for measuring brain activity in the articles were determined as invasive and non-invasive according to the sensor placement method that had been used [2, 7]. Invasive methods were ECoG (electrocortigography) and MEA (multi-electrode array) while non-invasive methods were classified as immobile and mobile. MEG (magnetoencephalography) and fMRI (functional magnetic resonance imaging) were considered as immobile while EEG (electroencephalography) and NIRS (near-infrared spectroscopy) were considered as mobile brain activity acquisition methods.

7. *Applied BCI signal processing*: In this section the methods used in articles for interpreting brain activity were determined. First, filtering should be applied to the acquired brain activity to remove noise or body movement related artifacts. Articles were analyzed according to applied filtering method such as low-pass, high-pass, band-pass or notch filtering or ICA (Independent Component Analysis) [9] in the first sub-section here. Then which features that were extracted for the BCI systems were analyzed based on Hwang et al.'s [4] classification scheme which covered five groups of PSD (power spectral density), ERP (event related potential), use of more than two feature types, phase information and others. Finally in the signal processing section, articles were analyzed according to the classification algorithms that had been used. Classification algorithms used were LDA (Linear discriminant analysis), SVM (support vector machine), use of more than one classifier, Bayesian classifier, finding max. value, LR (Linear regression), thresholding, NN (Neural networks), and others [4].

2.2   Systematic Mapping Process

In the scope of this study, BCI-related articles published in the proceedings of HCI International Conference between years 2005 and 2015 were mapped according to the developed protocol. The article list related with BCI studies were gathered from previous years' conference web sites based on their titles. Afterwards articles were gathered from the conference proceedings' publisher database. However very few number of 2005 articles could only be gathered from general search engines. Some articles were removed from the list since they were realized that they were not in the scope of BCI research during the mapping. The total number of mapped articles can be seen in Table 2. Only full papers rather than posters were included in the mapping process.

Table 2. Total number of articles mapped

Year	# of articles mapped
2005	5
2007	24
2009	48
2011	38
2013	36
2014	28
2015	28
TOTAL	207

Articles were mapped by two authors independently first and then two came together and compared their results to reach a consensus. Articles assigned at least one category in each section but they could be assigned more than one category whenever possible. Therefore, the number of total articles mapped in each category showed some variance.

3 Results

In the scope of this research a systematic mapping was conducted regarding with the BCI related articles presented in HCI International Conference between 2005 and 2015 years. Based on the systematic mapping protocol defined in Sect. 2.1, articles were mapped to identify the BCI research types, general aims, BCI paradigm used, practical application areas, signal acquisition and processing methods used in studies and the countries and institutions that contributed to the BCI research in the conference. Detailed findings are presented in the following subsections.

3.1 BCI Research Types Studied

Research types conducted in BCI area were mapped according to four categories defined by Bruner et al. [8]. Majority of articles belonged to emerging applications not related to communication and control and basic research group, while there were less number of articles in clinical/translational research and consumer products as can be seen in Fig. 2. When these findings were evaluated according to the years, it was revealed that there were more articles in basic research group during the early years while there were more articles in emerging applications not related to communication and control group in recent years.

3.2 Aims of BCI Related Articles

Aims of the presented articles at the conferences were mapped according to Hwang et al.'s [4] classification scheme defined for BCI related researches. Many of the studies

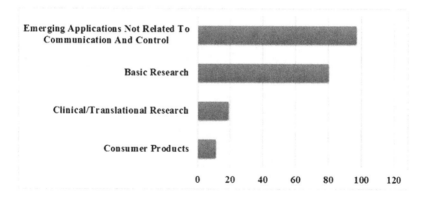

Fig. 2. BCI research types published in HCI International 2005-2015 Conferences

conducted were related with practical applications of BCI technologies. Second most conducted studies were related with development or improvement of methodologies for signal processing, feature extraction and classification. The details can be seen in Fig. 3. When the results were investigated in details according to years, it was revealed that in earlier years, development and improvement of methodologies studies were conducted more while later years practical application of BCI technologies gained more popularity.

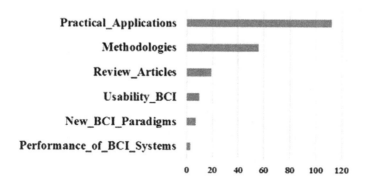

Fig. 3. Aim of BCI related articles

3.3 BCI Paradigm Used in the Articles

When the articles were investigated according the BCI paradigm they adopted, it was revealed that many of the papers adopted visual P300 paradigm for gathering brain activities. Steady state visual-evoked potentials (SSVEP), motor imagery, auditory stimuli or non-motor mental imagery paradigms were used less compared to visual P300 paradigm as can be seen in Fig. 4. There were also some other paradigms applied in few articles such as kinesthetic stimuli, vestibular stimuli or some hybrid stimuli of the mentioned paradigms.

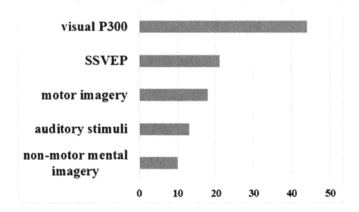

Fig. 4. BCI paradigm used in the articles

3.4   Practical Applications of BCI Technologies

Articles were mapped according to the related practical BCI application that were targeted. It was revealed that articles reported mostly BCI technologies applied for mental or cognitive load detection, emotion detection or attention detection. Other practical applications reported in the articles could be listed as brain-controlled smart home systems, brain controlled game applications, mental speller or mouse control applications as can be seen in Fig. 5.

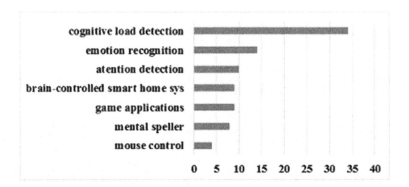

Fig. 5. Practical applications of BCI technologies targeted in the articles

3.5   BCI Signal Acquisition and Signal Processing Methods

Articles were investigated regarding BCI signal acquisition equipment used in the studies as well as signal processing methods. Main equipment used in studies for signal acquisition were EEG and NIRS which were non-invasive devices for measuring brain activity. There are also some articles that reported hybrid use of these equipment.

In addition in some studies they were used together with some other psycho-physiological devices for detecting heart rate, skin conductivity level as well as eye trackers (Fig. 6).

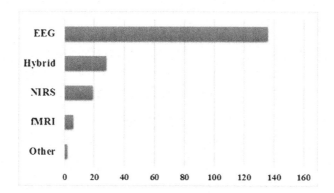

Fig. 6. Brain activity measuring devices used in the articles

For the interpretation of brain activities, gathered brain signals are processes through three main steps which were pre-processing or filtering, then feature extraction and finally classification. Articles were investigated regarding these steps as well. In order to filter noise in acquired signals, bandpass filter was the most used method. Following methods were independent component analysis (ICA), low-pass filter, notch filter and high-pass filter respectively as can be seen in Fig. 7.

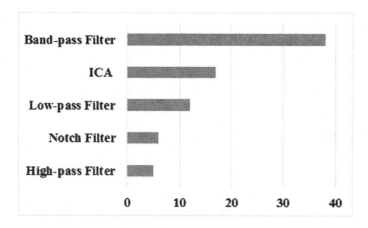

Fig. 7. Filtering methods reported in the articles

After preprocessing step, brain signals are processed through feature selection method. Event-related potentials and power spectral density were the mostly reported method for feature selection in the articles. Researchers applied fast Fourier transformation in many of the PSD based studies. Wavelength transformation, and short-term Fourier transformation were also applied in some studies.

Finally applied classification methods reported in the studies were linear discriminant analysis (LDA), linear regression, (LR), support vector machine (SVM), thresholding, Bayesian classifier and neural networks (NN) respectively as can be seen in Fig. 8. Use of more than one classifier was also reported in many of the articles as well.

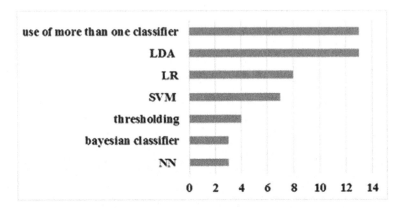

Fig. 8. Classification methods reported in the articles

3.6   Contributing Research Institutions and Countries

Contributing institutions and countries were also investigated. Authors were mapped according to their first affiliation. Institutions and countries were marked once when there were more than one contributing author from the same institution or country. There were more than 900 distinct authors, 250 institutions and 30 countries contributing with research related to BCI research area. Top five contributing institutions were Advanced Bran Monitoring, Inc., Drexel University, Swartz Center for Computational Neuroscience, Electrical Geodesics, Inc. from USA and Guger Technologies OG from Austria. On the other hand, top five contributing countries were USA, Japan, Germany, The Netherlands and Austria.

4   Conclusion

In the scope of this research, a systematic mapping was conducted regarding with the BCI related articles presented in HCI International Conference between 2005 and 2015 years to determine BCI research trends. According to the results of the mapping, research type of BCI articles were mainly in the category of the emerging applications not related to communication and control while a trend could be seen from basic research to this area in the later years. General aim of the articles was determined as practical applications of BCI technologies first and then development or improvement of methodologies for signal processing issues. Visual P300 was the mostly applied BCI paradigms and SSVEP and motor imagery followed next. Most of the articles had reported EEG as a signal acquisition method, ICA or bandpass filter as a preprocessing or filtering method, ERP as a feature type and LDA and LR as a classification algorithm method.

Although findings based on a single conference would not be sufficient to make a general conclusion, the results of this study is expected to provide some general trends related with BCI. This would help and guide researchers who would like to study on this subject area. As a future work it is planned to investigate more articles published at other HCI related conferences and journals. One of the limitation to be considered in these kind of studies is the reliability of the results. Therefore, the study was conducted iteratively. Authors first mapped articles alone and then came together to form consensus about their findings so researcher bias was tried to be overcome.

References

1. Wolpaw, J.R., Birbaumer, N., McFarland, D.J., Pfurtscheller, G., Vaughan, T.M.: Brain–computer interfaces for communication and control. Clin. Neurophysiol. **113**(6), 767–791 (2002)
2. Gürkök, H., Nijholt, A.: Brain–computer interfaces for multimodal interaction: A survey and principles. Int. J. Hum. Comput. Interact. **28**(5), 292–307 (2012)
3. Nam, C.S., Schalk, G., Jackson, M.M.: Current trends in Brain-Computer interface (BCI) research and development. Intl. J. Hum. Comput. Interact. **27**(1), 1–4 (2010)
4. Hwang, H.J., Kim, S., Choi, S., Im, C.H.: EEG-based brain-computer interfaces: a thorough literature survey. Int. J. Hum. Comput. Interact. **29**(12), 814–826 (2013)
5. Mason, S.G., Bashashati, A., Fatourechi, M., Navarro, K.F., Birch, G.E.: A comprehensive survey of brain interface technology designs. Ann. Biomed. Eng. **35**(2), 137–169 (2007)
6. Mason, S.G., Birch, G.E.: A general framework for brain-computer interface design. Neural Syst. Rehabil. Eng. IEEE Trans. **11**(1), 70–85 (2003)
7. Lin, C.T., Ko, L.W., Chang, M.H., Duann, J.R., Chen, J.Y., Su, T.P., Jung, T.P.: Review of wireless and wearable electroencephalogram systems and brain-computer interfaces–a mini-review. Gerontology **56**(1), 112–119 (2009)
8. Brunner, P., Bianchi, L., Guger, C., Cincotti, F., Schalk, G.: Current trends in hardware and software for brain–computer interfaces (BCIs). J. Neural Eng. **8**(2), 025001 (2011)
9. Bi, L., Fan, X.A., Liu, Y.: EEG-based brain-controlled mobile robots: a survey. Hum. Mach. Syst. IEEE Trans. **43**(2), 161–176 (2013)
10. HCI International: Home (n.d.). Retrieved October 4, 2015. http://www.hci.international/index.php?&MMN_position=1:1
11. Kitchenham, B.A., Dyba, T., Jorgensen, M.: Evidence-based software engineering. In: Proceedings of the 26th International Conference on Software Engineering, pp. 273–281. IEEE Computer Society (2004)
12. Petersen, K., Feldt, R., Mujtaba, S., Mattsson, M.: Systematic mapping studies in software engineering. In: 12th International Conference on Evaluation and Assessment in Software Engineering, vol. 17, no. (1) (2008)
13. Kitchenham, B., Budgen, D., Brereton, O.P.: The value of mapping studies – a participant-observer case study. In: EASE 2010 Proceedings of the 14th International Conference on Evaluation and Assessment in Software Engineering, pp. 25–33 (2010). http://www.bcs.org/upload/pdf/ewic_ea10_session2paper1.pdf
14. Turdaliev, N., Bilgin, B., Deniz, G., Durdu, P.O., İncebacak, D., Mutlu, A.: UYMS Araştırma Eğilimleri: Bir Sistematik Eşleme Çalışması 9. National Software Engineering Symposium (2015). http://ceur-ws.org/Vol-1483/58_Bildiri.pdf

Optimal User Interface Parameters
for Dual-Sided Transparent Screens
in Layered Window Conditions

Hae Youn Joung[✉], Se Young Kim, Seung Hyun Im,
Bo Kyung Huh, Heesun Kim, Gyu Hyun Kwon, and Ji-Hyung Park

Center for Robotics, Korea Institute of Science and Technology,
Hwarang-ro 14-gil 5, Seongbuk-gu, Seoul 02792, Korea
haey.joung@gmail.com, swsy52@gmail.com,
ish@gmail.com, pure4eva@gmail.com
ghkwon@hanyang.ac.kr
{090748,jhpark}@kist.re.kr

Abstract. In this research, we assess a set of optimal user interface parameters for a dual-sided transparent display in a collaborative working environment. To provide an experiment setup, we develop a prototype that simulates a dual-sided transparent display using two conventional displays and associated simulation software. The user interface parameters controlled in the experiment include the transparency level and the overlapped (or layered) size of foreground and background user interface windows, where a target marker (being searched by subjects) is presented along with distraction markers. To evaluate the optimal parameter setting, we measure the response time and correct response rate from the subject input to both the foreground and background displays. From the pilot study, we found that appropriate levels of transparency and windows overlapping potentially enhance the visibility of a user interface realized on layered multiple windows. Based on this finding, we propose an extended user research, where a *depth factor* and a *contour effect* are employed in addition to the user interface parameters, which may enhance the user response time especially in cases where the windows are highly overlapped.

Keywords: Transparent display · Both-sided interaction · Transparency · Layered interface

1 Introduction

Recent studies on transparent displays have aimed to address new interaction techniques and to identify potential applications such as face-to-face communication systems [1], social engagement tools, augmented-reality messaging applications [2], 3D interaction tools [3, 4]. In particular, a transparent display can be used as a face-to-face collaboration tool between collaborators located on the opposite side, while they use a common user interface projected on the same screen. In such a usage scenario, however, the transparent characteristic of the display potentially generates interruptive (or disruptive) user experience conditions [2, 5], where the objects or environment in

M. Kurosu (Ed.): HCI 2016, Part II, LNCS 9732, pp. 162–169, 2016.
DOI: 10.1007/978-3-319-39516-6_15

background are penetrated to foreground or the background user interface windows are overlapped to the foreground windows. Among these considerations, the overlapped (or layered) window issue can be particularly problematic if a dual-sided transparent display is employed in a collaboration environment, where the two users are situated face-to-face as shown in Fig. 1.

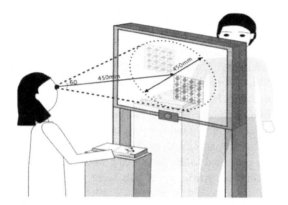

Fig. 1. Transparent display equipment for the experimental environment

To address the transparent, overlapped window issue, researchers studied various usage scenarios with a prototype emulating transparent user interface windows with a partial overlap. In [6], the potential use cases of transparent displays are presented with a fabric-based prototype for the collaboration of users on the opposite side. In [7], the usage scenario and usability evaluation of a transparent display prototype that is capable of controlling the transparency level are provided. These publications, however, are focused on evaluating a usage scenario from the application point of view without providing fundamental, empirical experiment results, which can be used to evaluate the feasibility of using a transparent display in a realistic use environment.

To fill such a gap revealed in previous usability researches, we performed a pilot study, which was based on the following question: Can the partially overlapped interface windows with a certain degree of transparency be effectively used in a collaborative work environment using a transparent dual-sided display? We developed an empirical prototype that emulates the characteristics of a transparent display using two conventional displays and associated simulation software. In this pilot study, we conducted the statistical analysis of experimental data in terms of response time and correct response rate to evaluate the user performance in a controlled test environment by programming the transparency level and the size of layered windows.

In an extended research based on the pilot study, we include contrast (or contour) effects in the controlled user interface parameters to further study the feasibility of using highly overlapped windows. This research potentially provides fundamental, empirical user research data such as the maximum allowed layered window size, optimal transparency and contrast level, to the field of user experience research for a transparent display used in a collaboration environment, where two (or more) users share the same display placement on the opposite side.

2 Method

Participants. 30 university students (20 male, 10 female) were paired in 15 groups (the average age of the participants is 27). All participants had normal or corrected-to-normal vision capability. A local committee approved the Institutional Review Board (IRB). Participants gave a user testing consent form.

Equipment. As shown in Fig. 1, we simulate a dual-sided transparent display by using two conventional 42" LCD displays (resolution: 2560 by 1440 pixels), front-facing embedded cameras and associated simulation software (developed by using the Unity game engine). The LCD displays provide the participants with stimuli, where foreground and simulated background windows with arrow (target and distraction) markers were shown. The behavior of participants was captured by the front-facing cameras and its mirrored image was projected to the participant on the opposite side in real time by using the simulation software. Arrow keyboards were given as an input device.

Stimuli. Stimuli are provided to participants within a viewing angle of 60° and a distance of 450 mm, as shown in Fig. 1. A foreground window and a background window (4×4 bins each) are projected on a simulated transparent display with the variable area of overlap between them: The overlapped (or layered) window size used in this experiment consists of (1×1)-bin, (2×2)-bin, (3×3)-bin cases. Each window presents a unique distractive arrow, and one of the two windows displays a target arrow marker that is distinct from the distractive arrows (among the four arrow types: left, right, up and down). For instance, in Fig. 2(b), a target arrow is highlighted in a red circle, and the other 31 distract arrows are shown. The location of a target arrow is randomly determined: It can be on either the foreground or background window, and on either the overlapped or non-overlapped area. To simulate the transparency condition of the user interface windows, we used four distinct transparency levels defined in an alpha value (a measure in percentage) of a 32 bit-RGBA color space ranging between 0 and 255: 51 (20 %), 102 (40 %), 153 (60 %), and 204 (80 %).

Procedure. The 4×3 factorial design used for our user experiments is illustrated in Fig. 3, where the transparency level factor and the layered window size factor are used. Participants are asked to detect a target arrow marker, which presents along with distractor arrows on the display and to press a matching arrow key on the keyboard provided to them. A total of 192 trials (after 10 practices) are conducted for each pair of participants in approximately 15 min. The position of a target arrow, the transparency level and the layered window size are randomly determined for each trial. The response time (RT) and correct response rate (CRR) are recorded by the simulation software for data post-processing and analysis. Since the study explores the feasibility of collaboration tasks with a transparent display, the experiment session remains active if one of the participants continues to search for the targeted arrow. We conducted user interviews at the end of each task.

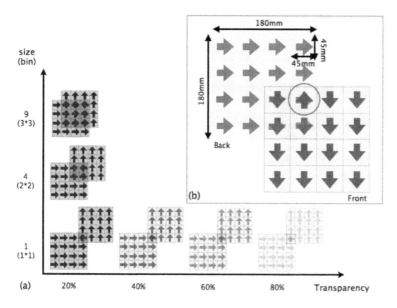

Fig. 2. 4 × 3 factorial design: (a) transparency and layered size combination; (b) stimuli based on visual search model.

Data Analysis. Experiment data are analyzed within a pair (collaborator A and B) in terms of RT and CRR. Two sets of data were excluded from the high error rate, and uncorrected data was discarded. Prior to analyzing the performance data, normality tests are performed. Since normality is not assumed in data post-processing, non-parametric statistical analysis techniques are used such as the Friedman test (*Fri.) and Wilcoxon signed-rank test (**Wil.) to assess the differences among transparency levels, layered sizes, and interaction effects for two factors with the significant p-value at a 5 % level.

3   Observation

We analyze the user behavior data obtained from the pilot study in two distinct categories: [*Overlapping Case*] where the target arrow marker is presented in the overlapped area of the two (foreground and background) windows, and [*Non-overlapping Case*] where the target maker is in the non-overlapped area. The user performance is analyzed in terms of RT and CRR (averaged values obtained from both the foreground and background users).

Transparent Level Effect. In Fig. 3, RT and CRR measured at various transparent levels are shown: RT (*Fri.: $\chi^2(3) = 31.062$, p < 0.01) and CRR (*Fri.: $\chi^2(3) = 10.113$, p < 0.05), where a noticeable variation in both RT and CRR is observed across transparency levels. Figure 3(a) shows that a higher transparency level increases the response time (in both [Overlapping Case] and [Non-overlapping Case].

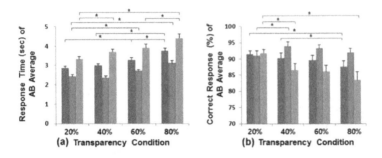

Fig. 3. Transparency level control: (a) response time and (b) correct response rate

This fact is potentially because of the *visual interference* of the background objects in the experiment environment to the user in the foreground in a higher transparency level case.

As shown in Fig. 3(b), the CRR of [*Overlapping Case*] shows a decreasing trend as the transparency level increases (**Wil.: 20 %/80 %, p < 0.05; 40 %/80 %, p < 0.01), which can be explained by the fact that a lower transparency level (i.e. 20 %) generates a higher contrast factor to the user interface windows, which helps the user correctly detect the target marker. In comparison, CRR of [*Non-overlapping Case*] measured at the 20 % transparency level is lower than that measured with the 40 % transparency level, which is considered a *threshold* in the plot.

The 40 % transparency level is the *optimal index* for the usage scenario of a transparent display with potentially overlapped windows, which is consistent with Harrison's hypothesis [1].

Layered Size Effect. Figure 4 shows the user detection performance measured in RT and CRR measured at various overlapped window sizes. In Fig. 4(a), RT values measured in [Overlapping Case] show meaningful differences across various over-lapped sizes (*Fri.: $\chi^2(2)$ = 19.846, p < 0.01), where the (1 × 1)-bin overlapped case results in a faster RT as compared to the (2 × 2)- or (3 × 3)-bin overlapped case, while [Non-overlapping Case] does not show a meaningful variation.

As shown in in [Non-overlapping Case] of Fig. 4(b), it is noticeable that CRR of the (2 × 2)-bin overlapped case is higher than that of the other cases. This implies that a *smaller visual field* (or reduced total area of search) enhances the user detection per-formance in the non-overlapping region, which makes it relatively easy for the user to find a target marker in the windows. In comparison, the user might have experienced overloaded search areas [6] in the (3 × 3)-bin case, which results in reduced CRR as compared to the (2 × 2)-bin case. Note that the (2 × 2)-bin overlapping case presents a consistently stable RT and CRR performance in both [Overlapping Case] and [Non-overlapping Case]. This experiment result shows that it is promising to use windows with a certain degree of overlapping, not just to pursue as a small area of overlapping as possible.

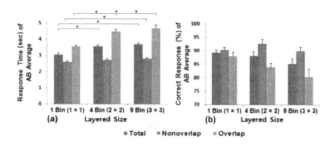

Fig. 4. Layered window size effect: (a) response time and (b) correct response rate

Transparency and Layered Size Effect Interaction. Finally, the interaction effects of transparencies and layered sizes were examined. There were significant interaction transparencies and layered sizes in RT performance (Fried, χ^2 (11) = 87.568, p < 0.01) and CR (Fried, χ^2 (11) = 27.958, p < 0.01). Each transparency level set according to layered size was shown as follows. In the RT performance, all transparency levels revealed significant differences among pairs of 1 and 4bin (Wil, 20 %, p < 0.01; 40 %, p < 0.01; 60 %, p < 0.05; 80 %, p < 0.01), 1 and 9bin (Wil, 20 %, p < 0.01; 40 %, p < 0.01; 60 %, p < 0.05; 80 %, p < 0.01). Both 4 and 9bin showed similar results in RT. Overall, regardless of transparency level, layered size affected the results, as shown in Fig. 5(a).

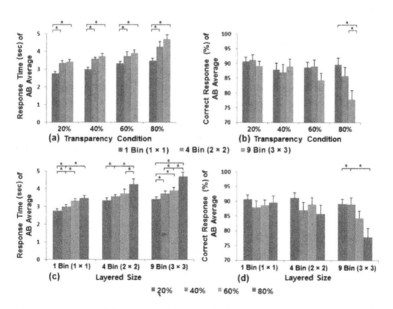

Fig. 5. Collaborators A and B average: (a) layered size as transparency condition in response time: (b) correct response; (c) transparency condition as layered size in response time; (d) correct response.

In the CR performance, of the two pairs of 1 and 9bin (Wil, p < 0.01), 4 and 9bin (Wil, p < 0.01) in the 80 % level showed significant differences, as depicted in Fig. 5(b). Although there were no significant differences of CR, the CR of 1 and 4bin was higher than that of 9bin in the highest transparency level. In addition, each layered size according to transparency level was demonstrated, as shown in Fig. 5(c and d). In the RT performance, the higher the transparency level, the longer the RT, as mentioned in the transparency results section. For CR performance, the CR of the 20 % and 40 % levels was higher than that of the 80 % level. Based on the results, the 80 % level with the 9bin combination may cause the worst performance for users of TDs.

Interface Guideline. In summary, to guide users, the TD would be most effectively used at a transparency level between 20 % and 40 %. The *'contrast'* effect may influence all transparency levels during collaboration. In addition, the layered size efficiency showed the best performance in the 1bin condition. Based on the results in the previous section, we suggest that the 40 % level with 1bin is the most effective condition for a collaboration environment. Alternatively, 4bin (25/100 area) presented a consistently stable performance across transparency levels. Therefore, we suggest that 4bin is likewise an efficient condition with broad transparency usage.

4 Extended Study

From the pilot study, we found that appropriate levels of transparency and windows overlapping potentially enhance the visibility of a user interface realized on layered multiple windows: The increase in either transparency level or overlapped window size generally degrades the user detection performance with a certain degree of *threshold*.

To further investigate the feasibility of using a layered, transparent window condition and to identify a complete set of the interface parameters that need to be tuned for the optimal user performance, we propose an extended user research (work-in-progress), where a *depth factor* or a *contour effect* are employed as an additional user interface parameter in the experiment. The use of a depth factor, especially in the overlapped area of the foreground and background windows, may help enhance the user response time to detect the target marker (or generally enhance the user performance). In summary, we employ the controlled interface parameters in our extended study to investigate a complete set of interface parameters for using transparent, layered windows in a work-in-progress:

- Transparency level
- Overlapped window size
- Depth factor
- Contour effect

Acknowledgements.   This work was supported by the IT R&D program of MOTIE/KEIT. [10042418, UI and User Interaction Technology for more than 60 HD-level Transparent Flexible Display Applied Product Using Eye-tracking and Space Recognition].

References

1. Harrison, B.L., et al.: Transparent layered user interfaces: an evaluation of a display design to enhance focused and divided attention. In: Proceedings of the CHI 1995, pp. 317–324. ACM Press (1995)
2. Ishii, H., Kobayashi, M.: ClearBoard: a seamless medium for shared drawing and conversation with eye contact. In: Proceedings of the CHI 1992, pp. 525–532. ACM Press (1992)
3. Hirakawa, M., Koike, S.: A collaborative augmented reality system using transparent display. In: Proceedings of the MSE 2004, pp. 410–416. IEEE Press (2004)
4. Hilliges, O., et al.: HoloDesk: direct 3D interactions with a situated see-through display. In: Proceedings of the CHI 2012, pp. 2421–2430. ACM Press (2012)
5. Lee, J., et al.: SpaceTop: integrating 2D and spatial 3D interactions in a see-through desktop environment. In: Proceedings of the CHI 2013, pp. 189–192. ACM Press (2013)
6. Li, J., Greenberg, S., Sharlin, E., Jorge, J.: Interactive two-sided transparent displays: designing for collaboration. In: DIS 2014, pp. 395–404 (2014)
7. Lindlbauer, D., Aoki, T., Walter, R., Uema, Y., Hochtl, A., Haller, et al.: Tracs: transparency-control for see-through displays. In: UIST 2014, pp. 657–661. ACM (2014)

Bimodal Speech Recognition Fusing Audio-Visual Modalities

Alexey Karpov[1(✉)], Alexander Ronzhin[1], Irina Kipyatkova[1],
Andrey Ronzhin[1], Vasilisa Verkhodanova[1], Anton Saveliev[1],
and Milos Zelezny[2]

[1] St. Petersburg Institute for Informatics and Automation of the Russian
Academy of Sciences, SPIIRAS, Saint-Petersburg, Russian Federation, Russia
{karpov,ronzhinal,kipyatkova,ronzhin}@iias.spb.su
[2] University of West Bohemia, Pilsen, Czech Republic
zelezny@kky.zcu.cz
http://hci.nw.ru
http://www.kky.zcu.cz

Abstract. In this paper, we present a novel bimodal speech recognition technique that fuses both audio information (sound signal) and visual information (movements of lips) for Russian speech recognition. We propose an architecture of the automatic system for bimodal recognition of audio-visual speech, which uses one stationary microphone Oktava and one high-speed camera JAI Pulnix (200 frames per second at 640 × 480 pixels) to get audio and video signals. We describe also developed software for audio-visual speech database recording, phonemic and visemic structures of the Russian language, as well as probabilistic models of bimodal speech units based on Coupled Hidden Markov Models. Realization of a transformation method from a Coupled Hidden Markov Model into an equivalent 2-stream Hidden Markov Model is presented as well.

Keywords: Automatic speech recognition · Audio-Visual speech processing · Speech technology · Information fusion · Automatic Lip-reading · Bimodal system and interface

1 Introduction

At present, there are some Russian automatic speech recognition (ASR) systems based on audio-only signal captured via a microphone developed by some International industrial companies, such as Google (Google Now software), Nuance (Dragon Naturally Speaking software), Apple (Siri software for iPhone 6), Microsoft (software for Xbox One and Cortana for Windows 8), Samsung, as well as by some Russian commercial companies, leading state Universities and Institutes of the Russian Academy of Sciences [1, 2].

However, present performance of audio-only Russian ASR is not satisfactory for the most of end-users. However, it is well known from some recent works [3–6], that audio and visual modalities (cues) of speech supplement each other very well and their joint multimodal processing can improve both accuracy and robustness of ASR.

© Springer International Publishing Switzerland 2016
M. Kurosu (Ed.): HCI 2016, Part II, LNCS 9732, pp. 170–179, 2016.
DOI: 10.1007/978-3-319-39516-6_16

In this paper, we present a bimodal automatic speech recognition technique that fuses both audio information (speech sound signal) and visual information (lip movements) for the Russian speech recognition.

The paper is structured as follows: Sect. 2 presents general architecture of the bimodal speech recognition system, Sect. 3 describes probabilistic models of audio-visual speech units based on Coupled Hidden Markov Models, and conclusions are outlined in Sect. 4.

2   Architecture of the Bimodal Speech Recognition System

General architecture of a typical bimodal speech recognition system, which fuses both audio and visual modalities, is presented in Fig. 1. As any state-of-the-art speech recognition system our system operates in two modes: (1) model training and (2) speech decoding/recognition.

In this system, we use one high-speed camera JAI Pulnix (200 fps at 640×480 pixels) and one dynamic microphone Oktava in order to capture both video and audio signals. High frequency of video frames is crucial for analysis of dynamical images, since visible articulation organs (lips, teeth, tip of tongue) change their configuration quite fast at speech production and duration of some phonemes (e.g. explosive consonants) is within 10–20 ms (duration of each video at 25 fps frame is 40 ms that is too long). So recordings made by a standard camera with 25–30 fps cannot catch fast dynamics of lips movements and most of the important information is missing in these signals.

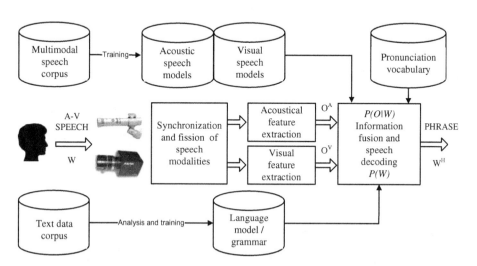

Fig. 1. General architecture of the bimodal speech recognition system

In our bimodal speech recognition system, 12-dimentional Mel-frequency cepstral coefficients (MFCC) are extracted as acoustical features, calculated from 26 channel filter bank analysis of 20 ms long frames with 10 ms step [7]. Visual features of speech are calculated as a result of the following signal processing steps using the open source computer vision library OpenCV [8]: multi-scale face detection in video frames from a video-camera using a cascade classifier with AdaBoost method based on the Viola-Jones algorithm [9, 10] with a trained face model; mouth region detection with two cascade classifiers (for a mouth and mouth-with-beard) within the lower part of the face [11]; normalization of detected mouth image region to 32×32 pixels; mapping to a 32-dimensional feature vector using the principal component analysis (PCA); visual feature mean normalization; viseme-based linear discriminant analysis (LDA). The video signal processing module produces 10-dimentional articulatory feature vectors.

In order to train probabilistic language models and acoustic-visemic models, text and audio-visual speech corpora are required. Figure 2 shows the architecture of software for audio-visual speech database recording. The audio-visual speech recording system is intended for formation of an audio-visual speech database to train probabilistic models of the speech recognition system.

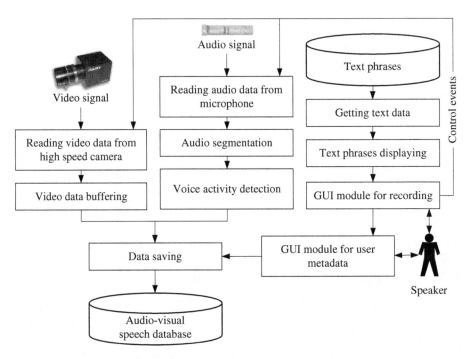

Fig. 2. Architecture of the audio-visual speech database recording software

The software complex consists of four main modules: (1) video data capturing and buffering; (2) audio data capturing, processing and segmentation; (3) text data displaying; (4) GUI for interaction with a user (speaker). The developed software has two GUI modules for interaction with user and receiving metadata. The modules of GUI provide two modes for data recording: (1) an "expert" mode, where the user manages start and end points; (2) an "automatic" mode, where fragments of recording are determined by a voice activity detection (VAD) method. In the "automatic" mode, capturing and processing of audio signal is carrying out continuously, as well as video data is buffered in RAM memory for the last 60 frames (300 ms at 200 fps). This buffering option is based on some aspects of human speech production. After the recording phrase, audio and video data of a current speaker are saved into the speech database; for synchronizing audio and video signals, the software calculates frame mistiming.

One major problem in machine audio-visual speech recognition is to implement a correct method for synchronization and unification of different speech modalities. The problem is that the two modalities naturally become desynchronized, i.e., streams of corresponding phonemes and visemes are not perfectly synchronous in real life due to natural constraints in the human speech production process, inertia in human articulation organs, and coarticulation (interdependence and interaction of adjacent elements in spoken speech) which has different effects on acoustic and visual speech components, leading to desynchronization. It is known that visemes always lead in phone-viseme pairs; at that in the beginning of a phrase visual speech units usually lead more noticeably (up to 150-200 ms for stressed rounded vowels) over the corresponding phonemes than in the central or ending part of the phrase.

3 Probabilistic Models of Audio-Visual Speech Units

To take into account the temporal desynchronization between the streams of corresponding acoustic and visual features, which is natural for human speech, we propose to apply Coupled Hidden Markov Models [3, 12]. Figure 3 presents a topology of such a model for an audio-visual speech unit (a phoneme–viseme pair) with several states for each stream of feature vectors. Circles denote HMM states that are hidden for observation; squares indicate mixtures of normal distributions of observation vectors in the states. A coupled Hidden markov model (CHMM) is a set of parallel HMMs, one per information flow (modality). Model states at some moment of time t for each HMM depend on hidden states at time moment $t-1$ for all parallel HMMs. Thus, the entire state of a CHMM is defined by the collection of states for two parallel HMMs. One advantage of such a topology is that it lets several streams of feature vectors independently walk through the model states, which gives us a possibility to model admissible temporal inconsistencies in both audio and video data.

In the topology of CHMM audio-visual speech units we use three hidden states per each parallel stream of feature vectors, assuming that the first states correspond to a dynamical transition from the previous speech unit, the third states, to a transition to the next unit, and the second states of the unified model (the most lengthy ones) correspond to the stationary central segment of the speech unit. In order to define a CHMM $\lambda = <L, D, B, \gamma>$ for an audio-visual speech unit, we have to specify the following parameters:

(1) Number of hidden states in the model– L (states for speech audio and video modalities are shown with circles in Fig. 3 and denoted as A and V respectively).

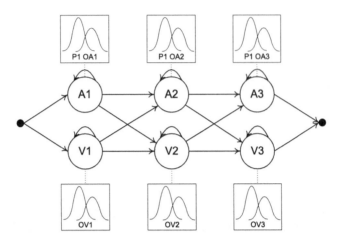

Fig. 3. Topology of a Coupled Hidden Markov Model for an audio-visual unit

(2) Matrix of transition probabilities between model states– $D = \{d_{ij}\}$, $1 \leq i \leq L, 1 \leq j \leq L$

(3) Probability distributions for the feature vector in model states (shown in squares in Fig. 3) – $B = \{b_j(O)\}$. We use mixtures of Gaussian distributions:

$$b_j(O) = \sum_{m=1}^{M} c_{jm} N(O, \ \mu_{jm}, \ \sigma_{jm}^2), \sum_{m=1}^{M} c_{jm} = 1, 1 \leq j \leq L,$$

where O is the feature vector being modeled (for the audio or video signal), C_{jm} is the weight coefficient of component m in a state j, N is the distribution density (usually a Gaussian distribution density) with mean (expectation) μ_{jm} and variance (standard deviation) σ_{jm}^2 for mixture component m in the state j, M is the number of Gaussian components in the mixture (up to 16).

(4) Information weights (importance) $\gamma = \{\gamma^A, \ \gamma^V\}$ of speech modalities (audio and video streams); they are tuned during system training or adaptation, and they always sum up to the constant: $\gamma^A + \gamma^V = 2$.

The Russian language contains several dozens of various context-independent phonemes (different researchers and phoneticians distinguish 40–50 phonemes, in our system we use 48 phonemes, see Table 1), so there are as many different CHMMs in the automatic speech recognition system. However, there exist fewer number of various visemes in Russian speech; only about 10–12 depending on the speaker's articulation (in our system we use 10 visemes, see Table 1) [13, 14]. Each CHMM represents one phoneme-viseme pair, and to model audio speech signals, we need more HMMs than for the visual speech modeling only.

In order to cope with this problem, it is proposed to tie distributions of observation vectors for visual components in the states of different CHMMs. The total number of CHMMs in the system equals the number of phonemes being recognized, but some models have common states and parameters; it simplifies the training process. Figure 4 shows the scheme of tying parameters of a CHMMs pair for 2 phonemes corresponding to 1 viseme. After tying the output densities of corresponding viseme models according to the mapping in Fig. 4, we can get 30 tied probability densities for the visual data stream and 144 untied ones for the acoustical feature stream.

A simple method to transform a CHMM into an equivalent HMM, which keeps all the properties of the former model, was proposed in [15] and later used by the authors in [16]. This method is used in our recognition system as well. Transformed HMM for an

Table 1. Visemes and phoneme-to-viseme mapping for Russian speech

Viseme	Viseme class	Corresponding phonemes
/v1/	silence (neutral position)	/sil/(pause)
/v2/	wide-opened mouth unrounded vowels	/a/,/a!/,/e!/
/v3/	unrounded vowels (unstressed and stressed)	/i/,/i!/,/y/,/y!/,/e/
/v4/	rounded vowels	/o!/,/u/,/u!/
/v5/	labial consonants (hard and soft)	/b/,/b'/,/p/,/p'/,/m/,/m'/
/v6/	labio-dental consonants	/f/,/f'/,/v/,/v'/
/v7/	alveolar fricatives	/sh/,/zh/,/ch/,/sch/
/v8/	alveolar sonorants	/l/,/l'/,/r/,/r'/
/v9/	dental consonants	/d/,/d'/,/t/,/t'/,/n/,/n'/, /s/,/s'/,/z/,/z'/,/c/
/v10/	velar consonants	/g/,/g'/,/k/,/k'/,/h/,/h'/,/j/

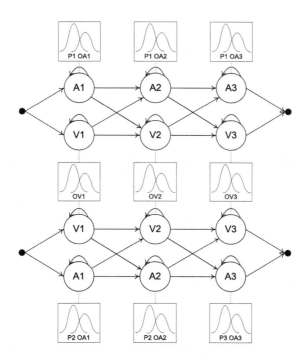

Fig. 4. Tying probability distributions of a pair of the Coupled Hidden Markov Models for two phonemes corresponding to one viseme.

audio-visual speech unit contains all the combinations of parallel states of the corresponding CHMM. In the CHMM model, the two streams are independent; the output distribution of a joint state is calculated by the output densities of both streams. In the equivalent 2-stream HMM, the output distribution is obtained as a product of the two output densities. To avoid tripling of the output densities in the model, it is proposed to tie the appropriate output densities in the 2-stream HMM according to CHMM-to-HMM conversion of the hidden states. The resulting 2-stream HMM is shown in Fig. 5. We use CHMM with 3 emitting states per feature stream. Therefore, all their combinations produce 9 states in the equivalent left-to-right HMM. Increment of the number of the states in comparison with the original CHMM increases the memory allocated for the model, but does not reduce the speed of speech decoding. The parameters of 2-stream HMMs are obtained by the Baum-Welch (expectation-maximization) algorithm with maximum likelihood estimation using bimodal training data.

In order to recognize (decode) speech, we apply a modified token passing algorithm based on the Viterbi optimization algorithm for multi-threaded HMMs [7, 17], which finds probabilities of generating observation symbols (sequences of feature vectors) in

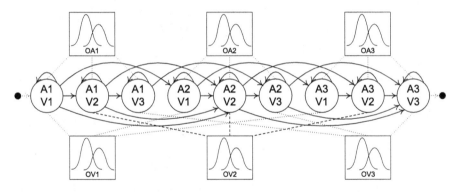

Fig. 5. Transformation of a CHMM into the equivalent 2-stream HMM

this model and sequences of the model's hidden states traversed along the way. The essence of our method is as follows: to model possible phrases, we construct a unified probabilistic model (graph) with all possible transitions between HMMs of minimal speech units (constrained by the recognition dictionary) and between HMMs of individual words (constrained by the language model). Then with dynamical programming (Viterbi) we find the maximum likelihood sequence/path of hidden states (that contain information about speech units) in the model to generate the processed sequence of observations [7]. As a result of decoding the speech signal, the automated system can output one or several best recognition hypotheses of the said phrase. The final solution for choosing the recognition hypothesis is made by maximizing the probabilities of generating hypotheses obtained in signal analysis.

The AVSR system processes acoustical and visual observations in parallel, and it has to weight the informativity of one speech modality over the other. In standard CHMMs, it is made by setting audio and video stream weights and using them as exponents of the observation probabilities. However, we suppose that some phoneme and viseme models may be more reliable than others in varying environment and their contribution to the overall recognition performance may be bigger. So we propose to assign individual modality significance weights to each phoneme-viseme model. In this case, the observation probabilities in hidden states of HMMs are calculated as:

$$P(O_t|\lambda_{avunit}) = \prod_{s\in\{A,V\}} P(O_t^s|\lambda_{avunit})^{\gamma_{avunit}^s}$$

where O_t is the audio-visual observation vector at time t, whereas O_t^s represents the observation vector of one (audio or visual) stream s at time t, λ_{avunit} represents HMM parameters of a particular viseme-phoneme model, and γ_{avunit}^s means the significance weight of visual/audio stream for the given AV speech unit model.

For experimental research, we are collecting an audio-visual Russian speech database. According to our preliminary results the bimodal speech recognition that fuses both audio and visual modalities allows increasing the accuracy (word recognition rate) with respect to unimodal audio- or video-based speech recognition systems, especially in noisy conditions. In our future research, the developed multimodal ASR system will be a part of the universal assistive information technology [18, 19].

4 Conclusion

In the paper, we have presented the new bimodal speech recognition technique that fuses audio and visual information for the Russian speech recognition. We have proposed the general architecture of the automatic system for bimodal recognition of audio-visual speech; it uses the stationary microphone Oktava and the high-speed camera JAI Pulnix to get audio and video signals. We have also described the architecture of the developed software for audio-visual speech database recording, phonemic and visemic structures of the Russian language, as well as the probabilistic models of audio-visual speech units based on Coupled Hidden Markov Models and equivalent 2-stream Hidden Markov Models. For the experimental research, we have collected a part of the audio-visual Russian speech database. According to our preliminary results the bimodal speech recognition that fuses both audio and visual modalities allows improving the word recognition rate with respect to unimodal audio- or video-based speech recognition systems, especially in noisy conditions.

Acknowledgements. This research is financially supported by the Ministry of Education and Science of the Russian Federation, agreement № 14.616.21.0056 (reference RFME-FI61615X0056), project "Research and development of audio-visual speech recognition system based on a microphone and a high-speed camera", as well as by the Czech Ministry of Education, Youth and Sports, project № LO1506.

References

1. Karpov, A., Markov, K., Kipyatkova, I., Vazhenina, D., Ronzhin, A.: Large vocabulary Russian speech recognition using syntactico-statistical language modeling. Speech Commun. **56**(1), 213–228 (2014)
2. Besacier, L., Barnard, E., Karpov, A., Schultz, T.: Automatic speech recognition for under-resourced languages: A survey. Speech Commun. **56**(1), 85–100 (2014)
3. Katsaggelos, A., Bahaadini, S., Molina, R.: Audio-visual fusion: challenges and new technologies. Proc. IEEE **103**(9), 1635–1653 (2015)
4. Stewart, D., Seymour, R., Pass, A., Ming, J.: Robust audio-visual speech recognition under noisy audio-video conditions. IEEE Trans. Cybern. **44**(2), 175–184 (2014)
5. Noda, K., Yamaguchi, Y., Nakadai, K., Okuno, H., Ogata, T.: Audio-visual speech recognition using deep learning. Appl. Intell. **42**, 722–737 (2015)
6. Deng, L., Li, X.: Machine learning paradigms for speech recognition: an overview. IEEE Transa. Audio Speech Lang. Process. **21**(5), 1060–1089 (2013)
7. Young, S., et al.: The HTK Book (for HTK Version 3.4). Cambridge University Press, Cambridge (2006)
8. Kaehler, A., Bradsky, G.: Learning OpenCV 3. O'Reilly Media, California (2015)
9. Viola, P., Jones, M.: Rapid object detection using a boosted cascade of simple features. In: Proceedings of the IEEE International Conference on Computer Vision and Pattern Recognition CVPR-2001, USA, pp. 511–518 (2001)
10. Liang, L., Liu, X., Zhao, Y., Pi, X., Nefian, A.: Speaker independent audio-visual continuous speech recognition. In: Proceedings of the International Conferenceon Multimedia and Expo ICME 2002, Lausanne, Switzerland, pp. 25–28 (2002)
11. Castrillyn, M., Deniz, O., Hernandez, D., Lorenzo, J.: A comparison of face and facial feature detectors based on the Viola-Jones general object detection framework. Mach. Vis. Appl. **22**(3), 481–494 (2011)
12. Nefian, A.V., Liang, L.H., Pi, X., Xiaoxiang, X., Mao, C., Murphy, K.: A coupled HMM for audio-visual speech recognition. In: Proceedings of the International Conference ICASSP-2002, Orlando, USA, pp. 2013–2016 (2002)
13. Karpov, A.A.: An automatic multimodal speech recognition system with audio and video information. Autom. Remote Control **75**(12), 2190–2200 (2014)
14. Karpov, A., Kipyatkova, I., Železný, M.: A framework for recording audio-visual speech corpora with a microphone and a high-speed camera. In: Ronzhin, A., Potapova, R., Delic, V. (eds.) SPECOM 2014. LNCS, vol. 8773, pp. 50–57. Springer, Heidelberg (2014)
15. Chu, S.M., Huang, T.S.: Multi-modal sensory fusion with application to audio-visual speech recognition. In: Proceedings of the Multi-Modal Speech Recognition Workshop-2002, Greensboro, USA (2002)
16. Karpov, A., Ronzhin, A., Markov, K., Zelezny, M.: Viseme-dependent weight optimization for CHMM-based audio-visual speech recognition. In: Proceedings of the International Conference, INTERSPEECH-2010, ISCA Association, Makuhari, Japan, pp. 2678–2681 (2010)
17. Benesty, J., Sondhi, M., Huang, Y., et al.: Springer Handbook of Speech Processing. Springer, New York (2008)

18. Karpov, A., Ronzhin, A.: A universal assistive technology with multimodal input and multimedia output interfaces. In: Stephanidis, C., Antona, M. (eds.) UAHCI 2014, Part I. LNCS, vol. 8513, pp. 369–378. Springer, Heidelberg (2014)

19. Karpov, A., Ronzhin, A., Kipyatkova, I.: Automatic analysis of speech and acoustic events for ambient assisted living. In: Antona, M., Stephanidis, C. (eds.) UAHCI 2015. LNCS, vol. 9176, pp. 455–463. Springer, Heidelberg (2015)

Towards Enhancing Force-Input Interaction by Visual-Auditory Feedback as an Introduction of First Use

Akemi Kobayashi[1(✉)], Ryosuke Aoki[1], Norimichi Kitagawa[2],
Toshitaka Kimura[2], Youichi Takashima[1], and Tomohiro Yamada[1]

[1] NTT Service Evolution Laboratories,
Nippon Telegraph and Telephone Corporation, 1-1 Hikarinooka,
Yokosuka, Kanagawa, Japan
{kobayashi.akemi,aoki.ryosuke,takashima.youichi,
yamada.tomohiro}@lab.ntt.co.jp
[2] NTT Communication Science Laboratories,
Nippon Telegraph and Telephone Corporation,
3-1 Morinosato Wakamiya, Atsugi, Kanagawa, Japan
{kitagawa.norimichi,kimura.toshitaka}@lab.ntt.co.jp

Abstract. Force-input interfaces are now attracting research interest and feedback schemes that yield high accurate operation are being investigated. Extrinsic feedback can help the user to operate a device with high accuracy and/or efficiency. However, for learning force control, the effectiveness of multimodal augmented feedback has not been investigated enough. This paper focuses on foam objects for learning force control and describes an experiment conducted to verify the effectiveness of augmented visual and auditory feedback. In the experiment, participants apply pushing force (using their thumb) to a foam cube under different augmented feedback conditions: (1) visual feedback, (2) auditory feedback and (3) visual-auditory feedback. Training and retention tests are conducted. The results show that just five minutes of practice similar to playing a musical instrument can enhance force reproduction skills and make subsequent force inputs more accurate.

Keywords: Force-input · Motor learning · Visual-auditory feedback and anticipate force control

1 Introduction

There are various force-input devices and force-input operation has been gradually become common with the adoption of touch-input panels. Recent research results include augmented feedback [1,2] and force-input interaction on foam objects [3,4], and the field of force-input interaction continues to be developed. However, force control remains more difficult to learn than position or velocity control. This is because force control, unlike position/velocity control, relies mainly on somatic feedback with only slight visual/auditory feedback.

© Springer International Publishing Switzerland 2016
M. Kurosu (Ed.): HCI 2016, Part II, LNCS 9732, pp. 180–191, 2016.
DOI: 10.1007/978-3-319-39516-6_17

The understanding is that augmented feedback will help users to operate devices with high accuracy and/or efficiency, e.g. visual feedback helps text input. Many studies use augmented feedback to enhance manipulation capability, but an unwanted side effect is that users come to rely too much on augmented feedback, especially with augmented visual feedback [5]. A familiar example is touch typing. In initial training, visual feedback (looking at the keyboard) helps users to develop skill in typing, but then it hinders the acquisition of true touch-typing skill. On the other hand, study [5] showed that learning based on auditory feedback allows users to learn to perform equally well with or without feedback. Recent work examined the effectiveness of some kind of multimodal augmented feedback [6], and this work focuses on the effect of augmented visual-auditory feedback in learning how to control force.

The aim of this paper is to introduce a method that supports users when initially learning how to use force-input devices. We examine what kind of feedback best enhances the learning of force-input interaction in terms of motor skills. In this paper, we focus on the acquisition of learning force control, not operation, and investigate the learning effect of augmented feedback. Once users learn to operate a device without feedback, they will operate the device more rapidly with reduced user burden, like eyes-free operation. For force-input operation, learning to operate devices without feedback means to acquire anticipatory force control. As rapid learning is more effective, long practice times bother users, our case study examines if short-term visual-auditory feedback training can promote the acquisition of highly accurate force control without feedback.

We conduct an experiment in which participants applied pushing force (using their thumb) to a foam cube under different augmented feedback conditions: (1) visual feedback, (2) auditory feedback and (3) visual-auditory feedback; the feedback provides an experience similar to playing a musical instrument. The experiment uses eight levels of pushing force, and we examine how accurately the subjects could produce the levels of pushing force under each feedback condition. We tested whether the performance enhancement achieved with feedback remained in the absence of the feedback. The results confirmed that augmented visual-auditory feedback was more effective for learning pushing force control than just augmented visual or auditory feedback in isolation.

2 Related Works

2.1 Force-Input Interaction

There are various force-input devices and several studies have examined force-input interaction. Force-input interaction can be used as an alternative to touch-input and a supplement to enhance existing input interaction. Several different approaches to augmented feedback have been investigated. Study [7] conducted experiments to examine levels of pressure that users could easily discriminate with visual feedback given target selection task by varying a stylus' pressure. Study [2] introduced force-input that gives the feeling of being pressed and study [8] showed how to enrich the representation methods. However, these feedback studies focused on improving input operation. Our intention is to achieve the situation in which users can use force control without augmented feedback, and so we focus on the effectiveness of feedback-based learning.

Recently, force-input interaction on foam objects has been researched and methods for interacting through foam objects attached to smart phones [3], or cushions [4] have been developed. This paper focuses on foam objects. Foam objects allow users to better feel finger resistance and help users to learn force control. In fact, they are also used for rehabilitation for force control.

2.2   Motor Learning and Augmented Feedback

Motor skills have the aspects of both feedback control and feed-forward control. In feedback control, real-time feedback is used to control the present motion. In feed-forward control, an initial command is sent to the muscle (internal proprioceptive) to effect the push, and feedback information is used to raise the accuracy of the next motion, not the present motion. Rapid motion control and anticipatory motion control are components of feed-forward control. Effective anticipatory motion control reduces the user's burden, and so we focus on feed-forward force control.

To improve the accuracy of feed-forward motion control, it is necessary to develop a better internal model, and inverse models are to be preferred. The understanding is that good inverse models are constructed through feedback error learning [9], and providing accurate sensory feedback information leads to the acquisition of high accuracy motion control. Many researchers have investigated the effects of augmented feedback, also known as extrinsic feedback in motor learning [10]. In general, augmented feedback has been shown to be highly effective.

Study [5] focused on learning for a wrist bimanual coordination pattern and their results show that people who use augmented visual feedback become dependent on it; accuracy is high only if the feedback is provided, whereas the auditory feedback group performed equally well with or without feedback. Recent work has examined the effectiveness of some kind of multimodal augmented feedback. On the other hand, real time continuous feedback has been shown to degrade time control learning [11,12]. It is thought that some types of feedback create dependencies rather than skills. Thus, feedback design considering feedback timing and kinds of feedback is important.

2.3   Force Control and Augmented Feedback

In force control, given a target value, the trajectory reaches an extreme value (called peak value hereafter), and thereafter approaches the target value. It is thought that the peak value reflects the degree of anticipatory force control and the convergent period reflects feedback force control. As to pushing force control, study [12] showed that continuous visual feedback degraded the accuracy of force control, except after a peak value. Study [13] focused on the effects of auditory feedback for prolonged force control, manual and oral force. However, their experiments focused on just one force level and on just visual or auditory feedback.

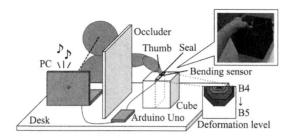

Fig. 1. Experimental layout and deformation level

We conducted an experiment to verify the effectiveness of multimodal feedback in learning pushing force control, especially anticipatory force control. In the experiment, participants were trained to produce eight levels of pushing force under three combinations of augmented feedback: (1) visual feedback, (2) auditory feedback and (3) visual-auditory feedback.

3   Experiment

3.1   Participants

Twelve adults (5 females, 7 males) aged between 23 and 36 (mean = 27) years participated. The experiment was conducted for each hand under the different augmented feedback conditions (8 persons by each feedback condition). The order of dominant hand and the order of feedback condition were counterbalanced.

3.2   Experimental System Design

Figure 1 is a schematic illustration of the experimental set-up. The experiment used a foam cube, the target of the pushing action, and a PC (MacBook Air 11 in.) controlled the augmented visual and auditory feedback. The cube had sides of 20 cm, and a bending sensor (SFESEN-08606, 4.5 in.) was attached to the middle of one face of the cube (target face). Participants were told to push the central point of the target face, which was marked by a sticker. The bending sensor was connected to an Arduino Uno connected to the PC. When the target face of the cube was pushed, the Arduino Uno captured the change in the resistance values of the sensors and sent the results to the PC, which calculated the degree of surface deformation every 100 ms. The cube and the PC were placed on a desk with an occluder (60 cm × 40 cm) between them, so that the participants could not see their hand during the experiment. The distance between middle of the cube and participants' body was 50 cm. The PC was placed 40 cm in front of the participants.

In handling or using the cube, the level of force changes with the softness of the surface, so we used the level of object deformation (captured by the bending sensor) instead of strict weight values. The right lower panel of Fig. 1

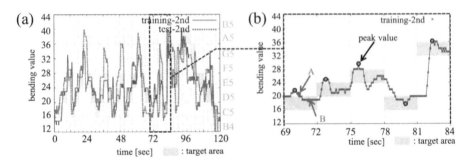

Fig. 2. (a) The blue line shows the trajectory of deformation over time at the 2nd training and the green line shows that at the 3rd test. The pink area shows the target level. When the participants controlled their force of thumb pushing appropriately, the system counted the event as a correct answer. (b) An enlargement of the area delineated by the dotted line in (a). (Color figure online)

shows simplified changes of the level of surface deformation. These changes were grouped into eight levels (B4, C5, D5, E5, F5, G5, A5, B5) called deformation levels here. The value of the feedback change depends on the value of the bending sensor deformation, which is not a linear indication of the deformation of the target surface. This is reasonable as we want to know whether users can learn new force levels, not a linear relation. The number of levels was, according to a preliminary experiment with three participants (none participated in the formal experiment), set to be neither too difficult nor too easy because we wanted to verify if participants could discriminate the level of pushing force properly.

The PC changed the feedback in a step-like manner in response to the force produced by the participants. The augmented feedback was realized by a line and bar on a visual display and/or simple tones; where height and tone indicated the deformation level (Figs. 1 and 2). Details are shown below. (1) Visual feedback: The resolution of PC display was 1366 × 768 pixels and the size of the visual display was 800 × 600 pixels. The target was presented as a black line and the present force level was presented as by a green bar (10 × 50 pixels) on the display. (2) Auditory feedback: The target and the present force level were described by sound tones. The sound signal output, a single sine-wave (frame rate = 60 Hz, portamento speed = 200 ms), was fed to the PC's speaker. B4-B5 were named after piano tones (329.63, 349.23, 392.00, 440.00, 493.88, 523.25, 587.33, 659.26 Hz). (3) Visual-auditory feedback: mixture of (1) and (2)

3.3   Experimental Procedure

In this experiment, participants were instructed to push the target surface to reach the presented target deformation level as soon as possible. During training, both the target deformation level and the present deformation level produced by the participants were given to participants. After training, participants took the retention test; only the target deformation level was given. In training, each

Table 1. Questionnaire items

Category	Question (0: I do not think so at all - 5: I really think so)
Effort	I used effort to control with this feedback combination
Ease	I felt it was easy to learn with this feedback combination

level triggered one kind of augmented feedback. Participants were instructed to push the cube with the thumb of the specified hand. The experiment was conducted for each hand under different augmented feedback combinations. Each participant followed the order of 1st training, 1st test, 2nd training, 2nd test and 3rd test on each hand. Based on recent findings on augmented visual feedback [11, 12], augmented feedback was given after the peak value was reached. To raise the effectiveness of the training, participants were told that feedback would be given only after the pushing force became stable. At the end of the experiment, participants answered the questionnaire shown in Table 1 with scores ranging from 0 to 5 (0: I do not think so at all, 5: I really think so).

Task. Each target deformation level corresponded to one tone of a melody of a well-known children's song, analogous to playing a musical instrument. This approach should make learning similar to playing a musical instrument, and thus motivate participants in performing the experiment and form an unconscious association between force and feedback, which is expected to yield more accurate force control. The target deformation level was proposed along with the melody in order, and participants were told to push the target surface with their thumb to reach the proposed level. Training and test used five target deformation levels. From the 1st training to the 2nd test, the same song "Tulip" and five target deformation levels (C5, D5, E5, G5, A5) were used; total target number was 33. From the 1st training to the 2nd test, participants were considered to learn not only the proposed 5 levels but also F5 (appears in the 3rd test) which corresponds to the gap between E5 and G5 and the level beyond A5 and level below C5 (not touched), i.e., eight levels in total. Each target deformation level was presented for 3 s regardless of the rhythm of the melody, after which the system automatically switched to the next level. The time interval was decided from the results of a preliminary experiment. Figure 2(a) shows target deformation levels and an example of surface deformation in the 2nd training and the 2nd test. Figure 2(b) shows an enlarged area of Fig. 2(a). Each test and training session took about two minutes. Through the task, participants were trained to distinguish relative force changes, not absolute force levels. To know whether participants could learn the absolute deformation level or not, participants took the 3rd test. In the 3rd test, a different song, "Bienchen Summ Herum!" and five target deformation levels (different from above, (C5, D5, E5, F5, G5)) were used and the total target number was 32.

Training. Figure 3 shows how larger surface deformation raised the height of the visual feedback bar on the display and the tone of the auditory feedback signal

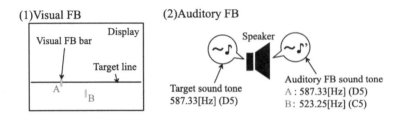

Fig. 3. The feedback modes are described, (1) Visual feedback, (2) Auditory feedback. Visual-auditory feedback is combination of (1) and (2). This exam-ple shows the feedback for data points A and B in Fig. 2(b).

during training. The target value and level produced by the participant were presented as follows. (1) Visual feedback: On the display, the target deformation level was presented as the target line and augmented feedback was shown as the height of the visual feedback bar, see Fig. 3(1). (2) Auditory feedback: From the speaker of the PC, the target deformation level was presented as a sound tone and augmented feedback was output as a sound tone, see Fig. 3(2). (3) Visual-auditory feedback: combination of (1) and (2).

Test. After training, a learning test was conducted to determine how well the participants had learned deformation level control. In this test, the target deformation level was presented in the same way as in training but no feedback was provided.

3.4   Determination of Accuracy

We used all data except the first 3 s part of songs and last 3 s parts when the same sound continued. Given a trajectory of strength of force over time, the first extreme value (peak value) reflects anticipatory force control and the following convergence region reflects feedback control [12,14] (Fig. 2(b)). We used this values in determining participant performance. We focused on the peak value mainly, and if it was inside the target deformation level (a range), we counted it as a correct response. The method of determining accuracy was informed to the participants in advance.

3.5   Result

Figure 4(i) shows the correct answer rate in training session and test and Fig. 4(ii) shows the correct answer rate in each training session and test. We did t-test with Bonferroni correction for trainings, and there was significant difference between the visual feedback and auditory feedback ($p < 0.001$) and there was significant difference between the auditory feedback and visual-auditory feedback ($p < 0.001$). In the 3rd test, ANOVA identified a marginally significant effect of feedback type ($F_{(2,18)} = 3.456$, $p = 0.0769$), no significant effect of hand used ($F_{(1,18)} = 0.402$, $p = 0.5418$), and these effects

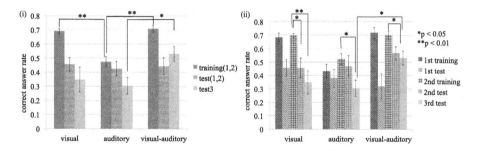

Fig. 4. (i) The correct answer rate in each training and test. (ii) The correct answer rate in training and test.

did not interact (F (2,18) = 0.675, p = 0.5329). With Bonferroni correction, there was a significant difference between auditory feedback and visual-auditory feedback (p = 0.038) and there was no significant difference between visual feedback and visual-auditory feedback (p = 0.279). For each feedback condition, we did t-tests between the 2nd training and the 2nd tests and the 3rd test. With Bonferroni correction, for visual feedback, there was a significant difference between the 2nd training and the 2nd test (p = 0.019) and there was a significant difference between the 2nd training and the 3rd test (p=0.001). For auditory feedback, there was a significant difference between the 2nd training and the 3rd test (p = 0.012) with Bonferroni correction. For visual-auditory feedback, there was a significant difference between the 2nd training and the 3rd test (p = 0.011) with Bonferroni correction. Figure 5 shows the difference in absolute value from the center value of the correct area in the 3rd test. ANOVA identified a significant effect of feedback type (F (2,381) = 19.906, p < 0.001), significant effect of hand used (F (2,381) = 26.5, p < 0.001), and these effects interacted (F (2,381) = 12.819, p < 0.001). With Bonferroni correction, on dominant hand, there was a significant difference between auditory feedback and visual-auditory feedback (p = 0.012) and there was no significant differ-

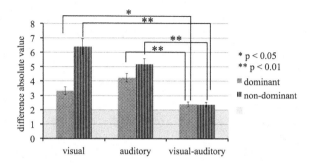

Fig. 5. The difference absolute value from the center value of a correct area in the 3rd test.

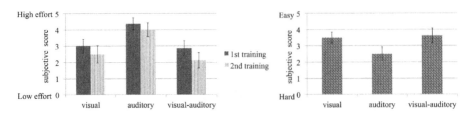

Fig. 6. The subjective score of effort of training (left). The subjective score of ease of learning (right).

ence between visual feedback and visual-auditory feedback (p < 0.001), and on non-dominant hand, there was a significant difference between auditory feedback and visual-auditory feedback (p < 0.001) and there was no significant difference between visual feedback and visual-auditory feedback (p < 0.001)

The left of Fig. 6 is the result of the subjective evaluation of burden of training and the right of Fig. 6 is the result of the subjective evaluation of ease of learning.

4   Discussions

We evaluated the learning effect of each feedback in terms of three items, (i) high correct answer rates in test (ii) small difference in correct answer rate between training and test (i.e., strong learning retention) (iii) less burden.

(i) High Correct Answer Rates in Test. To determine whether the participants could learn the deformation level independently of the task, we focus on the results of the 3rd test, which used a different song. The results show that visual-auditory feedback gives higher accuracy than auditory feedback, regardless of the order in which the changes in the pattern are presented. It is thought that visual-auditory feedback offers better training of force control than auditory feedback independently.

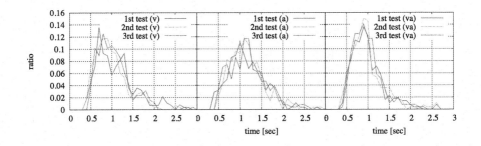

Fig. 7. The distribution of reaction time

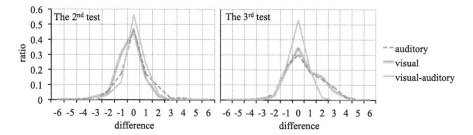

Fig. 8. The distribution of each difference from a target deformation level in the 2nd test and the 3rd test.

For more detail, Fig. 5 shows the difference in absolute value from the center value of the correct area in the 3rd test with regard to dominant hand. It shows learning proficiency with non-dominant hand with visual and auditory feedback is not sufficient, whereas with visual-auditory feedback, there is the potential for high learning proficiency regardless of dominant hand.

(ii) Strong Learning Retention. For visual feedback and auditory feedback, the correct answer rate tends to decrease from the 2nd test to the 3rd test (Fig. 4). These results show that visual feedback fails to maintain the correct answer rate, which agrees with the known characteristics of visual feedback [5]. Figure 8 shows the distribution of each difference from the target deformation level in the 2nd test and the 3rd test. In the 2nd test, all feedback types had the highest rate at zero difference (mean correct answer) and yielded sharp response curves. In the 3rd test, the sharp shape was kept only for visual-auditory feedback training. Visual and auditory feedback training yielded broad plots. This suggests that visual-auditory feedback allowed the participants to remember the deformation level with high retention rate, regardless of changes in the target pattern.

(iii) Less Burden. Subjective evaluations were made of the effort in training and the ease of learning. Figure 6 shows that auditory feedback training made participants feel more effort and less easiness compared with visual-auditory feedback and visual feedback training, and the load of auditory feedback may be mitigated if combined with visual feedback. One possible reason is that auditory information provides lower spatial resolution than visual information. Some participants answered that it was difficult to discern sound tone because their inexperience with music. This suggests that using more clearly different tones would probably enhance auditory feedback performance.

Other. Figure 7 shows the distribution of reaction time in the tests. It shows that visual and visual-auditory feedback yield response curves that are shaper and shifted more to the fast side than auditory, which leads to more stable training.

We found that F5 (which was never offered in training and was used in the 3rd test for the first time) had basically the same correct rate as the other levels. It is considered that participants could acquire the gap level without being directly trained.

The interview responses indicated that participants said that they if knew the melody, they could anticipate the next target deformation level more easily with auditory feedback and that the experience was enjoyable. This suggests that using well-known songs will not only motivate the user but also allow the user to predict the next target deformation level easily and reduce the effort needed to identify the target deformation level. This would lead users to pay more attention to control force than when randomly selected target deformation levels are used.

In the experiment, the total training time was about 5 min and the correct answer rate remained at 70 %, so proficiency is not really adequate. Moreover, few participants undertook the experiments, so we couldn't examine training effectiveness independent of individual. Future work includes more training time and more participants and clarifying the mechanism underlying the learning characteristics of each sensory modality.

Overall, the results confirm the effectiveness of visual-auditory feedback as a tool for learning how to control pushing force in short-term training. It is thought that visual-auditory feedback yields better force control during both training (due to visual feedback) and testing (due to auditory feedback) than visual feedback or auditory feedback independently.

5 Conclusion

This paper conducted an experiment to verify the effectiveness of multimodal feedback for training people to control pushing force. The experimental setup linked the degree of deformation of a foam object to visual feedback, auditory feedback, or both. Participants were told to control their pushing force and to learn the push level during training and the accuracy of level reproduction was checked in the absence of feedback. As a result, visual-auditory feedback was confirmed to be more effective than either visual feedback or auditory feedback in isolation. We can apply the results of this study to enhance the first use of force-input devices. Just five minutes of practice similar to playing a musical instrument can enhance force reproduction skill and make subsequent force inputs more accurate.

References

1. Mizobuchi, S., Terasaki, S., Keski-Jaskari, T., Nousiainen, J., Ryynanen, M., Silfverberg, M.: Making an impression: Force-controlled pen input for handheld devices. In: CHI 2005 Extended Abstracts on Human Factors in Computing Systems. pp. 1661–1664. ACM (2005)

2. Kildal, J.: 3D-press: Haptic illusion of compliance when pressing on a rigid surface. In: International Conference on Multimodal Interfaces and the Workshop on Machine Learning for Multimodal Interaction. ACM (2010)

3. Watanabe, C., Cassinelli, A., Watanabe, Y., Ishikawa, M.: Generic method for crafting deformable interfaces to physically augment smartphones. In: CHI 2014 Extended Abstracts on Human Factors in Computing Systems, pp. 1309–1314. ACM (2014)

4. Sugiura, Y., Kakehi, G., Withana, A., Lee, C., Sakamoto, D., Sugimoto, M., Igarashi, T.: Detecting shape deformation of soft objects using directional photoreflectivity measurement. In: Proceedings of the 24th Annual ACM Symposium on User Interface Software and Technology, pp. 509–516. ACM (2011)

5. Ronsse, R., Puttemans, V., Coxon, J.P., Goble, D.J., Wagemans, J., Wenderoth, N., Swinnen, S.P.: Motor learning with augmented feedback modality-dependent behavioral and neural consequences. Cerebr. Cortex 21(6), 1283–1294 (2011)

6. Sigrist, R., Rauter, G., Riener, R., Wolf, P.: Augmented visual, auditory, haptic, and multimodal feedback in motor learning: A review. Psychon. Bull. Rev. 20(1), 21–53 (2013)

7. Ramos, G., Boulos, M., Balakrishnan, R.: Pressure widgets. In: Proceedings of the SIGCHI Conference on Human Factors in Computing Systems, pp. 487–494. ACM (2004)

8. Lai, C.H., Niinimaki, M., Tahiroglu, K., Kildal, J., Ahmaniemi, T.: Perceived physicality in audio-enhanced force input. In: Proceedings of the 13th International Conference on Multimodal Interfaces, pp. 287–294. ACM (2011)

9. Kawato, M., Gomi, H.: A computational model of four regions of the cerebellum based on feedback-error learning. Biol. Cybern. 68(2), 95–103 (1992)

10. Schmidt, R.A., Wrisberg, C.A.: Motor learning and performance: A Situation-Based Learning Approach with Web Study Guide, 4th edn. Human Kinetics Publishers (2007)

11. Schmidt, R.A., Wulf, G.: Continuous concurrent feedback degrades skill learning: Implications for training and simulation. Hum. Factors 39(4), 509–525 (1997)

12. Doyo, D.: A basic study on the visual feedback in the pushing-power control training (in Japanese). Jpn J. Ergon. 42(4), 227–233 (2006)

13. Torrey, M.J.L., Ofori, E., Sosnoff, J.J.: Force control under auditory feedback: Effector differences and audiomotor memory. Percept. Mot. Skills 114(3), 915–935 (2012)

14. Potter, N.L., Kent, R.D., Lindstrom, M.J., Lazarus, J.A.C.: Power and precision grip force control in three-to-five-year-old children: velocity control precedes amplitude control in development. Exp. Brain Res. 172(2), 246–260 (2006)

Book-Like Reader: Mirroring Book Design and Navigation in an E-Book Reader

Yuto Kotajima$^{(\boxtimes)}$ and Jiro Tanaka

University of Tsukuba, Tsukuba, Japan
{kotajima,jiro}@iplab.cs.tsukuba.ac.jp

Abstract. This paper describes our design of the Book-Like Reader, an e-book reader interface that mirrors paper books. This study focuses on the characteristics of flexibility and lightweight navigation in paper books. We consider the important requirements for navigation to be the control method, the behavior of paper pages, and lightweight bookmarking. By satisfying these requirements, the user can handle an e-book intuitively like a paper book. Our reader is capable of the same user-friendly navigation as a paper book.

We have developed a prototype (as an Android application) with an Android tablet, two force sensitive resistors, and a microcomputer board. The touch display and the resistors are sufficient to detect the input. The application visualizes e-books (consisting of image files) like paper books using an OpenGL ES. Our Book-Like Reader has the aforementioned characteristics of paper books.

Keywords: Electronic book · Mobile device · User interface · Android application

1 Introduction

As portable devices (such as tablets) become increasingly widespread, electronic books are becoming increasingly popular. However, these kinds of books do not offer the same advantages as paper books, such as flexible navigation and viewing multiple documents placed side by side. These functions have an important role in reading books. This study focuses on flexibility and lightweight navigation as two of the most important characteristics of paper books. By reproducing behaviors such as flipping, lightweight bookmarking, and tactile/acoustic feedback, we aim to obtain the same user-friendly navigation of a paper book on an e-book.

2 System Design

2.1 Requirements for the User-Friendly Navigation

We believe that the factors contributing to a user-friendly navigation in paper books are the following.

© Springer International Publishing Switzerland 2016
M. Kurosu (Ed.): HCI 2016, Part II, LNCS 9732, pp. 192–200, 2016.
DOI: 10.1007/978-3-319-39516-6_18

Control Method. When reading a paper book, the reader commonly holds a book with both hands: pressing down the front of the book with the thumbs and holding the back of the book with the other fingers (Fig. 1(a)). Then, the reader flips through the book by bending it: applying pressure to the back of the book and shifting the thumb outside to the front of the book (Fig. 1(b)). The reader can control the flipping speed and the number of pages flexibly and precisely by adjusting the pressure applied and the movement of the thumb.

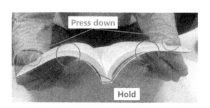
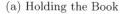
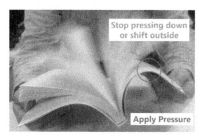

(a) Holding the Book   (b) Flipping the Book

Fig. 1. Control method of paper book

Behavior of Pages and Feedback. A lot of information can be obtained from the pages of a paper book. Flipping is accompanied by a sound as well as visual cues and sensory ones (touching/grazing the pages). The reader knows how many pages are turned judging by the thickness. Furthermore, using the same thickness, it is easy to tell how much of the book has already been read and how much is left (Fig. 2(a)). The thickness of the closed book is used as a criterion of reopening as a rule of thumb (Fig. 2(b)). All these pieces of information support flexible navigation.

Lightweight Bookmarking. A paper book can be bookmarked by putting a marker between the leaves of the book. The reader can use a variety of things as a marker, even his/her own finger (Fig. 3(a)). In addition, bookmarking and turning to a bookmarked page are very easy to achieve (Fig. 3(b)).

2.2 Design of the Book-Like Reader

We propose the Book-Like Reader as a design of an e-book reader device and application, which has the aforementioned functions for mirroring the user-friendly navigation of a paper book. We chose tablet devices as the platform because of their sufficiently large size and the many built-in sensors for reproducing a paper book. Moreover, they use stripped-down sensors that allow maintaining the characteristics of e-books, e.g., the ease of carrying many books.

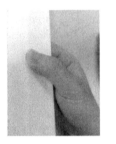 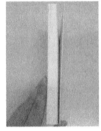  

(a) Thickness of Side Pages

(b) Thickness of Closed Book

(a) Finger Bookmark

(b) Turning to Bookmark

Fig. 2. Thickness of pages   **Fig. 3.** Lightweight bookmarking

Built-in or attached sensors are capable of detecting the input: both thumbs are shifted to the front of the device, and pressure is applied from other fingers (Fig. 4). A Book-Like Reader application loads the e-book data, then it handles the e-book through the input detected by the sensors (Fig. 5).

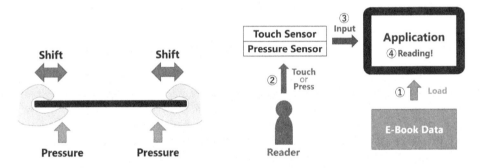

Fig. 4. Detecting input   **Fig. 5.** System flow

3   Implementation Prototype

3.1   Prototype Device and Application

The prototype of the Book-Like Reader device is shown in Fig. 6. As previously stated, as much as possible, the prototype is not equipped with additional sensors. Only two force sensitive resistors are attached to the back of the device. The sensors convey the detected values to the device through the Arduino board with a USB OTG host cable.

The prototype of the Book-Like Reader software is implemented as an Android application; the detected data are processed using this application. In this prototype, the e-book data format loaded by the application is restricted to a set of image files compressed into a zip file.

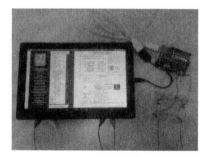

(a) Device Connected to Arduino   (b) Back of Device, Equipped with Two Force Sensitive Resistors

Fig. 6. Prototype device

3.2   Detecting Input Method

Just like when bending a paper book, the Book-Like Reader is controlled by shifting both thumbs to the front of the device and by applying pressure with other fingers. The input from the front of the device can be detected using the touch display to detect these actions with the tablet. The input from the back is detected by two force sensitive resistors (because the tablet does not have pressure sensors on the back) (Fig. 7). The e-book reader is controlled according to these detected values.

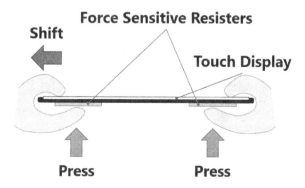

Fig. 7. Detecting input

An example of the relationship between the values measured by these force sensitive resistors and the user's behavior is shown in Fig. 8. The value measured by both sensors is clearly different, depending on whether the user performs no action, holds the device, or presses the back of the device. These states can be differentiated according to whether the sensor values are higher or lower than the threshold: 50 or 400. In addition, when the user taps the sensor twice, the values repeat the transition from high to low values.

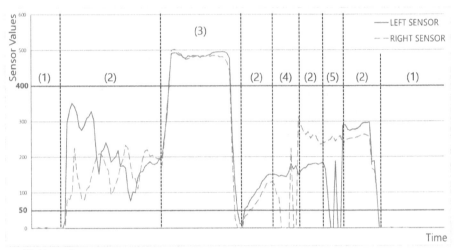

(1) No action
(2) Hold the device
(3) Press back of the device
(4) Double tap the right sensor
(5) Double tap the left sensor

Fig. 8. Pressure values and related action

3.3 Visualizing Similar to a Paper Book

On the assumption that the user handles the tablet device with horizontal orientation, the Book-Like Reader displays two pages at once, like an opened paper book (Fig. 9). This e-book is rendered by using an open source application, android_page_curl [1], which creates a page curl and flip effect using OpenGL ES [2]. The page images are loaded before being shown. Due to the issue of the device's memory capacity, the application keeps some nearby pages, which are resized to fit into the display.

(a) Displaying Two Pages   (b) Curl Effect

Fig. 9. Application screenshot

Visualizing the Book Thickness. We developed a function to visualize the thickness of the e-book, similar to a paper book. When both sensors on the back of the device are pressed over a specified value (Fig. 10(a)), the contents area becomes narrow, and the thickness of the e-book is visualized on both sides on the display (Fig. 10(b)). This thickness is drawn at a fixed width to leave enough space to show the contents. The number of pages is indicated by the depth of gradation in the background and by the number of drawn vertical lines in the visualized thickness area.

When both thumbs are swiped towards the center of the display (Fig. 10(c)), the thickness of the closed e-book is visualized (Fig. 10(d)). It is possible to turn to the selected page by tapping the thickness.

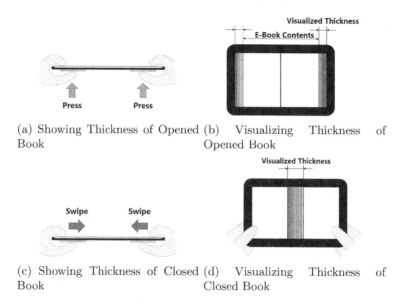

(a) Showing Thickness of Opened Book

(b) Visualizing Thickness of Opened Book

(c) Showing Thickness of Closed Book

(d) Visualizing Thickness of Closed Book

Fig. 10. Visualizing E-book thickness

Continuous Flipping Animation and Feedback. The Book-Like Reader performs flipping animation and gives feedback to the user when the two sensors are pressed over a given threshold and when one of the thumbs is swiped towards the outside of the display (Fig. 11(a)). The user is given feedback through vibration of the device and sound (Fig. 11(b)). Keeping the state that the thumb was shifted, the user can continue flipping. The flipping speed and the number of pages correspond to the detected sensor values.

However, the application can render animation for only one page; thus, it cannot turn pages as fast as those of a paper book.

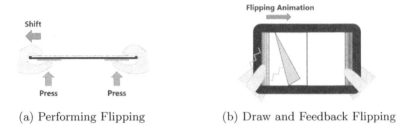

(a) Performing Flipping   (b) Draw and Feedback Flipping

Fig. 11. Flipping pages like those in paper books

3.4 Lightweight Bookmarking

Similar to a paper book, the Book-Like Reader can bookmark and enable turning to the bookmarked page with a simple action. The user can bookmark by
tapping either force sensitive resistor twice. Moreover, the user can return to
the bookmarked page by releasing the finger that tapped the sensor. As shown
in Fig. 8, when the user taps the sensor twice, the values measured by either
of the force sensitive resistors changes from a low value to a high value twice
successively. The application remembers the page where this transition of the
values was detected. Then, it returns to the page by using the decrease in the
values as a trigger.

4   Related Work

4.1 Natural Interaction with a Physical Object Like Paper

Some studies obtained natural interaction like paper books using a physical
object as an interface of digital content. The Listen Reader and Sequence Book
consist of a paper book with RFID tags embedded in each page [3,4]. Watanabe
et al. developed an interface consisting of two thin plastic sheets for browsing
content [5]. Fujita et al. proposed a novel book-shaped device for flipbooks,
embodying some physical features and e-book interactivity [6]. These studies
can give users a natural interface and can offer the advantages of paper books.
However, many books cannot be carried as easily as portable devices can.

4.2 Obtaining Characteristics Using Additional Devices

Several studies obtained characteristics of paper books on portable devices using
additional sensors or devices. Chen et al. designed a dual-display e-book reader,
which supports embodied interactions like paper books [7]. TouchMark [8] introduced physical tabs on each side of the device to enable gestures such as page
thumbing and bookmarking. Izawa et al. proposed Flip Interface, which obtained
flipping using two flip sensors that consist of multiple film-like capacitive sensors
[9]. These studies offer natural interaction easily. However, they only ensure a
part of the characteristics.

4.3   Expansions of E-Books

There are several studies in which the e-book readers are capable of interacting naturally, in the same way as paper books. Yoon et al. introduced Touch-Bookmark, a lightweight technique for E-books [10]. To use this technique, users can bookmark and turn pages to do simple finger gestures on a touch screen. Kim et al. designed a novel touchscreen interaction technique for lightweight navigation; it enables consecutive flipping to do a bezel gesture on a tablet [11]. These studies enable lightweight navigation only with a tablet device. However, these techniques cannot be controlled as intuitively as paper books.

Our work has solved the aforementioned problems. However, the interface described in this study is not as natural as those that use a physical interface.

5   Conclusions

We developed a prototype of an e-book reader called Book-Like Reader, which obtains the same user-friendly navigation of a paper book using a tablet device and a few sensors. Our Book-Like Reader behaves like a paper book, and users can interact with it in a similar way. However, some characteristics of paper books have not been achieved, like quick navigation. In future work, we intend to improve the application behavior to make it more similar to paper books and more user-friendly. In addition, we intend to enhance our application so that it can handle major e-book formats, like epub.

References

1. android_page_curl. https://github.com/harism/android_page_curl/
2. OpenGL ES. https://www.khronos.org/opengles/
3. Back, M., Cohen, J., Gold, R., Harrison, S., Minneman, S.: Listen reader: An electronically augmented paper-based book. In: Proceedings of the SIGCHI Conference on Human Factors in Computing Systems, CHI 2001, pp. 23–29. ACM, New York (2001)
4. Yamada, H.: Sequencebook: Interactive paper book capable of changing the storylines by shuffling pages. In: CHI 2010 Extended Abstracts on Human Factors in Computing Systems, CHI EA 2010, pp. 4375–4380. ACM, New York (2010)
5. Watanabe, J., Mochizuki, A., Horry, Y.: Bookisheet: Bendable device for browsing content using the metaphor of leafing through the pages. In: Proceedings of the 10th International Conference on Ubiquitous Computing, UbiComp 2008, pp. 360–369. ACM, New York (2008)
6. Fujita, K., Itoh, Y., Kidokoro, H.: Paranga: An electronic flipbook that reproduces riffling interaction. Int. J. Creat. Interaces Comput. Graph. 4(1), 21–34 (2013)
7. Chen, N., Guimbretiere, F., Dixon, M., Lewis, C., Agrawala, M.: Navigation techniques for dual-display e-book readers. In: Proceedings of the SIGCHI Conference on Human Factors in Computing Systems, CHI 2008, pp. 1779–1788. ACM, New York (2008)

8. Wightman, D., Ginn, T., Vertegaal, R.: Touchmark: Flexible document naviga- tion and bookmarking techniques for e-book readers. In: Proceedings of Graphics Interface 2010, GI 2010. pp. 241–244. Canadian Information Processing Society, Toronto, Ont., Canada (2010)
9. Izawa, K., Suzuki, N., Akabane, K., Yamakawa, H., Maruyama, J., Aikawa, T., Kubomoto, R., Sibayama, F., Takenaka, H., Kobayashi, S.: A proposal of new inter- actions with directly-manipulable 'mekuri' interface. In: IPSJ Interaction 2011, pp. 123–130, (2011). in Japanese
10. Yoon, D., Cho, Y., Yeom, K., Park, J.H.: Touch-bookmark: A lightweight navi- gation and bookmarking technique for e-books. In: CHI 2011 Extended Abstracts on Human Factors in Computing Systems, CHI EA 11, pp. 1189–1194. ACM, New York (2011)
11. Kim, S., Kim, J., Lee, S.: Bezel-flipper: Design of a light-weight flipping interface for e-books. In: CHI 2013 Extended Abstracts on Human Factors in Computing Systems, CHI EA 2013, pp. 1719–1724. ACM, New York (2013)

Temporal and Spatial Design of Explanations in a Multimodal System

Florian Nothdurft[1]([⊠]), Frank Honold[2], and Wolfgang Minker[1]

[1] Institute of Communications Engineering, Ulm University, Ulm, Germany
{florian.nothdurft,wolfgang.minker}@uni-ulm.de
[2] Institute of Media Informatics, Ulm University, Ulm, Germany
frank.honold@uni-ulm.de
https://www.uni-ulm.de/in/nt/research/ds.html
https://www.uni-ulm.de/in/mi.html

Abstract. Modern dialog systems are known to act user-specific. They apply individual decisions for content presentation and course adaptation. However, it is still an open research question how additional, but required explanations should be integrated best into a given dialog structure. Previous research focused on the improvement of user knowledge models and its fine-grained use in human-computer interaction, but does not directly address the temporal and spatial aspects of presentation when it comes to explanations. In this paper, we introduce different strategies for an ad-hoc integration of required explanations. We describe a user study, and show which parameters from the fields of user experience, personality, and cognitive load theory have what effects on the applied strategies. We expect that our findings can help to increase usability and decrease unwanted cognitive load.

Keywords: Dialog · Adaption · Multimodal · Explanation · HCI

1 Introduction

Modern dialog systems evolve from simple task solvers into intelligent assistants that are able to assist the user in a variety of challenging tasks. These are, for example, *Companion*-Systems, which are "continually available, co-operative, reliable and trustworthy assistants which adapt to a user's capabilities, preferences, requirements, and current needs" [14]. However, because of the increasing capabilities and functionalities of these systems, they also become increasingly complex to operate, and less intelligible for the user. One of the main reasons for this is that the interaction between human and dialog system may exceed the users' knowledge, or capabilities. Hence, such systems should adapt its content and course of interaction to the user's knowledge. One of the most important means of this undertaking are explanations. Explanations can be used, for example, to clarify concepts, provide information on how to perform a task, or justify decision-making. Therefore, they are vital and appropriate instruments

© Springer International Publishing Switzerland 2016
M. Kurosu (Ed.): HCI 2016, Part II, LNCS 9732, pp. 201–210, 2016.
DOI: 10.1007/978-3-319-39516-6_19

for adapting a dialog to the user. Previous research, e. g., in the field of *intelligent tutoring* [1], or *expert systems* [9], focused on the improvement of user knowledge models and its fine-grained use in human-computer interaction (HCI) (e. g., in [4,5,10]).

However, not only the modelling and appropriate selection of knowledge is important, but also how it is presented to the user. If knowledge needs to be imparted, several factors influence how pleasant and effective this will be for the user. Future cooperative *Companion*-Systems behave as interactive peers, which support their users in arbitrary decision making processes of their daily lives. Therefore, here we describe how temporal and spatial distances of providing explanations relative to a selection task in a cooperative decision-making process affect the user experience (UX). We aimed at gathering insights into how different users assess the different variants based on their individual sensation to help to derive layout criteria, select appropriate media types, and structure the dialog in future cooperative *Companion*-Systems. This vision of cooperative systems comes with two implications that are of interest in this paper.

2   Demo System and Scenario

Since the application domain of such systems is not specified but universal, their implementation cannot be realized in an all-embracing manner. Therefore, as the first implication, such systems will act as multimodal interpreters (almost like today's web browsers). They will render the desired user interface (UI) in a model-driven manner. That is why we apply a model-driven prototypical *Companion*-System system [3,7] for our study, which automatically generates a multimodal UI as described in [8].

The aspect of universal application leads to the second implication. Such systems shall be able to provide dynamically-generated explanations whenever they are of need [2,12]. Since complex issues can be explained more convenient with the use of pictures, we use multi-media explanations that consist of text and pictures. Based on that, we focus on the challenging situations, in which an extensive explanation in combination with the underlying selection may exceed the size of the screen. The realization of such an UI would either result in a wizard-like sequence of multiple screens (explanations plus selection) or in one, but scrollabel UI (see Fig. 1), hence varying the spatial and temporal distances between explanation and selection task. As baseline condition we also assessed UX during a selection task without explanations, to compare it to the various conditions.

In this scenario the user's task was to create individual strength training workouts using said prototype. In each strength training workout at least three different muscle groups had to be trained and exercises chosen accordingly. The user was guided through the process by the system, which provided a selection of exercises for training each specific muscle group necessary for the workout. The user was assisted during these selection tasks using the following conditions, which are explained in the following.

3   Methodology

For this evaluation, the temporal and spatial distance of explanations relative to a selection task were varied. The following conditions were implemented (see Fig. 1) and tested:

Joint Explanations beforehand (JE-B) showed collectively all respective explanations temporally prior to the upcoming selection. This means that *one* additional dialog step was created to present *all* explanations at once. As a result of the limited space the explanations were text-only.

Seperate Explanations beforehand (SE-B) showed all respective explanations separately prior to the upcoming selection. Thus, for *every* explanation, a *separate* dialog step was created that presented the explanation, as text and picture, temporally before the upcoming selection.

Joint Explanations during (JE-D) showed collectively *all* explanations plus the related selection within the same dialog, meaning that during the selection, the necessary explanations could be easily accessed and seen by the user. However, as a result of the limited space the explanations were text-only.

No Explanations (NE) acted as the baseline. In known fashion, the user was confronted with a selection with no prior help by additional explanations. However, the users could still manually request explanations via an additional explicit user interaction. In these cases, the selection dialog was hidden and the requested explanation was shown instead of the selection (as in SE-B). After a user-given confirmation, the former selection dialog was presented; again without any additional explanation.

These four settings allow to vary the temporal distance (i. e., before or during the selection), as well as the spatial distance (i. e., separately, jointly, or only on request) between the explanations and the related selection.

After cleaning the data (e. g., because of incomplete questionnaires) a total of 72 participants were used for the analysis. The participants were distributed through a random-function to the variants, resulting in 18 participants for the baseline condition NE, 28 for JE-D, 13 for SE-B, and another 13 for JE-B.

For measuring UX and other interesting aspects, different standardized and validated questionnaires were used. The *AttrakDiff* questionnaire [6] allows to assess dialog systems or software in general. Its items range from the limited view of usability, representing mostly pragmatic qualities, to the integration of scales measuring hedonic qualities, and the attractiveness in general. *Cognitive load* comprises of three types of load: intrinsic, extraneous, and germane. Therefore, we included an experimental questionnaire developed by Klepsch and Seufert [11] that measures all three types of cognitive loads separately. In addition, the analysis of the *big five personality traits* (Big 5) provides insights in broad dimensions of human personality, using the BFI-K [13].

We expect differences for the AttrakDiff questionnaire in general. The various conditions and the limitation of the content should have some effect on the

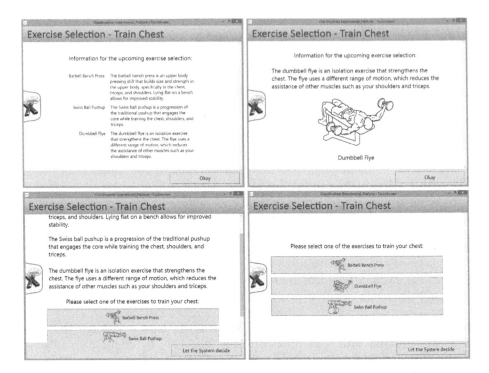

Fig. 1. The conditions. On the *top-left*, the explanations are presented jointly before the selection (JE-B); on the *top-right*, the SE-B condition showed all respective explanations separately prior to the upcoming selection; on the *bottom-left*, the explanations are presented jointly during the selection (JE-D); and on the *bottom-right*, the baseline condition, the user was confronted with a selection with no prior, proactively provided, help by additional explanations.

perceived attractiveness of the system; especially in terms of presented modalities when presenting collective explanations. We expect the joint explanations (JE-B/D) to perform worse than the separate explanations (SE-B) because the SE-B condition might leave sufficient space to also present a picture of the exercise. However, we expect the separate presentation to lead to a higher cognitive load, compared with presenting no proactive explanations at all, because the system behaviour is different than before. Providing explanations during the selection (JE-D) is expected to perform worst because of the sheer amount of content presented in one dialog step, including the limitation that not all content is visible without scrolling.

4   Results

AttrakDiff. The AttrakDiff questionnaire is based on oppositional word pairs (see Fig. 2). There were statistically significant differences between the groups (despite the low number of participants for some conditions) as determined by one-way ANOVA for *ugly—attractive* ($F(3, 68) = 5.714, p = .005$), and marginal significance for *unpleasant—pleasant* ($F(3, 68) = 4.299, p = .071$).

Post hoc comparisons, using the Fisher LSD test, revealed for *ugly—attractive* that the JE-B condition ($M = 3.15, SD = 1.34$) performed significantly worse ($p = .028$) than providing no explanations (NE) ($M = 4.05, SD = 1.16$), significantly worse ($p = .000$) than SE-B ($M = 4.77, SD = .92$), and also significantly worse ($p = .040$) than providing explanations during the selection screen (JE-D) ($M = 3.92, SD = 1.01$). Providing explanations on separate screens prior to the selection (SE-B) was also rated significantly more attractive ($p = .026$) than explaining during the selection (JE-D), and marginally significant better ($p = .080$) than showing no additional explanations (NE), thus performing best overall. For the word pair *unpleasant—pleasant* the post hoc tests showed that providing separate explanations beforehand ($M = 4.84, SD = 1.21$) was perceived significantly better ($p = .010$) than providing them jointly beforehand (JE-B) ($M = 3.46, SD = 1.45$), as well as marginal significant better ($p = .061$) than providing the explanations jointly during the selection (JE-D) ($M = 4.00, SD = 1.27$).

Additionally, we found that for *cautious—bold*, providing no proactive explanations ($M = 3.611, SD = 1.09$) performed significantly worse ($p = .025$) than providing explanations separately beforehand (SE-B) ($M = 4.38, SD = .96$). For the word pair *discouraging—motivating*, no explanations ($M = 4.00, SD = 1.23$) performed as well significantly worse ($p = .029$) than the SE-B condition ($M = 4.92, SD = .95$).

Cognitive Load. For measured cognitive load, statistically significant results were found between the groups for *general cognitive load* ($F(3, 97) = 7.979$, $p = .001$), assessed classically by one item, and for *difficulty* of the task ($F(3, 97) = 7.419, p = .004$).

Post-hoc comparisons, to find the origin of significant differences, using Fisher's LSD, showed that the *general cognitive load* was the lowest when providing no explanations (NE) ($M = 1.61, SD = .63$). It was significantly lower ($p = .000$) than the JE-B condition ($M = 2.94, SD = 1.61$), significantly lower ($p = .003$) than the SE-B condition ($M = 2.70, SD = 1.38$), and marginal lower ($p = .072$) than providing the explanations during the selection (JE-D) ($M = 2.16, SD = 1.08$). For the perceived *difficulty* of the task the results are similar. The NE condition ($M = 1.57, SD = .80$) performed best, with a significantly lower perceived difficulty ($p = .002$) than separate explanations (SE-B) ($M = 2.80, SD = 1.39$), significantly lower ($p = .003$) than joint explanations beforehand (JE-B) ($M = 2.73, SD = 1.36$), and significantly lower ($p = .041$) than explaining during the selection (JE-D) ($M = 2.25, SD = 1.38$). However, for *germane load*, which is a good type of load, because it measures that the participants are willing to put effort into creating a schema, presenting no explanations (NE) ($M = 3.14, SD = 1.44$) performed significantly worse ($p = .046$) than joint explanations beforehand (JE-B) ($M = 4.20, SD = 1.38$), and marginal worse ($p = .079$) than separate explanations beforehand(SE-B) ($M = 4.07, SD = 1.49$).

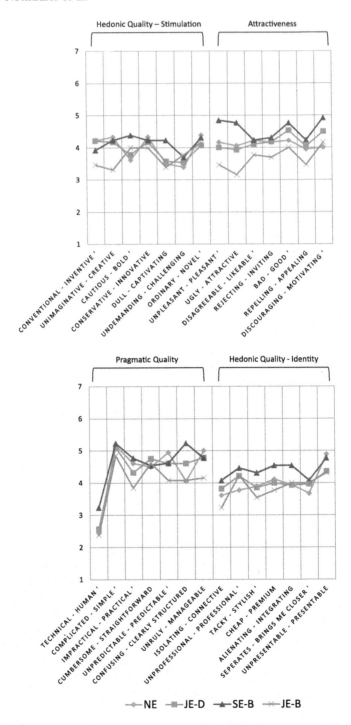

Fig. 2. Average means of the AttrakDiff comparing the explanation conditions on a seven-point Likert scale. The apostrophe (') indicates inverted scales, in the interest of readability.

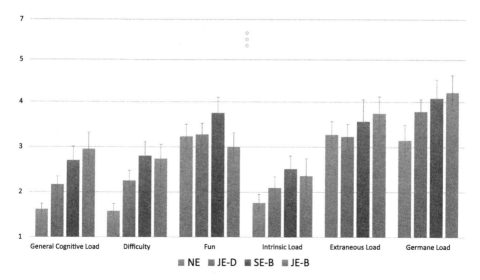

Fig. 3. Average means of the Cognitive Load comparing the explanation conditions on a seven-point Likert scale.

Big 5 Personality Traits. Analysing the Big 5 Personality Traits question-naire, and its relationship with the other instruments, we found several condition-dependent correlations, using a Pearson correlation test.

For the condition of presenting the explanations jointly during the selection, a significant positive correlation between *Extraversion* and *unpleasant—pleasant* ($r = .400, n = 28, p = .035$) was found. For the Big 5 dimension of *Agreeableness* significant positive correlations with the word pairs *unpresentable—presentable* ($r = .458, n = 28, p = .014$), and *conventional—inventive* ($r = .466, n = 28, p = .012$) were indicated by the data.

For the average means of the participants receiving the explanations sepa-rately before the selection, positive correlations between *Extraversion* and the AttrakDiff dimension *Hedonic Quality—Identity* ($r = .699, n = 13, p = .008$), with the dimension of *Hedonic Quality—Stimulation* ($r = .605, n = 13, p = .029$), and with the dimension of *Attractiveness* ($r = .586, n = 13, p = .035$) were found in the data. Besides positive correlations between *Extraversion* and some of the corresponding word pairs of the significant correlating dimensions, also a positive correlation was found with the word pair *technical—human* ($r = .563, n = 13, p = .045$).

For the Big 5 dimension of *Agreeableness* a negative correlation was found with the AttrakDiff dimension *Hedonic Quality—Identity*, $r = -.566$, $n = 13, p = .044$. This negative correlation originates from the negative correla-tion in the word pairs *unprofessional—professional* ($r = -.633, n = 13, p = .020$) and *tacky—stylish* ($r = -.645, n = 13, p = .017$). Additionally, also a negative correlation was found with *ugly—attractive*, $r = -.606, n = 13, p = .028$.

For the Big 5 dimension of *Openess to Experience* there were positive correlations with *conventional—inventive* ($r = .582, n = 13, p = .037$), and *conservative—innovative* ($r = .625, n = 13, p = .022$).

When presenting the explanations jointly in one dialog before the selection, there were negative correlations between *Neuroticism* and the AttrakDif dimensions *Hedonic Quality—Identity* ($r = -.742, n = 13, p = .004$) and *Attractiveness* ($r = -.607, n = 13, p = .028$). Additionally, negative correlations were found between *Neuroticism* and the word pairs *unpredictable—predictable* ($r = -.769, n = 13, p = .002$), and *confusing—clearly structured* ($r = -.701, n = 13, p = .008$), both belonging to the *Pragmatic Quality* of the system.

5 Discussion

The data indicates that providing explanations separately before presenting the selection itself (SE-B) performs best. This is perceived particularly more attractive than providing them jointly in advance, but also better than jointly during decision-making. Naturally, this can be attributed to the fact that separate explanations allow for a graphical representation of the exercise, unlike joint explanation conditions. Therefore, we do not think that separating explanations is always the recommended method, but it can be used in cases where the presentation form is limited by the amount of content. The graph in Fig. 2 represents the average mean values of the word pairs. It shows that the condition that presents the explanations separately performs mostly best or as well as the others. However, we think that at least some of these effects can be attributed to the automatically generated layout of the presentation. Comparing the conditions of joint explanations, which only differ in their temporal distance to the selection, and not the modalities, the presentation during the selection performs better. This variation is perceived as more practicable, manageable, connective, or motivating. We think that this can be attributed to the fact that a direct connection between the explanations and decision-making, in the form of the selection, can be made.

The cognitive load (see Fig. 3) is, as expected, the lowest when no additional explanation is provided because this is the system behaviour with which the participants are familiar. However, this also results in the lowest germane load compared with the other conditions. The general cognitive load is modest for the condition that presents explanations during the selection, performing second best. Because most of the other dimensions measure cognitive load (i. e., difficulty, fun, intrinsic load, extraneous load), they are also at least second best (to no explanation); from this perspective, presenting explanations during the selection seems to be the best option when explanations are needed.

In addition, Personality traits seem to have an impact on system perception, as well. We found several correlations between the Big 5 Personality Traits and other measurements. However, it is always important to mention that correlation does not imply causation. When presenting explanations separately in advance, more extraverted persons tend to affiliate higher hedonic qualities and attractiveness to the system compared with not so extraverted individuals, because for all of these dimensions, a significant positive correlation between *Extraversion* and the respective dimensions can be found. Extraverted persons, who are sociable, outgoing, and positive, seem to enjoy this variation with included graphical representations. In addition, for the dimension of *Agreeableness*, which relates on the positive side to more cooperative, trustful, and compassionate people, there is a positive correlation for the dimension of *Hedonic Quality—Identity*. Hence, people with higher agreeableness tend to have a higher perceived identity with the system in this condition, attributed by characteristics such as *connective* or *integrating*. The correlations indicate that presenting the explanations separately in advance seems to be more suitable for extraverted persons.

Contrary to that, we found especially strong negative correlations for the Big 5 dimension of *Neuroticism* in the condition of presenting the explanations jointly in advance. There are negative correlations between *Neuroticism* and *Hedonic Quality—Identity* and *Attractiveness*. Hence, participants with a higher neuroticism score generally perceive the system as less attractive and could identify less with the system. For the other conditions, no correlations to *Neuroticism* could be found, leaving potentially the difference in using graphical representations, and not the joint presentation, as one of the probable reasons for these correlations.

6   Conclusion

The results show that providing explanations separately in advance makes sense when the amount of content would impair the presentation form. However, if a convenient method for presenting the explanation content on the same dialog is possible without impairing the modality choice, for example, this is the best option. We were able to show that both temporal and spatial distances of the presentation of explanations relative to decision-making (i. e., the selection) influence user experience. If these strategies shall be applied in a purely model-driven UI process, additional attributes have to be added, marking these respective items as explanation. Such an attribute can be used to influence the automatic temporal and spatial layout processes, in order to achieve the desired effects. In addition, by analysing the existent correlations, we show that extraverted participants seem to profit from the presentation of graphics, whereas neurotic persons seem to suffer from a low quality of explanation dialogs because for the jointly, only-textual, presentation, neuroticism correlated negatively with the perceived system attractiveness and hedonic system qualities (especially the identification dimension).

Acknowledgement. This work was supported by the Transregional Collaborative Research Centre SFB/TRR 62 "Companion-Technology for Cognitive Technical Systems" which is funded by the German Research Foundation (DFG).

References

1. Anderson, J., Boyle, C., Reiser, B.: Intelligent tutoring systems. Science **228**, 456–462 (1985)

2. Behnke, G., Ponomaryov, D., Schiller, M., Bercher, P., Nothdurft, F., Glimm, B., Biundo, S.: Coherence across components in cognitive systems - one ontology to rule them all. In: Proceedings of the 25th International Joint Conference on Artificial Intelligence (IJCAI 2015). AAAI Press (2015)

3. Bercher, P., Richter, F., Hörnle, T., Geier, T., Höller, D., Behnke, G., Nothdurft, F., Honold, F., Minker, W., Weber, M., Biundo, S.: A planning-based assistance system for setting up a home theater. In: Proceedings of the 29th National Conference on Artificial Intelligence (AAAI 2015), pp. 4264–4265. AAAI Press (2015)

4. Brusilovsky, P., Millán, E.: User models for adaptive hypermedia and adaptive educational systems. In: Brusilovsky, P., Kobsa, A., Nejdl, W. (eds.) Adaptive Web 2007. LNCS, vol. 4321, pp. 3–53. Springer, Heidelberg (2007). http://dl.acm.org/citation.cfm?id=1768197.1768199

5. Fischer, G.: User modeling in human–computer interaction. User Model. User-Adap. Inter. **11**(1–2), 65–86 (2001)

6. Hassenzahl, M., Burmester, M., Koller, F.: AttrakDiff: Ein Fragebogen zur Messung wahrgenommener hedonischer und pragmatischer Qualität. In: Szwillus, G., Ziegler, J. (eds.) Mensch & Computer 2003: Interaktion in Bewegung, pp. 187–196. B. G. Teubner, Stuttgart (2003)

7. Honold, F., Bercher, P., Richter, F., Nothdurft, F., Geier, T., Barth, R., Hoernle, T., Schüssel, F., Reuter, S., Rau, M., Bertrand, G., Seegebarth, B., Kurzok, P., Schattenberg, B., Minker, W., Weber, M., Biundo, S.: Companion-technology: Towards user- and situation-adaptive functionality of technical systems. In: 10th International Conference on Intelligent Environments (IE 2014), pp. 378–381. IEEE (2014)

8. Honold, F., Schüssel, F., Weber, M.: Adaptive probabilistic fission for multimodal systems. In: Proceedings of the 24th Australian Computer-Human Interaction Conference, OzCHI 2012, pp. 222–231. ACM, New York, 26–30 November 2012

9. Jackson, P.: Introduction to Expert Systems, 2nd edn. Addison-Wesley Longman Publishing Co., Inc., Boston (1990)

10. Jokinen, K., Kanto, K.: User expertise modelling and adaptivity in a speech-based e-mail system. In: Proceedings of the 42nd Annual Meeting on Association for Computational Linguistics, p. 87. Association for Computational Linguistics (2004)

11. Klepsch, M., F.W., Seufert, T.: Differentiated measurement of cognitive load: Possible or not? (2015, in press)

12. Nothdurft, F., Minker, W.: Using multimodal resources for explanation approaches in technical systems. In: Proceedings of the 8th Conference on International Language Resources and Evaluation (LREC 2012), pp. 411–415 (2012)

13. Rammstedt, B., John, O.P.: Short version of the 'Big Five Inventory' (BFI-K). Diagnostica : Zeitschrift für psychologische Diagnostik und differentielle Psychologie **4**, 195–206 (2005)

14. Wendemuth, A., Biundo, S.: A companion technology for cognitive technical systems. In: Esposito, A., Esposito, A.M., Vinciarelli, A., Hoffmann, R., Müller, V.C. (eds.) COST 2012. LNCS, vol. 7403, pp. 89–103. Springer, Heidelberg (2012)

Automatic Facial Recognition: A Systematic Review on the Problem of Light Variation

Kelvin S. Prado[1], Norton T. Roman[1(✉)], Valdinei F. Silva[1],
João L. Bernardes Jr.[1], Luciano A. Digiampietri[1], Enrique M. Ortega[2],
Clodoaldo A.M. Lima[1], Luis M.V. Cura[3], and Marcelo M. Antunes[2]

[1] University of São Paulo, São Paulo, SP, Brazil
`norton@usp.br`
[2] Central Kung-Fu Academy, Campinas, SP, Brazil
[3] Campo Limpo Paulista Faculty, Campo Limpo Paulista, SP, Brazil

Abstract. In this systematic review we approach the problem of light variation in tasks related to automatic facial recognition, a feature that can significantly affect the performance of automatic systems. We then carry out a broad research on the state of the art, describing and comparing current research in this subject. The review relies on a set of processes for searching, analysing and describing research that is considered relevant to this work, and which are reported in more detail in this article. In analysing the results, we could notice that the problem of light variation is still one of the greatest challenges in the area of facial recognition, which translates in a good deal of research directly tackling this problem, trying to solve it or, at least, mitigate it somehow, so as to improve the performance of facial recognition techniques and algorithms. Finally, results also show that this is a problem of great concern by researchers in the field, insomuch that even those articles that do not directly deal with it still make explicit the researchers' concern about it.

1 Introduction

The ability to promptly recognise faces is something people automatically do in their everyday lives [12]. Despite the apparent lack of effort in doing so, the amount of processing people actually do make such a process a hard task for a computer to perform. Part of this difficulty is due to the fact that this is a multifaceted problem, where one has not only to deal with pose variations, but also image resolution and light variation.

With current computers' computational power and low cost, the interest in the automatic processing of images and graphical videos has increased, with practical applications in the most varied areas of human knowledge. Existing systems for facial recognition usually operate in either of two ways [12]:

1. Face verification or authentication, which consists in a one-to-one comparison where some face in a database is compared to the face to which authentication is required; or

M. Kurosu (Ed.): HCI 2016, Part II, LNCS 9732, pp. 211–221, 2016.
DOI: 10.1007/978-3-319-39516-6_20

2. Face identification or recognition, which consists in a one-to-many comparison where some image is matched against all images in a data base, so as to determine the identity of the consulted face.

In uncontrolled environments, where there mainly is a significant amount of pose and light variation, along with constant movement, automatic facial recognition systems still finds a whole lot of challenges that can significantly affect their performance. Such challenges may be found in some literature reviews already made in the field (e.g. [7,19,21,22]). These, however, usually focus on aspects such as pose variation and image resolution, amongst others, either in video or in static pictures, with very little reference, if any, to light variation in video recordings.

As a feature, light variation plays a paramount role in the task of identifying the person or object under examination and, more specifically, the task of face recognition, for changes in the light level may affect other features, such as perceived colour and shape (by adding shadows to the image, for instance). As a result, it comes as no surprise that light variation may drastically affect the performance of facial recognition systems [1].

Hence, and to help fill in this gap, in this article we present a systematic literature review we carried out on this subject. Our main goal with this review was to build a broad picture of the current state of the art in techniques used to approach the problem of light variation in video, when applied to automatic face recognition, by seeking and comparing work that deal either directly or indirectly with this problem. Our aim, with this review, is to contribute to future work in this area, by saving research time which can be directed to the search for solutions for other more specific issues.

To do so, we start out by describing the procedure we followed in our review, from the initial exploratory searches to the analysis of the final results. We also describe the steps in defining the review protocol and the decisions we had to make along the way. Executed during the month of May 2015, the review was conducted over the IEEE and ACM databases, resulting in a total of 104 articles, of which only 24 remained after the selection/rejection criteria were applied.

As it turned out, the problem of light variation is reported as one of the greatest challenges in the area of automatic facial recognition. Interestingly, although over 60 % of the articles do recognise light variation to be an important feature, not all of them approach the problem in a direct way. Some, in fact, limit themselves to acknowledging its importance, but with no practical proposal for its solution.

Still, many of them try to directly approach the problem. From these, we have set up a list of explored techniques, along with statistics about their popularity amongst the reported researches. As it turned out, Viola Jones and Principal Component Analysis are the most popular methods, from a total of seven different approaches we found.

Through this systematic review, we could determine that the problem of light variation is one of great concern for researchers in the area, and which is still an open question. With this effort, we hope to help other researchers in the field to approach this problem not only by summing up the major techniques their peers are currently using, but also by presenting it in the form of a reproducible systematic review, thereby allowing for comparisons to be significantly made with other existing or forthcoming related work.

The rest of this article is organised as follows. Section 2 describes the steps followed in this systematic review, from the starting exploratory search to the conduction of the review itself. Results are then presented in Sect. 3, whereas in Sect. 4 we make a discussion of the main findings, pointing out some challenges in the field. Finally, Sect. 5 concludes this work, also presenting some limitations of the current research.

2 Materials and Methods

According to Mian et al. [15], a systematic review is a scientific methodology that goes beyond a simple overview of the state of the art about some subject. It is an actual research capable of identifying, selecting and producing data related to some specific topic, which can also be used to identify gaps in the current state of knowledge. Differently from a simple literature review, then, a systematic review consists in a logical sequence of processes that can be reproduced by other researchers. Figure 1 illustrates the steps taken in our review. In what follows, we will describe these processes, as we move along them in our research.

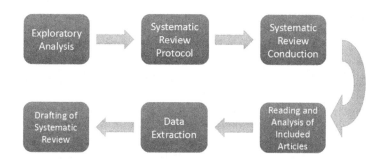

Fig. 1. Processes' flow in the systematic review.

2.1 Exploratory Search and Review Protocol

The first step we took in this research was to identify which data bases would be sought for research articles and which terms should build the search string for these bases. The chosen bases were IEEE Xplore[1] e ACM Portal[2], given their size and focus on the area of Computer Science.

---

[1] http://ieeexplore.ieee.org.
[2] http://dl.acm.org/.

The bases were then searched using some terms related to the field. From this initial search, we could characterise the review protocol, whose main goal is to put in details how the systematic review will be conducted, serving as a guide throughout the review process. As such, the protocol covers, amongst other things, research goals, keywords used in the search, along with criteria for adding and excluding articles in the research corpus. In our research, the research protocol comprises:

- *Research goal*: To determine the state of the art in the area of automatic image processing, more specifically the problem of facial recognition, focusing in uncontrolled environments with light variation.
- *Research question*: "What are the main techniques used for facial recognition in uncontrolled environments with light variation?".
- *Sources*: ACM Portal and IEEE Xplore.
- *Keywords*: Image processing, face recognition, face detection, face tracking, multiple object recognition, low resolution, surveillance camera, illumination invariance, pose invariant, person recognition.
- *Criteria for inclusion*: Should be considered relevant articles which (a) describe techniques for facial recognition; (b) define image processing and facial recognition concepts; (c) are related to facial recognition in real-life uncontrolled environments with light variation; and (d) deal with facial recognition using low-resolution cameras.
- *Criteria for exclusion*: Should be excluded from the set of retrieved articles those (a) not related to facial recognition; (b) using facial recognition techniques, but in controlled environments where, for example, high resolution cameras are used or there is good light; (c) presenting shallow evaluations, without giving details about the methods and techniques investigated; (d) using 3D models for facial recognition; (e) which did not undergo a peer-reviewed evaluation process; and (f) not dealing with the problem of light variation.
- *Criteria for primary study quality*: As a quality criteria for the investigated primary studies we defined the assessment of the techniques reported in the article and their relevance to this review's goal.
- *Selection of primary studies*: Primary studies were queried in the data bases using search strings build from the keywords defined in this protocol. These strings should be used in the search engines of the data bases defined in this protocol, during the execution of the review.
- *Assessment of the primary studies quality*: We selected only articles that satisfied one or more criteria for inclusion. If an article satisfies criteria both for inclusion and exclusion, it must be read entirely to decide for its inclusion or exclusion.
- *Information extraction strategy*: Articles should be first analysed by reading their titles, abstracts and, whenever necessary, conclusions.
- *Results summarisation*: From the selected articles we extracted the reported techniques, variables and final results. With this information it would be possible to determine the main advantages of the applied techniques, as well as to identify existing gaps in the current state of the art.

2.2   Review Conduction and Data Extraction

The review itself consisted in searching the data bases using the search strings built from the keywords defined in the review protocol. Searches were made in May 2015 and, for each database, we had a different search string, better suited to the base's search engine. The strings used in each data base were:

- ACM Portal: ((face recognition OR face detection OR face tracking OR person recognition) AND (low resolution OR surveillance camera) AND (illumination invariance OR pose invariant))
- IEEE Xplore: ("face recognition" OR "face detection") AND ("low resolution" OR "surveillance camera" OR "illumination invariance" OR "pose invariant")

The search in ACM returned 77 articles, of which only 10 satisfied the criteria for inclusion. Over IEEE the search retrieved a total of 27 articles, with one duplicated (in comparison to ACM) and six satisfying the criteria for inclusion. When reading the articles, another one was excluded for reporting a literature review (*i.e.* a secondary study). As a result, we ended up with 15 articles considered relevant to our research. These 15 articles were then read in their entirety, in the search for information such as the research contributions, applied techniques, approached variables and results found.

3   Results

From the extracted data, we could notice that the problem of light variation is real and a relevant one for the process of facial recognition, for it is present in all of the articles found in our research. Figure 2 illustrates this result, along with the main variables found in the 15 included articles.

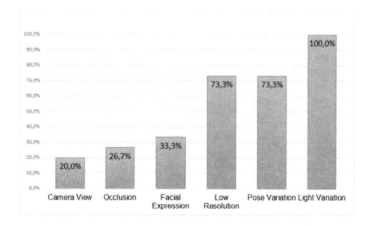

Fig. 2. Main variables found in the research.

Articles that passed the criteria for inclusion may be divided in two sets: those reporting research that directly deals with the problem of light variation and those that deal with it indirectly. In the first group, we find the research by Arandjelovic and Cipolla [2], who deal with the role colours play in automatic facial recognition. In their work, the authors claim that light variation is the most challenging aspect of this task, for different light may drastically change the performance of automatic systems. The way they found to overcome this problem was to exclude non-informative regions of the image, that is, pixels whose luminosity was lower than 3 % or higher than 97 % of the maximum luminosity in the image, thereby removing those pixels with greater light variation. For the face detection, the authors used Principal Component Analysis and the Viola-Jones algorithm.

Another approach tried by the same authors was to propose an algorithm for "reillumination" [4] that takes two image sequences as input and outputs a synthetic sequence, with the same poses of the first sequence, combined with the illumination of the second. Using Viola-Jones to detect faces and the proposed "reillumination" algorithm, the authors have improved facial recognition accuracy. This algorithm was also tested along with Probabilistic Principal Component Analysis (PPCA), in another article by the same authors [6]. In yet another work [3], they present two approaches based on generative models (illumination cones and 3D morphable model) for light variation in images, also proposing the use of Gamma Intensity Correction (GIC) to compensate for bright variation, along with a normalization of the light subspace to mitigate the problem of light variation.

Alternatively, Arandjelovic, Hammoud and Cipolla [5] approach the difficulty facial recognition algorithms have to deal with pose contrast and light variation by relying on thermal images. As a resource, these images have the desired characteristic of being almost insensitive to light variation. On the other hand, there is a loss of facial information that could be relevant to the recognition process. The authors then propose the fusion of both visual and thermal images which, according to their tests, raised the facial recognition accuracy up to 97 % in a test set with great light variation.

Following a similar path, Heo, Savvides and Vijayakumar [11] also propose the use of thermal images and correlation filters, especially in images with light variation and low resolution. Results showed that correlation filters improved the face recognition performance in low resolution images, both when dealing with visual and thermal ones. When comparing them, face recognition with thermal images outperformed the test on the visual ones under light variation and facial expression variation conditions, despite the loss of relevant facial information that thermal images present when compared to visual ones.

A different approach to mitigate the light variation problem is proposed by Wang and Li [17]. In their work, they focus on eliminating the effect that uneven light has on faces. To do so, they propose a new way to classify illumination orientation, and then compensate or eliminate its variation. Since this procedure reduces the quality of the image, they also propose an image fusion rule. Throughout their work, different techniques were tested, such as Lambert Illumination Model and PCA, amongst others.

Also relying on methods to compensate for light variation, Bicego et al. [9] propose to use not only nose, eyes and mouth as characteristic areas for facial recognition, but also the space around them. This approach conceptually differs from others, which rely on specific parts of the face only. With a mean error rate around 10.93 %, the authors claim this to be a feasible alternative, compared to other state of the art methods. Finally, to mitigate the problem of light and pose variation, occultation and low resolution, Mishra and Subban [16] examine a fusion strategy based in skin shade segmentation and highlight for face detection. The authors work in a YCbCr orthogonal colour space, since the superposition between skin and non-skin regions is small. Results were significantly good, with the additional advantage of this being a simple and low complexity approach.

Amongst the articles that deal with the problem of light variation indirectly, that is those that usually limit themselves to presenting the problem as a challenge or to showing that their methods are robust in such conditions, we find the work by Bedagkar-Gala and Shah [8], which deal with the problem of reidentification based on facial characteristics and colours, in a multi-camera environment. In this case, the authors point out that light variation is an important variable that should not be set aside, for even regions with greater variation contribute to improve their model. Still in the realm of reidentification, Bak et al. [10] approach it in a camera network environment which, by itself, implies a good deal of light variation, along with pose variation and occultation. The authors show that by normalising the covariance matrix, they managed to absorb rotation and light variations.

Louis, Plataniotis and Ro [14], in turn, propose a face detector that combines results from two classifiers. The authors try out different algorithms such as Viola-Jones, AdaBoost and GentleBoost, amongst others. The system was tested by artificially adding noise, with one of them being light variation (from -100 % to +100 %). Even in the presence of such noise, their detector proved capable of dealing with great light variation, outperforming Lienhart's detector. Louis and Plataniotis [13] also integrate two types of Local Binary Pattern (LBP) characteristics for the same task. Here, they used a Circular LBP, which targets the pixels in the image, and a Histogram LBP, in which whole regions are the target. According to their results, LBP has proved capable of dealing with the problem of light variation.

Alternatively, Wang et al. [18] introduce an incremental learning approach for video-based facial recognition. Through their "visual words" algorithm, sequences of images of faces are clustered according to their descriptors. Representative images are then extracted from each cluster. With these images' descriptors, the algorithm builds a "code book". A voting algorithm is then used to determine the face identity in the video. The authors claim that their approach is robust even under pose, light and facial expression change conditions. Used algorithms were Adaboost, Camshift and Viola-Jones, amongst others.

Finally, Wang, Miao and Zhang [20] propose a framework for the extraction of low resolution facial images in video sequences under light variation, which uses a skin detection algorithm in each frame of the sequence to help on the face detection task. Although citing the problem of light variation, the authors did not try to solve or extenuate it.

4   Discussion

As the results illustrate, the problem of light variation is still an open one, severely affecting the automatic recognition of faces. Given its complexity, however, not all of the retrieved articles deal with this question directly, despite the fact that all of them take this problem to be relevant. As a workaround, some researchers constrain their work to thermal images only, which are not sensitive to light variation. The drawback to this approach, however, is the loss of relevant facial information, such as colour for example, which might be relevant to the performance of the recogniser.

Another approach taken by researchers is to try to mitigate the problem, by running a "reillumination" algorithm, in order to normalise the light in the image. In our review, the main strategies we found to tackle, mitigate, or even move around this problem are:

- Use of thermal images;
- Exclusion of "non-informative" pixels, that is those with greater light variation;
- Light compensation and/or generalisation;
- Use of "reillumination" algorithms;
- Use of colours to improve the performance of grey-scale based algorithms;
- Use of methods for skin detection in images.

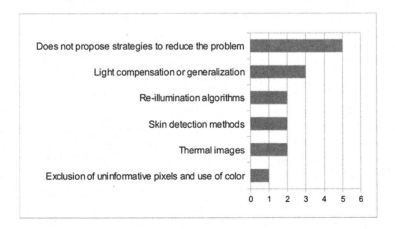

Fig. 3. Strategies adopted in the retrieved articles (and number of articles applying them).

Figure 3 shows the number of articles adopting each of the strategies, while Fig. 4 presents the main algorithms used for facial recognition. As can be seen, the preferred technique for facial recognition is Principal Component Analysis (PCA) and its variations, followed by Viola-Jones algorithm. Besides being very popular in the area, both seem to outperform other state-of-the-art techniques. Along with these, other algorithms are also found, and new ones are proposed.

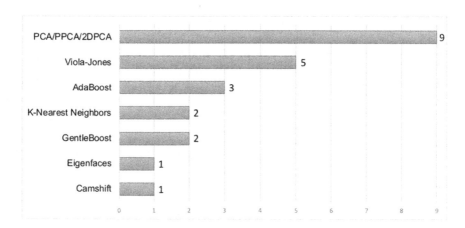

Fig. 4. Main algorithms applied to automatic facial recognition (and number of articles using them).

5 Conclusion

In this article we presented the results of a systematic review we carried out in the field of automatic face recognition, in an attempt to identify how the sub-problem of light variation is being approached by current research. Besides presenting a snapshot of the current state of the art in the field, results showed the main techniques and algorithms used both to tackle this problem, or to avoid it (or even to diminish its influence).

We understand this work to be useful for researchers who are willing to enter the field, or to students who want to learn more about it. As a limitation of our work, we cite the focus on two data bases only (IEEE and ACM). However useful and trustworthy, there can be found other data bases, which might be searched for a broader view on the subject.

References

1. Adini, Y., Moses, Y., Ullman, S.: Face recognition: The problem of compensating for changes in illumination direction. Pattern Anal. Mach. Intell. IEEE Trans. **19**(7), 721–732 (1997)

2. Arandjelovi, O., Cipolla, R.: Colour invariants for machine face recognition. In: 8th IEEE International Conference on Automatic Face Gesture Recognition, FG 2008, pp. 1–8, September 2008

3. Arandjelovi, O., Cipolla, R.: A pose-wise linear illumination manifold model for face recognition using video. Comput. Vis. Image Underst. **113**(1), 113–125 (2009). http://dx.doi.org/10.1016/j.cviu.2008.07.010

4. Arandjelovi, O., Cipolla, R.: Achieving robust face recognition from video by combining a weak photometric model and a learnt generic face invariant. Pattern Recogn. **46**(1), 9–23 (2013). http://dx.doi.org/10.1016/j.patcog.2012.06.024

5. Arandjelovi, O., Hammoud, R., Cipolla, R.: Thermal and reflectance based personal identification methodology under variable illumination. Pattern Recogn. **43**(5), 1801–1813 (2010). http://dx.doi.org/10.1016/j.patcog.2009.11.023

6. Arandjelović, O., Cipolla, R.: Face recognition from video using the generic shape-illumination manifold. In: Leonardis, A., Bischof, H., Pinz, A. (eds.) ECCV 2006. LNCS, vol. 3954, pp. 27–40. Springer, Heidelberg (2006)

7. Barr, J.R., Bowyer, K.W., Flynn, P.J., Biswas, S.: Face recognition from video: A review. Int. J. Pattern Recogn. Artif. Intell. **26**(05), 1266002 (2012)

8. Bedagkar-Gala, A., Shah, S.K.: Part-based Spatio-temporal Model for Multi-person Re-identification. Pattern Recogn. Lett. **33**(14), 1908–1915 (2012). http://dx.doi.org/10.1016/j.patrec.2011.09.005

9. Bicego, M., Grosso, E., Lagorio, A., Brelstaff, G., Brodo, L., Tistarelli, M.: Distinctiveness of faces: a computational approach. ACM Trans. Appl. Percept. **5**(2), 11:1–11:18 (2008). http://doi.acm.org/10.1145/1279920.1279925

10. Bk, S., CorvE, E., BrMond, F., Thonnat, M.: Boosted human re-identification using riemannian manifolds. Image Visi. Comput. **30**(6–7), 443–452 (2012). http://dx.doi.org/10.1016/j.imavis.2011.08.008

11. Heo, J., Savvides, M., VijayaKumar, B.: Performance evaluation of face recognition using visual and thermal imagery with advanced correlation filters. In: IEEE Computer Society Conference on Computer Vision and Pattern Recognition - Workshops, 2005. CVPR Workshops, p. 9, June 2005

12. Jain, A.K., Li, S.Z.: Handbook of face recognition, vol. 1. Springer, Heidelberg (2005)

13. Louis, W., Plataniotis, K.: Frontal face detection for surveillance purposes using dual Local Binary Patterns features. In: 2010 17th IEEE International Conference on Image Processing (ICIP), pp. 3809–3812, September 2010

14. Louis, W., Plataniotis, K., Ro, Y.M.: Enhanced weakly trained frontal face detector for surveillance purposes. In: 2010 IEEE International Conference on Fuzzy Systems (FUZZ). pp. 1–8, Jul 2010

15. Mian, P., Conte, T., Natali, A., Biolchini, J., Travassos, G.: A systematic review process for software engineering. In: Proceedings of the 2nd Experimental Software Engineering Latin American Workshop (ESELAW 2005), Brazil (2005)

16. Mishra, R., Subban, R.: Face detection for video summary using enhancement-based fusion strategy under varying illumination conditions. In: 2014 International Conference on Science Engineering and Management Research (ICSEMR), pp. 1–8, November 2014

17. Wang, C., Li, Y.: Combine image quality fusion and illumination compensation for video-based face recognition. Neurocomput **73**(7–9), 1478–1490 (2010). http://dx.doi.org/10.1016/j.neucom.2009.11.010

18. Wang, C., Wang, Y., Zhang, Z., Wang, Y.: Incremental learning patch-based bag of facial words representation for face recognition in videos. Multimedia Tools Appl. **72**(3), 2439–2467 (2014). http://dx.doi.org/10.1007/s11042-013-1562-1

19. Wang, Z., Miao, Z., Wu, Q.J., Wan, Y., Tang, Z.: Low-resolution face recognition: a review. Vis. Comput. **30**(4), 359–386 (2014)
20. Wang, Z., Miao, Z., Zhang, C.: Extraction of high-resolution face image from low-resolution and variant illumination video sequences. In: Congress on Image and Signal Processing, CISP 2008. vol. 4, pp. 97–101. IEEE (2008)
21. Zhang, X., Gao, Y.: Face recognition across pose: A review. Pattern Recogn. **42**(11), 2876–2896 (2009)
22. Zhao, W., Chellappa, R., Phillips, P.J., Rosenfeld, A.: Face recognition: a literature survey. ACM Comput. Surv. **35**(4), 399–458 (2003). http://doi.acm.org/10.1145/954339.954342

The Contribution of a Virtual Self and Vibrotactile Feedback to Walking Through Virtual Apertures

Daniel R. Mestre[1(✉)], Céphise Louison[1,2], and Fabien Ferlay[2]

[1] CNRS, Institute of Movement Sciences, Aix-Marseille University, Marseille, France
daniel.mestre@univ-amu.fr
[2] CEA, IRFM, Saint-Paul-Lez-Durance, France
{cephise.louison,fabien.ferlay}@cea.fr

Abstract. We previously demonstrated that behavioral adjustments to environmental properties constituted an objective indicator of presence in Virtual Reality (VR). The subject's task was to walk through virtual apertures of variable width. Subjects exhibited a behavioral transition, from frontal walking to body rotation, while walking from broad to narrow apertures. Here, we tested the same basic protocol, using a Head-Mounted Display (HMD). Overall, results show the same basic behavior (shoulder rotation through a narrow door). However, optimal adaptive behavior (avoiding collision with the door's borders) required both the presence of a dynamic representation of the subject's body (in the visual display) and of a vibrotactile feedback, signaling approach of the subject's shoulder towards the doorpost.

Keywords: Virtual environments · Affordance · Virtual body · Vibrotactile feedback

1 Introduction

We previously suggested that behavioral adjustments to environmental properties could be an indicator of presence in virtual environments (VE) [1]. Using Warren & Whang [2] original experimental protocol, the subject's task was to walk through a virtual aperture of variable width. In this particular affordance [3], subjects exhibited a behavioral transition, from frontal walking (for broad apertures) to body rotation (for narrow apertures). This adaptive behavior was also observed in a VE, using a CAVE setup [1]. In a CAVE, the subject sees his/her own body. This is no longer the case when s/he wears a head mounted display (HMD). This raises the question of the role of the perception of one's own body (a virtual self) during behavioral adjustments to environmental properties (here the virtual door's variable width). Our general hypothesis was that, when the subject wears a HMD, the presence of a (visual, co-localized)) virtual self favors perceptual calibration of the body/environment relationships (and the processing of body-scaled information [2]).

Another reason to test the subject's behavior while wearing a HMD is that we previously observed [4] that, when the subject's body approaches a virtual object (or worse passes through that object), this latter has a tendency to become transparent (destroying

© Springer International Publishing Switzerland 2016
M. Kurosu (Ed.): HCI 2016, Part II, LNCS 9732, pp. 222–232, 2016.
DOI: 10.1007/978-3-319-39516-6_21

the feeling of presence). This, of course, is no longer the case with a HMD (and a virtual body representation).

Furthermore, in line with recent studies, we supposed that vibrotactile feedback (signaling, in our study, that one's shoulder is approaching the (virtual) door) might also contribute to behavioral calibration. If visual rendering of virtual environments is satisfying nowadays, haptic rendering remains difficult to use, without a physical hardware (force-feedback arm and/or physical objects inside the virtual environment, constraining the subject's posture and movements). The lack of haptic feedback results in incomplete sensorial feedback, as soon as the subjects interacts with virtual objects. For example, collisions of the body with virtual objects do not typically result in proprioceptive and haptic feedback: nothing is actually there to stop the subject's movement. This deficiency might lead to a lack of user's presence in VE, and be one reason for inappropriate behavior, with respect to reality. In a recent study [4], we started investigating the effect of vibrotactile stimulation while interacting with virtual objects, and asked whether vibrotactile stimulation might act as a substitute for haptic stimulation (see also [5–7]). The general hypothesis is that vibrotactile feedback (signaling approach to- or contact with a physical surface) enhances collision awareness, and spatial perception in general.

2   Materials and Methods

2.1   Subjects

Twenty male subjects voluntarily took part in this experiment. They have been chosen in the student and university staff, with an age range between 20 and 39 years (mean = 24.15; SD = 5.1). All participants gave written informed consent prior to the study, in accordance with the 1964 Declaration of Helsinki. The study was approved by the local institutional review board (IRB) from the Institute of Movement Sciences. The logic for choosing only male subjects was the same as in [1], which is mainly a morphological reason: "In males, the body rotation while walking through an aperture is known to depend upon the shoulder width, i.e., the widest frontal body dimension. In females, the same behavior is potentially more complex since it could depend not only on the shoulder width but also on the bust size" (quoted from [1]).

Subjects were naïve as concerns the purpose of the experiment. All subjects reported normal vision and sense of touch and were free from any locomotor disorder. Their stereoscopic acuity was tested using the Randot® Graded Circles test (Stereo Optical Company Inc, Chicago, IL, USA) and their inter-pupillary distance (IPD) was measured (using the Oculus configuration utility software). IPD ranged from 61.4 to 67.8 mm (mean = 64.1; SD = 1.4), and was used to adjust stereoscopic rendering to each individual. The subjects were not selected regarding their stature. Their shoulders' width ranged from 42.5 to 51 cm (mean = 45.9; SD = 2.2) and their standing height ranged from 168 to 185 cm (mean = 177.1; SD = 5.1).

2.2 Apparatus

The experiment was conducted in a square area (3 × 3 meters), being the inside of the CAVE setup at CRVM (www.crvm.eu). Subjects were equipped with an Oculus Rift DK2 device. This HMD allows stereoscopic 3D rendering of virtual environments, with a 960 × 1080 pixels resolution per eye. It uses a combination of 3-axis gyros, accelerometers, and magnetometers, which makes it able to achieve precise absolute (relative to earth) head orientation tracking. The HMD was connected by wire to the graphics PC, running Unity software. The wire came from the top and was long enough to minimally disturb the subject's locomotion (see Fig. 1, left). The CAVE tracking system (ArtTrack®) with eight cameras, using infrared recognition of passive markers, was used to monitor the subject's translational movements, in particular the subject's head position and to update stereoscopic image relative to the subject's point of view (a configuration of markers was placed on the HMD, see Fig. 1). Additionally, the ART tracking system was used to monitor the subject's all-body position, with passive markers placed all over the subject's body (feet, legs, thighs, waist, hands, arms, forearms and shoulder), in order to record the subject's movements, and eventually connect these to a real-time and co-localized virtual representation of the subject's body (see Fig. 1, right). The real-time VR system operated at 60 Hz.

Fig. 1. *Left.* A subject in the experimental setup. He wears the HMD, equipped with an ART target for the tracking of the head's translational movements. He also wears an ART all-body capture set. *Right.* The recording of all-body movements are used to build a co-localized avatar (the subject's head was not actually represented in the experiment). The spheres' centers represent the vibrating actuators position on the subject's shoulder. Their size represents the spatial domain in which the actuators were active (that is when the subject shoulder's distance to a virtual object was inferior to their radius). See text for details.

Moreover, visual feedback (virtual environment and eventually self-avatar) could be augmented by a vibrotactile feedback. The vibrotactile device was developed previously [1]. This device is based on an Arduino-like microcontroller (ChipKit Max32™), equipped with a Bluetooth module for communicating with the PC on which the simulation was running. The controller can address up to 20 vibrators with 11 levels of amplitude (from 0 to 100 % of the amplitude), using Pulse-width modulation (PWM) and two vibration patterns (continue or discontinuous). The controller activates vibrators

(DC motor with an eccentric mass), connected by wires. The controller is powered by two rechargeable batteries (one for the board power supply and the other for the vibrators supply). In the present experiment, two actuators were used. They were positioned on the subject's shoulders (see Fig. 1, right).

The VR loop (motion capture to sensorial rendering) was controlled by a PC and a 5.1 surround sound system was used to render spatialized sound (door sliding movements). The experimental application was built with Unity3D, to allow experimental control, data recording and all scenario actions. The logical, geometrical, real-time connection between the Oculus and the ART tracking system was realized using a home-made distribution software (VRdistrib, developed by J.M. Pergandi at CRVM).

2.3 Virtual Environment

The virtual environment (VE) was designed using 3D modeling software (3DSmax®), imported into Unity3D to control the experimental scenario. The VE was composed of a small corridor, enclosed by a fence on one side and opening onto a shed on the other side (see. Figs. 2 and 3, below). There was some furniture behind the fence and in the shed, in order to provide static and dynamic depth cues. This corridor was 3 meters wide (the actual size of the physical space in the CAVE). A sliding door was positioned in the middle of the corridor (being also the middle of the physical space). The size congruence between the virtual environment and the "real" physical space was meant to enable real walking of the subject in the experiment, which appears to be an effective way to get rid of locomotion interfaces and cybersickness (and to favor presence [1]).

Fig. 2. The virtual environment (with representation of the subject crossing the aperture)

The door consisted of two mobile panels (height = 250 cm, thickness = 20 cm). It could be opened or closed by lateral translation. There were five different width apertures, ranging from 40 cm to 80 cm, with 10 cm steps (40, 50, 60, 70, 80 cm). A rattle spatialized sound was associated with the closing and opening movements of the door. Two dark-gray disks/

marks were positioned on the floor, 1 m from the door on each side. These disks were used to indicate departure and arrival points.

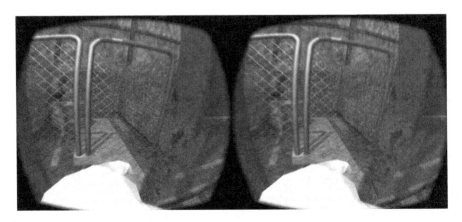

Fig. 3. Subjective view inside the HMD (with representation of the virtual body). The reader may see the 3D scene by cross-fusing both images.

2.4   Procedure

Each subject was first received in a meeting room, where the experimenter read the instructions. The subject's stereoscopic acuity was tested and he was asked to fill a questionnaire about his susceptibility to motion sickness (Motion Sickness Suscepti- bility Questionnaire Short-form [8]). This procedure was used to reject subjects who had significant motion sickness symptoms during transportation in real life, to prevent potential cybersickness. Once a subject was recruited for the study, his shoulders' width was measured with an anthropometric device from the tip of the left humerus to the right humerus, with the shoulder relaxed. His interpupillary distance was measured, using the Oculus Rift Configuration Utility. This value was used to calibrate stereoscopic rendering of the VE.

The subject was equipped with tracking markers and with the vibrotactile device. The two vibrotactile actuators were placed on the tip of the left and right humerus. Once equipped, the subject was taken to the experimentation area and equipped with the head- mounted display. The initial VE was displayed with the door completely open and an avatar in a T pose at the doorstep. Different calibration and configuration steps were made. The initial Oculus field of vision was calibrated to match the tracking system reference. The Bluetooth connection between the PC and the vibrotactile device was established and tested.

The Avatar morphology was calibrated regarding the shoulder width and the height of the subject. Avatar calibration was performed to fit the avatar limbs with the subject limbs measured by the tracking system. At the end of this setup, the avatar was optimally co- localized with the subject's own body, reproducing the subject's movements in real-time.

The subject was next presented with a training session. He was required to walk straight from the starting point to the arrival point and to stop at this point. He was then asked to turn around and do the same thing in the other direction. The door was still fully open. During this phase, he could get familiar with the task and with his virtual body. In a second time, he experienced a short vibrotactile training session. The door was entirely closed and the subject was asked to slowly approach the door with one of his shoulders until he felt the vibrotactile feedback. He then could try the different feedback modes (see below), by getting closer or getting in contact with the door.

After these training sessions, the subject was asked to return to the starting point. The door was fully opened, and the first trial could begin. One trial consisted in the following sequence: the subject was standing on one of the marks on the floor, while the door was moving to the next aperture width. At the beep, the subject had to walk straight to the other mark, on the other side of the door. When he arrived at the mark, the door was opened. The subject had to turn around. The door was moved to the next aperture width and another trial could start in the other direction.

2.5 Experimental Conditions

There were two independent crossed variables. The first one was the type of feedback. It could be only visual or augmented with vibrotactile stimulation. Vibrotactile feedback operated as a radar (similar to those in cars). When the subject approached his shoulder from virtual object (a side of the door in our case) a discontinuous vibration was sent to the corresponding actuator. The closer the shoulder was from an object, the more intense was the vibration. If the shoulder collided the door a continuous vibration at maximum intensity was sent. The "radar" was a sphere with a radius around 10 cm, situated on each shoulder (see Fig. 1, right). This size was chosen in reference to the minimal security distance adopted by subjects in [1]. The collision detection was realized by placing a collider (simple collision detection algorithm) covering the shoulder and forearm of the avatar. The system always computed the radar and collision detection, but, depending on the feedback condition, the vibrotactile controller was activated or not. All collisions and distances to the doorpost were recorded during the experimentation. The level of amplitude of the radar was recorded from 1 to 10, 0 meaning no detection (distance between any shoulder and any doorpost superior to 10 cm) and 11 meaning collision.

The second condition was the presence (or not) of a virtual body (co-localized with the subject's body). Once again, like for collision detection, the avatar was always active in the simulation software. However, it could (or not) be present in the displayed visual scene).

2.6 Task

Subjects were simply asked to walk straight from a starting point to a target position (both marked on the floor). Each subject carried out four sessions: one for each of four conditions, resulting from the combination of two "Avatar" conditions (with and without a virtual body representation in the HMD) and two "Vibrotactile" conditions (with or without activation of the actuators).

The experimentation was interrupted by a short break between each session. During these breaks the subject could rest and had to fill a questionnaire about cybersickness (SSQ [9]). Each session consisted of 20 trials. Each trial corresponded to one of 5 aperture: 40, 50, 60, 70, 80 cm, and each aperture condition was repeated four times. Within a given session, the aperture-width succession order was randomized across subjects. The subjects were split into four groups. Subjects were randomly assigned to one group, each group having a different (pseudo-random) succession order of the four experimental conditions.

2.7   Data Recording and Analysis

During the experiment, several behavioral indicators and events were recorded. In this paper, we will focus 1) on the maximal angle of shoulder rotation while the subject was passing through the aperture, indicating a qualitatively appropriate behavior of the subject, as a function of the doors' width, and 2) on the eventual presence of a collision between one shoulder and a doorpost, which is a finer indicator of adaptive behavior.

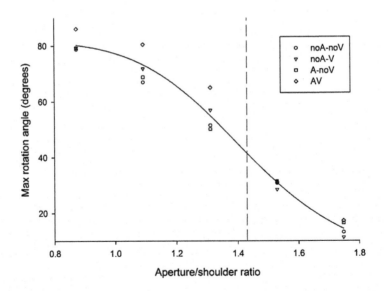

Fig. 4. Representation of the average maximal shoulder rotation when the subject crossed the aperture, as a function of the ratio between each subject shoulder and the aperture width. As the aperture becomes smaller, subjects systematically change their posture from frontal walking (shoulder rotation close to zero for ratios superior to 1.6) to sideways walking (shoulder rotation close to 80–90 degrees for ratios inferior to 1). Data for average values observed in the four experimental conditions were fitted with a logistic function (noA-noV: no avatar, no vibrotactile feedback; noA-V: no avatar, vibrotactile feedback; A-noV; avatar, no vibrotactile feedback; AV: avatar, vibrotactile feedback).

3   Results

From the 20 subjects who were included in the experiment, two were removed from data analysis, due to recording issues. Results show that, in all conditions, the door's aperture width had a significant effect on the subjects' shoulder rotation (ranging from 0 to 90 degrees), with a significant increase in shoulder rotation for a ratio between each subject's shoulder width and the door width for a value of approximately 1.4 (see Fig. 4).

This result is coherent with the outcome of previous studies [1, 2]. More precisely, [1] found a critical aperture width (the aperture width for which a significant shoulder rotation is observed) of about 1.3 (similar to the value observed in [2]). Here, we calculated the average shoulder rotation for all subjects, as a function of the four experimental conditions and the five aperture widths (Fig. 4). We fitted these value with a four parameter logistic curve (Eq. 1).

$$y = min + \frac{max - min}{1 + (\frac{x}{ec})^\wedge slope} \tag{1}$$

The obtained regression coefficient was superior to .999. The "ec" parameter (see Eq. 1), represents the inflexion point of the fitted curve. We took it as an approximation of the critical aperture width. It is represented in Fig. 4 as a vertical dash-line.

This first result shows that, across all four experimental conditions, subjects exhibited an adapted behavior, starting to rotate their shoulder when the ratio between their shoulder width and the aperture width became inferior to about 1.4.

This result indicates that, overall, subjects exhibited an adapted behavior, using body-scaled information [2], and that our experimental setup triggered behavioral presence. Using repeated-measures ANOVA, a significant effect of door width was observed (as expected). No significant simple effect of the experimental conditions was observed on shoulder rotation. However, an interaction effect between the "Vibrotactile" condition and door width, with shoulder rotation being significantly higher (closer to 90 degrees) as the door aperture became smaller, when the vibrotactile feedback was present ($p < .01$).

We further analyzed the percentage of collisions between the subjects' shoulders and the door, as they crossed the aperture. In short, for small apertures, results show that both conditions significantly affected the occurrence of collisions, these being minimal when both vibrotactile feedback and a virtual body were present ($p < .01$), with no significant interaction effect between both factors. In other words, the positive effects of these factors appear to be additive.

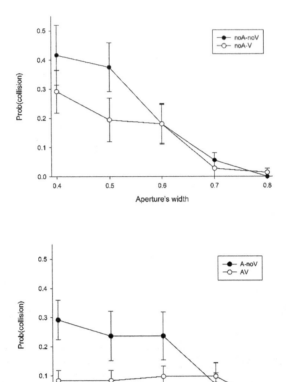

Fig. 5. Average probabilities of a collision between the body and door (with standard deviation), as a function of aperture width. Top: Without an avatar, vibrotactile feedback reduces the occurrence of collisions (for small apertures). Bottom: the same effect is observed in the presence of an avatar: collisions are minimal when both the avatar and vibrotactile feedback are present (AV).

4 Conclusion

In the present experiment, we confirmed that adaptive behavior (rotating the shoulder to pass through a narrow aperture), previously observed in natural conditions and in a CAVE setup, are actually basically similar when participants wear a Head-Mounted Display (HMD).

The experimental interest of using a HMD is that, by default, the subject does not see his/her own body when using such device. This enabled us to investigate the effect of seeing or not a (co-localized) representation of one's own-body (avatar) when interacting with a virtual environment. One first outcome of this experiment is that subjects exhibited an adaptive behavior, even in the absence of an avatar. This result is not surprising and confirms that presence is obtained while wearing an HMD, even without a representation of one's own-body.

However, looking closer into the data, it appears that, in the absence of an "avatar", subjects collided with the doorpost (for small apertures), in almost 50 % of the trials (Fig. 5, top). Here, adding a vibrotactile "radar" feedback (signaling approach to the doorpost) helps, enabling the subjects to calibrate the perception of their body-environment relationships (using body-scaled information). This result can be taken as further evidence of visual distance perception compression in virtual environments [10].

On the other hand, the presence of a co-localized avatar also improved distance perception, as compared to the condition without an avatar and vibrotactile feedback. However, optimal performance was only observed when both the avatar and vibrotactile feedback were present. This last result requires further investigation, since it can be related to different hypotheses.

It might be that the avatar helps the subjects feel present in the virtual environment and consequently improves distance perception [11]. Subjects using a HMD without any self-representation often complain of a feeling of "floatation" (you do not see your feet, so do not know where you are as compared to the ground surface). However, such body-appropriation would not be sufficient to get rid of the depth-compression effect in VEs, such that vibrotactile feedback would be necessary to further calibrate spatial perception.

It might also be that the "quality" of the avatar was not sufficient in our conditions to be fully effective and/or that the co-localization between the real and virtual body was imperfect (spatially and temporally), resulting in distorted spatial perception.

Acknowledgments. The authors wish to thank the CRVM (www.crvm.eu) team for decisive assistance in the experimental process. They also acknowledge the contribution of Jean-Claude Lepecq to this line of research. Céphise Louison is supported by a doctoral grant form INSTN (http://www-instn.cea.fr/).

References

1. Lepecq, J., Bringoux, L., Pergandi, J., Coyle, T., Mestre, D.: Afforded actions as a behavioral assessment of physical presence in virtual environments. Virtual Reality **13**, 141–151 (2009)
2. Warren, W., Whang, S.: Visual guidance of walking through apertures: Body-scaled information for affordances. J. Exp. Psychol. Hum. Percept. Perform. **13**, 371–383 (1987)
3. Gibson, J.J.: The Ecological Approach to Visual Perception. Houghton Mifflin, Boston (1979)
4. Louison, C., Ferlay, F., Keller, D., Mestre, D.: Vibrotactile feedback for collision awareness. In: Proceedings of the 2015 British HCI Conference on Human-Computer Interaction, pp. 277–278, Lincoln, UK (2015)
5. Bloomfield, A., Badler, N.: Virtual training via vibrotactile arrays. Presence: Teleoperators Virtual Environ. **17**, 103–120 (2008)
6. Lindeman, R., Page, R., Yanagida, Y., Sibert, J.: Towards full-body haptic feedback. In: Proceedings of the ACM Symposium on Virtual Reality Software and Technology - VRST 2004 (2004)
7. Li, Y., Jeon, W., Nam, C.: Navigation by vibration: effects of vibrotactile feedback on a navigation task. Int. J. Ind. Ergon. **46**, 76–84 (2015)

8. Golding, J.F.: Predicting individual differences in motion sickness susceptibility by questionnaire. Person. Individ. Differ. **41**, 237–248 (2006)

9. Kennedy, R.S., Lane, N.E., Berbaum, K.S., Lilienthal, M.G.: Simulator sickness questionnaire: an enhanced method for quantifying simulator sickness. Int. J. Aviat. Psychol. **3**, 203–220 (1993)

10. Messing, R., Durgin, F.H.: Distance perception and the visual horizon in head-mounted displays. ACM Trans. Appl. Percept. **2**, 234–250 (2005)

11. Interrante, V., Ries, B., Anderson, L.: Distance perception in immersive virtual environments, revisited. In: Proceedings of the IEEE conference on Virtual Reality, pp. 3–10, Washington DC, USA (2006)

In-Depth Analysis of Multimodal Interaction: An Explorative Paradigm

Felix Schüssel[1]([⊠]), Frank Honold[1], Nikola Bubalo[2], Anke Huckauf[2], Harald Traue[3], and Dilana Hazer-Rau[3]

[1] Institute of Media Informatics, Ulm University, Ulm, Germany
{felix.schuessel,frank.honold}@uni-ulm.de
[2] Department of General Psychology, Ulm University, Ulm, Germany
{nikola.bubalo,anke.huckauf}@uni-ulm.de
[3] Section of Medical Psychology, Ulm University, Ulm, Germany
{harald.traue,dilana.hazer}@uni-ulm.de
https://www.uni-ulm.de/in/mi.html
https://www.uni-ulm.de/en/in/psy-paed
http://www.emotion-lab.org

Abstract. Understanding the way people interact with multimodal systems is essential for their design and requires extensive empirical research. While approaches to design such systems have been explored from a technical perspective, the generic principles that drive the way users interact with them are largely unknown. Literature describes many findings, most of them specific to certain domains and sometimes even contradicting each other, and thus can hardly be generalized. In this article, we introduce an experimental setup that – despite being rather abstract – remains generic and allows in-depth exploration of various aspects with potential influence on users' way of interaction. We describe the gamified task of our setup and present different variations for empirical research targeting specific research questions. Applying the experimental paradigm offers the chance for new in-depth insights into the general principles and influencing factors of multimodal interaction, which could in turn be transferred to many real-world applications.

Keywords: Multimodal interaction · Experimental paradigm · Empirical research · Interaction histories · Pressure of time and success · Cognitive load

1 Introduction

Multimodal interaction has been a topic of research for some while now. There has been a lot of progress concerning how to model and process multimodal inputs. Still, little is known about the generic principles that apply, e.g. the choice of modalities, the temporal relations of multimodal inputs, and what may be an even more important factor, the contextual parameters that influence multimodal interaction. To tackle these questions, we have designed an abstract, but still generic, experimental paradigm that allows the exploration of these questions

© Springer International Publishing Switzerland 2016
M. Kurosu (Ed.): HCI 2016, Part II, LNCS 9732, pp. 233–240, 2016.
DOI: 10.1007/978-3-319-39516-6_22

in a flexible but controlled manner. Based on the developed paradigm, individual applications are generated and applied in different experimental setups.

2   Related Work

There have been a number of approaches on how to design multimodal interfaces and on how to model multimodal inputs from a system's perspective (see [5] for an overview). A more generic perspective on multimodal interaction is examined by Turk [13]. Two of the open challenges stated therein are a thorough understanding of the issues relating to the cognitive load of users, and the development of better guidance and best practices for the design and evaluation of multimodal systems (ibid.). Tackling these challenges requires empirical evidence. Accordingly, there has been a lot of empirical research in multimodal interaction, mostly specific to a certain domain, including map interactions [4, 7–9], augmented reality [6], image manipulation [2], and music players [3].

Comparing the results of these studies reveals considerable differences. Although the domain and tasks in the work of Oviatt et al. [7–9] and Haas et al. [4] are quite similar, their results are in parts contradictory. While the former reports on users predominantly showing a simultaneous use of modalities, the latter reports on no users showing a simultaneous use of modalities. Similarly, the dependency on task difficulty remains ambiguous. The findings of [2, 6] are even more specific to their respective domains. Although these provide some insights, their generalizability and transferability to other applications seems doubtful. Dumas et al. take a broader perspective and present a test bed for the evaluation of fusion engines using a music player as example [3]. They conclude that more work is necessary on fusion engine's adaption to context (i.e. environment and applications), as well as usage patterns and repetitive errors. This shows, that basic research on universal principles, which govern common tasks found in many applications, is still rare.

One aspect of the context is the influence of time pressure and the pressure of success onto the interaction behavior of a user. Getting the right ticket at the ticket vending machine in the train station last minute before the train leaves would be an example for such a situation. Including game elements to the study enables the simulation of such pressures on the user in laboratory settings. Respective gamification methods include feedback [1] on success and time pressure as well as a reward system [12]. These elevate both the intrinsic and extrinsic motivation of the user to complete the given tasks as reasoned by [10] based on the self determination theory.

3   A Visual Search Task for Empirical Research

In search of a task that is common to many different applications, we can identify *operations on objects* as a joint characteristic. Figure 1 shows different application examples.

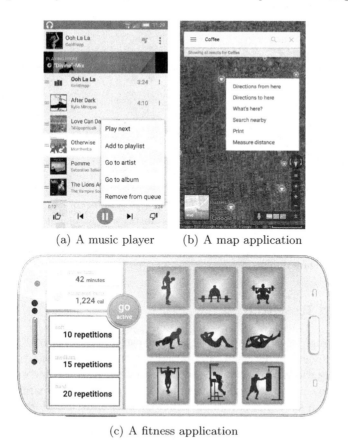

(a) A music player   (b) A map application

(c) A fitness application

Fig. 1. Different applications allowing operations on presented objects.

These kinds of tasks are found throughout many applications and are thus chosen for our research. Empirical research poses additional requirements as well, e.g. tasks must be performed repeatedly without becoming routine or dull, and participants' motivation must be kept high throughout the course of an experiment. In order to remedy these issues, we chose to use a gamified version of the task. In matters of the domain the tasks should take place in, we decided to use abstract representations of objects and operations.

Our solution is a visual search task, where the user has to identify the visually unique object and then specify its location and color (as a replacement for an arbitrary operation). Figure 2 shows a screenshot of the game. In the central area of Fig. 2, objects with differing shapes and colors are presented. In the given example, the green rectangle on position 3 is the unique object to be spotted by the user. The expected input can be provided either by using exclusive touch, exclusive speech, exclusive mouse or a combination of those modalities (e.g. touching the object and naming its color or vice versa).

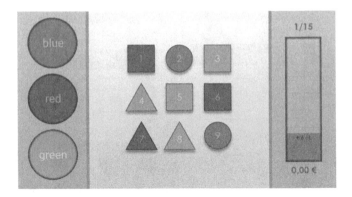

Fig. 2. Screenshot of the game that serves as abstract replacement of operations on objects found in many applications. The user has to spot the single unique object and designate it's location and color. In the above screenshot, the unique object is the red triangle. (Color figure online)

4   Planned Research

The generic design of our setup enables the investigation of isolated factors such as the users previous experience, contextual parameters, and cognitive demand. The following sections provide further details on how the presented experimental paradigm can easily be adjusted to facilitate the respective research. Although they are based on the same paradigm, different setups are used for each focus of research. Where applicable, first results are presented as well.

4.1   A User's Previous Experience: Individual Interaction Histories

In order to investigate the influence of individual user-centered interaction histories, the experimental paradigm is applied as shown in Fig. 3. The applied modalities are speech and touch inputs in any possible multimodal combination as described in Sect. 3. The inclusion of an *induction phase*, which requires users to solve the tasks applying only one of the possible four modality combinations, enables the investigation of the influence of individual interaction histories in the *free interaction phase*. We are particularly interested in the modality preferences of the free interaction phase, depending on the induced modality combination. Is there a favorite modality combination (regarding to error rates) and how long does it take users to apply it when induced otherwise? This could provide insights on the learning behavior of multimodal inputs.

Additionally, this experimental setup allows for an in-depth analysis of temporal relations of multimodal inputs, particularly with regard to the contradicting findings of the related work concerning the predominance of simultaneous and sequential interaction patterns. Results of a user study with this setup are reported in [11]. It is shown that a classification into simultaneous and sequential users may not be feasible in general. Instead, a more differentiated inspection of individual behavior is proposed and possible uses are discussed (cf. [11]).

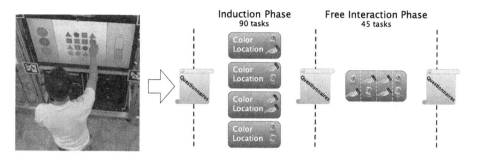

Fig. 3. The experimental procedure to investigate individual interaction histories. The *induction phase* induces a certain modality combination for each subject. In the *free interaction phase*, users can perform inputs in any modality combination.

4.2   Contextual Parameters: Pressure of Success and Time

Regarding contextual parameters, we investigate the influence of pressure to succeed in the task and time pressure, by varying the reward system and the available time to complete a task. These factors are supposed to have a significant influence not only on the error rate, but also on the way people interact with a system. To this end, an experiment was conducted in which we compared two groups of subjects which differed in the amount of auditory and visual feedback given by the system as well as the monetary reward given for the participation. Contrary to the *Feedback* group, the *No-Feedback* group got no auditory or visual feedback whether their input was correct, no timer was presented and consequently no performance dependent monetary rewards were given. Both groups underwent the same experimental procedure (see Fig. 4). Preliminary results indicate that users in the *Feedback* condition try to increase their success by interacting significantly faster than the *No-Feedback* group at the expense of significantly higher error rates. Furthermore, users from the *Feedback* condition chose multimodal interaction (33 % of trials) more often compared to the *No-Feedback* group (29.7 % of trials). Given that the *Feedback* group earns significantly higher monetary rewards, this difference in interaction behavior proves to be an effective way to increase success under pressure.

Regarding the in-depth analysis of the temporal patterns of interaction, temporal interaction parameters like modality overlaps and individual durations are measured under very different contextual conditions while the task is held fixed. We hypothesize that temporal interaction patterns become shorter when the users are under pressure. This could have implications on the fusion of user inputs and their adaption to context within the same application. Preliminary results suggest that the users do indeed act faster in the pressure condition. To be more specific, the temporal overlap of modalities decreases, while the durations of each modality themselves remain almost the same.

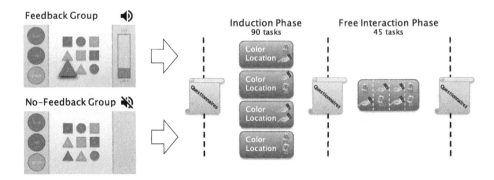

Fig. 4. The experimental procedure to investigate the effects of time pressure and pressure to succeed. One group is set under pressure (*Feedback*), while the other is not (*No-Feedback*). In the *induction phase*, each subject is restricted to use specific modalities. In the *free interaction phase*, users can perform inputs using any modalities. (Color figure online)

4.3   Cognitive Load: Induction of Overload and Underload

Given that users can be overwhelmed by the options and corresponding operations presented to them, diminishing the users' satisfaction with the system in general and thus affecting the user-system interaction, we intend to investigate the effects of cognitive load. Based on the present paradigm, an experiment was conducted to induce cognitive overload and underload in the subjects and investigate their effects by analyzing the users' individual reactions and subjective feedbacks.

The induction of cognitive overload and underload is generated by varying the number of objects and their colors within a task as well as the available given time to solve that task. These variables influence the difficulty of a given task and also affect the user's interaction with the system. Cognitive overload is induced by increasing the task field objects and colors as well as decreasing the available time, while cognitive underload is induced by decreasing the task field objects and colors and increasing the available time. Figure 5 depicts the two variants and the overall experimental procedure.

The interaction modality used during the induction phase can be either speech or mouse and is defined at the beginning of the experiment. Standardized questionnaires are filled by the subjects prior starting the experiment. Further, various kinds of subjective feedbacks including free speech, emotional rating and direct questions as well as baseline breathing phases are also implemented.

In order to enable an easy-to-handle workflow, the course of events within the experiment as well as the used modalities may be completely managed through an external *task set*. Within a task set, the workflow setting of the sequences can be defined individually for every task and every subject, allowing a high flexibility and generalization of the course setup.

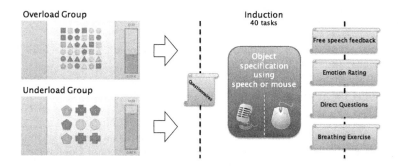

Fig. 5. The experimental procedure to induce and investigate the effects of cognitive load. Both groups (*Overload* and *Underload*) undergo the same procedure, while cognitive load is increased by increasing the task field objects and colors as well as decreasing the time. The modality during the induction phase is set up at the beginning of the experiment. (Color figure online)

5 Conclusion

The presented experimental paradigm enables a controlled investigation of the general laws and principles associated with multimodal interaction and the cognitive load of users, while the results are kept generalizable to a vast number of different implementations of multimodal interaction. Based on the paradigm, we presented three implemented setups covering a broad range of research topics. This includes an investigation of the role of users' previous multimodal interaction experience (their so-called interaction history). The resulting insights into the individuality of multimodal temporal relations will help to improve the fusion of inputs in future systems [11]. The second implementation shows that the influence of contextual parameters like pressure of success and time can be examined by slightly varying the provided feedback. Using fine grained variations of the task's difficulty, one gains control over the amount of cognitive demand imposed on the users, reaching from underchallenged to well overstrained.

In addition to such flexibility, the presented paradigm has several other advantages over using a specific real-world application for research, such as its easy implementation, the possibility to deploy it on different hardware setups with different modalities, as well as its suitability for lengthy laboratory studies with a lot of repetitions due to its gamified design. Thus, it allows researchers to meet the goal of gaining knowledge of multimodal interaction that is diverse and in-depth, yet still generalizable.

Acknowledgments. This work was supported by the Transregional Collaborative Research Center SFB/TRR 62 "Companion-Technology for Cognitive Technical Systems", which is funded by the German Research Foundation (DFG). It is also supported by a Margarete von Wrangell (MvW) habilitation scholarship funded by the Ministry of Science, Research and the Arts (MWK) of the state of Baden-Württemberg for Dilana Hazer-Rau. Some icons from Fig. 1 were designed by www.Freepik.com.

References

1. Cheong, C., Cheong, F., Filippou, J.: Quick quiz: A gamified approach for enhancing learning. In: PACIS, p. 206 (2013)
2. Dey, P., Madhvanath, S., Ranjan, A., Das, S.: An exploration of gesture-speech multimodal patterns for touch interfaces. In: Proceedings of the 3rd International Conference on Human Computer Interaction, IndiaHCI 2011, pp. 79–83. ACM, New York (2011). http://doi.acm.org/10.1145/2407796.2407808
3. Dumas, B., Ingold, R., Lalanne, D.: Benchmarking fusion engines of multimodal interactive systems. In: Proceedings of the 2009 International Conference on Multimodal Interfaces, ICMI-MLMI 2009, pp. 169–176. ACM, New York (2009)
4. Haas, E.C., Pillalamarri, K.S., Stachowiak, C.C., McCullough, G.: Temporal binding of multimodal controls for dynamic map displays: A systems approach. In: Proceedings of the 13th International Conference on Multimodal Interfaces, ICMI 2011, pp. 409–416. ACM, New York (2011). http://doi.acm.org/10.1145/2070481.2070558
5. Lalanne, D., Nigay, L., Palanque, P., Robinson, P., Vanderdonckt, J., Ladry, J.F.: Fusion engines for multimodal input: a survey. In: Proceedings of the 2009 International Conference on Multimodal Interfaces, ICMI-MLMI 2009, pp. 153–160. ACM, New York (2009). http://doi.acm.org/10.1145/1647314.1647343
6. Lee, M., Billinghurst, M.: A wizard of oz study for an ar multimodal interface. In: Proceedings of the 10th International Conference on Multimodal Interfaces, ICMI 2008, pp. 249–256. ACM, New York (2008). http://doi.acm.org/10.1145/1452392.1452444
7. Oviatt, S., Coulston, R., Lunsford, R.: When do we interact multimodally? Cognitive load and multimodal communication patterns. In: Proceedings of the 6th International Conference on Multimodal Interfaces, ICMI 2004, pp. 129–136. ACM, New York (2004)
8. Oviatt, S., Coulston, R., Tomko, S., Xiao, B., Lunsford, R., Wesson, M., Carmichael, L.: Toward a theory of organized multimodal integration patterns during human-computer interaction. In: Proceedings of the 5th International Conference on Multimodal Interfaces, ICMI 2003, pp. 44–51. ACM, New York (2003)
9. Oviatt, S., Lunsford, R., Coulston, R.: Individual differences in multimodal integration patterns: what are they and why do they exist? In: Proceedings of the SIGCHI Conference on Human Factors in Computing Systems, CHI 2005 pp. 241–249. ACM, New York (2005)
10. Ryan, R.M., Rigby, C.S., Przybylski, A.: The motivational pull of video games: A self-determination theory approach. Motiv. Emot. **30**(4), 344–360 (2006)
11. Schüssel, F., Honold, F., Weber, M., Schmidt, M., Bubalo, N., Huckauf, A.: Multimodal interaction history and its use in error detection and recovery. In: Proceedings of the 16th ACM International Conference on Multimodal Interaction, ICMI 2014, pp. 164–171. ACM, New York (2014)
12. Smith, A.L., Baker, L.: Getting a clue: creating student detectives and dragon slayers in your library. Reference Services Review **39**(4), 628–642 (2011)
13. Turk, M.: Multimodal interaction: A review. Pattern Recogn. Lett. **36**, 189–195 (2014)

Portable Tabletops: A Low-Cost Pen-and-Touch Approach

Marisol Wong-Villacres[1]([⊠]), Vanessa Echeverría Barzola[2], Roger Granda[2], and Katherine Chiluiza Garcia[1]

[1] Facultad de Ingeniería en Electricidad y Computación,
Escuela Superior Politécnica del Litoral, ESPOL,
Campus Gustavo Galindo Km 30.5 Vía Perimetral, P.O. Box 09-01-5863,
Guayaquil, Ecuador
lvillacr@espol.edu.ec

[2] Centro de Tecnologías de Información, Escuela Superior Politécnica del Litoral,
ESPOL, Campus Gustavo Galindo Km 30.5 Vía Perimetral, Guayaquil, Ecuador

Abstract. This paper describes the design and implementation of a low-cost portable tabletop to be used in classrooms. This solution enables pen and touch interactions over a projected canvas. Twelve users participated in a user study that gauged the system's effectiveness to support drawing and moving objects on the surface. Additionally, a stress test to evaluate users' identification was conducted. Results showed that the system exhibited a fair effectiveness when users draw or move objects. Average errors of 5.6 % to 6.5 % were found when differentiating users. In general, the proposed tabletop is a promising solution at an affordable price; nevertheless, three key challenges need to be addressed before a full deployment of the solution: a better precision to draw complex shapes, a better gesture intepretation when rotating objects and achieving a minimum error for user differentiation.

Keywords: Multi-touch · Portable · Pen-and-touch · Low-cost · User differentiation · Depth camera · User study

1 Introduction

Multi-touch tabletops have the potential to enhance collaborative learning in the classroom by fostering a playful, enjoyable environment that promotes communication [6], awareness of others [10] and equity of participation [24]. Nonetheless, the conventional multi-touch technology approach of enabling interaction by augmenting surface instrumentation, does not provide the portability and economical feasibility needed for widespread classroom deployments. In this context, Wilson's proposal of using a front mounted depth camera to furnish interactive capabilities to any physical surface [25] becomes promising. Explorations around this author's initiative have shown that touch input can in fact be achieved on everyday surfaces [13,17].

© Springer International Publishing Switzerland 2016
M. Kurosu (Ed.): HCI 2016, Part II, LNCS 9732, pp. 241–252, 2016.
DOI: 10.1007/978-3-319-39516-6_23

Although the results of these studies are highly indicative of portable table-tops' potential for the classroom, further explorations are still required to fully understand how this technology can support typical classroom activities such as sketching, designing and painting. Former research has shown that pen and touch tabletop support can boost the rich interactions required for engaging in such type of creative tasks [5,11]; while the dominant hand engages in fine-precision actions with the pen, the non-dominant hand can lend itself to activities that do not require high levels of dexterity, such as zooming, rotating and tapping [12,14]. In fact, a previous experiment [5] demonstrated that the pen and touch approach offers a good support for drawing as a mean for problem solving. More-over, supporting pen and touch can enable students to seamlessly move from the physical to the digital world [3], decreasing the cognitive load the user faces when having to shift from one world to the other. Despite all the advantages of the pen and touch approach, the technological support for this interaction still poses practical challenges for low-cost portable tabletops; most initiatives in the area have focused on supporting pen and touch either on high-cost interactive surfaces such as Microsoft Surface Hub[1] and Wacom[2]; or on non-portable low-cost ones such as the one proposed in [11].

Furthermore, the exploration of widespread tabletop classroom deployments should offer support for user differentiation: touch/stroke identification that allows a tabletop to associate objects with the users' identity. This ability becomes vital for supporting educational activities' features such as enforced turn-taking and the analysis of groups' dynamics. Previous studies that have required user differentiation for pen-based multi-touch surfaces, have mostly relied on commercial high-cost devices that do not work on portable projectable tabletops; some examples are the Mimio pen [8], the Promethean Activeboard pen [15], and the Anoto pen[3].

Additionally, former research that has proposed new pen-based initiatives to enable user identification on portable tabletops, has not aim at low-cost approaches [4]. This lack of low-cost explorations in the area of users' pen strokes differentiation for portable tabletops, can potentially avert this tabletop technol-ogy from effectively buttressing educational experiences in the classroom. The current study poses that low-cost portable tabletops initiatives, need to better address pen and touch support as well as user stroke identification in order to achieve a real ubiquitous status in educational settings.

In this paper, we present a low-cost portable multi-touch pen-based tabletop that recognizes the pen strokes of up to three different users using a depth camera as well as infrared pens. The total cost of the hardware solution is around USD $450. In line with validation approaches used by similar works on projectable tabletops [7,13], we conducted a user study to quantify the proposed system's support for simple gestures and drawings, as well as a stress testing to gauge user differentiation accuracy. Our findings demonstrated that our tabletop has

---

[1] https://www.microsoft.com/microsoft-surface-hub.

[2] http://www.wacom.com.

[3] http://www.anoto.com.

a strong technological potential to support pen and touch interactions; the proposed solution allows the user to draw and move objects with almost no difficulty within an acceptable time response (0.1–0.13 s). Moreover, the proposed system was able to differentiate users' pen strokes with an error rate lower than the one reported in similar works [7,20]. Nevertheless, the hardware used for recognition tasks needs to be reviewed before a full deployment of the system in terms of achieving successful execution of some pen-based actions (drawing of complex figures), as well as touch-based gestures (rotating objects).

This paper is structured as follows: first, a related work section is presented and the proposed low-cost portable multi-touch tabletop is described. Then, the research context, evaluation and corresponding results are detailed. Finally, a conclusion section along with reflections about further research is proposed.

2   Related Work

Numerous multi-touch technologies enable tabletops to sense touches; among them are: capacitance, optical, LCD and computer vision-based approaches. The latter is particularly popular because it can be enabled by low-cost devices [9]. Nonetheless, most of the tabletops that rely on this technology require a fixed-positioned table to allow physical interaction [19]. Early work presented by Wilson [25], explored multi-touch detection in a non-flat surface using a Kinect sensor as a depth camera. This author's work triggered other explorations on how to use a depth-sensing camera to deliver interactive capabilities to any physical surface: HuddleLamp is a desk lamp with an integrated low-cost RGB-D camera that detects and tracks smaller displays on tables [22], and OmniTouch is a wearable projection system that enables surfaces, such as an individual's body, to become interactive [13].

Additionally, there have been initiatives to enhance depth cameras' touch detection mechanisms; Klompmaker et al. proposed dSensingNI [16], a framework for depth-camera sensing that tracks user fingers and hand palms to enable recognition of gestures such as grasping, grouping and stacking; and Murugappan et al. [19] proposed an extended multi-touch approach for low-cost tabletops that can recover finger, wrist and hand posture of the user. Our work differs from this latter initiative, in the approach used to validate the precision of pen and touch interactions; while they focus on gestures used to control actions (e.g. navigation), we propose validating gestures that allow the manipulation of 2D objects.

On the area of pen-and-touch support for interactive surfaces, research has mostly been conducted on non-portable tabletop solutions such as capacitive multi-touch tabletops [14,15]. Likewise, most of the approaches proposed to enable pen and touch interactions cannot be considered low-cost solutions; well-known products that are an example of this are the Anoto pen used for tabletop interactions, Wacom, and Microsoft Surface Hub. In addition, current digital pen technology still exhibits basic issues that hinder natural interactions: existing devices are bulky and pose restrictions on the type of movements an individual can perform with them [3].

In the context of vision-based systems, seldom initiatives have used the visual signature of the pen for user differentiation and recognition. For example, Qin et al. describes the implementation of Ppen, a pressure sensitive pen with an active IR-emitting tip, a laser emitter for remote interaction, three buttons and a RF module for user identification and data transmission [20]. However, this device tends to rely on high-cost technologies. Among the few studies that seek to achieve user's pen strokes differentiation, is the work of Chen et al., who proposed IR pens as writing tools on a low-cost tabletop [7]. Nonetheless, their solution is not a hand touch technology. Although our work builds on theirs, we propose a less bulky device that allows drawing on a muti-touch low-cost portable surface.

3   Proposed Solution: Portable Tabletop

In order to achieve a low-cost portable tabletop design that supports collaborative pen and touch interactions as well as user differentiation, the proposed solution implements the following design guidelines:

- *Support simultaneous user actions of up to three users:* As suggested by [23], to engage users into tabletop activities, multiple users' inputs should be supported by the surface.
- *Allow users to freely move and regulate their workspace:* Xambó [26] warned against the harmful effects on creativity and free collaborative activities that tabletops with territorial constraints can cause. Following recommendations presented in [15], this solution let users to choose where to work, just as they would do on a table.
- *Allowing for pen and touch inputs:* A pen and touch tabletop can boost creative classroom activities by enabling digital interactivity while supporting behaviors found on the pen and paper approach [2].
- *Portability and low-cost:* This guideline aims at enabling tabletop solutions to easily integrate into educational settings.
- *Distinguishing users work*: Awareness of individual contributions makes a successful collaborative work [18].

In order to support these requirements, a combination of hardware and software solution was deployed. Afterwards, an evaluation was carried out in terms of accuracy of user's pen strokes identification and a user testing of the proposed solution.

3.1   Hardware Solution

The hardware solution is built using low-cost components: (1) up to four color-tracking pens, (2) two web cameras for pen tracking (60fps), (3) one Kinect sensor (version 1, 30fps) for touch interaction and, (4) a projector for presenting the image of a canvas, where the users can interact with the system. Colored-tracking pens were constructed placing an infrared led on each pen's tip and a colored ball on each pen's top. The projector, the Kinect sensor and the web cameras are located above a flat surface, which becomes the projected area of interaction. Depending on the projector capabilities, this area can be expandable. Figure 1 depicts the proposed solution and a scheme with the current settings of the system, which covers a projected area of 43 in.

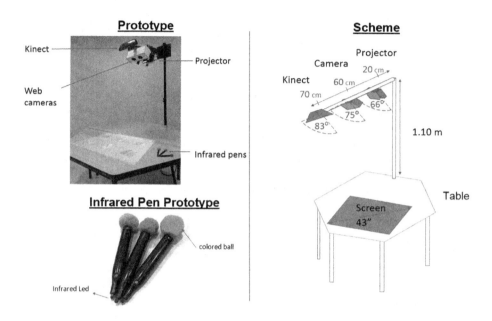

Fig. 1. Prototype and scheme of the proposed solution

3.2   Software Solution

The software solution had to address several challenges to enable the tabletop's low-cost and portable approach:

- Low performance of pen identification due to low resolution of web cameras.
- Inaccurate hand tracking due to the low resolution and the related sensor noise of Kinect (version 1).
- The unavailability of a centralized controller that can handle the events generated both by pens and touch interactions.

To tackle these issues, we designed a client-server architecture that handles interactions triggered by pen-and-touch inputs. Next, we describe the architecture's components: a pen-tracking server, a hand-tracking server, and a user interface client component.

1. ***Pen-Tracking server component:*** Its purpose is to recognize and identify each pen by tracking it through infrared (IR) and color web cameras. IR tracking is used to identify pen tips. A binarization process is applied to each frame of the IR camera, which enables the recognition of one or more IR led lights. Position and timing of detection of IR light sources are stored temporarily in memory. Color tracking is used to identify the colored ball located at the top of the pen. In this process, each RGB frame from the color camera is converted to a HSV color space. Then, a process of color filtering is applied to the HSV frame using the HSV values of the colored pens. This process generates the positions of the tracked colors, which are ultimately given to the Camshift algorithm [1]. Camshift is responsible of doing tracking of each colored pen over the interaction. In case Camshift looses track of a particular color, the color filtering process is used again to find the correspondent color. Pairs of IR and color points are used to detect a pen. The criterion used for this pairing is to use the nearest IR and colored points. Once a pen is recognized and identified by its color, a multi-touch event is created and delivered to the system's User Interface-client component.

2. ***Hand-Tracking server component:*** Hand-tracking is achieved through: a scene capturing process, a depth-image thresholding process, and a blob tracking process. First, a process captures the initial 3D scene of the projection surface. Next, a background subtraction between each frame and the initial 3D scene is calculated. This subtraction is used to recognize 3D objects that were not previously presented into the 3D scene. The depth-image thresholding process is used to detect fingers or hands near the projection table. This process consists on substracting any object located five centimeters or more above the flat surface. This substraction results in depth information about the objects over the surface. Depth information is transformed to a binary image. Since each finger or hand produces a shadow in the binary image, this information is suitable to be used for blob tracking. When a blob is detected, the hand-tracking server creates and delivers a multi-touch event. In order to prevent false recognition of a pen as a hand, the system requires a minimum and maximum area to confirm a blob is in fact a hands' blob.

3. ***User Interface client component:*** This component is responsible of receiving and interpreting each touch event, storing the status of each object and rendering the user interface. Touch events coming from the hand-tracking server are used to move objects on the projected surface. The touch events generated by the pen-tracking server are used to draw colored strokes according to the color of each pen.

4   Tools and Frameworks

A set of several tools and frameworks were used to build the components described in the previous section. For deploying the pen-tracking server component, the Openframeworks library[4] was used at the top level.

---

[4] http://openframeworks.cc/.

In addition, the OpenCV library[5] helped to process images using a set of algorithms such as: RGB to HSV transformation, binarization and Camshift. As for the hand-tracking server component, a modified version of Kinect Core Vision software[6] was used to process data coming from Kinect. The connection between Kinect Core Vision and hardware itself is controlled by the libfreenect library[7]. Furthermore, multi-touch events were implemented using TUIO multi-touch protocol[8] across all components. Finally, the user-interface client component uses Kivy framework[9] to easily deploy multithreaded applications for multi-touch aplications.

The implemented solution presents the following technical characteristics: a latency of 0.1 s for pen-drawing, and 0.133 s for hand interactions; a disparity of 4 mm between the real pen's tip position and the position showed by the system; and a multi-touch accuracy of approximately 10 mm. Moreover, the pen-tracking server component works at 48 fps, while the hand-tracking server component works at 29 fps.

The overall hardware cost is around \$450. We used the following devices to deploy this solution: an Axxa pico projector (\$319.99), a Kinect sensor v1 (\$99.99) and 2 web cameras (\$16.98 both). The price of the computer is not considered in the overall price.

5   Evaluation

Two testings were conducted to assess the performance of the low-cost portable tabletop. The first was based on user evaluations of the system and attempted to gauge accuracy-related variables of both pen and touch interactions, whereas the second focused on stress testing and measured the accuracy of the color recognition algorithm that enables user differentiation.

5.1   User Study

Twelve people (7 males and 5 females, average age 28) with previous experience using multi-touch surfaces, participated in a one-session user study. The study sought to gauge how much time and effort the user had to invest in successfully drawing and moving objects on the tabletop. For this purpose, participants were asked to perform tasks on a tabletop application which consisted of a canvas with a rectangular 2D object that a user could move with their hands (Fig. 2b). Furthermore, the canvas allowed users to draw using the IR proposed pen (Fig. 2a). At the beginning of the session, participants were given an average time of two minutes to get familiar with the tabletop application. After this, they were assigned a set of 11 tasks; they had to use the pen to draw five different

---

[5] http://opencv.org/.
[6] https://github.com/patriciogonzalezvivo/KinectCoreVision.
[7] https://openkinect.org.
[8] http://www.tuio.org/.
[9] https://kivy.org/.

figures on the tabletop (line, square, circle, fork-like figure, spoon-like figure), as can be seen in Fig. 2c; and they had to perform seven object movement tasks to manipulate the rectangle projected on the tabletop left to right (L-R), right to left (R-L), upward and downward movements; circular movements; and object rotations). Participants were instructed to attempt a task as many times they felt they needed to successfully finishing it. At the end of task, participants were required to fill a questionnaire. For pen-related tasks, the questionnaire asked the number of attempts required to successfully execute the task, the time invested in successfully finishing the task, and whether the final result resembled the participant's original intention. For movement-related tasks, the first two questions were the same; and the last question asked whether the participant was able to successfully finish the task.

(a) Pen interaction   (b) Hand interaction   (c) Figures drawn with pens

Fig. 2. Tabletop application used in evaluation

5.2   Stress Testing

We measured the accuracy of the system to differentiate users' pen strokes. A stress testing was used and consisted of the following:

- **One-minute stress testing:** Three users were asked to simultaneously make the maximum number of strokes they could in a one-minute period. The count of strokes made by each individual during this period was gathered, as well as, the number of number of times the system misidentified each pen.
- **Thirty-strokes stress testing:** Three users were asked to simultaneously make thirty strokes on a random area of the tabletop. They were asked to count the number of misidentifications of their colored pen. A misidentification is counted when the color of a stroke on the canvas does not match a pen's color.

6   Results

The outcomes of the user test are summarized in Tables 1 and 2. Table 1 shows the results related to drawing tasks. As can be seen, most of the participants required less than three attempts to finish a given task; one participant had difficulties in drawing squares, forks and spoons and two participants faced challenges when drawing circles. Additionally, most participants agreed that the final version of their drawings resembled their intended drawing. As for the time used to perform a drawing task, users reported investing 5 to 7 s for drawing squares, forks and spoons. Table 2 shows the results from the movement related tasks. It is evident that the users experimented difficulties rotating objects. In the rest of the tasks, few users (1 or 2) reported investing more than three attempts. The percentages of successful completion of the assigned tasks were high, with the exception of the rotation movement task, which only reached 50 %. Regarding the average time per task, the circular movement and object rotation took eight and twelve seconds, respectively.

In terms of the one-minute stress testing, results showed a colored detection average error of 5.56 %, whereas the thirty-strokes stress testing presented an error rate of 6.46 %.

Table 1. Drawings section of User Testing Results

Measure	Line	Square	Circle	Fork	Spoon
Less than 3 attempts	100 %	91.67 %	83.33 %	91.67 %	91.67 %
Resemblance to intended drawing	100.0 %	100.0 %	91.7 %	100.0 %	83.3 %
Average time (s)	3	7	4	5	5

Table 2. Object movements User Testing Results

Measure	L-R	R-L	Upwards	Downwards	Circular	Rotation
Less than 3 attempts	91.67 %	83.33 %	100.00 %	91.67 %	83.33 %	50.00 %
Successful completion of the task	100.0 %	100.0 %	100.0 %	100.0 %	91.7 %	50.0 %
Average time (s)	4	3	2	3	8	12

7   Conclusions and Further Work

The proposed system integrates pen and touch interactions with low-cost portable tabletop technologies. The main goal of this proposed solution is to enable tabletop widespread usage in educational settings; therefore the reported system was designed to allow more than two users to interact with the tabletop using pen and touch, regardless of their location. This approach differs from other proposed solutions; while [7] enabled two users to simultaneously interact with a projected tabletop, [27] does not report a portable solution. We validated our approach by quantifying the time and effort users had to invest in successfully drawing and moving objects on the tabletop. Moreover, we measured the proposed tabletop's ability to identify different user's stroke. The fact that all participants had previous experience interacting with multi-touch surfaces minimized the time invested in learning how to use the proposed system. Results showed that seldom times users had to engage in more than one attempt to draw figures on the proposed tabletop. In contrast, users had to execute an average of two attempts when having to manipulate 2D objects on the tabletop. Additionally, the system exhibited low rates of users' strokes misidentification. To our knowledge, these results cannot be compared to other initiatives; previous work on projectable tabletops has had a different focus than ours, it has explored mostly: technology's support for gesture analysis [16,19]; pen-based interactions [7]; or has neither attempted to identify different users nor published results[10]. In general, the proposed tabletop is a promising solution at an affordable price. Nevertheless, before a full deployment of the system, the following challenges must be addressed in further work:

– **Challenge 1:** More drawing precision is required. In average, 6 % of the attempts when drawing complex shapes required more than three attempts to resemble the intended drawing.
– **Challenge 2:** More effectiveness in interpreting gestures is needed. Rotating an object became a challenge for users.
– **Challenge 3:** A lower error rate for users' strokes differentiation needs to be achieved. Even though error rates on user identification are better or similar to other reviewed solutions, for tabletops to achieve a massive usage in the classroom, error rates should be minimum. [7,21]

Overall, the first two challenges could be overcome by exploring the usage of devices that can more accurately sense user's movement, such as Kinect 2. The user recognition challenge could be improved through a shape recognition algorithm.

References

1. Allen, J.G., Xu, R.Y.D., Jin, J.S.: Object tracking using camshift algorithm and multiple quantized feature spaces. In: Proceedings of the Pan-Sydney Area Workshop on Visual Information Processing, VIP 2005, pp. 3–7. Australian Computer Society Inc., Darlinghurst, Australia, Australia (2004). http://dl.acm.org/citation.cfm?id=1082121.1082122
2. Annett, M., Anderson, F., Bischof, W.F., Gupta, A.: The pen is mightier: Understanding stylus behaviour while inking on tablets. In: Proceedings of Graphics Interface 2014, GI 2014, pp. 193–200. Canadian Information Processing Society, Toronto, Ont., Canada, Canada (2014). http://dl.acm.org/citation.cfm?id=2619648.2619680
3. Annett, M., Gupta, A., Bischof, W.F.: Exploring and understanding unintended touch during direct pen interaction. ACM Trans. Comput. Hum. Inter. (TOCHI) **21**(5), 28 (2014)

---

[10] http://www.ubi-interactive.com/.

4. Bi, X., Shi, Y., Chen, X.: uPen: A smart pen-liked device for facilitating interaction on large displays. In: First IEEE International Workshop on Horizontal Interactive Human-Computer Systems, TableTop 2006, p. 7. IEEE (2006)
5. Brandl, P., Forlines, C., Wigdor, D., Haller, M., Shen, C.: Combining and measuring the benefits of bimanual pen and direct-touch interaction on horizontal interfaces. In: Proceedings of the Working Conference on Advanced Visual Interfaces, pp. 154–161. ACM (2008)
6. Buisine, S., Besacier, G., Aoussat, A., Vernier, F.: How do interactive tabletop systems influence collaboration? Comput. Hum. Behav. **28**(1), 49–59 (2012)
7. Chen, R., Chen, P.J.R., Feng, R., Liu, Y.E., Wu, A., Mazalek, A.: SciSketch: A tabletop collaborative sketching system. In: Proceedings of the 8th International Conference on Tangible, Embedded and Embodied Interaction, TEI 2014, pp. 247–250, NY, USA (2013). http://doi.acm.org/10.1145/2540930.2540973
8. Collins, A., Kay, J.: Collaborative personal information management with shared, interactive tabletops. In: Proceedings of PIM 2008 CHI Workshop (2008)
9. Dang, C.T., Straub, M., André, E.: Hand distinction for multi-touch tabletop interaction. In: Proceedings of the ACM International Conference on Interactive Tabletops and Surfaces, pp. 101–108. ACM (2009)
10. Falcão, T.P., Price, S.: Interfering and resolving: How tabletop interaction facilitates co-construction of argumentative knowledge. Inter. J. Comput. Support. Collab. Learn. **6**(4), 539–559 (2011)
11. Frisch, M., Heydekorn, J., Dachselt, R.: Diagram editing on interactive displays using multi-touch and pen gestures. In: Goel, A.K., Jamnik, M., Narayanan, N.H. (eds.) Diagrams 2010. LNCS, vol. 6170, pp. 182–196. Springer, Heidelberg (2010)
12. Guiard, Y.: Asymmetric division of labor in human skilled bimanual action: The kinematic chain as a model. J. Motor Behav. **19**(4), 486–517 (1987)
13. Harrison, C., Benko, H., Wilson, A.D.: Omnitouch: wearable multitouch interaction everywhere. In: Proceedings of the 24th Annual ACM Symposium on User Interface Software and Technology, pp. 441–450. ACM (2011)
14. Hinckley, K., Yatani, K., Pahud, M., Coddington, N., Rodenhouse, J., Wilson, A., Benko, H., Buxton, B.: Manual deskterity: an exploration of simultaneous pen+touch direct input. In: CHI 2010, Extended Abstracts on Human Factors in Computing Systems, pp. 2793–2802. ACM (2010)
15. Kharrufa, A., Leat, D., Olivier, P.: Digital mysteries: designing for learning at the tabletop. In: ACM International Conference on Interactive Tabletops and Surfaces, pp. 197–206. ACM (2010)
16. Klompmaker, F., Nebe, K., Fast, A.: Dsensingni: a framework for advanced tangible interaction using a depth camera. In: Proceedings of the Sixth International Conference on Tangible, Embedded and Embodied Interaction, pp. 217–224. ACM (2012)
17. Liu, Y., Weibel, N., Hollan, J.D.: Interactive space: a prototyping framework for touch and gesture on and above the desktop. In: CHI 2013 Extended Abstracts on Human Factors in Computing Systems, pp. 1233–1238. ACM (2013)
18. Martínez, R., Collins, A., Kay, J., Yacef, K.: Who did what? who said that?: Collaid: An environment for capturing traces of collaborative learning at the tabletop. In: Proceedings of the ACM International Conference on Interactive Tabletops and Surfaces, ITS 2011, pp. 172–181. ACM, NY, USA, New York (2011)
19. Murugappan, S., Elmqvist, N., Ramani, K., et al.: Extended multitouch: recovering touch posture and differentiating users using a depth camera. In: Proceedings of the 25th Annual ACM Symposium on User Interface Software and Technology, pp. 487–496. ACM (2012)

20. Qin, Y., Yu, C., Jiang, H., Wu, C., Shi, Y.: ppen: enabling authenticated pen and touch interaction on tabletop surfaces. In: ACM International Conference on Interactive Tabletops and Surfaces, pp. 283–284. ACM (2010)
21. Qin, Y., Yu, C., Jiang, H., Wu, C., Shi, Y.: ppen: Enabling authenticated pen and touch interaction on tabletop surfaces. In: ACM International Conference on Interactive Tabletops and Surfaces, ITS 2010, pp. 283–284, NY, USA (2010). http://doi.acm.org/10.1145/1936652.1936717
22. Rädle, R., Jetter, H.C., Marquardt, N., Reiterer, H., Rogers, Y.: Huddlelamp: Spatially-aware mobile displays for ad-hoc around-the-table collaboration. In: Proceedings of the Ninth ACM International Conference on Interactive Tabletops and Surfaces, pp. 45–54. ACM (2014)
23. Scott, S.D., Grant, K.D., Mandryk, R.L.: System guidelines for co-located, collaborative work on a tabletop display. In: Kuutti, K., Karsten, E.H., Fitzpatrick, G., Dourish, P., Schmidt, K. (eds.) ECSCW 2003, pp. 159–178. Springer, Heidelberg (2003)
24. Wallace, J.R., Scott, S.D., MacGregor, C.G.: Collaborative sensemaking on a digital tabletop and personal tablets: prioritization, comparisons, and tableaux. In: Proceedings of the SIGCHI Conference on Human Factors in Computing Systems, pp. 3345–3354. ACM (2013)
25. Wilson, A.D.: Using a depth camera as a touch sensor. In: ACM International Conference on Interactive Tabletops and Surfaces, pp. 69–72. ACM (2010)
26. Xambó, A., Hornecker, E., Marshall, P., Jordà, S., Dobbyn, C., Laney, R.: Let's jam the reactable: Peer learning during musical improvisation with a tabletop tangible interface. ACM Trans. Comput. Hum. Interact. **20**(6), 36: 1–36: 34 (2013). http://doi.acm.org/10.1145/2530541
27. Xu, S., Manders, C.M.: Building a multi-touch tabletop for classrooms. In: Chang, M., Hwang, W.-Y., Chen, M.-P., Müller, W. (eds.) Edutainment 2011. LNCS, vol. 6872, pp. 131–138. Springer, Heidelberg (2011)

Mobile and Wearable Interaction

A Survey of Text Entry Techniques
for Smartwatches

Ahmed Sabbir Arif$^{(\boxtimes)}$ and Ali Mazalek

Synaesthetic Media Laboratory, Ryerson University, Toronto, ON, Canada
{asarif,mazalek}@ryerson.ca

Abstract. The growing interest in wearable devices has resulted in a wave of novel and improved text entry techniques for smartwatches and other ultra-small devices. These techniques are not only diverse in nature but also evaluated in different experimental conditions. This makes it difficult for designers and researchers to compare the techniques, and their performances in terms of speed and accuracy. This paper reviews the most important text entry techniques for smartwatches and other ultra-small devices. It categorizes all techniques based on whether they use (a variant of) the standard QWERTY keyboard, a novel keypad or keyboard, or handwriting recognition, and discusses the design and evaluation of the techniques. It includes a table that displays the performances of these techniques in the most common text entry performance metrics.

Keywords: Input and interaction · Text entry · Text input · Smartwatches · Smaller devices · Ultra-small devices · Touchscreen · Gesture · Wearables

1 Introduction

Smartwatches and other wearable devices are becoming increasingly popular among mobile users [19]. Users nowadays can use several applications on their smartwatches, and can interact with the applications installed on a paired smartphone without ever touching the smartphone. Yet interaction with smartwatches is mostly limited to checking emails, texts, and social networking posts. This is primarily due to the unavailability of an effective text entry technique for smartwatches. Most other tasks (e.g., replying to a text message) require text entry in some capacity, thus to perform those tasks users are forced to use a more text entry friendly device (e.g. a smartphone or tablet).

Researchers from both academia and industry are attempting to address this issue by designing and developing novel and improved text entry techniques for smartwatches. Unfortunately, experimental data on smartwatch text entry performance reported in the literature varies widely due to the use of different development platforms, devices, and performance metrics. This makes it difficult to compare studies or to extract meaningful average performance data from this body of work. This makes it hard for designers and researchers to use and apply these results and works against the synthesis of a larger picture. This can cause re-exploration of design philosophies, slowing down the overall development process in the area.

© Springer International Publishing Switzerland 2016
M. Kurosu (Ed.): HCI 2016, Part II, LNCS 9732, pp. 255–267, 2016.
DOI: 10.1007/978-3-319-39516-6_24

To provide designers and researchers with a better understanding of the current developments in the area, this paper reviews the most important text entry techniques for smartwatches and other ultra-small devices. It categorizes all techniques based on whether they use (a variant of) the standard Qwerty keyboard, a novel keypad or keyboard, or handwriting recognition, and discusses the design and evaluation of these techniques. It excludes all techniques that, in theory, cannot function individually (i.e., require either additional devices or external sensors to function). It also excludes all speech recognition techniques.

Table 1 shows performances of the reviewed techniques from empirical evaluations, both in terms of speed and accuracy, when available. In most evaluations, participants were asked to transcribe short English phrases from the MacKenzie and Soukoreff set [24] using the examined technique(s). However, some studies used words [7] or phrases from a different set [20]. Most studies instructed participants to transcribe the phrases as fast and accurately as possible, and to correct their mistakes as they notice them. Table 1 displays entry speed in the standard words per minute (WPM), and accuracy in Error Rate (ER), Total Error Rate (TER), or Character Error Rate (CER) metrics [2]. For some techniques these metrics were derived from the other data reported in the literature.

2 The QWERTY Layout

The standard QWERTY is the most dominant keyboard layout in personal computers and handheld devices [3]. Therefore, many use a variant of QWERTY in text entry techniques for smartwatches with the hope that a familiar layout will encourage users to use it and will accommodate a faster transition from novice to expert. Although not optimized for ultra-small devices, many have also explored the possibility of using a miniature version of the standard QWERTY on smartwatches [16]. This section reviews all techniques that use the QWERTY layout in some capacity.

Virtual Sliding QWERTY (VSQ). This technique loads a smartphone QWERTY keyboard on smartwatches, but displays only a part of it on the screen (Fig. 1). To see an invisible region, the user has to change the view by dragging the keyboard to the intended direction [5]. To enter a character with this technique, the user first navigates to the region where it is located, providing it is not already in the visible area, then taps on the corresponding key. In addition to using the space and backspace keys, the user can also enter a space and backspace by performing left and right swipes on the input area, respectively.

Fig. 1. The Virtual Sliding QWERTY (VSQ). To enter a character with this technique, the user drags the keyboard to a particular region and then taps on the intended key.

SplitBoard. Similar to VSQ [5], SplitBoard displays a partial view of a larger keyboard [17]. It divides the standard QWERTY into two main sections and includes an extra section for the digits, symbol, caps, and enter keys that enable the entry of numbers, symbols, and uppercase characters (Fig. 2). To enter a character, the user first navigates to the section where the character is located by performing horizontal swipes, providing it is not already in the visible area, then taps on the corresponding key. The space and backspace keys are located at the bottom of the screen, and can be selected by touching the bezel.

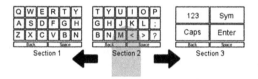

Fig. 2. The SplitBoard. To enter a character with this technique, the user navigates to a region by performing left and right swipes, and then taps on the intended key.

Swipeboard. Swipeboard [13] divides the standard QWERTY into nine regions (Fig. 3). Entering any character with this technique requires two swipes: the first swipe specifies the region where the character is located, and the second specifies the character within that region. These swipes can be performed anywhere on the screen, which eliminates the need for precise target selection. For space and backspace, the user has to perform a double-swipe diagonally down to the right and left, respectively. In addition, a double-swipe up switches to symbols and numbers.

Fig. 3. The Swipeboard. In this picture, the user first performs a left swipe to select one of the nine regions, and then a right swipe to select the character 'D'.

A smart eyewear adaptation of Swipeboard, called **SwipeZone**, slightly modifies the QWERTY layout and divides it into three regions, each containing three rows of keys [14]. To enter a character, the user first swipes vertically on a region to select one of its three rows, and then swipes horizontally towards the direction where the intended character is located. In a user study with Google Glass, SwipeZone reached up to 8.73 WPM with on average 24.9 % ER, including hard and soft errors.

Fig. 4. The ZoomBoard. When the user taps on the miniature QWERTY keyboard, it iteratively magnifies the touched region. The user then can tap on a particular key to enter the corresponding character. The keyboard goes back to its original state immediately after that.

ZoomBoard. ZoomBoard displays a miniature standard QWERTY on the screen [26]. To enter a character, the user roughly taps on the region where it is located, and the system iteratively magnifies the region until the keys are large enough for the user to select (Fig. 4). The user then enters the character by tapping on the corresponding key. The keyboard transforms back to its original state immediately after entering a character. ZoomBoard also enables space and backspace entry through a left and a right swipe on the keyboard, respectively. In addition, an up swipe switches the keyboard to symbols and numbers.

Callout and ZShift. Both Callout and ZShift are inspired by the callout feature of many modern virtual keyboards for smartphones. When a user touches a region of a miniature QWERTY keyboard, the Callout technique [22] displays a callout containing the currently selected character above the keyboard (Fig. 5). The user then can refine the selection by slightly moving the finger, and when satisfied, enter the character by lifting up the finger. One disadvantage of this technique is that the user has to rely on his/her spatial memory when refining a selection, as the fingertip usually covers most of the keyboard. ZShift [22] addresses this issue by showing a magnified version of the occluded region in the callout. It provides the user with visual feedback on the currently selected character by highlighting it in the callout, illustrated in Fig. 5, right.

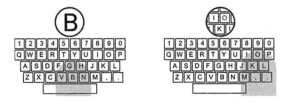

Fig. 5. The Callout and ZShift, respectively. The former displays the currently selected character in the callout, while the latter displays a magnified version of the occluded region and highlights the currently selected character. With both techniques, the user can refine the selection by slightly moving the finger, and enter a selected character by lifting the finger.

SlideBoard. SlideBoard [17] consists of fifteen keys laid out in a 5 × 3 grid, each containing two characters (Fig. 6). With this technique, the user swipes right on a key to enter the right character and swipes left to enter the left character. The enter, space, and backspace keys are located at the bottom of the screen, and can be selected by touching the bezel.

DualKey. DualKey [15] uses a very similar keyboard template as SlideBoard [17], see Fig. 6, but leverages the distinction between the index and middle fingers to enable single tap character entry. In DualKey, the first fourteen keys contain two characters,

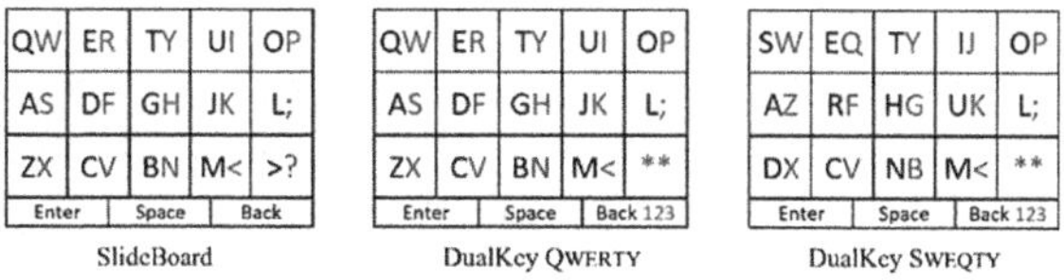

QW	ER	TY	UI	OP
AS	DF	GH	JK	L;
ZX	CV	BN	M<	>?
Enter		Space		Back

SlideBoard

QW	ER	TY	UI	OP
AS	DF	GH	JK	L;
ZX	CV	BN	M<	**
Enter		Space		Back 123

DualKey QWERTY

SW	EQ	TY	IJ	OP
AZ	RF	HG	UK	L;
DX	CV	NB	M<	**
Enter		Space		Back 123

DualKey SWEQTY

Fig. 6. The SlideBoard, DualKey QWERTY, and SWEQTY. With SlideBoard, the user swipes left or right on a key to enter the left or right character, respectively. In DualKey, the left and right characters associate with the index and middle fingers, respectively. Therefore, the user uses the index finger to enter the left character and middle finger to enter the right. The '**' key enables swapping a character with its same-key counterpart. SWEQTY is an optimized layout for DualKey that reduces the time required between two taps and the total finger switching instances.

where the right character associates with the middle and the left associates with the index finger. The '**' key enables swapping a character with its same-key counterpart, e.g., tapping on the key immediately after entering a 'Q' will replace it with a 'W'. The enter, space, and backspace keys are located at the bottom of the screen. A middle finger tap on the backspace switches the keyboard to symbols and numbers.

The SWEQTY layout attempts to increase the performance of DualKey by reducing the time and finger switching instances between subsequent taps. It deliberately maintains a closeness to QWERTY to accommodate faster learning (Fig. 6).

Fig. 7. Screenshots of Fleksy and Minuum, respectively. Both are predictive techniques that correct and disambiguate input at both character and word levels based on the sequence of keys pressed.

Fleksy. Fleksy is a commercial predictive keyboard, available for several touchscreen-based devices [10], including smartwatches [21]. Its predictive system autocorrects the entry at character-level as the user types based on the previous input and context. Fleksy also enables word prediction and autocorrection. In case of an incorrect autocorrection, the user can swipe down anywhere on the screen to see alternative suggestions. A long press on the screen enables symbols and number entry. The user can also delete one word at a time by swiping left on the screen. Figure 7 illustrates the technique.

Minuum. Minuum is a commercial predictive keyboard, originally designed for tablets [23], but can be used on various touchscreen devices, including smartwatches [33]. It condenses the three rows of keys in the standard QWERTY layout into a single line. The system disambiguates the input based on the sequence of keys pressed. It also includes an extra line for symbols and numbers (Fig. 7). Minuum also supports gestures. A right swipe on the screen enters a space, a left swipe deletes a full word, and two right swipes changes to symbols. There is no empirical evaluation available for Minuum on smartwatches.

Fig. 8. Screenshots of Swype and WatchWriter [13], respectively. Both are predictive techniques that enable gesture typing. The user enters one character per tap or one word per gesture. The traces in the picture indicate the gestures drawn to enter 'Swype' and 'please', respectively.

Swype. Swype is a commercial predictive keyboard, designed mainly for smartphones, that supports both touch and gesture typing [31]. With Swype, the user enters either one character per tap or a word per gesture (Fig. 8). It features a suggestion bar that displays the best predictions based on the preceding input and context. The user accepts a prediction by either tapping on the prediction bar or the space key. When a prediction is selected, the system automatically enters a space following the word. Further, Swype automatically corrects all likely incorrect words. Although not optimized for ultra-small devices, Swype has been evaluated on a smartwatch [6].

WatchWriter. WatchWriter supports both touch and gesture typing on smartwatches [13]. Similar to modern gesture keyboards, the user enters either a character per tap or a word per gesture. It also features a suggestion bar (Fig. 8) that displays the two best predictions based on a language model during gesture typing. During tap typing, the bold suggestion on the left displays the best prediction and the right suggestion displays the literal string. If the most likely prediction matches the literal string, the left suggestion displays the second most likely prediction. The user can accept a prediction by tapping on it, which also enters a space following the word. The backspace key is located beside the prediction bar. It operates at a word-by-word level, that is, deletes one word per tap.

3   Novel Keyboard Layouts

Many have also proposed novel text entry techniques for smartwatches. Most of these techniques map multiple characters onto a single key to account for the smaller screens and use different strategies to disambiguate an ambiguous entry. This section reviews all these techniques.

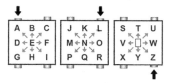

Fig. 9. The TiltType. To enter a character, the user tilts the device and presses one or more physical buttons. A character is entered based on the button(s) pressed and the direction and angle of the tilt.

TiltType. TiltType is a novel text entry technique for wristwatches [27] that utilizes four physical buttons (two above and two below the device) and eight compass directions for text entry (Fig. 9). It assigns all letters alphabetically and the space character to three different views that the user selects by pressing the top two and the bottom right physical buttons, respectively. To enter a character, the user tilts the device towards the direction where the character is located, and then presses the button respecting the view containing the character. Leveling the device selects the character in the center position. The user can refine the selection when holding the button by changing the tilt direction and angle. The fourth button (bottom left) is used for backspace and other special features. Pressing it without tilting enters a backspace, while tilting the device in different directions and angles enters uppercase characters, numbers, and symbols. TiltType requires two hands to operate, thus devices using this method must be easily removable from its wrist-strap. Unfortunately, there is no empirical evaluation available for the technique.

DragKeys. DragKeys [8], also known as Tipckle [32], consists of an array of circu- larly arranged keys that continuously follows the text cursor. It has two levels of key arrays, where each array contains multiple keys, and each key contains multiple characters (Fig. 10). To enter a character, first the user drags an ambiguous key con- taining multiple letters to the cursor. This loads the second-level non-ambiguous keys. The user then drags a non-ambiguous key to the cursor to enter the corresponding character. Skipping the second step enters the character in the center of the first-level key. The most frequently used characters are placed in that position, so that they can be entered with a single stroke. Unfortunately, there is no empirical evaluation available for the technique.

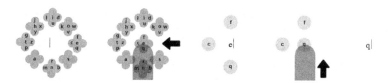

Fig. 10. The DragKeys. To input the letter 'Q', the user drags the right most key to the cursor to see the second-level keys containing the letters from the dragged key, and then drags 'Q' key to the cursor to input it. Skipping the second step enters the letter in the center 'E'.

Qwerty-like Keypad (QLKP). QLKP consists of nine keys laid out in a 3 × 3 grid, each containing multiple characters [18]. The keypad places the left characters of the Qwerty on the left column and the right characters on the right column to maintain a resemblance to the standard Qwerty layout (Fig. 11). Similar to Multi-tap [3], to enter a character with this technique the user taps on a key repeatedly until he/she gets the intended character. Although primarily designed for feature phones, this technique has been evaluated on a smartwatch [17]. The smartwatch version includes the enter, space, and backspace keys at the bottom of the screen that can be selected by touching the bezel.

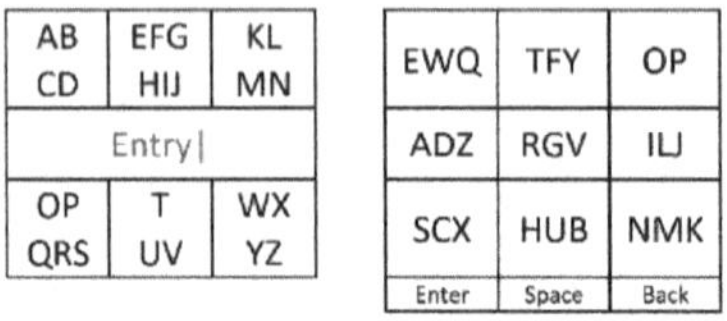

AB CD	EFG HIJ	KL MN
Entry|		
OP QRS	T UV	WX YZ

EWQ	TFY	OP
ADZ	RGV	ILJ
SCX	HUB	NMK
Enter	Space	Back

Fig. 11. The Optimized Alphabetic Layout (OAL) and Qwerty-like Keypad (QLKP), respectively. To enter a character with OAL, the user taps on the ambiguous keys and the system disambiguates the input based on the tap sequence. With QLKP, similar to Multi-tap on a standard 12-key keypad, the user taps on a key repeatedly until he/she gets the intended character.

Optimized Alphabetic Layout (OAL). OAL consists of six large ambiguous keys, three above and three below the input area [20]. The layout maps the letters onto the keys in alphabetic order (Fig. 11), but methodically splits them to reduce ambiguity errors and subsequent target distances. The keyboard uses a predictive system to disambiguate the input, that is, predicts the intended character based on tap sequences. It also suggests word completion that the user can accept by swiping right on the screen. A first tap on the central area enters a space, while the subsequent taps rotate through alternative suggestions that match the ambiguous entry. Similarly, a left swipe enters a backspace and a down swipe switches the layout to symbols and numbers.

UniWatch. UniWatch [29] is the smartwatch variant of a mobile text entry technique called UniGlyph [28]. It categorizes all characters into three groups based on the primary shape they are composed of. All characters that contain diagonal strokes are categorized as 'diagonal' characters, all other characters that contain loops or curves are categorized as 'curve' characters, and the remaining characters are categorized as 'line' characters. Accordingly, the UniWatch template consists of three keys, representing the three shapes (Fig. 12). To enter a character, the user taps on the key that represents its primary shape. As these shapes are shared between multiple characters, the technique disambiguates the input based on the sequence of keys pressed. Currently there is no empirical evaluation available for this technique. Relevantly, a text entry technique for smartphones, called UOIT, also exploits the shapes of the characters [1].

Table 1. Performances of text entry techniques for smartwatches from the literature. A "*" signifies results from a simulation.

Technique	Reference	Participant	Device	Diagonal Display mm	Keyboard Size mm	Key Size mm	Entry Speed WPM	Error Rate %	KSPC
NON-PREDICTIVE QWERTY									
QWERTY	16	18	Samsung Galaxy Gear	41.44	29.3×21.3	1.6×3.0	9.74	28.3^TER	-
					22.9×16.6	2.3×4.1	12.12	19.2^TER	-
					16.5×11.2	2.9×5.3	14.42	19.9^TER	-
	17	12	Samsung Galaxy Gear	41.44	-	2.9×5.3	12.90	21.4^TER	-
Virtual Sliding QWERTY (VSQ)	5	20	Microsoft Surface Pro 3	40.0	40.0×21.0	3.0×3.0	10.76	-	1.05
					50.0×26.5	4.0×4.0	11.66	-	1.03
					60.0×31.0	5.0×5.0	11.26	-	1.03
					70.0×36.5	6.0×6.0	10.64	-	1.02
					80.0×41.0	7.0×7.0	10.04	-	1.02
SplitBoard *	17	24	Samsung Galaxy Gear	41.44	-	4.8×6.5	14.75	7.5^TER	-
	16	18	Samsung Galaxy Gear	41.44	29.3×21.3	2.7×3.7	10.66	13.9^TER	-
					22.9×16.6	3.8×5.1	11.67	11.1^TER	-
					16.5×11.2	4.8×6.5	15.07	7.9^TER	-
Swipeboard	7	8	Apple iPad 3	-	12.0×12.0	1.5×1.5	19.58	17.5^ER	-
ZoomBoard	26	6	Apple iPad 3	-	16.5×6.1	1.5×1.5	9.30	-	2.15
	16	18	Samsung Galaxy Gear	41.44	29.3×21.3	1.6×1.6	8.02	10.1^TER	-
					22.9×16.6	2.3×2.3	9.09	6.7^TER	-
					16.5×11.2	2.9×2.9	9.26	7.3^TER	-
	17	12	Samsung Galaxy Gear	41.44	-	2.9×2.9	9.20	7.1^TER	1.85*
	22	20	Samsung Nexus S	25.46	16.0×6.5	1.5×1.5	6.00	15.3^TER	2.7
				33.94	21.3×8.6	2.0×2.0	7.80	8.0^TER	2.2
				45.25	28.4×11.4	2.6×2.6	8.20	7.3^TER	2.1
Callout	7	8	Apple iPad 3	-	16.5×6.1	1.5×1.5	17.08	19.6^ER	-
	22	20	Samsung Nexus S	25.46	16.0×6.5	1.5×1.5	4.30	19.9^TER	1.8
				33.94	21.3×8.6	2.0×2.0	7.10	14.8^TER	1.5
				45.25	28.4×11.4	2.6×2.6	8.30	12.4^TER	1.4
ZShift	22	20	Samsung Nexus S	25.46	16.0×6.5	1.5×1.5	5.40	15.4^TER	1.5
				33.94	21.3×8.6	2.0×2.0	7.20	13.9^TER	1.4
				45.25	28.4×11.4	2.6×2.6	9.10	12.3^TER	1.3
SlideBoard	17	12	Samsung Galaxy Gear	41.44	-	5.6×6.5	12.08	7.9^TER	1.85*
DualKey^QWERTY	15	10	LG G Watch	41.86	-	5.6×6.5	19.61	5.3^TER	-
PREDICTIVE QWERTY									
Fleksy	6	18	Samsung Galaxy Gear	41.44	-	5.66×-	20.3	16.0^TER	-
Swype	6	18	Samsung Galaxy Gear	41.44	-	4.10×-	29.3	9.0^TER	-
WatchWriter^Gesture	13	18	LG G Watch R	33.02	-	-	24.0	3.7^CER	0.4
WatchWriter^Tap	13	18	LG G Watch R	33.02	-	-	22.0	1.5^CER	1.5
NOVEL NON-PREDICTIVE									
QLKP	17	12	Samsung Galaxy Gear	41.44	-	9.5× 6.4	9.20	4.3^TER	1.53*
DualKey^SWBQTY	15	8	LG G Watch	41.86	-	5.6×6.5	21.59	3.27^TER	-
NOVEL PREDICTIVE									
OAL	20	20	Sony Smart-Watch 2	39.05	-	-	8.08	~5.7^CER	-
HANDWRITING RECOGNITION									
EdgeWrite	9	5	Breadboard	58.6	-	-	3.9	6.4^TER	-

ABCDEFGHIJKLMNO
PQRSTUVWXYZ

$$\boxed{\text{V/}}\ \boxed{\text{( )}}\ \boxed{\text{─I}}$$

Fig. 12. UniWatch consists of three keys, representing the 'diagonal', 'curve', and 'line' shapes. The dark parts of the letters (above) signify their primary shapes. To enter a letter, the user taps on the key that represents its primary shape, the technique disambiguates the input.

4   Handwriting Recognition

Researchers are also exploring handwriting recognition for text entry on smartwatches. Unlike virtual keyboards, where many keys share a small screen, handwriting can offer most of the screen for each character, allowing much more comfortable character entry [25]. In addition, prior investigations showed that some handwriting systems can be used without looking at the screen [11], enabling eyes-free text entry.

EdgeWrite. EdgeWrite is a unistroke-based technique for users with motor impairments [34]. Unlike natural handwriting, unistroke-based techniques limit user behaviors by allowing only a single way of drawing each character to avoid segmentation and other handwriting recognition related problems [4]. The EdgeWrite alphabet maintains a resemblance to its printed counterpart to maximize the user's ability to guess (Fig. 13). It requires the user to input characters by traversing the edges and diagonals of a square screen. Then a gesture is recognized not through patterns, but based on the sequence of corners that are hit. Recently, this technique has been evaluated in the context of a smartwatch [9].

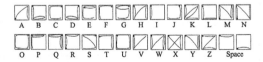

Fig. 13. EdgeWrite unistroke gesture alphabet. Here, a dot represents the start point of a stroke.

Analog Keyboard. Analog Keyboard [25] enables natural handwriting on smartwatches. With this technique, the user writes one character at a time on the screen using a finger. The system then recognizes the character, including digits and symbols, and inputs it. The keyboard also includes two narrow buttons in the left and right sides of the screen for backspace and space, respectively. Unfortunately, there is no empirical evaluation available for the technique.

5   Results and Discussion

Results suggest that predictive techniques perform relatively better than non-predictive techniques, both in terms of speed and accuracy. This is not surprising, considering users usually make more mistakes when typing on smaller screens, most of which predictive techniques can automatically correct. This improves the overall performance by reducing errors and error correction efforts. Most predictive techniques yielded over 20 WPM in empirical evaluations, while entry speeds for non-predictive techniques ranged from 4 to 22 WPM. Similarly, the lowest reported error rate was about 2 % with WatchWriter, a predictive technique. Error rates for non-predictive techniques ranged from 4 to 28 %. EdgeWrite yielded the lowest entry speed (4 WPM), which is not surprising considering it was designed for users with motor impairments.

To assist precise selection of smaller keys, most QWERTY-based techniques break up each key selection into a multi-step operation. However, the results do not indicate an immediate benefit of this approach. In studies, these techniques yielded on average 10 WPM, ranging from 4 to 20 WPM, while miniature QWERTY keyboards yielded on average 12 WPM. Both Swipeboard and ZoomBoard yielded noticeably better entry speed than QWERTY, roughly 20 and 17 WPM, respectively. However, the fact that these techniques were evaluated in longitudinal studies and on an Apple iPad may have contributed towards this. In other studies, ZoomBoard yielded on average 9 WPM. Hence, performances with these techniques may improve with practice. Error rates were mostly comparable between all techniques (~ 12 %). Some predictive techniques were relatively more accurate, but did not account for in-vocabulary errors in the studies, which would have increased their error rates. This suggests that these techniques are error prone, therefore demand extra correction efforts. This highlights the need for effective error correction methods for smartwatches.

Although some studies found significant effects of keyboard and key sizes on text entry performance [16], this survey failed to find a clear indication of this. This is most likely because performances do not differ substantially when keyboard and key sizes are within a certain range. Results of a prior study also support this assumption [22].

Interestingly, many are exploring techniques for feature phones on smartwatches, as these techniques also attempt to map all letters, digits, and symbols onto a smaller area [34]. Prior work in mobile text entry left a rich body of work, thus further investigations are necessary to fully understand whether (and how) these techniques, or modified versions of them, can be used on smartwatches. Further, most current techniques are designed for square-faced smartwatches. The support for round-faced devices is also important, as they are becoming increasingly popular among users [30]. Although modified versions of these techniques may function on round devices, thorough investigation is necessary to determine how that would impact their performances. Moreover, none of the current systems, apart from handwriting, explore eyes-free text entry. With eyes-free text entry users can reach their maximum entry speed, hence considered as the final step of the novice-expert transition [3]. This can also increase the usability of smartwatches. Thus, further investigation is necessary to design and develop methods that enable touch typing.

6 Conclusion

This document reviewed the most important text entry techniques for smartwatches. It categorized all techniques based on whether they use (a variant of) QWERTY, a novel keypad or keyboard, or a handwriting system. It discussed the design and motivation for all current techniques and presented their performances from the literature, both in terms of speed and accuracy, in a table. Finally, it concluded with a discussion of the remaining challenges and future possibilities in the area.

References

1. AbuHmed, T., Lee, K., Nyang, D.: UOIT keyboard: a constructive keyboard for small touchscreen devices. IEEE Trans. Hum.-Mach. Syst. **45**(6), 782–789 (2015)
2. Arif, A.S., Stuerzlinger, W.: Analysis of text entry performance metrics. In: IEEE Toronto International Conference—Science and Technology for Humanity, pp. 100–105. IEEE Press, Washington (2009)
3. Arif, A.S.: Predicting and Reducing the Impact of Errors in Character-Based Text Entry. York University, Toronto (2013)
4. Buxton, W.A.S.: Touch, gesture, and marking. In: Baecker, R.M., Grudin, J., Buxton, W., Greenberg, S. (eds.) Readings in Human Computer Interaction: Toward the Year 2000, pp. 469–524. Morgan Kaufmann, San Francisco (1995)
5. Cha, J.M., Choi, E., Lim, J.: Virtual sliding QWERTY: a new text entry method for smartwatches using Tap-N-Drag. Appl. Ergon. **51**, 263–272 (2015)
6. Chaparro, B.S., He, J., Turner, C., Turner, K.: Is touch-based text input practical for a smartwatch? In: Stephanidis, C. (ed.) 17th International Conference on Human-Computer Interaction. Posters' Extended Abstracts, pp. 3–8. Springer, Heidelberg (2015)
7. Chen, X.A., Grossman, T., Fitzmaurice, G.: Swipeboard: a text entry technique for ultra-small interfaces that supports novice to expert transitions. In: 27th Annual ACM Symposium on User Interface Software and Technology, pp. 615–620. ACM Press, New York (2014)
8. Cho, H., Kim, M., Seo, K.: A text entry technique for wrist-worn watches with tiny touchscreens. In: Adjunct Publication of the 27th Annual ACM Symposium on User Interface Software and Technology, pp. 79–80. ACM Press, New York (2014)
9. Darbar, R., Sen, P.K., Dash, P., Samanta, D.: Using hall effect sensors for 3D space text entry on smartwatches. In: 7th International Conference on Intelligent Human Computer Interaction. Elsevier, Philadelphia (2015)
10. Fleksy Keyboard. https://fleksy.com
11. Goldberg, D., Richardson, C.: Touch-typing with a stylus. In: INTERACT 1993 and CHI 1993 Conference on Human Factors in Computing Systems, pp. 80–87. ACM Press, New York (1993)
12. Gong, J., Tarasewich, P.: Alphabetically constrained keypad designs for text entry on mobile devices. In: SIGCHI Conference on Human Factors in Computing Systems, pp. 211–220. ACM Press, New York (2005)
13. Gordon, M., Ouyang, T., Zhai, S.: WatchWriter: tap and gesture typing on a smartwatch miniature keyboard with statistical decoding. In: 34th Annual ACM Conference on Human Factors in Computing Systems. ACM Press, New York (2016)
14. Grossman, T., Chen, X.A., Fitzmaurice, G.: Typing on glasses: adapting text entry to smart eyewear. In: 17th International Conference on Human-Computer Interaction with Mobile Devices and Services, pp. 144–152. ACM Press, New York (2015)
15. Gupta, A., Balakrishnan, R.: DualKey: miniature screen text entry via finger identification. In: 34th Annual ACM Conference on Human Factors in Computing Systems. ACM Press, New York (2016)

16. Hong, J., Heo, S., Isokoski, P., Lee, G.: Comparison of three QWERTY keyboards for a smartwatch. In: Interacting with Computers (2016)

17. Hong, J., Heo, S., Isokoski, P., Lee, G.: SplitBoard: a simple split soft keyboard for wristwatch-sized touch screens. In: 33rd Annual ACM Conference on Human Factors in Computing Systems, pp. 1233–1236. ACM Press, New York (2015)

18. Hwang, S., Lee, G.: Qwerty-like 3x4 keypad layouts for mobile phone. In: CHI 2005 Extended Abstracts on Human Factors in Computing Systems, pp. 1479–1482. ACM Press, New York (2005)

19. IC Insights.: Research Bulletin: Wearable Systems Give Major Boost to Total IoT Sales in 2015 (2015). http://www.icinsights.com/news/bulletins/Wearable-Systems-Give-Major-Boost-To-Total-IoT-Sales-In-2015

20. Komninos, A., Dunlop, M.: Text input on a smart watch. IEEE Pervasive Comput. 13(4), 50–58 (2014)

21. Lee, N.: Fleksy Keyboard Brings Predictive Touch Typing to the Galaxy Gear. Engadget (2014). http://www.engadget.com/2014/01/09/fleksy-galaxy-gear

22. Leiva, L.A., Sahami, A., Catala, A., Henze, N., Schmidt, A.: Text entry on tiny QWERTY soft keyboards. In: 33rd Annual ACM Conference on Human Factors in Computing Systems, pp. 669–678. ACM Press, New York (2015)

23. Li, F.C.Y., Guy, R.T., Yatani, K., Truong, K.N.: The 1line keyboard: a QWERTY layout in a single line. In: 24th annual ACM Symposium on User Interface Software and Technology, pp. 461–470. ACM Press, New York (2011)

24. MacKenzie, I.S., Soukoreff, R.W.: Phrase sets for evaluating text entry techniques. In: CHI 2003 Extended Abstracts on Human Factors in Computing Systems, pp. 754–755. ACM Press, New York (2003)

25. Microsoft Research: The Analog Keyboard Project. http://research.microsoft.com/en-us/um/redmond/projects/analogkeyboard

26. Oney, S., Harrison, C., Ogan, A., Wiese, J.: ZoomBoard: a diminutive qwerty soft keyboard using iterative zooming for ultra-small devices. In: 31st Annual ACM Conference on Human Factors in Computing Systems, pp. 2799–2802. ACM Press, New York (2013)

27. Partridge, K., Chatterjee, S., Sazawal, V., Borriello, G., Want, R.: TiltType: accelerometer-supported text entry for very small devices. In: 15th Annual ACM Symposium on User Interface Software and Technology, pp. 201–204. ACM Press, New York (2002)

28. Poirier, F., Belatar, M.: UniGlyph: only one keystroke per character on a 4-button minimal keypad for key-based text entry. In: 9th International Conference on Human-Computer Interaction, pp. 479–483. Springer, Heidelberg (2007)

29. Poirier, F., Belatar, M.: UniWatch - some approaches derived from UniGlyph to allow text input on tiny devices such as connected watches. In: Kurosu, M. (ed.) Human-Computer Interaction. LNCS, vol. 9170, pp. 554–562. Springer, Heidelberg (2015)

30. Sung, D.: Round v Square Faced Smartwatches: We Ask the Experts which is Best. Wareable (2015). http://www.wareable.com/smartwatches/round-v-square-smartwatches-which-is-best

31. Swype. http://www.swype.com

32. Tipckle. https://play.google.com/store/apps/details?id=esrc.korea.ac.kr.tipckle_ime

33. Typing On a Watch. http://minuum.com/minuum-on-smartwatch

34. Wobbrock, J.O., Myers, B.A., Kembel, J.A.: EdgeWrite: a stylus-based text entry method designed for high accuracy and stability of motion. In: 16th Annual ACM Symposium on User Interface Software and Technology, pp. 61–70. ACM Press, New York (2003)

MobiCentraList: Software Keyboard with Predictive List for Mobile Device

Georges Badr[1(✉)], Antoine Ghorra[2], and Kabalan Chaccour[1]

[1] TICKET LAB, Université Antonine, Hadat-Baabda, Lebanon
{georges.badr,kabalan.chaccour}@ua.edu.lb
[2] Université Antonine, Hadat-Baabda, Lebanon
antoine.ghorra1@gmail.com

Abstract. Software keyboards were designed to provide accessibility to mobile users as well as to people with motor disability. Text entry is henceforth made possible on portable devices such as mobile phones, tablets, pads. Despite their obvious utility, these keyboards present major drawbacks in terms of speed of acquisition and induced fatigue comparatively to conventional physical keyboards. Optimization efforts have showed efficacy by adding prediction lists and dictionaries. Other researches have considered the effect of the position of characters and the prediction list relatively to the time of acquisition and performance. Those researches were designed for computer software keyboards. In this paper, the position of the prediction list is investigated on a mobile device. The "MobiCentraList" is the mobile version of a previous computer software keyboard "Centralist" which was developed for this purpose. The position effect of the prediction list is studied and compared to natural software keyboards.

Keywords: Software keyboard · Prediction list · Text entry speed · Dictionary · Mobile device

1 Introduction

Nowadays digital texting have become an extremely important activity in our daily life. Beyond writing on hard papers as part of office activities, digital writing is considerably increasing and changing the way we communicate. As a matter of fact, verbal communication which was previously a privilege is leaving more room for the written communication using digital means through the use of short messaging systems (SMS) or even multimedia messaging systems (MMS). This amendment, which uses the digital text entry, is also accompanied by a significant development of portable computing devices. Desktop computers are currently replaced by mobile devices (mobile phone, touch pad, etc.). For portability and mobility reasons, these computing devices are becoming smaller and generally are not equipped with keyboards for digital entry. Hence, alternative methods of text input to replace the standard keyboard has become an insisting need. The software keyboard is presented as an intuitive and natural way to replace the physical keyboard. The user interacts with the system using a pointing device like a mouse, a stylus or even a finger.

© Springer International Publishing Switzerland 2016
M. Kurosu (Ed.): HCI 2016, Part II, LNCS 9732, pp. 268–277, 2016.
DOI: 10.1007/978-3-319-39516-6_25

However, experiments have shown that these onscreen keyboards were less efficient than their physical counterparts (45 words per minute for QWERTY standard keyboard [1], 20 words per minute for the software keyboard with the same layout of the characters [2] and 5 words per minute for a person with a disability entering text on a software keyboard [3]).

The current research examines the performance of a software keyboard developed on a mobile device. The developed keyboard is optimized in terms of character arrangement and prediction list position to increase the efficiency of digital data acquisition. We developed a mobile version of a previous computer software keyboard "CentraList". Performance indicators are also compared to a natural software keyboard that was also developed for this purpose to validate the previous results.

The paper is divided into four sections. A literature review on software keyboards is compiled in the first section. A state of the art on keyboards associated with a predictive list is detailed. In the second section, a new software keyboard model coupled to a prediction list is proposed for mobile devices. The third section presents the evaluation of our model in terms of performance, extraction and analysis of results. The fourth section concludes the paper.

2   Related Works

For portability and mobility reasons, the use of desktop computers follows an inclined road. As a result, physical standard keyboards will no longer exist. The most intuitive alternative to replace theses keyboards is to develop a software keyboard. In terms of input means, the user can hold a pointer, stylus or even use his fingers to enter text. Controversially, experiments carried out by MacKenzie [1, 2] showed the effectiveness of the results achieved by the physical keyboards compared to those obtained on software keyboards. These results were confirmed by Le Pévédic [3] for people with reduced mobility. The prestigious QWERTY or AZERTY arrangements were first introduced to slow down the text entry speed when typing on old typewriters. In fact, the speed caused the character bars of the machines to overlap. This constraint disappeared with the introduction of software keyboards. In this intuitive data entry application, text entry speed must be accelerated. To speed up character entry; optimizations must be made on the software keyboard. The literature reviews many optimizations techniques. These are either changing the shape of the keyboard or coupling it with a prediction system. Mixed techniques are also found.

Some keyboards use a list of fixed words like UKO-II [4]. Other systems, display the prediction list next to the last inserted character like PO-Box [5]. FASTY [6] pops up the list near the writing cursor in order to reduce the pointer's distance. These lists could be used with pointing devices [5, 7], or with a scanning system [8]. These lists are coupled to a word (or text) prediction system. The reader may find a survey concerning on text prediction systems with word lists in [9] (Fig. 1).

The main goal of adding a list of predicted words is to reduce the number of keystrokes and the distance of the cursor. It also aims to increase the speed of writing. But according to [10], the text entry rate is still not optimized regardless of the increase in the keystroke saving rate. In all cases, the user has to move his cursor between the keyboard and the list. Moreover, in cases like PO-BOX, the list is covering an important part of the keyboard. This may charge additional cognitive effort on the user. Those cognitive and perceptual efforts result in tiredness of the user and make him loose his focus on both the keyboard and the list.

Fig. 1. On the left, PO-BOX interface: when selecting a character, the list appears directly on it. On the right, FASTY interface, the list appears next to the cursor.

In this context, the most intuitive or natural character configuration is the alphabetical order. While this arrangement does not reduce the distance and the cursor movement, it has the advantage of being known by everyone. In [11], Norman and Fisher distributed the letters on several lines (Fig. 2A). Based on their experiments, alphabetical keyboards are not more efficient than QWERTY keyboards. MacKenzie [1] proposes to reduce the keyboard in two lines containing 13 letters each (Fig. 2B). Their experiments do not show any difference in the text entry rate. Neither MacKenzie nor Norman advises the alphabetical arrangement of keyboards. The text entry rate remains lower than with an ordinary keyboard because of the great distance between characters.

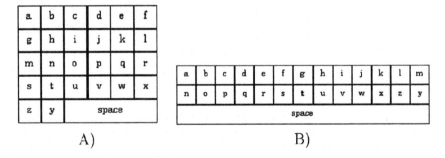

Fig. 2. Software keyboards with alphabetic arrangement

Far from the natural and intuitive solutions, we can find the methods that apply optimization algorithms. These methods compute a set of opportunities and keep only the best. The first system designed with such a method is the Getschow keyboard in [12]. The keyboard uses the construction algorithm (also named "greedy algorithm") and the frequency of occurrence of letters in the English language. The algorithm rearranges the character buttons to minimize average distances between them. Other proposed systems such as the GAG in [13] are based on genetic algorithms to generate a new keyboard design with an arrangement of characters that theoretically increase the speed of text entry. The proposed system would theoretically increase the speed of entering text with a stylus almost 50 % compared with QWERTY keyboards and soft AZERTY [13]. Others like Metropolis and Hooke [14] apply the laws of physics and thermodynamics to bi-gram tables to reduce the distances between the most frequently consecutive letters.

As simple as it may seem, creating a new keyboard arrangement would make the user lose his focus and eye gaze from both the keyboard and the list. This would dramatically slow the text entry rate and speed, and increase the tiredness of the user.

In the mobile world, systems couple their keyboard with a prediction algorithm in order to optimize text entry. Word completion or a list of words is presented to the user, but interaction is still the same as on desktop computers and thus results are the same (Fig. 3).

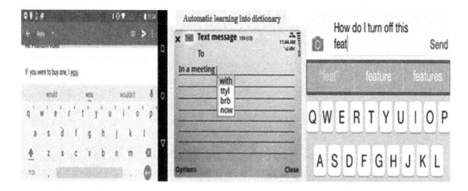

Fig. 3. Integration of list of predicted words on different mobile platforms

The present paper focuses on this problem of interaction. A mobile software keyboard model allied with a list of predicted words is proposed. The MobiCentraList is a mobile version of the previously designed software keyboard "Centralist" [15].

The previous study showed improvements in terms of speed and use of the list, as well as improvements in reducing the distance travelled by the cursor. Thus, the main objective was to validate the results obtained with CentraList on the desktop with MobiCentraList developed for mobile.

3   MobiCentralist

MobiCentraList is the new name of the mobile version of the CentraList. The latter was originally designed to place the prediction list in the center of attention of the user. The advantage is to keep the attention of the user in one place without hiding the keyboard characters. As shown in Fig. 4, letters were located around the prediction list in a square-like shape. CentraList keyboard was developed for desktop computers. MobiCentraList inherits the same properties of the desktop version. It aims to reduce the user's tiredness by minimizing the distance between the list and keys.

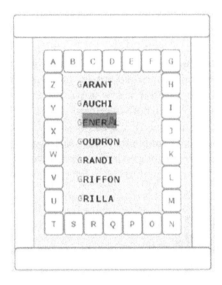

Fig. 4. CentraList desktop interface

3.1 Design

As shown in Fig. 5, Character keys are distributed alphabetically so the user will never lose the reference. Letters surround the list of predicted words, in a square like shape. The keyboard has 4 space character buttons, each on a side of the keyboard, as it is the most selected character. This configuration allows the user to select the nearest space to the last input letter.

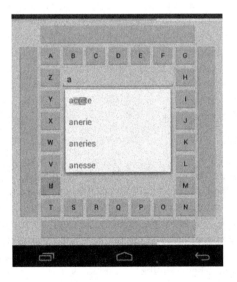

Fig. 5. MobiCentraList mobile interface

3.2 Experiments

To prove our hypothesis, MobiCentraList should be evaluated. The main idea is to validate the results of CentraList on a different platform.

Participants. Eight people (six men and two women) participated in this experiment. They were all volunteers aged between 21 and 43. The participants were all regular users of mobile and desktop QWERTY keyboards. They do not use the prediction list.

Apparatus and Equipment. The program was developed with JAVA for mobile using Android Studio 4.0.1 platform running on a Toshiba laptop with Windows 10. The program was then deployed on a 7 inches Android Tablet of the brand "ELEMENTS".

Evaluation. MobiCentraList is compared to a standard alphabetical keyboard with a list of prediction words (cf. Fig. 6). Both systems are limited with the 26 characters of the Latin alphabet and the space. They both have the same interactive list designed in [16] and use the same prediction algorithm based on the lexicographical tree. Same dictionary is also used by both systems. Participants had two exercises. They had to copy 40 words, with lengths greater than 5 letters, on both keyboards. The words were the same for the two exercises. The order of the exercises was counterbalanced. The first subject starts his first exercise with MobiCentraList then switches to the standard alphabetical keyboard. The second participant starts with the alphabetical keyboard then MobiCentraList and so on.

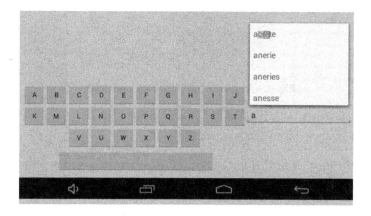

Fig. 6. Alphabetical keyboard interface.

Procedure. Participants were asked to copy as quickly as possible and with the least possible errors the list of 40 words using one finger only. At the end of each typed word, the user pressed the space bar to validate his entry and move to the next word and the list is re-initialized to its original state. Experimentations data were collected in an "XML" file when typing. These data are the words entered, the characters clicked, the coordinates (x, y) of the characters, the time taken to click the character and time of each word.

Results. The following variables were computed: the input speed (CPS), the distance between two consecutive strokes, the error rate, the key stroke per character (KSPC), and the hit rate (HR).

CPS. The input speed or character per second (CPS) is the number of characters entered per unit of time (e.g. second). This speed is obtained by dividing the number of characters (N) by the time. The entry time is usually taken between the first character to enter and the last character. In this case, $N - 1$ is the total number of character.

$$CPS = \frac{\text{Number of characters entered} - 1}{\text{time}} \text{(Error! Bookmark not defined.)}$$

The analysis of the results (Fig. 7) shows that the users have gained speed while typing on MobiCentraList compared with the alphabetic keyboard. In fact, the number of characters clicked per one second has increased.

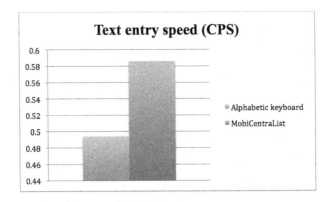

Fig. 7. Text entry speed for both keyboards

On average, CPS has increased from 0.494 with alphabetic keyboard to 0.586 with MobiCentraList showing an average gain of 18.6 %.

KSPC and Hit Rate. KSPC is the number of operations required to enter a word or character. If no list is present, each character requires one click on the keyboard (KSPC is equal to one). When the list is present, and the user selects the word from it, the number of operations needed is reduced, thus, KSPC is less than one.

$$KSPC = \frac{\text{Number of characters entered}}{\text{Total number of characters}} \text{(Error! Bookmark not defined.)}$$

Hit Rate represents the percentage of times the user selects his word from the prediction list. The results of this experiment showed that MobiCentraList has drawn user's attention to the list and thus he is using the list further. In fact, the use of the prediction list has increased by 8.3 % when copying words with the new system.

The frequent use of the list is shown by the decrease of the KSPC's value. This means that the user requires fewer operations to enter a word. The result shows a significant reduction in the average number of operations needed to enter a character from 0.831 actions on the alphabetic keyboard to 0.756 actions on MobiCentraList (a decrease of 9.9 %). In comparison, a standard software keyboard requires an action by character (Fig. 8).

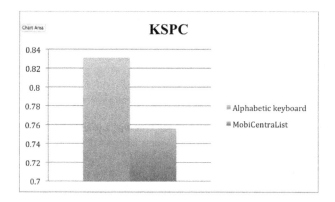

Fig. 8. KSPC for both keyboards

Distance between Two Strokes. This measures the distance of the path travelled by the finger between letters themselves and between letters and the prediction list. As far as the distance is reduced, the user's fatigue is reduced, thus, the performance of the user is increased.

Our hypothesis was that when placing the prediction list in the center of the keyboard, this would lead to a reduction in the distance between two strokes. The results of the experiments confirmed that hypothesis. Thus, we obtained a reduction in term of distance the user has to do between two clicks. In fact, the pointer (finger in our case) travelled an average distance of 1638.6 pixels with the classical keyboard and an average distance of 1484.97 pixels on MobiCentraList. This will give the user a benefit of about 9.3 %.

Error Rate. The error rate is the percentage of typos made when entering a number of words. Whenever a mistake is made, the system records it. During the exercises, error was recorded when the current character differed from the expected character. In average, the error rate was less than 3 % for both keyboards. (1.9 % for the classical keyboard and 1.8 % with MobiCentralist).

4   Conclusion

In this article, we presented a software keyboard for mobile operating systems with a list of predictions (MobiCentraList). This paper was to confirm the results obtained with the same design implemented on a desktop computer (CentraList). The keyboard is constituted with the 26 alphabetic letters positioned around a list of prediction. By this arrangement, the user may focus his eye-gaze on the center of the keyboard, and select the word from the list once it appears. By this, he will improve his text entry speed and reduce the number of operations he needs to enter a word, thus reduce his fatigue. We also evaluated the system and compared it with a classical alphabetical keyboard. The results showed a benefit for the users in terms of speed and reduction of the distance. Those results confirmed the ones we obtained using the desktop version.

References

1. Mackenzie, I.S., Zhang, X.S.: The design and evaluation of a high performance soft keyboard. In: Proceedings of the ACM Conference on Human Factors in Computing Systems. ACM Press, New York, pp. 25–31 (1999)
2. Mackenzie, I.S., Zhang, X.S., Soukoureff, R.W.: Text entry using soft keyboards. Behav. Inf. Technol. **18**, 235–244 (1999)
3. Le Pévédic, B.: Prédiction morphosyntaxique évolutive dans un système d'aide à la saisie de textes pour les personnes handicapées physiques. Rapport de thèse, Université de Nantes, France (1997)
4. Harbusch, K., Hasan, S., Hoffmann, H., Kühn, M., Schüler, B.: Domain-specific disambiguation for typing with ambiguous keyboards. In: Proceedings of the 2003 EACL Workshop on Language Modeling for Text Entry Methods. ACL Workshops. Association for Computational Linguistics, Morristown, NJ, pp. 67–74 (2003)
5. Masui, T.: An efficient text input method for pen-based computers. In: Proceedings of the ACM Conference on Human Factors in Computing Systems, CHI 1998 (1998)
6. Beck, C., Seisenbacher, G., Edelmayer, G., Zagler, W.L.: First user test results with the predictive typing system FASTY. In: Miesenberger, K., Klaus, J., Zagler, W.L., Burger, D. (eds.) ICCHP 2004. LNCS, vol. 3118, pp. 813–819. Springer, Heidelberg (2004)
7. Keystrokes on-screen keyboard, user manual. http://www.assistiveware.com/files/KeyStrokesXmanualA4.pdf
8. Wandmacher, T., Antoine, J.Y., Poirier, F., Départe, J.P.: SIBYLLE, an assistive communication system adapting to the context and its user. ACM Trans. Access. Comput. **1**(1), 1–30 (2008)
9. Garay-Vitoria, N., Abascal, J.: Text prediction systems: a survey. Univ. Access Inf. Soc. **4**(3), 188–203 (2006). Springer-Verlag
10. Newell, A.F., Booth, L., Beattie, W.: Predictive text entry with PAL and children with learning difficulties. Br. J. Educ. Technol. **22**(1), 23–40 (1991)
11. Norman, D.A., Fisher, D.: Why alphabetic keyboards are not easy to use: keyboard layout doesn't much matter. Hum. Fact. **24**, 509–519 (1982)
12. Getschow, C.O., Rosen, M.J., Goodenough-Trepagnie, C.: A systematic approach to design of a minimum distance alphabetical keyboard. In: Proceedings of Rehabiliation Engineering Society of North America ñ RESNA 9th Annual (1986)
13. Raynal, M.: Claviers GAG: claviers logiciels optimisés pour la saisie de texte au stylet. In: Proceedings of the 18th International Conference of the Association Francophone d'Interaction Homme-Machine. ACM (2006)
14. Zahi, S., Hunter, M., Smith, B.A.: The Metropolis Keyboard - an exploration of quantitative techniques for virtual keyboard design. In: Dans Actes de The 13th Annual ACM Symposium on User Interface Software and Technology (UIST), pp. 119–218, San Diego, California (2000)

15. Badr, G., Raynal, M.: Centralist. In: European Conference for the Advancement of Assistive Technology in Europ, Maastricht, 31/08/2011–02/09/2011. IOS Press, pp. 944–951, September 2011

16. Badr, G., Raynal, M.: WordTree: results of a word prediction system presented thanks to a tree. In: Stephanidis, C. (ed.) UAHCI 2009, Part III. LNCS, vol. 5616, pp. 463–471. Springer, Heidelberg (2009)

Cognitive Load and Attention for Mobile Applications: A Design Perspective

Upasna Bhandari[1(✉)], Wen Yong Chua[1], Tillmann Neben[2], and Klarissa Chang[1]

[1] Department of Information Systems, School of Computing,
National University of Singapore, Singapore, Singapore
upasna.bhandari@u.nus.edu.sg, changtt@comp.nus.edu.sg
[2] Chair of General Management and Information Systems,
University of Mannheim, Mannheim, Germany
neben@uni-mannheim.de

Abstract. Aesthetics has been the success factor of Apple products. Despite of knowing aesthetics as a success factor, researchers and practitioners have limited aesthetics to purely defining it without any factors of practicability being instilled to it. Two factors of practicability could be design balance and complexity. To fill the gap of the need for practicability factors to be instilled into the understanding of aesthetics, this studies draws upon the Gestalt theory to examine how design balance and complexity could be applied on mobile app design. As a research in progress, we plan to validate the effects of design balance and complexity empirically.

Keywords: Mobile applications · Attention · Cognitive load · Aesthetics

1 Introduction

The success of Apple products is of no surprise to anyone (Brosch et al. 2010). The company has established their reputation of having aesthetically designed products. This beauty has been associated with a strong emotional desire from consumers that results in an increased desire to own them (Norman 2005). Aesthetics is a major dimension when designing products. Aesthetics is however a broad term and has been explored with different focuses. All these definitions have an underlying common dimension of beauty embedded in them (Kant 2000).

Concept of aesthetically designed IT products has been used for websites in the past (Lynch 2009; Papachristos and Avouris 2011; Van der Heijden 2003). It was observed the aesthetics and design in general can impact an array of factors affecting user's attitudes towards website. Broadly speaking, the concept of usability has been the most popular when measuring user's response to product like websites and other IT products (Nielsen 1994). However this phenomenon has not been explored in case of mobile applications. Some research has found evidence that is similar to websites, mobile applications designed with aesthetic parameters in consideration impact the quality perception of the applications (Bhandari et al. 2015).

© Springer International Publishing Switzerland 2016
M. Kurosu (Ed.): HCI 2016, Part II, LNCS 9732, pp. 278–284, 2016.
DOI: 10.1007/978-3-319-39516-6_26

Specifically aesthetics has been looked at frequently to understand and open the black box of how users form judgments towards IT products. Multiple scales have been created to measures aesthetic for websites. Lavie and Tractinsky (2004) has developed the perceived visual aesthetic scale that sub classifies aesthetics into classic and expressive aesthetics which can be used to evaluate whether websites have followed a particular aesthetic bent (Lavie and Tractinsky 2004). Despite of having the understanding of the importance of aesthetics, efforts in this direction has been limited to only defining what design means resulting in major gaps. First, these studies did not test the dimensions of aesthetics with real world products to examine the reaction of the users.

Second, it is still unclear why these aesthesis dimensions have an impact on how we process information specifically design processing mechanism. Does it appeal to certain cognitive or affective dimension that drives the subsequent behavior and judgments? This is an important question to answer if we want to move towards a more customize experience for users.

Self-report measures have been used to have retrospective measures of factors like attractiveness, intention to use, attitude which are central to user's reacting to IT products. A major criticism of transitional psychometric measures is self-reporting which might be far from real time evaluations. In this vein, researchers are now looking at supplement traditional psychometric measures with more objective measures for e.g. physiological measures which can help in measuring constructs like emotions, attractiveness, attention, cognitive engagement etc. This can further strengthen the confidence of refreshers and practitioners in phenomenon under focus.

Keeping these gaps in mind this study addresses above-mentioned issues. First of all we manipulate design factors specifically to see their effect on cognitive processing of design and subsequent effect on attitude towards applications. Also we uncover the black box of design processing on the context of mobile applications. Finally we use combination of subjective and objective measures for measuring the processing mechanism.

2 Theoretical Background

Achieving harmony is in important design principle to achieving greater usability (Dilman 2005). The word harmony is often interchangeable by the word unity. They are being referred to as a complete concord among the elements in a design. For instance, they appear as though they were being brought together through some visual connection, thus, giving them a sense of belonging together (Lauer and Pentak 2011). Therefore, we propose that unity in designing mobile applications can be achieved through balance and visual complexity.

2.1 Design Factor-Balance

According to Lauer, balance refers to the allocation of visual weight within a screen. In accessing pictorial balance (screen on the mobile app), an individual would expect to see some form of equal distribution on both sides using the center vertical axis as a separator. Using a seesaw as an example, the vertical axis would act as the fulcrum and the two sides will need to be in equilibrium. When equilibrium is not achieved, an individual will feel that something is just not right. The individual will feel that there is a need to rearrange the elements on the screen. According to Lauer, Balance can be achieved through multiple ways (Lauer and Pentak 2011).

First, it could be achieved through bilateral symmetry. Bilateral symmetry could be applied by repeating similar shapes on the exact positions on both axes. It is also commonly known as formal balance (Lauer and Pentak 2011). This is inline with the law of similarity in the Gestalt theory (Fisher and Smith-Garatto 1998–1999). In this law, individuals will be attracted to it by grouping the similar objects together. Individuals will be able to recognize them because they look similar in the same arrangement (Fultz 1999).

Second, balance can also be attained through value. Value is determined by the amount of contrast, which describes the lightness, or darkness of the hue. For instance, black gives a powerful contrast than grey against white. The addition of 'white' color creates a tint, which increases the value of the color. On the other hand, the addition of 'black' produces a shade which lowers the value of the color (Lauer and Pentak 2011). Hence, choosing a dark color against a light color commonly does this, as it would attract the individual's attention.

Last but not least, balance could also be achieved through color. It is commonly used to create the focal point of the picture. For instance, individual will be attracted to brighter colors such as yellow as compared to darker colors like grey or black. Hue is one of the properties of color. It simply refers to the name of the color that is red, orange, green or purple that could be mixed to produce other colors such as pink or red. According to Lauer, "hue describes the visual sensation of the different parts of the color spectrum" (Lauer and Pentak 2011).

2.2 Design Factor-Complexity

Geissler et al.'s (2001) in his study found that visual complexity has the notion of how many elements occupy the design space. This density can further impact how users react to the design in terms of first impressions. Similar to Heissler's results other studies have also found complexity to majorly impact user judgments. Findings regarding the influence of amount of text, number of links, and number of graphics on user's perceived complexity of webpage have been found (Deng and Poole 2005).

Other way of understanding this is in terms of the output of variations in visual complexity. Studies found that by manipulating complexity it can impact aesthetic processing, fluency processing and other derivatives (Reber et al. 2004).

When varying the amount of information in the stimuli increases complexity it will require higher amount of cognitive resources for aiding information processing. This can result in users developing liking towards certain stimuli and impact usability parameters like attention.

3   Hypothesis Development

According to Lauer (Lauer and Pentak 2011), symmetry could be achieved through a balance of color or value. An interface that is designed with high symmetry consists of text and images that are aligned along either of the axis. This alignment could be achieved through the usage of colors. On the other hand, an interface that is designed with low symmetry will not have equally aligned text and images. This will cause the user to feel that something is just not right which results in a reduced attention span. Therefore, the individual will feel that there is a need to rearrange the elements on the screen for a better cognitive processing of information on the interface.

H1 (a) Higher balance will negatively affect the cognitive load associated with mobile applications.

H1 (b) Increased balance will positively affect the attention associated with mobile applications.

While balance deals primarily with alignment and grouping of information, complexity deals with amount of information. Higher complexity is achieved by having higher density of interface elements. When user is exposed to highly complex information, it increases the cognitive resources required to process the information. This leads to a higher cognitive load.

H2 (a) Higher complexity will positively affect the cognitive load associated with mobile applications

On the other perspective, it can also lead to increased attention. However the subsequent user judgment of this effect may not be positive. Heightened attention can often result in disliking if it is accompanied by increase in cognitive load. This we hypothesize:

H2 (b) Higher complexity will positively affect the attention associated with mobile Higher

Information processing perspective, more information is more resources needed.

Usability has been at the centre of a number of studies but they have different focuses ranging from satisfaction to visual appeal to trust etc. Studies have linked usability with cognitive processing of design elements (Van der Heijden 2003) and also the affective component of initial impressions. In this study we look at the cognitive aspect of design only. When the individual has to encounter an interface that requires a high cognitive load, the individual will have to spend more time processing the information on the screen, which results in a lower satisfaction. Therefore, we hypothesize,

H3: Higher cognitive load will negatively affect the attitude towards mobile applications

An individual is often attracted to an interface with higher degree of balance and a lower complexity. Such attraction will increase the individual's satisfaction towards the application and user will be more willing to use mobile application. Therefore, we hypothesize,

H4: Higher attention will positively affect the attitude towards mobile applications.

4 Research Methodology and Data Analysis

The main objective of this study is to find how aesthetic based design attributes impact the cognitive dimension and attention parameters of design processing. We thus manipulate balance and complexity to induce high and low levels of balance and complexity. Within subject experiments are designed and exposing participants to the manipulated stimuli can collect data. The analyses involved preprocessing of neurophysiological data to get objective measurements for cognitive load and attention. This can be used to run repeated measures ANOVA to find within subject and between subject differences.

4.1 Stimuli

In this study we choose to study 6 applications that have been ranked under *Top 30 applications* in the iTunes applications store. The reason is because we want to explore what works with top performing applications with regards to design. These applications are chosen to have high or low complexity (text), high/low complexity (images) and high/low (balance). We hence operationalized two independent variables: complexity and balance. For low balance interfaces, text and images are not aligned along either of the axis. Mirroring of visual composition is not done in these designs to achieve difficulty in information processing. Balance makes it easier for us to process the information and thus a low balance interface needs to have lack of alignment across horizontal or vertical axis. For complexity, manipulations can be done for image and text both. Limiting the number of images and textual space can offer clean manipulations for complexity. We designed two levels of complexity (complexity increases from low to high) in the stimuli by manipulating numbers if links, graphics and text.

4.2 Eye Tracking

Part of the problem with using just subjective measures is common method bias and also ambiguity in measurement and complex interpretations. Physiological measurements are used less in measuring first impressions and don't suffer from being overshadowed by extreme retrospective processing in self-reported measures. Measuring the physiological changes of users enables assessing their reaction to the experienced applications. Research suggests that physiological tools can be effectively used to measure reaction to design base interfaces (Strebe 2011). Popular techniques include using screen saving, facial and eye movement tracking. We use eye tracking as it can measure unbiased and immediate reaction as the stimulus presents itself. The users have little control over their physiological reaction to the stimuli and it can capture even before they actively start analyzing the design. Another advantage if eye tracking is that we can do area of interest analysis. We divide the stimuli into various areas and these can be compared across the board with other stimuli.

We measure cognitive demand objectively by pupil dilation as our first dependent variable (Palinko et al. 2010). Fixations and saccades are recorded to measure attention. Fixation count and saccades are an important physiological measure for understanding how users are processing the design and thus can be used to measure attention, which is our second dependent variable. The important thing to note is that we restrict the amount of time the stimuli shows in order to restrict over processing. What we are capturing is the instant first impression reaction of users. We aim to add understanding of how design factors affect design processing amongst users. Also practically for mobile application designers this study can guide them on important design considerations to bear in mind while designing their applications (Fig. 1).

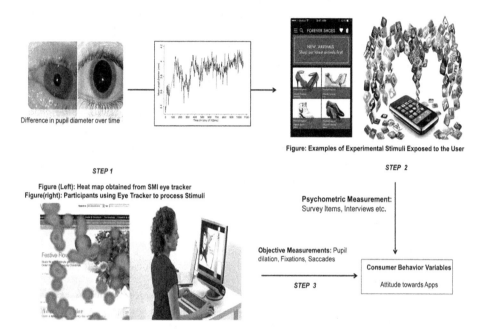

Fig. 1. Schematic diagram of the research model

5 Conclusion

Smartphone users across the globe are using their devices to do all kind of tasks. From online shopping to personal entertainment to travel based tasks. They achieve these using special programs called mobile applications or popularly known as "applications". In such a scenario it has become more than ever critical to understand what "clicks" with users from design perspective. Usability perspective has long helped solve this problem. However a new issue is emerging where users have multiple options for smart phone application. A common scenario is when users are overloaded with choices and possess only restricted information to make this decision. Design can be crucial in such cases and the main factor driving the purchase or in this case download decision. User often has to make a choice whether to download this app or not. This decision in such a case can be dependent on design mostly. This is because it is the only thing that users get exposed to at this stage. Information processing based perspective can offer insight to this problem with a special focus on design information.

References

Bhandari, U., Neben, T., Chang, K.: Understanding visual appeal and quality perceptions of mobile apps: an emotional perspective. In: Kurosu, M. (ed.) Human-Computer Interaction. LNCS, vol. 9169, pp. 451–459. Springer, Heidelberg (2015)

Brosch, T., Pourtois, G., Sander, D.: The perception and categorisation of emotional stimuli: a review. Cogn. Emot. **24**(3), 377–400 (2010)

Kant, I.: Critique of the Power of Judgment. Cambridge University Press, Cambridge (2000)

Lavie, T., Tractinsky, N.: Assessing dimensions of perceived visual aesthetics of web sites. Int. J. Hum. Comput. Stud. **60**(3), 269–298 (2004)

Lynch, P.: Visual decision making. A List Apart: For People Who Make Websites (286) (2009)

Nielsen, J.: Usability inspection methods. In: Conference Companion on Human Factors in Computing Systems. ACM, pp. 413–414 (1994)

Norman, D.A.: Emotional Design: Why We Love (or Hate) Everyday Things. Basic books, New York (2005)

Papachristos, E., Avouris, N.: Are first impressions about websites only related to visual appeal? In: Campos, P., Graham, N., Jorge, J., Nunes, N., Palanque, P., Winckler, M. (eds.) INTERACT 2011, Part I. LNCS, vol. 6946, pp. 489–496. Springer, Heidelberg (2011)

Van der Heijden, H.: Factors influencing the usage of websites: the case of a generic portal in the Netherlands. Inf. Manage. **40**(6), 541–549 (2003)

Dillman, D.A., Gertseva, A., Mahon-Haft, T.: Achieving usability in establishment surveys through the application of visual design principles. J. Off. Stat. **21**(2), 183 (2005). http://search.proquest.com/docview/1266791770?accountid=13876

Lauer, D., Pentak, S.: Design Basics. Cengage Learning, Boston (2011)

Fisher, M., Smith–Gratto, K.: Gestalt theory: a foundation for instructional screen design. J. Educ. Technol. Syst. **27**(4), 361–371 (1998–1999)

Fultz, J.: Theory of Gestalt Psychology (1999). http://users.anderson.edu/~jfultz/gestalt.html. Accessed 21 Oct 2000

Reber, R., Schwarz, N., Winkielman, P.: Processing fluency and aesthetic pleasure: is beauty in 40 the perceiver's processing experience? Pers. Soc. Psychol. Rev. **8**(4), 364–382 (2004)

Cox, D., Cox, A.D.: Beyond first impressions: the effects of repeated exposure on consumer 6 liking of visually complex and simple product designs. J. Acad. Mark. Sci. **30**(2), 119–130 (2002)

Arnheim, R.: Order and complexity in landscape design. In: Arnheim, R. (ed.) Toward a Psychology of 20 Art. University of California Press, Berkeley, Los Angeles (1966)

Nadkarni, S., Gupta, R.: A task-based model of perceived website complexity. MIS Q. **31**(12), 501–524 (2007)

Data Visualization in Mobile Applications: Investigating a Smart City App

Andrei Garcia[✉], Cristina Camacho, Marina Bellenzier, Marina Pasquali, Tiago Weber, and Milene S. Silveira

PUCRS, Faculdade de Informática, PUCRS, Porto Alegre, Brazil
{andreig,pasquali,tiago.weber}@hp.com,
cristinarcamacho@gmail.com, marinabellenzier@gmail.com,
milene.silveira@pucrs.br

Abstract. After the popularity of smartphones, a large number of different applications have been developed with a view to facilitate the users' life and their community. Among this scenario, Smart Cities applications intended to offer ideas, services or content adding value to a city or community. Generally built based on maps, these applications provide a large amount of data. In this research, we aim to analyze data visualization in a map-based application, investigating zooming and panning functionalities from a diverse user perspective. The selected application is Colab.re, an online collaboration system which allows the users to report urban issues based on their location. The main idea is to observe if potential users could perform the needed gestures to navigate in the map, and understand the information received.

Keywords: Data visualization · Map-based application · Smart cities

1 Introduction

Nowadays the use of mobile applications (apps) to improve community collaboration is increasing. Collective intelligence and crowdsourcing have become a common approach to many problems that cannot be easily solved or that need human feedback explicitly [1]. Supported by this concept, these apps can offer services, ideas or content.

In the context of Smart Cities, many citizen apps have been using collective intelligence to address urban problems. These applications can appear in multiple flavors and different dimensions regarding their data source, goals and types of urban problem they tackle [2]. Thus, in order to contextualize community information, many of them are built based on maps [3, 4], which is the case of Colab.re[1].

On Colab.re, citizens can identify and report urban problems, suggest improvements and rate public services using a map view. The usability of mobile map applications depends not only on data visualization, but also on the interaction with map and device [5]. Regarding mobile devices, the use of gestures such as pinch to zoom and drag to pan is frequent because they generally have small screens. In addition, the interaction with maps usually requires the exploration of large spaces, increasing the mentioned interactions [6].

---

[1] www.colab.re.

© Springer International Publishing Switzerland 2016
M. Kurosu (Ed.): HCI 2016, Part II, LNCS 9732, pp. 285–293, 2016.
DOI: 10.1007/978-3-319-39516-6_27

Focusing on map interactions and their data visualization, the present research intends to better understand the user's interaction with maps in this class of apps. To perform this user study, we have selected a sample divided by users with and users without previous knowledge of map-based applications. The main goal of this separation was to examine if users could perform the gestures that are necessary to navigate in the map and comprehend the information received.

The remaining of this paper is organized as follows. In the next section, we discuss background on map-based interfaces and their interactions such as zooming and panning. Following that, we describe our method divided in application definition, planning, pilot test, observation, and data analysis. Thereafter we report the results based on the user study. Finally, we draw some conclusions from this work and point out further research on this topic.

2   Background

The idea of data visualization is to transform complex data sets in visual representation, presenting data in various forms with different interactions. Thus, the user can spot patterns, structures and features to understand the underlying data [7]. For mobile applications in multi-touch devices, data visualization also needs to handle available screen space and user interactions [8].

One of the most common multi-touch interactions is the pinch gesture. The pinch gesture is dated from early 80's [9] and it can be defined as a lateral motion expanding or contracting the finger spread [10]. This continuous action, performed with two fingers, is called zooming, which enables users to zoom in or zoom out an image or a map, for example.

In the map context, zooming functionality allows users to change the map scale. Along with zooming there is panning, which is the ability to reposition the map on the screen [11]. The panning action can be performed with hold and drag gestures in any direction, generally with one finger. Zooming and panning are used to navigate in 2D spaces that are too large to be displayed within a single window.

Beyond the pinch and drag interactions, there are some other available gestures that can be performed in map applications to accomplish zooming and panning. One of them is the Double-Tap gesture, which allows zooming in with only one hand by using a double tap with one finger. Another one, introduced by Google Maps, is Double-Tap-and-Hold + Drag. This gesture allows zoom adjustments with one finger, tapping twice, holding the screen the second time and then moving the finger upwards to zoom out, or downwards to zoom in. Furthermore, there is Two-Finger-Tap, used by Google Maps and Apple Maps, that allows zooming out by tapping the screen with two fingers [6].

Regarding zooming and panning functionalities, Jokisch et al. [12] performed an empirical research where the main goal was to examine if users could find and use gestures on a multi-touch device. They examined three gestures used to interact with a virtual globe, which were drag to pan, pinch to zoom and tilt to change the inclination angle of the camera. To carry out their study they used the multi-touch version software Google Earth. The first main test was performed with adults aged between 20 and 30 years old with no background in computer science, and the second main test was performed with children from a primary school. Their findings were that many but not all adults knew intuitively how to operate the multi-touch device, even if they did not have experience with this technology. Children interacted faster and more frequently with the device, having more difficulty to find the right gestures. Although this study focused on users with no background, it did not studied older users.

3   Method

The user study was composed of the following phases: application selection, planning, pilot test, observation, and data analysis [13].

In the first phase, we investigated different apps related to spatial data visualization that allow observation of functionalities as zooming and panning. With respect to planning the study, we decided to investigate zooming and panning functionalities in map-based application and observe users with or without previous knowledge of this type of system. We also defined the observation scenario, tasks and a questionnaire to collect data about the users' profile and their impression about the app. After planning, a pilot test was run with a 31-year-old female user, and the results of this observation were used to refine the questionnaires. In the observation phase, there were 24 participants. Of this amount, 50 % have had familiarity with map systems and the other 50 % have never used them.

3.1   Application Selection

In this stage, we explored different mobile applications that met the Smart City concept and allowed spatial data visualization. The criteria used to select this app were popularity and location. Considering both criteria and background, we were able to choose Colab.re application. The popularity of the app was relevant because of the amount of data available in the app. Colab.re is being used by several city halls and is available on Android and Apple platforms [14]. Regarding location, the app should be accessible in the city of Porto Alegre, where the study was performed; the case of Colab.re.

The proposal of Colab.re is to support city management through cooperation between citizens and city halls. By making use of it, users have the possibility to identify and pinpoint urban problems, suggest improvements and evaluate solutions. The main advantage of problem identification is that it accelerates the process of problem resolution by making the city hall aware of a problem [2]. These data create a collaborative map, containing pictures and location of an issue, which support concerned authorities to take assertive actions.

Citizens can use a smart phone to take a picture of a problem related to infrastructure, street cleaning, unlit lampposts, broken roads, litter, etc. The application automatically detects its location using the phone's GPS and allows the user to categorize and add comments about the problem. In addition, the user can track the progress of all reported issues through a map view and follow the issues of interest (Fig. 1). The city hall by its turn, can handle the problem assigning it to the specific public agency, and it can also inform citizens about the status of a reported problem. Once the problem is solved, it disappears from the map.

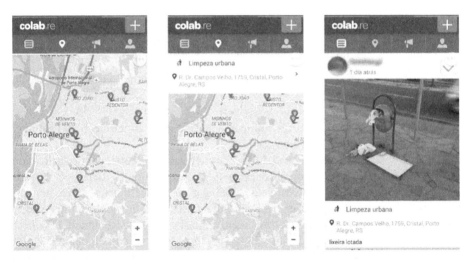

Fig. 1. Colab.re screenshots. From left to right: (1) Main map view pointing city problems; (2) a popup showing details about a selected problem; (3) details about a problem containing a picture, category and street address

According to Desouza and Bhagwatwar's [2] classification scheme, Colab.re can be classified as follows: Problem Identification regarding its goal, User Feed related to its data source, Mobile Device and Web Based App related to its platform deployment, and National regarding its range. Furthermore, Colab.re uses Google Maps as a basis for its map view.

3.2 Planning

In order to observe the zooming and panning functionalities and data visualization in the map-based application, we created a data collection tool, consisting of one questionnaire to collect data about the participants' profile, a user scenario and a questionnaire to collect their impression about the app after its use. In addition, an ethical protocol was presented to the participants with an informed consent form.

The sample was divided in people with previous knowledge in map-based applications, hereafter called experienced, and people with no prior knowledge in map-based apps, called beginners. The goal of this separation was to observe if potential users could perform the required gestures to navigate in the map, and identify data visualization issues. To guide the observation method, a scenario and two main tasks were defined:

Scenario: You are in the city of Porto Alegre and someone tells you there is an app to help you check urban problems, called Colab.re.

Task 1:   You decide to go through the system to verify if there is any problem near the place where you are.

Task 2:   After checking the first problem, you decide to find another one near your house/work. By choosing any problem that calls your attention, you decide to verify all details about the issue including resolution/status/progress.

3.3 Pilot Test

In this stage, we validated the scenario performing a pilot test. This preliminary study was performed with a 31-year-old female user, who have had previous knowledge in map-based applications. This test was not recorded. However, we could evaluate the study's feasibility and estimate the necessary time for each test. The results of this observation were used to refine the scenario and questionnaires.

3.4 Observation

The observation took place on the University campus. The user observations were performed with a sample of 24 participants, being 12 experienced and 12 beginners. Experienced participants' age ranged between 24 and 44 years old, and beginners' age ranged between 30 and 78. Seven experienced participants were male and five female. From beginners, five participants were male and seven female.

The participants were asked if they wanted to participate in a short user study focusing on evaluating a mobile application. After that, they were invited to answer a few questions about their profile and their experience using map-based applications. Afterwards they were given a short overview about Colab.re and the defined scenario with its tasks, and they were observed during the use of the app. Finally, after the observation, the interviewer asked some questions about the participants' experience and feelings during the observation. All observations were recorded for further analysis. One interviewer monitored the studies and another recorded the videos. Finally, it was possible to identify several issues by analyzing the recorded videos and the observations made during the study.

3.5 Data Analysis

Graphics were generated from questionnaires' results, which were used for quantitative data analysis. These data were used to compare the level of difficulty between the first and the second task used in the scenario, as well as to associate the user's profile. In addition, all comments about the participant's feedback were reviewed to find similar answers. Afterwards, a detailed video analysis has enabled the results' polishment.

4 Results

After the data and video analysis, we could compare information between people with previous knowledge and without prior knowledge. Moreover, we highlighted some issues that came up during the observations and became clear during the video analysis.

All experienced participants could use zooming and panning functionalities without great effort. However, not all beginners found out the needed gestures to perform zoom and pan. Two participants could not find the drag gesture to pan the map, and instead of that, they tried to navigate by tapping the problem's pins, which centralizes the map in the tapped pin. Besides that, the same two participants could not find the pinch gesture and could not zoom, using the map in the default zoom level to complete the tasks. In total, four participants could not find the pinch gesture, or any other gesture to perform zoom. One participant found only the pinch to zoom in and, before performing the gesture, he/she asked if he/she could "enlarge the map", referring to zooming in. As an alternative to pinch to zoom out, this participant used the Zoom Control (minus button) located in the bottom right corner of the map (Fig. 2-a).

Fig. 2. Observation: (a) use of zoom control; (b) use of index and middle fingers to zoom

The Zoom Control, which is a default control from Google Maps[2], was used by only three participants, two from experienced and one from beginners' group. Experienced participants used pinch in various ways. Besides the most common used fingers, thumb and index, to perform zooming, three participants used two thumbs, and two participants used index and middle fingers to zoom (Fig. 2-b). However, experienced participants did not use any different gestures to zoom, while two beginners performed Double-Tap to zoom in while they were trying to find possible gestures. Neither participants from experienced nor from beginners' group used no other gestures such as Double-Tap-and-Hold + Drag and Two-Finger-Tap.

During the execution of the first task, three main questions stood out. The first most cited was about the icons' size, followed by the lack of an auto-locate button, and the pin color, respectively. Regarding icons' size, ten beginners and four experienced participants reported that the icons inside pins were very small. Comments such as *"I cannot see the icon very well even when there is 100 % of zoom in"* became evident during the video analysis, when participants persisting to zoom in tried to magnify icons without success. In addition, six beginner participants reported problems to understand what some icons represented. One participant said the lamppost icon, represented by a bulb, symbolizes an idea to him.

---

[2] https://developers.google.com/maps/documentation/javascript/controls.

Another issue was related to the lack of an auto-locate button, which was reported by five participants right after they started the task. One participant stated he was not good with maps and the application could do the "*difficult work*" for him. Despite that, the participant could perform panning and zooming to complete the task. Finally, as mentioned before, the third highlighted issue was about the pin color. The application uses a green pin to draw all reported problems. Four participants said that green does not remind them of a problem and maybe the pin should be red to better symbolize it.

As shown in Fig. 3, two experienced participants considered hard or very hard to find their location in the first task. However, both mentioned the auto-locate button and said they are not good with geo location. In the meantime, most experienced participants considered easy or very easy to find their location. All beginners considered easy or moderate to find their location in the map, despite the fact some of them could not find some gestures.

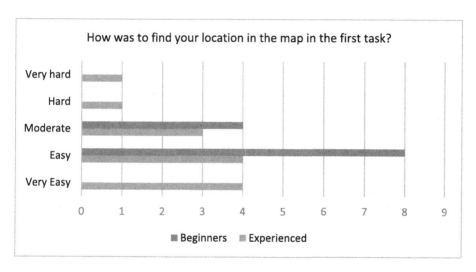

Fig. 3. Comparison between beginners and experienced participants related to first task

In the second task, participants should locate another problem, tap in the overview popup, and navigate to a different screen to see its details (Fig. 1). Three beginner participants could not see the popup in more than three attempts and then the interviewer indicated where they should tap to proceed with the task. Nevertheless, in this task, participants were able to locate themselves on the map easier than in the first task. Most of the participants considered easy or very easy to use the map in the second task (Fig. 4).

The oldest beginner participant, aged 78 years old, considered being easy to interact with the map in both tasks. He said that he did not know how to adequately handle the smartphone and whenever he needs anything, he asks his grandson. However, when he started interacting with the map, his first question was "Can I enlarge that?", and soon after he was performing pinch to zoom and asking "is it that way?" already zooming in. After the observation, when asked why he performed that gesture, he stated he had seen his grandson interacting with the device that way.

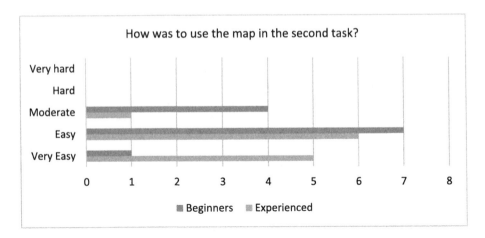

Fig. 4. Comparison between beginners and experienced participants related to second task

5 Conclusions and Future Work

The user study shows that not all beginners could easily use gestures to interact with the map. However, they used more gestures to interact with the map, using double-tap besides pinch to zoom. Some of them stated that they learned those gestures by looking at other people interacting on their multi-touch devices. Pinch seems to be the most common gesture to perform zoom among experienced participants, and none of them used other gestures during the observations.

Lack of features, such as an auto-locate button, was mentioned specially by experienced participants. They also reported issues concerning icons, but most reports related to icons were from beginner participants. The relation between participants' age and the icon size can be further investigated, as well as the understanding of the icon.

The present study focused on data visualization in map-based applications, investigating gestures to interact with a map. The main idea was to observe if potential users could perform the needed gestures to navigate in the map, and understand in-formation. As future work, other map-based applications can be used in user observations and also with different age ranges.

References

1. Sigg, S., Fu, X.: Social opportunistic sensing and social centric networking. In: Proceedings of 2014 ACM International Workshop on Wireless Mobile Technologies for Smart Cities - WiMobCity 2014, pp. 83–90 (2014)
2. Desouza, K.C., Bhagwatwar, A.: Citizen apps to solve complex urban problems. J. Urban Technol. **19**(3), 1–30 (2012)
3. Neis, P., Zielstra, D., Zipf, A.: The street network evolution of crowdsourced maps: OpenStreetMap in Germany 2007–2011. Futur. Internet **4**, 1–21 (2012)
4. Hudson-Smith, A., Batty, M., Crooks, A., Milton, R.: Mapping for the masses. Soc. Sci. Comput. Rev. **27**, 524–538 (2009)

5. Looije, R., te Brake, G.M., Neerincx, M.A.: Usability engineering for mobile maps. In: Proceedings of 4th International Conference on Mobile Technology, Applications, and Systems and The 1st International Symposium on Computer Human Interaction Mobile Technology, pp. 532–539 (2007)

6. Bellino, A.: Two new gestures to zoom: enhancing online maps services. In: Proceedings of 24th International Conference on World Wide Web Companion, WWW 2015, pp. 167–170 (2015)

7. Fayyad, U.M., Wierse, A., Grinstein, G.G.: Information Visualization in Data Mining and Knowledge Discovery. Morgan Kaufmann, San Francisco (2002)

8. Carmo, M.B., Afonso, A.P., Matos, P.P.: Visualization of geographic query results for small screen devices. In: Proceedings of the 4th ACM Workshop on Geographical Information Retrieval - GIR 2007, p. 63 (2007)

9. Bill, B.: Multi-Touch Systems that I Have Known and Loved. http://www.billbuxton.com/multitouchOverview.html

10. Hoggan, E., Nacenta, M., Kristensson, P.O., Williamson, J., Oulasvirta, A., Lehtiö, A.: Multi- touch pinch gestures: performance and ergonomics, pp. 4–7 (2013)

11. Harrower, M., Sheesley, B.: Designing better map interfaces: a framework for panning and zooming. Trans. GIS **9**, 77–89 (2005)

12. Jokisch, M., Bartoschek, T., Schwering, A.: Usability testing of the interaction of novices with a multi-touch table in semi public space. In: Jacko, J.A. (ed.) Human-Computer Interaction, Part II, HCII 2011. LNCS, vol. 6762, pp. 71–80. Springer, Heidelberg (2011)

13. Rubin, J., Chisnell, D.: Handbook of Usability Testing: How to Plan, Design, and Conduct Effective Tests. Wiley, New York (2011)

14. Colab. http://www.colab.re/

Should My Device Learn My Identity and Personality?

Minal Jain[✉], Sarita Seshagiri, and Aditya Ponnada

Samsung R&D Institute India, Bangalore, India
{minal.jain,sarita.s}@samsung.com, aditya1990.p@gmail.com

Abstract. Understanding user identity and personality is vital for designing effective user experiences. Researchers have recognized that identity and personality are a confluence of various constructs. In our study, we examined identity orientation, personality traits and their manifestation on different platforms for 17 software professionals in urban Bangalore. We explored personality distribution of 1174 employees of our organization. Findings showed users to have high personal and relational identity orientations. Our sample was also high on openness and neuroticism and low on conscientiousness, extraversion and agreeableness. We established co-relations between these constructs and examined the self-observer asymmetry in perceiving them. These results inform user experiences on personal devices (including core applications), particularly for individuals who are oriented to their social and personal circles and less towards their community, or more towards accruing social approval than conquering personal challenges.

Keywords: Identity · Personality · Group · Personalization

1 Introduction

Identity is composed of different constructs. Signelis designed a scale to measure the strength of an individual's independent and interdependent self-construal [1].The tripartite model of the self, also known as the RIC model [2, 3], recognizes three selves, namely, relational, individual and collective self. Individual identity (also known as personal identity) refers to one's goals, emotions, values, beliefs, aims and so on, while relational identity refers to one's role in relation to others along with the importance one gives to maintaining those relationships. Collective identity indexes individuals to groups based on their race, ethnicity, political affiliation and religion to name a few. Personal or individual identity can be mapped to independent self-construal while collective and relational identity relate to the interdependent self-construal. A fourth component was added to the model of identity by Cheek et al. [4] called the public or social identity which is based on James' model of social self [5] or social representation. This was recognized along with relational and collective identity as the third aspect of interdependent self thereby giving way to a tetra-partite model of self-concept as opposed to the previous tripartite model. In our study, we adopted the tetra-partite model that includes personal, relational, social and collective identity orientations.

However, it has been posited that not all aspects of people's identity are equally central to them [6, 7]. Only those components that individuals find central to their

© Springer International Publishing Switzerland 2016
M. Kurosu (Ed.): HCI 2016, Part II, LNCS 9732, pp. 294–301, 2016.
DOI: 10.1007/978-3-319-39516-6_28

identity will integrate into their sense of self-concept. It is hence worthwhile to recognize the central aspects to understand a person better. Identity and personality traits of people which form a part of their self as observed by them, differs from those perceived by others. Vazire posits a Self-Other Knowledge Asymmetry model [8] whereby the self is more accurate in predicting low observability personality traits such as neuroticism, whilst others are better at judging traits high in evaluativeness like intellect. This actor-observer asymmetry is useful for exploring identity orientations, since not all aspects of identity are easily discernable by others. The perception of self could be biased for certain aspects, which only a closer study can reveal. Our study involved a comparison between the self and observer perception of identity orientation and personality traits.

Prominence of specific personality and identity traits on public platforms determines the observers' perception of any individual. Different personality types engender varied usage of social media including Facebook or Twitter (e.g. posting pictures, posts etc.) [9–11]. Similarly, perception of identity orientations of any individual is highly influenced by its manifestation on public platforms. However this is an area not widely explored yet.

In our study we aimed at understanding the identity orientation of a closed group of software professionals in urban Bangalore. Bangalore, also called India's Silicon Valley has seen influx of people from all parts of the country, giving it a cosmopolitan nature [12]. The aim of our study was to understand identity orientation and personality traits of such a varied population both from self and observer point of view. We also explored the possible co-relation between one's identity orientation and the personality traits they exhibited. There was also a need to understand how identities are manifested on public platforms and how that influences the observer perception.

2   Method

The study comprised of three major objectives – measuring personality (traits), measuring identity orientation and studying their manifestation on different platforms. We describe each of these parts in subsequent paragraphs.

For measuring personality, the Big-Five Inventory (BFI) was used. It assumes personality model to be comprising of five dimensions, namely, extraversion, openness, conscientiousness, agreeableness and neuroticism. We used a 44-item Likert scale ranging from strongly agree to strongly disagree which consists of 8 items for extraversion (sample item: "I see myself as someone who is talkative"), 9 items for agreeableness (sample item: "I see myself as someone who is helpful and unselfish with others"), 9 items for conscientiousness (sample item: "I see myself as someone who does a thorough job"), 8 items for neuroticism (sample item: "I see myself as someone who can be moody") and 10 items for openness (sample item: " I see myself as someone who has a few artistic interests").

Due to the absence of a standard rubric to evaluate BFI, we conducted a personality survey in our organization. Responses from 1174 employees (23.9 % females: 74.95 % in the age group 20–30, 23.4 % in the age group 30–40, 0.02 % on the age group > 40) were gathered. In turn, these responses were divided into 3 categories – top 27 percentile (the high scoring group), bottom 27 percentile (the low scoring group) and the rest as medium-scoring group.

This formed the basis for creating local norms for each personality construct. This locally established rubric was utilized for examining the position of our participants on all personality traits across this sample of 1174 similar people. Table 1 mentions the mean and standard deviation scores.

Table 1. Mean and standard deviation of personality scores

	Mean	Std dev
Extraversion	3.28	0.67
Agreeableness	3.90	0.55
Conscientiousness	3.59	0.62
Neuroticism	2.82	0.73
Openness	3.61	0.47

In order to measure identity orientation, we used the 35-item Aspects of Identity Questionnaire – IV or AIQ [13] on a 5 point likert scale ranging from "not important" to "extremely important to the sense of who I am". It consists of 10 items for personal (sample item: "My personal values and moral standards"), 10 items for relational (sample item: "Having close bonds with other people"), 8 items for collective (sample item: "My race or ethnic background") and 7 items for public identity centrality (sample item: "My popularity with other people").

17 participants (6 females and 11 males; 10 people between 20–30 years and 7 between 30–40 years) were recruited for the main study. They had similar job profile as those from our organization to make the comparison on personality scale relevant. For each of these participants (U), 4 other people (U1, U2, U3, U4) with varying degrees of closeness from the primary participants were recruited (who we refer to as secondary participants) for the study. Each participant was required to fill the AIQ-IV questionnaire and BFI questionnaire for himself and his/her secondary participants were also required to fill both for him/her.

Subsequently, a card sorting activity was scheduled with primary participants. Each of them was given cards with 25 attributes written on them (one attribute on each card and multiple cards for each attribute). These attributes were adapted from the AIQ-IV and BFI questionnaires (some examples being, "values and morals", "race/ethnicity" and so on). Along with these, users were given another set of 16 cards with different platforms or spaces written (for example "office desk", "Facebook profile", "WhatsApp" etc.). They had to sort the first set of cards under the second type to show which of their attributes manifested on a platform implicitly or explicitly. Users were free to add more attributes or platforms if needed. Later, an open ended interview session was held with respondents where we discussed how different attributes manifested themselves on different platforms according to their categorization.

3   Results

10 out of 17 respondents had strong personal and relational identity orientation with 7 participants being common between the two clusters. Strong social identity orientation was limited to 5 participants and similarly a strong collective identity orientation was found in 5 participants out of 17. The Venn diagram in Fig. 1 shows people at intersections of all identity orientations. It demonstrates that identity orientations and their combinations varied greatly among people. While more than 2 aspects of identity were important for 7 participants, all aspects were low for 2.

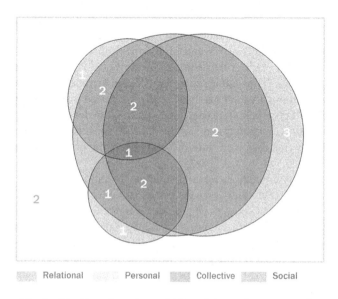

Relational   Personal   Collective   Social

Fig. 1. Identity orientations of 17 participants from our study.

Personal Identity was manifested in personal spaces like home and on public platforms like social media. Its expression though is indirect, for e.g. sharing articles or artefacts to imply one's personal beliefs. However, Relational Identity is only implicitly manifested in the presence of members from one's personal network. Consequently, people assumed and therefore incorrectly estimated Relational Identity through social norms. Sharing pictures of friends and family is a small example of its expression on social media. Interestingly, Collective Identity was not a strong aspect among most of our sample. Yet, it was overestimated by one's social circles. Its manifestations are usually limited to personal spaces like home. Strong collective identity is experienced among the diaspora, who are physically removed from their collective or home. In such cases, manifestations extend from personal to public spaces. Social identity points to the desire for social acceptance. Seeking 'likes' on Facebook or 'followers' on Twitter is a manifestation of this aspect.

We tried to compare deviations in the scores given by 4 members of a user's social circle. Maximum deviation was seen in Relational Identity Orientation (RIO) followed by Collective Identity Orientation (CIO), Personal identity Orientation (PIO) and Social Identity Orientation (SIO). A significant difference in this deviation was found in the case of RIO and SIO ($p = 0.0076$) via the Wilcoxon test. It indicates that RIO is difficult to evaluate for anyone but the self. It is not expressed publicly and can be misconstrued according to one's social role or generic social norms. SIO though, is easy for others to judge and hence observer-reported scores are closest to the self-reported scores.

Personality data of all was similarly analyzed. 17.6 % people ranked high on extraversion, 47 % ranked low and 35.3 % lay in the medium range. For agreeableness, 29.4 % were in the high range, 17.6 % lay in the mid-range and 52.3 % were low on agreeableness. 5.8 % participants were in the high range of conscientiousness, 35.3 % in the medium range and 58.9 % in the low range. 47 % of our users were high on neuroticism, followed by 41.2 % in the medium range and 11.8 % in the low range. 58.9 % participants were high on openness, while 29.4 % and 11.8 % medium and low on the same respectively. This distribution of observed traits can be attributed to the demographics of the chosen captive user base. The sample primarily included members between 20–30 years, who had joined the company after having recently graduated from college which might be critical for their high proclivity to new experiences, low levels of conscientiousness and high neuroticism (low emotional stability). Since most people were recent urban migrants, it is likely that they were cautious and hence low on extraversion and agreeableness.

Similar to identity orientation, we compared the deviations in the scores given by a participant's social circles to the scores the participant gave himself for the BFI personality traits. Wilcoxon test showed significant difference between the deviations in conscientiousness and agreeableness ($p = 0.0335$), conscientiousness and openness ($p = 0.0093$), agreeableness and neuroticism ($p = 0.0092$) and neuroticism and openness ($p = 0.0174$). Similar to earlier studies [8], we found innate qualities such as conscientiousness and neuroticism, difficult for social circles to gauge, but openness and extraversion were easily estimated.

We computed the spearman rank correlation coefficient for self-reported identity and personality measures. Moderate correlations occurred between neuroticism and PIO ($\rho = 0.527$, $p = 0.03$) and openness and RIO ($\rho = 0.512$, $p = 0.036$). So, people high on PIO can be assumed to be very particular about their ideas, beliefs, thoughts and goals. This engenders low emotional stability (high neuroticism), thereby explaining the co-relation. Users high on openness might seek new experiences to expand their horizons. In the process, they will increase and strengthen their network/relationships, thereby causing high relational identity.

No significant co-relation was found between deviations observed in identity scores reported by members of users' social circle to the self-reported personality scores of users. Moderate co-relation was observed between average deviation in the scores reported by social circles in PIO to the self-reported SIO of the primary participant ($\rho = 0.557$, $p = 0.02$), also indicating that PIO of people high on SIO tends to be misjudged by observers. It reinforces the fact that PIO gets masked by conspicuous SIO. Average score on CIO reported by social circles was positively moderately co-related to the self-reported CIO of the user ($\rho = 0.512$, $p = 0.036$). This shows that collective identity is easily revealed and recognized on public platforms or face-to-face. Average score on SIO reported by social circles is also co-related to self-reported scores of CIO ($\rho = 0.544$, $p = 0.024$), personal identity ($\rho = 0.664$, $p = 0.003$) and social identity ($\rho = 0.63$, $p = 0.0067$). Thus, people with high CIO, SIO or PIO are evaluated high on SIO by their social circles. Social identity is easily manifested and perceived by others. For PIO and CIO though, this correlation could be due to the nature of social media where sharing anything on that platform is seen as seeking social approval through 'likes', 'comments', 'following' or 'endorsement'. This is true of sharing personal communications, face-to-face too.

Card sorting data yielded certain insights. Sexual Orientation for participants from LGBT groups was critical. For users with high 'openness' and 'extraversion' it was widely expressed on public platforms through their physical appearance or posts on social media, while for others low on these aspects, it was expressed within personal networks alone. Most people expressed their hobbies (a vital aspect of PIO) on different platforms. Phone wallpapers for certain personality types were a reflection of their current thoughts, mood, hobbies or goals. This was contrary to those who neither changed their wallpapers nor customized the device. Emotions and feelings were also differently expressed by different personalities. While certain users withheld expressing emotions that evoked deep feelings (especially negative ones), others widely used social media or publicly visible spaces such as WhatsApp status to express themselves. Conversing on public platforms with many friends was uncommon in people with low 'extraversion', who maintained personal blogs to express themselves. Image sharing behavior also varied across participants. Some abstained from displaying pictures even on semi-personal platforms (WhatsApp) while others freely shared images on open media such as Facebook. Display pictures such as avatars or icons were preferred on other platforms.

4 Discussion

Our research presented here helped us understand the identity and personality orientation of a segment of IT professionals in urban Bangalore. We computed the co-relations that existed between these traits and how their varied manifestation led to a self-observer asymmetry in identity and personality perception. Such an exploration is worthwhile for user-experience designers and researchers in developing experiences on mobile platforms and wearables (to name a few) that are tailored to a user's identity and personality. Needs and expectations of a user with a strong PIO will be quite different from those with strong RIO. It will hold true for users with CIO and SIO too. Moreover, users' personality determines their acceptance or behavior towards a product. A person high on openness could be an early adopter for a new technology or feature, as against someone low on that trait.

Identity is critical to personalize the device for the user. This is especially needed when the device is a personal mobile assistant or device, which will be used by an individual time and again. There are differences in terms of how people personalize their wallpaper on the mobile. Someone with high RIO may adorn their wallpapers with snaps of family members and friends. At other times, wallpaper may include motivational quotes, or images of artifacts created by users themselves. Such instances may imply that PIO is high for users. It is worth examining how users change their wallpapers on special occasions such as festivals, ceremonies and events. Some of our users revealed that they liked to have snaps of lighted *diyas* (candles) during *Diwali* (festival of lights) or send family snaps and e-cards to each other. Others sent self-created digital artifacts (patterns or paintings) to each other. It is probable that users experience high CIO or RIO at such times. For people with dominant PIO, Diwali holidays may well be a time to undertake an online course or module.

Apart from Wallpapers, understanding the patterns of search results could be rewarding. For instance, queries and searches done by users could be curated according to their interests, which in turn are influenced by their identities. Contact List or Address Book on mobile phones is another area that should be explored. It will be worthwhile to examine how they store their contacts, i.e. what names do they use to store their contacts under. It is likely that users will organize their contacts in terms of their profession or their relation with the user. An observation like this will need further investigation to check if it reflects that such users have either one aspect of RIO or even CIO.

Different aspects of a user's identity can show up at certain times or events, which indicates that identity manifestation is contextual. As technology providers, we have to be sensitive to such converged and contextual identities and accordingly provide features, applications and services. Sensitivity in understanding and responding to such identities will decide whether or not a product/experience gains user appeal. Ideally, such experiences can even boost self-esteem of users.

Going forward, we also will explore how personality affects manifestation of emotion based on the use of paralinguistic elements and how this is perceived by different personality types. Along with this, we also want to examine media preference of various personality types for expression of emotions. An attempt to answer these can then lead to design and development of intelligent user interfaces.

There were certain limitations in our present study phase. For instance, we found it difficult to find a pattern or inconsistency in behavior due to the varied backgrounds of our sample set. It will be interesting to replicate the same study with a bigger user sample with some variables held constant. Restricting the study to certain identity types and studying difference in personality traits and their manifestation can give richer insights into the effect of personality trait in identity manifestation. It will also be worthwhile to study how these identities and their manifestations change over a specific period of time.

We should also devise more methods to gather and analyze user activity on social media, whilst simultaneously observing their physical spaces (e.g. fly-on-the-wall). Such a method will provide data with greater accuracy on how different aspects of users' identity are manifested or withheld. However the tradeoffs to be considered in such a case are the risks it can pose to user privacy.

References

1. Singelis, T.M.: The measurement of independent and interdependent self-construals. Person. Soc. Psychol. Bull. **20**(5), 580–591 (1994)

2. Kashima, E.S., Hardie, E.A.: The development and validation of the relational, individual and collective self-aspect (RIC) scale. Asian J. Soc. Psychol. **3**, 19–48 (2000)
3. Sedikides, C., Brewer, M.B.: Individual Self, Relational Self, Collective Self. Psychology Press, Philadelphia (2001)
4. Cheek, N.N., Cheek, J.M., Grimes, J.O., Tropp, L.R.: Public displays of self: Distinctions among relational, social and collective aspects of the independent self. In: Poster Presented at the Annual Meeting of the Society for Personality and Social Psychology, Austin, TX (2014)
5. James, W.: The Principles of Psychology, vol. 1. Holt, New York (1890)
6. Brittian, A.S., Umaña-Taylor, A.J., Lee, R.M., Zamboanga, B.L., Kim, S.Y., Weisskirch, R.S., Castillo, L.G., Whitbourne, S.K., Hurley, E.A., Huynh, Q.L., Brown, E.J., Caraway, S.J.: The moderating role of centrality on associations between ethnic identity affirmation and ethnic minority college students' mental health. J. Am. Coll. Health **61**, 133–140 (2013)
7. Cheek, J.M., Briggs, S.R.: Self-consciousness and aspects of identity. J. Res. Person. **16**, 401–408 (1982)
8. Vazire, S.: Who knows what about a person? The self-other knowledge asymmetry (SOKA) model. J. Person. Soc. Psychol. **98**(2), 281–300 (2010)
9. Yee, N., Harris, H., Jabon, M., Bailenson, J.N.: The expression of personality in virtual worlds. Soc. Psychol. Person. Sci. **2**, 5–12 (2011)
10. Marcus, B., Machilek, F., Schutz, A.: Personality in cyberspace: personal websites as media for personality expression and impression. J. Person. Soc. Psychol. **90**, 1014–1031 (2006)
11. Li, L., Li, A., Hao, B., Guan, Z., Zhu, T.: Predicting active users' personality based on micro-blogging behaviours. PLoS ONE **9**(1), e84997 (2014)
12. Population of Bangalore (2015). http://www.indiaonlinepages.com/population/bangalorb-population.html. Accessed March 2015
13. Cheek, J.M., Smith, S.M., Tropp, L.R.: Relational identity orientation: a fourth scale for the AIQ. In: Paper Presented at the Meeting of the Society for Personality and Social Psychology, Savannah, GA (2002)

Mobile Application Tutorials: Perception of Usefulness from an HCI Expert Perspective

Ger Joyce[✉], Mariana Lilley, Trevor Barker, and Amanda Jefferies

School of Computer Science, University of Hertfordshire, College Lane, Hatfield,
Hertfordshire AL10 9AB, UK
gerjoyce@outlook.com,
{m.lilley,t.1.barker,a.1.jefferies}@herts.ac.uk

Abstract. Mobile application tutorials are an opportunity to educate users about a mobile application. Should a mobile application tutorial not be used, the number of frustrated users and uninstalled applications could increase, resulting in a substantial loss in revenue for mobile application developers. Yet, the historical ineffectiveness of printed documentation and online help may have a negative influence on the perception of usefulness of mobile application tutorials for more experienced HCI experts. This in turn may influence their design decisions, whereby they may choose to not design a mobile application tutorial when it may have been better for the user. Our research suggests that while there is a split in the perception of usefulness of mobile application tutorials within the HCI community, the length of time in an HCI role did not have a statistically significant effect on this perception.

Keywords: Mobile tutorials · Mobile applications

1 Introduction

Mobile application tutorials are the subject of a strong debate within the Human-Computer Interaction (HCI) community. On one hand, some researchers argue that mobile applications need to be intuitive (Lee et al. 2004), and the existence of a mobile application tutorial simply infers that the mobile application is not as usable and intuitive as it should be (Echessa 2014). On the other hand, other researchers suggest that learnability has always been important in any context, and that there are times when mobile application tutorials can be useful (Bedford 2014; Satia 2014). This is an important debate given the potential for a massive loss in revenue, as well as frustrated users, should mobile applications be uninstalled if they cannot be learnt quickly without mobile application tutorials being available.

Prior to mobile application tutorials, software and web application users had printed documentation and online help at their disposal. Yet, the availability of printed documentation and online help proved to be largely ineffective (Grayling 1998; Novick et al. 2006). Our research question was:

© Springer International Publishing Switzerland 2016
M. Kurosu (Ed.): HCI 2016, Part II, LNCS 9732, pp. 302–308, 2016.
DOI: 10.1007/978-3-319-39516-6_29

RQ1: Has the historical ineffectiveness of printed documentation and online help negatively influenced the perception of HCI experts in regard to mobile application tutorials?

In this work, the authors test this hypothesis. The results of this study could be important to the HCI community, including mobile application design teams, and others that wish to better understand the reasoning underpinning the mobile application tutorial debate, as well as other HCI researchers investigating this new, exciting, yet under-represented topic.

2   Related Work

The length of time it takes for a user to become capable in using any computer-based system or application has been a vital area of HCI for many years (Harrison 2013). Research suggests that the inability to become efficient in a system or application in a short period of time may affect the perceived usability of the system or application (Dumas et al. 1999; Ketola et al. 2001; Rogers et al. 2011). Further, given the distracted nature of mobile application users (Nilsson 2009; Oulasvirta et al. 2005), the ability to learn a mobile application quickly is even more important (Longaria 2004). To that end, a mobile application tutorial is one of the primary methods in assisting a user as they quickly learn how to use a mobile application (Clark 2010).

Yet, some researchers argue that mobile applications may not need tutorials, that they are simply blockers to using a mobile application (Echessa 2014). However, further research that has shown that users continue to expect some form of assistance for mobile applications (Bertini et al. 2006; Inostroza et al. 2012). Once a mobile application tutorial is available, a substantial proportion of first time users of a mobile application appear to interact with the mobile application tutorial either briefly or in-depth (Inbar et al. 2009; Tokárová et al. 2013). Well-designed mobile application tutorials, such as Intro Tours or Inline Cues (Hess 2010), will allow users to quickly scan content (Neil et al. 2014) and exit without the need to look at all pages within the tutorial (Higgins 2012). This allows the mobile application tutorial to be beneficial without being distracting nor a block to using a mobile application quickly.

3   Methodology

While each side debates their position for and against mobile application tutorials, few researchers consider if there is a reason that might better explain the difference in perspectives. Could that reason be the ineffectiveness of printed documentation and online help for desktop applications which may have influenced HCI experts, giving them a negative perception toward the usefulness of mobile application tutorials?

To explore this phenomena further, the authors examined data collected during a study which rated usability heuristics for mobile applications (Joyce et al. 2014). In particular, one of the heuristics concerned with mobile application tutorials. Survey participants were recruited through email, all of whom were authors of peer-reviewed HCI research papers. Of the 120 participants invited, 60 HCI experts hailing from

18 countries participated in the survey. 46 of the participants were HCI researchers, with the remainder primarily being HCI practitioners and HCI educators. During the survey, participants rated each heuristic using a five-point Likert Scale from 1 (Not Useful) to 5 (Very Useful) (Fig. 1), also offering free text comments. The quantitative and qualitative responses from the survey gave great insight into the perception of the usefulness of mobile application tutorials across the HCI community.

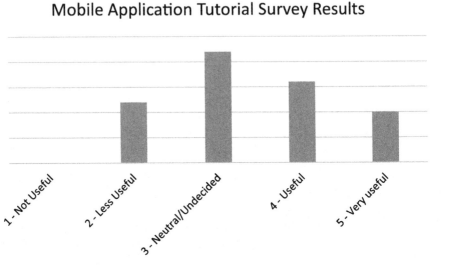

Fig. 1. Mobile application tutorial survey results (n = 60)

4   Results

The results from the survey were thought-provoking in that the split within the HCI community for and against mobile application tutorials was evident. This was reflected by 26 (43 %) participants that considered a heuristic for mobile application tutorials as being useful or very useful. In contrast, 12 (20 %) participants felt that a heuristic for mobile application tutorials as being less useful. Interestingly, 22 (36 %) participants were neutral/undecided on the subject (Fig. 1).

With the split in perceptions toward mobile application tutorials clearly visible, the authors wished to explore these differences further. To that end, the authors examined how the length of time in an HCI role might have an impact, given that HCI experts with at least 10 years in their role would recall the ineffectiveness of desktop-based printed documentation and online help. Length of time in an HCI role was, therefore, classified into four groups, namely "Less than 5 years", "5–10 years", "11–15 years" and "More than 15 years". Following this classification, the authors' initial results showed that the Likert Scale modal values were found to decrease for groups with 5 or more years' experience (Table 1). This suggested that length of time in an HCI role may have an effect the perception of the usefulness of mobile application tutorials.

Table 1. Mobile application tutorial survey responses likert scale modal values

Length of time in HCI role	Number of participants	Likert scale modal value
Less than 5 years	20	4
5–10 years	21	3
11–15 years	13	3
More than 15 years	6	3

Further statistical analysis would determine if this was correct. As the data collected from a Likert scale is ordinal in nature, and as there are more than 3 independent samples to compare, the authors utilized the Kruskal-Wallis H test (Kruskal et al. 1952), with SPSS being used to analyze the data. A visual inspection of the resulting boxplot showed that the distribution of scores were similar for all groups (Fig. 2).

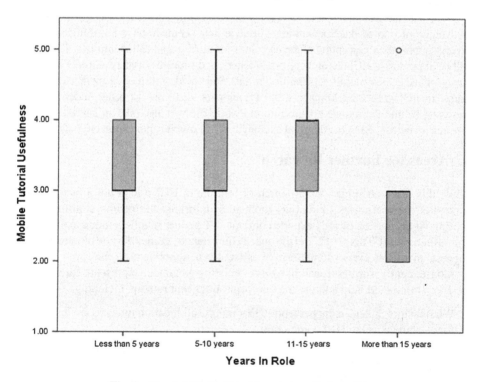

Fig. 2. Kruskal-Wallis H test boxplot results (n = 60)

The results of the Kruskal-Wallis H test confirmed that the modal values did decrease. However, the results from the Kruskal-Wallis H test also indicated that the differences were not statistically significant, $\chi2(3) = 1.660$, p = .646. Consequently, the authors' hypothesis was rejected.

5 Conclusion

Given the prevalence of mobile applications today (Newark-French 2011; Murphy 2012; Rosenberg 2012), the decision to use a mobile application tutorial or not when designing a mobile application is an important one. In this paper, the authors investigated a potential reason for the difference in perceptions toward mobile application tutorials. This reason could have been that mobile application tutorials fill a role similar to that of ineffective traditional printed documentation and online help. Therefore, the authors explored if HCI experts with 10 or more years' experience, who would have recalled traditional printed documentation and online help, had a negative impact toward the perception of usefulness of mobile application tutorials.

Following a survey of 60 HCI researchers, practitioners and educators in 18 countries, our research suggests that the number of years in an HCI role had no statistically significant effect on the perception of usefulness of mobile application tutorials.

This is an interesting result in that past experience with, and/or knowledge of, the ineffectiveness of printed documentation and online help seems to have not influenced HCI experts against their perception of the usefulness of mobile application tutorials. This result will be important to HCI researchers, practitioners, and educators as they consider the arguments for and against mobile application tutorials. Stakeholders on mobile application design teams, including Product Managers and Developers, that wish to better understand the reasoning behind the mobile application tutorial debate will also take an interest. As will researchers investigating the new and exciting topic of mobile application tutorials.

6 Areas for Further Research

While this research suggests that length of time in an HCI role is not a factor in the perception of usefulness of mobile application tutorials, the results confirm that a substantial proportion of HCI experts continue to consider mobile application tutorials as less than useful. This result, and the overarching debate, comes despite research which suggests that users expect some form of assistance in a mobile context.

Consequently, further research in this interesting, yet under-represented area within the Literature could help address the many questions that remain, including:

- What factors underpin the perception that mobile application tutorials are less useful for a segment of the HCI community?
- How effective are mobile application tutorials in assisting users as they learn to use mobile applications?
- Which types of mobile application tutorials are more successful?
- Why are these types of mobile application tutorials more successful?
- Which types of mobile application tutorials are less successful?
- Why are these types of mobile application tutorials less successful?
- To what extent does application type, type of user, or context-of-use have an impact on the success or failure of a mobile application tutorial?
- Which types of users utilize mobile application tutorials?
- Can the most effective mobile application tutorials be further improved?

In an effort to address some of these questions, the authors plan to hold further cross-sectional and longitudinal studies of both HCI experts and non-HCI experts which includes observation of users, surveys, and interviews.

Acknowledgments. The authors are grateful to the 60 HCI experts around the world that participated in the study. The authors are also grateful to the School of Computer Science at the University of Hertfordshire in Hatfield, United Kingdom for generously providing funding for this study, whereby for each survey response received, £2 was donated to Sands charity in the United Kingdom.

References

Hess, W.: Onboarding: Designing Welcoming First Experiences | UX Magazine. http://uxmag.com/articles/onboarding-designing-welcoming-first-experiences

Lee, V., Schneider, H., Schell, R.: Mobile Applications: Architecture, Design, and Development. Prentice Hall, Upper Saddle River (2004)

Echessa, J.: Improving Your App's Onboarding UX. http://www.sitepoint.com/improving-apps-onboarding-ux/

Bedford, A.: Instructional Overlays and Coach Marks for Mobile Apps. http://www.nngroup.com/articles/mobile-instructional-overlay/

Satia, G.: Mobile Onboarding: A Beginner's Guide. http://www.smashingmagazine.com/2014/08/11/mobile-onboarding-beginners-guide/

Grayling, T.: Fear and loathing of the help menu: a usability test of online help. Tech. Commun. **42**, 166–177 (1998)

Novick, D.G., Ward, K.: Why Don't people read the manual? In: Proceedings of 24th Annual Conference Design of Communication - SIGDOC 2006, p. 11 (2006)

Harrison, R., Flood, D., Duce, D.: Usability of mobile applications: literature review and rationale for a new usability model. J. Interact. Sci. **1**, 1–16 (2013)

Dumas, J.S., Redish, J.: A Practical Guide to Usability Testing. Intellect Books, London (1999)

Ketola, P., Röykkee, M.: The three facets of usability in mobile handsets. In: CHI 2001, Workshop: Mobile Communications: Understanding Users, Adoption & Design (2001)

Rogers, Y., Sharp, H., Preece, J.: Interaction Design: Beyond Human - Computer Interaction. Wiley, New York (2011)

Bertini, E., Gabrielli, S., Kimani, S.: Appropriating and assessing heuristics for mobile computing. In: AVI 2006, Proceedings of the Working Conference on Advanced Visual Interfaces, pp. 119–126 (2006)

Inostroza, R., Rusu, C., Roncagliolo, S., Jiménez, C., Rusu, V.: Usability heuristics for touchscreen-based mobile devices. In: Proceedings of the 9th International Conference on Information Technology, ITNG 2012, pp. 662–667. IEEE, Las Vegas, NV (2012)

Inbar, O., Lavie, T., Meyer, J.: Acceptable intrusiveness of online help in mobile devices. In: Proceedings of the 11th International Conference on Human-Computer Interaction with Mobile Devices and Services - MobileHCI 2009, p. 1. ACM (2009)

Tokárová, L., Weideman, M.: Understanding the process of learning touch-screen mobile applications. In: Proceedings of the 31st ACM International Conference on Design of Communication - SIGDOC 2013, pp. 157–164. ACM Press (2013)

Neil, T., Malley, R.: Rethinking Mobile Tutorials: Which Patterns Really Work? http://www.smashingmagazine.com/2014/04/22/rethinking-mobile-tutorials-which-patterns-really-work

Nilsson, E.G.: Design patterns for user interface for mobile applications. Adv. Eng. Softw. **40**, 1318–1328 (2009)

Oulasvirta, A., Tamminen, S.: Interaction in 4-second bursts: the fragmented nature of attentional resources in mobile HCI. In: Proceedings of the SIGCHI Conference on Human Factors in Computing Systems, pp. 919–928. ACM (2005)

Longaria, R.: Designing software for the mobile context : a practitioner's guide. Springer Science & Business Media, London (2004)

Clark, J.: Tapworthy: Designing Great iPhone Apps. O'Reilly Media, Sebastopol (2010)

Higgins, K.: First time user experiences in mobile apps. http://www.kryshiggins.com/first-time-user-experiences-in-mobile-apps

Joyce, G., Lilley, M.: Towards the development of usability heuristics for native smartphone mobile applications. In: Marcus, A. (ed.) DUXU 2014, Part I. LNCS, vol. 8517, pp. 465–474. Springer, Heidelberg (2014)

Kruskal, W.H., Wallis, W.A.: Use of ranks in one-criterion variance analysis. J. Am. Stat. Assoc. **47**, 583–621 (1952)

Newark-French, C.: Mobile Apps Put the Web in Their Rear-view Mirror. http://www.flurry.com/bid/63907/Mobile-Apps-Put-the-Web-in-Their-Rear-view-Mirror

Murphy, D.: Apple's App Store Hits 25 Billion Downloads: How Many Per iPhone? http://www.pcmag.com/article2/0,2817,2401122,00.asp

Rosenberg, J.: Google Play hits 25 billion downloads
http://officialandroid.blogspot.com/2012/09/google-play-hits-25-billion-downloads.html

Effects of Holding Ring Attached to Mobile Devices on Pointing Accuracy

Yuya Kawabata[✉], Daisuke Komoriya, Yuki Kubo, Buntarou Shizuki, and Jiro Tanaka

University of Tsukuba, Tsukuba, Japan
{kawabata,komoriya,kubo,shizuki,jiro}@iplab.cs.tsukuba.ac.jp

Abstract. It is difficult for a user to operate a touch screen device accurately under the eyes-free condition. The difficulties arise from the absence of visual or tactile feedback under this condition. This research focuses on the effectiveness of a holding ring attached to the back of mobile devices to improve pointing accuracy under the eyes-free condition. We explored the extent to which the holding ring improves the pointing accuracy by preparing three mobile devices with holding rings attached in different positions and a mobile device without a holding ring. The pointing accuracy was then evaluated by performing user studies. The result suggested that the pointing accuracy could be improved under the target condition, which is 15.4 mm × 10.4 mm, by attaching the holding ring.

Keywords: Eyes-free input · Back-of-device interaction · Tactile feedback · One-handed operation · Touch screen · Smartphone · Thumb-based input

1 Introduction

Using a mobile device with a touch screen (hereafter a mobile device) while walking has emerged as a social problem, because it consumes the user's visual attention and thus, causes of traffic accidents [1,2]. One of the solutions to this problem is an eyes-free touch input which enables the user to operate the mobile device without watching the display of the device. However, it is difficult to operate a mobile device without being able to look at the display [3] because there is neither visual nor tactile feedback.

Our idea to address the above issue was prompted by a previous solution and research. The user of a one-handed keyboard (e.g., Twiddler Tek Gear Inc.) uses a belt to hold the keyboard stably. Fukatsu et al. [4] and Corsten et al. [5] showed that the pointing accuracy in eyes-free touch input is improved by tactile landmarks on the back of the device. These solutions and research results suggest that the back of a device presents potential design space for improving the performance of the input via the touch screen located on the front of a mobile device.

© Springer International Publishing Switzerland 2016
M. Kurosu (Ed.): HCI 2016, Part II, LNCS 9732, pp. 309–319, 2016.
DOI: 10.1007/978-3-319-39516-6_30

Fig. 1. A holding ring.

Our idea in this research is to use a ring-shaped part, e.g., VENICEN Ring Holder2, on the back of a device to prevent the device from falling(hereafter, a holding ring). Our assumption was that attaching a holding ring would be able to improve the eyes-free pointing accuracy during one-handed operation (Fig. 1), because the user's gripping attitude is stabilized. In this research, we conducted user studies to measure the eyes-free pointing accuracy, using mobile devices to which a holding ring is attached in different positions to examine the above idea.

2   Related Work

2.1   Back of Device

Previous research showed that touch-enabling the back of a touch screen device improves the usability of the device. For example, Baudisch et al. [6] showed that touch-enabling the back of an ultra-small device improved the pointing accuracy on the front side. Wigdor et al. [7] proposed a tabletop system of which the back is touch-enabled, and which extended input vocabulary by detecting touch on the back of the table. LucidTouch [8] is a see-through mobile device which has touch sensors on its back. It improves the pointing accuracy and the usability of text entry on the front side because the see-through device allows the user to see the user's fingers and hand on the back of the device; it also showed bimanual input techniques which coordinately use the front and back.

Pointing accuracy in eyes-free touch input was shown to improve by tactile landmarks on the back of the device. For example, HaptiCase [5] provides back-of-device tactile landmarks that the user senses with their fingers to estimate the location of touch at the front, and thus allows the user to touch with high precision under the eyes-free condition. Fukatsu et al. [4] showed that tactile textures attached on the back of the device can improve pointing accuracy.

In contrast to the above research, we explore the effect of attaching a holding ring to the back of the device for eyes-free touch input.

2.2   Eyes-Free Input

Some research proposed eyes-free input methods. For example, Slide Rule [9] is a method that allows blind users to access touch screen applications in eyes-free by using voice guidance along with multi-touch interaction techniques. A user study with 10 blind people showed that Slide Rule was faster than a system based on a screen reader and participants preferred Slide Rule. BrailleTouch [10] is a method that allows users to input text in an eyes-free manner. It shows a Braille cell, which consists of a 3 by 2 binary matrix on the touch screen of a mobile touch screen device; where the user places their fingers in a one-to-one correspondence to a standard Braillewriter to input a character. Bragdon et al. [11] investigated the effect of various situations on touch screen interaction. One of the investigated situations was an eyes-free environment. As a result, these authors suggested that, in terms of performance, the most notable effect for touch screen interaction came from not looking at all times. Gustafson et al. [12] proposed palm-based imaginary interfaces that use a human palm as input surface mapped to an invisible GUI based upon the user's spatial memory such as the home screen GUI of a smartphone. They investigated pointing time under sighted and blindfolded conditions. Their results indicated the potential of imaginary interfaces for blind and eyes-free use.

In contrast to the above research, we focus on improving the accuracy of eyes-free input by attaching a holding ring.

2.3   Tactile Feedback

It is possible to improve pointing accuracy using tactile feedback. FingerFlux [13] is an output technique to generate near-surface haptic feedback by magnets. The technique can reduce drifting when operating on-screen targets in eyes-free condition. Kincaid [14] proposed tactile guide overlays for touch screens. An overlay is a transparent Lexan sheet cut and hollowed out to fit the buttons, sliders, and other components on touch screens. An evaluation shows that a tactile guide overlay can decrease task time compared to a bare touch screen. Touchplates [15] is an overlay for touch screens designed for accessibility. El-Glaly et al. [16] proposed augmenting a touch screen with a tactile overlay that consists of a border, a vertical ruler, horizontal lines, vertical lines, or landmarks. MudPad [17] is a system that can provide localized active haptic feedback on multitouch screens. This allows users to explore the interface haptically.

Various kinds of tactile feedback other than the above ones have been explored in the HCI field. For example, TeslaTouch [18] produces various kinds of tactile sensations by controlling electrostatic friction between a touch surface and the user's fingers by exploiting the principle of electrovibration. Ultra Haptics [19] is multi-point midair haptic feedback for touch surfaces radiated using a phased array of ultrasonic transducers. BaduumTouch [20] is an attractive force feedback interface using air suction.

In contrast to the above research, we use tactile feedback in the form of a holding ring attached to the back of a mobile device and to explore how the feedback affects the eyes-free pointing accuracy on the touch screen.

3   Evaluation

We conducted a user study to measure pointing accuracy using mobile devices with a holding ring attached in different positions.

3.1   Design

Participants. Six male participants including three of the authors ranging in age from 22 to 24 took part in the evaluation as volunteers. They were using mobile devices with touch screens on a daily basis. All participants were right-handed.

Apparatus. We used four mobile devices all of which ware Apple iPhone 4 S devices with a 3.5-inch screen (ring conditions). We attached a holding ring to three of them in three different positions as shown in Fig. 2 and used one of them as is. In summary, we tested the following four different ring conditions:

Top.
 We attached the holding ring to the back of the device 2.0 cm above the center of the touch screen.
Middle.
 We attached the holding ring at the back of the devices in the center of the touch screen.
Bottom.
 We attached the holding ring to the back of the device 2.0 cm below the center of the touch screen.
NoRing.
 Nothing was attached.

Fig. 2. Ring conditions (from left to right): Top, Middle, Bottom, and NoRing.

Procedure. We located a 17-inch display on a desk, to mirror the screen of the mobile device (Fig. 3). We asked the participants to sit down on a chair and hold the mobile device with their right hand. We also asked them to position their right elbow on the desk, and their middle finger through the holding ring at their proximal interphalangeal joint. Furthermore, we covered the participants' hand holding the mobile device to prevent the participant from observing the display of the mobile device.

Fig. 3. Setup of the evaluation.

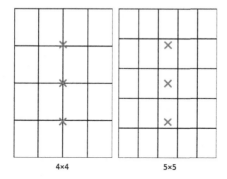

Fig. 4. Display of the mobile device on each split condition. The three X marks illustrate the positions of the holding rings under the Top, Middle, and Bottom conditions. Note that the X marks were not presented to the participants in this evaluation.

The screen of the mobile device, which is split into a 4×4 or 5×5 grid (split conditions) as shown in Fig. 4, was mirrored on the display. As a trial, a gray rectangle (hereafter target) was shown in one of the grids. We asked the participants to point (i.e., tap) the corresponding position on the screen of the mobile device as accurately as possible. Specifically, we also asked the participants to touch down on the touch screen with their finger, move their fingers on the touch screen to find the target, and then raise their fingers from the touch screen. We used the point where the fingers were raised (i.e., the coordinate of the touch up event) for analysis in pointing accuracy.

The following is the procedure according to which a participant carried out the task:

1. When the participant taps the target that is positioned on the upper left of the screen of the mobile device, the first trial starts: a target is shown on the display.
2. The participant points to the corresponding position on the touch screen of the mobile device.
3. Regardless of the success or failure of the pointing, a tap sound is played to promote the participant to move on to the next trial. The next target is shown on the display randomly.

Split conditions were changed in a randomized order between the participants to counterbalance the order effect. A task consists of 15 training trials (the participants watch the display of the mobile device), 15 training trials (the participants do not watch the display of the mobile device), and 50 trials (80 trials in total). Each participant carried out this task once in each ring condition in each split condition (i.e., 8 tasks = 640 trials in total) and completed all 8 tasks in approximately 40 min.

3.2   Result and Discussion

Figure 5 shows the pointing accuracy of each split condition. Table 1 lists the standard deviation of the distances between the target and the touch point (hereafter variance) in each split condition. Figure 6 shows the pointing accuracy of each target in each ring condition in each split condition. In Fig. 6, the darker the area is, the higher the accuracy of the area is. Figure 7 shows the center of gravity of the touch points in each target in each condition. In Fig. 7, the circles show the standard deviation of the variances in each split condition in each target; the points show the center of gravity of touch points in each split condition in each target.

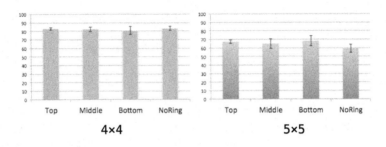

Fig. 5. Pointing accuracy of each split condition.

Table 1. Standard deviation of variances in each split condition.

Grid	Condition	SD (Deviation)	SD (x)	SD (y)
4 × 4	Top	42.45	23.01	35.67
4 × 4	Middle	40.91	20.05	35.67
4 × 4	Bottom	47.55	22.35	41.97
4 × 4	NoRing	42.72	21.24	37.07
5 × 5	Top	44.29	22.93	37.90
5 × 5	Middle	46.43	23.96	39.77
5 × 5	Bottom	45.99	22.91	39.88
5 × 5	NoRing	45.06	24.73	37.66

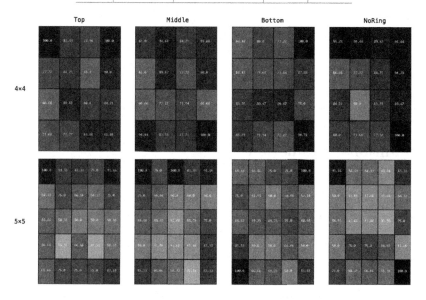

Fig. 6. Pointing accuracy of each target in each ring condition in each split condition.

The pointing accuracy is improved by attaching a holding ring in the 5×5 condition as Fig. 5 shows. In the 5×5 condition, there are significant differences between the Top and NoRing conditions ($p = .042 < .05$) and the Bottom and NoRing conditions ($p = .048 < .05$). In contrast, in the 4×4 condition, there were no significant differences between the four ring conditions. These results suggest that when a target is small (i.e., 5×5), attaching the holding ring to the back of a mobile device improves the pointing accuracy. The reason why the effect of the holding ring attached to the mobile device does not appear in the 4×4 condition would be because a target in the 4×4 condition is so large that the holding ring does not have a room to contribute to lower the pointing accuracy. On the other hand, on smaller targets (i.e., 5×5), the ring improves the pointing accuracy because participants need to touch the display more precisely. Figure 7 supports this observation. In Fig. 7, the circles in the 4×4 condition are larger than that in the 5×5 condition.

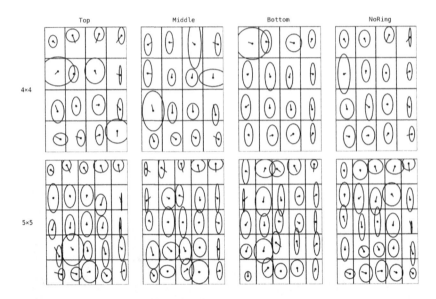

Fig. 7. Center of gravity of each target in each ring condition in each split condition.

4   Additional Evaluation

Since the result of the first evaluation suggests that the holding ring is effective in improving the pointing accuracy on smaller targets (i.e., 5 × 5), we conducted an additional evaluation. In this evaluation, we used the same four ring conditions as the first evaluation. However, this time we tested an even smaller split condition: a 6 × 6 grid. Figure 8 shows the display of the mobile device in 6 × 6 condition with the positions of the holding rings. Six participants ranging in age from 21 to 30 took part in the evaluation as volunteers. They differed from the participants who participated in the first evaluation. They were using mobile devices with touch screen on a daily basis. All participants were right-handed. In this additional evaluation, we did not display the grid lines because the target size is too small to touch. Moreover, an X mark illustrating the position of the holding ring *was presented* to the participants.

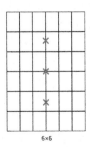

Fig. 8. Display of mobile device on 6 × 6 condition and positions of holding ring.

Table 2 shows the standard deviation of variances in each ring condition. Figure 9 shows the center of gravity of touch point of each target in the 6×6 condition. The result of the additional evaluation shows that there are significant difference between the Top and other conditions. The reason might be the fact that participants are forced to touch some of the targets in unusual postures caused by the holding ring. Especially, when participants touch the lowermost targets in the Top condition, the thumb takes an unusual posture. On the other hand, the variance at the Bottom condition is lower than the variance at the Top condition because the thumb can touch the uppermost targets just by reaching out the thumb when participants touch them in the Bottom condition. In summary, since this additional evaluation shows no significant difference between the four ring conditions in 6×6 while the pointing accuracy is improved in the Top and Bottom condition in 5×5 in this first evaluation, it is considered that the holding ring has the potential to improve the pointing accuracy when the target size is approximately $15.4\,\mathrm{mm} \times 10.4\,\mathrm{mm}$ (i.e., 5×5).

Table 2. Standard deviation of variances in 6×6 condition.

Grid	Condition	SD (Deviation)
6×6	Top	34.23
6×6	Middle	24.90
6×6	Bottom	29.29
6×6	NoRing	27.85

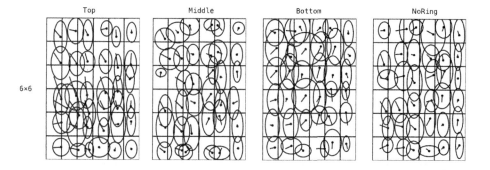

Fig. 9. Center of gravity of each target in each ring condition in 6×6 condition.

5   Conclusion and Future Work

We presented a holding ring attached to the back of a device has the potential to improve the pointing accuracy in one-handed eyes-free input. Specifically, the results of the user studies suggest that the pointing accuracy was improved in the 5×5 condition by attaching a holding ring.

In the future, we plan to conduct user studies to investigate the best attachment point of the holding ring. In addition, because we conducted the two user studies in this research in two separated periods, we plan to combine the two user studies to obtain precise results and analyze the results in detail.

References

1. Nasar, J., Hecht, P., Wener, R.: Mobile telephones, distracted attention, and pedestrian safety. Accid. Anal. Prev. **40**(1), 69–75 (2008)
2. Neider, M.B., McCarley, J.S., Crowell, J.A., Kaczmarski, H., Kramer, A.F.: Pedestrians, vehicles, and cell phones. Accid. Anal. Prev. **42**(2), 589–594 (2010)
3. Yi, B., Cao, X., Fjeld, M., Zhao, S.: Exploring user motivations for eyes-free interaction on mobile devices. In: Proceedings of the SIGCHI Conference on Human Factors in Computing Systems. CHI 2012, pp. 2789–2792. ACM, New York (2012)
4. Fukatsu, Y., Oe, T., Kuno, Y., Shizuki, B., Tanaka, J.: Evaluation of effects of textures attached to mobile devices on pointing accuracy. In: Marcus, A. (ed.) DUXU 2013, Part III. LNCS, vol. 8014, pp. 255–263. Springer, Heidelberg (2013)
5. Corsten, C., Cherek, C., Karrer, T., Borchers, J.: HaptiCase: Back-of-device tactile landmarks for eyes-free absolute indirect touch. In: Proceedings of the 33rd Annual ACM Conference on Human Factors in Computing Systems. CHI 2015, pp. 2171–2180. ACM, New York (2015)
6. Baudisch, P., Chu, G.: Back-of-device interaction allows creating very small touch devices. In: Proceedings of the 27th SIGCHI Conference on Human Factors in Computing Systems. CHI 2009, pp. 1923–1932. ACM, New York (2009)
7. Wigdor, D., Leigh, D., Forlines, C., Shipman, S., Barnwell, J., Balakrishnan, R., Shen, C.: Under the table interaction. In: Proceedings of the 19th Annual ACM Symposium on User Interface Software and Technology. UIST 2006, pp. 259–268. ACM, New York (2006)
8. Wigdor, D., Forlines, C., Baudisch, P., Barnwell, J., Shen, C.: Lucid Touch: A see-through mobile device. In: Proceedings of the 20th Annual ACM Symposium on User Interface Software and Technology. UIST 2007, pp. 269–278. ACM, New York (2007)
9. Kane, S.K., Bigham, J.P., Wobbrock, J.O.: Slide Rule: Making mobile touch screens accessible to blind people using multi-touch interaction techniques. In: Proceedings of the 10th International ACM SIGACCESS Conference on Computers and Accessibility. Assets 2008, pp. 73–80. ACM, New York (2008)
10. Romero, M., Frey, B., Southern, C., Abowd, G.D.: BrailleTouch: Designing a mobile eyesfree soft keyboard. In: Proceedings of the 13th International Conference on Human Computer Interaction with Mobile Devices and Services. MobileHCI 2011, pp. 707–709. ACM, New York (2011)
11. Bragdon, A., Nelson, E., Li, Y., Hinckley, K.: Experimental analysis of touchscreen gesture designs in mobile environments. In: Proceedings of the 29th SIGCHI Conference on Human Factors in Computing Systems. CHI 2011, pp. 403–412. ACM, New York (2011)
12. Gustafson, S.G., Rabe, B., Baudisch, P.M.: Understanding palm-based imaginary interfaces: The role of visual and tactile cues when browsing. In: Proceedings of the 31st SIGCHI Conference on Human Factors in Computing Systems. CHI 2013, pp. 889–898. ACM, New York (2013)

13. Weiss, M., Wacharamanotham, C., Voelker, S., Borchers, J.: FingerFlux: Near-surface haptic feedback on tabletops. In: Proceedings of the 24th Annual ACM Symposium on User Interface Software and Technology. UIST 2011, pp. 615–620. ACM, New York (2011)

14. Kincaid, R.: Tactile guides for touch screen controls. In: Proceedings of the 26th Annual BCS Interaction Specialist Group Conference on People and Computers, British Computer Society 339–344 (2012)

15. Kane, S.K., Morris, M.R., Wobbrock, J.O.: Touchplates: Low-cost tactile overlays for visually impaired touch screen users. In: Proceedings of the 15th International ACM SIGACCESS Conference on Computers and Accessibility. ASSETS 2013, pp. 22: 1–22: 8. ACM, New York (2013)

16. El-Glaly, Y.N., Quek, F., Smith-Jackson, T., Dhillon, G.: Touch-screens are not tangible: Fusing tangible interaction with touch glass in readers for the blind. In: Proceedings of the 7th International Conference on Tangible, Embedded and Embodied Interaction. TEI 2013, pp. 245–253. ACM, New York (2013)

17. Jansen, Y., Karrer, T., Borchers, J.: MudPad: Tactile feedback and haptic texture overlay for touch surfaces. In: ACM International Conference on Interactive Tabletops and Surfaces. ITS 2010, pp. 11–14. ACM, New York (2010)

18. Bau, O., Poupyrev, I., Israr, A., Harrison, C.: TeslaTouch: Electrovibration for touch surfaces. In: Proceedings of the 23rd Annual ACM Symposium on User Interface Software and Technology. UIST 2010, pp. 283–292. ACM, New York (2010)

19. Carter, T., Seah, S.A., Long, B., Drinkwater, B., Subramanian, S.: UltraHaptics: Multi-point mid-air haptic feedback for touch surfaces. In: Proceedings of the 26th Annual ACM Symposium on User Interface Software and Technology. UIST 2013, pp. 505–514. ACM, New York (2013)

20. Hachisu, T., Fukumoto, M.: VacuumTouch: Attractive force feedback interface for haptic interactive surface using air suction. In: Proceedings of the 32nd SIGCHI Conference on Human Factors in Computing Systems. CHI 2014, pp. 411–420. ACM, New York (2014)

The Influence of Matching Degree of the User's Inherent Mental Model and the Product's Embedded Mental Model on the Mobile User Experience

Tian Lei[1](✉), Xu Liu[1], Lei Wu[1], Ziliang Jin[1], Yuhui Wang[1], and Shuaili Wei[2]

[1] Department of Industrial Design,
Huazhong University of Science and Technology, Wuhan, China
andrew.tianlei@hust.edu.cn
[2] Jingdong ShangKe Information Technology Co., LTD, Shanghai, China

Abstract. A good user experience requires that the feedback generated by gestures is consistent with a user's existing cognitive habits and his learnt Mental Model. However, it remains unclear that to what extent and in what ways the consistency between a user's inherent Mental Model(UIMM) and a product's embedded Mental Model (PEMM) can affect a user's operating experience. This paper, by making two experiments, has explored the extent and the way in which the consistency between PEMM and UIMM influences the user experience. The results manifest that: (1) there is a high correlation between the two Mental Models' matching degree and the user experience. When the consistency, the matching degree between the two Mental Models, is high, a user's perception about the product's usability is also high; on the contrary, the user will feel a low product usability and a low user experience; (2) there is a significant correlation between the two Mental Models' matching degree and the task type. It is the tasks of "browsing news" and "adding comments", especially the former, that have a higher matching degree between UIMM and PEMM, and there is a lower one in the tasks of "viewing the detailed information", "viewing the comments" and "sharing the news". It shows that there is a bigger difference between users and designers in these three tasks.

Keywords: Inherent mental model · Embedded mental model · Mobile user experience · Consistency

1 Background

In the Mobile HCI, touching is one of the most significant interactions, which directly affects a user experience. Recent studies demonstrate that a good user experience requires that the feedback generated by gestures should be consistent with a user's existing cognitive habits and his learnt Mental Model. If a user's inherent Mental Model (UIMM) and his cognitive habits are consistent with a product's operating steps, information feedback, operation results, and the interaction logic, which are all mapped

© Springer International Publishing Switzerland 2016
M. Kurosu (Ed.): HCI 2016, Part II, LNCS 9732, pp. 320–329, 2016.
DOI: 10.1007/978-3-319-39516-6_31

out of a product, the user can gain a good experience; on the contrary, he may get a bad one. However, it remains unclear that to what extent and in what ways the consistency between UIMM and a product's embedded Mental Model (PEMM) would affect a user's operating experience.

This paper, by performing experiments, has studied the extent and the way in which the consistency between PEMM and UIMM influences the user experience. The first section was to extract the UIMM and PEMM, and the second one was to explore the affecting mechanism between the two Mental Models' matching degree and the user experience.

2 Literature Review

Since the 1950 s, academia has started to study Mental Model. The concept of Mental Model was first put forward by Kenneth Craik, and he thought that Mental Model was an explanation of someone's thought process about how something works in the real world [1]. Then, many researchers from different angles perfected and complemented it. Some scholars even came up with several new opinions. For example, Johnson Laird proposed that Mental Model described a human thinking pattern by using the existing knowledge to solve problems [2], and Indi Young thought Mental Model was the people's behavioral purpose, thinking processes, and the changes from emotions and thoughts in the process of implementing actions [3].

In short, Mental Models is the thinking mode and thoughts hidden in the human brain. It is an internal representation mapped by the external reality in the brain, and conversely affects a person's external behaviors. When he meets new things, Mental Models will be the first guidelines for his behaviors [4]. In HCI, Mental Model can help designers better understand the user, and also can help users better understand the product [5].

By researchers' constantly studying, several types of Mental Model were found. For example, Norman decomposed the interaction process into three models related to Mental Model, which were "design model", "user model", and "system model" [6]. Design model was a bridge between the system model and the user model, which determined the usability of the product. If the overlap ratio between the design model and the user model was high, the product's user experience would be improved. In the book of About Face 3, Alan Cooper also summarized the interaction system into three models: the implementation model, the user's mental model and the represented model. The practical operation models of the machine and the procedure were called the implementation model, which could be seen as a model of the engineer. The user's understanding of the system operation principles was named the user's mental model. And the way of displaying the system's functions by designers was called the represented model [7]. Mental Model was further refined by Martina Angela Sasse into the user model, the designer's user model, and the researchers' user model [8]. Although scholars have proposed many different theories about Mental Model, they all pay attention to two key concepts, the design model and the user model, which determine the product's visual presentation created by designers and the one expected by the real users. Based on these two models, we put forward two concepts of the "Product's Embedded Mental Model" (PEMM) and the "User's Inherent Mental Model" (UIMM).

This paper focused on the extent and the way of consistency between PEMM and UIMM influencing user experience from the two correlative experiments. The first one was the extraction of UIMM and PEMM, and the second one was a study of the affecting mechanism between the two Mental Models' matching degree and user experience.

3   Preparations for the Experiment

First, three typical Chinese App samples were confirmed, which were The Paper, ZAKER, and Netease News respectively. The reasons for selecting these news App are: (1) it is a representative interaction system from the real behaviors to the internet behaviors, and then to the mobile internet behaviors; (2) its contents and Information Architecture are relative simpler than other Apps; and (3) these three Apps have a large user base.

Second, the tasks suitable for extracting Mental Models were confirmed in this section. We analyzed three Apps' Information Architecture and all the task flows, and then classified each natural task flow into several function modules and the corresponding behaviors, and draw them into a mesh structure afterward.

Take Netease News for example. If a user accesses to the application, firstly, he needs to slide the App's homepage, then browses the default news list on the homepage, selects the target news item, and clicks the button of "confirm". When the page of detailed news appearing, he swipes up and down to view the news content and comments, or do other operations. From such a brief natural task flow, we can note that there are several different functions and behaviors involved in this natural task.

By analyzing the type and the amount of the functions and behaviors involved in all the typical News App samples, 5 groups of the frequent functions and behaviors were abstracted, as follows:

Group 1: Looking for a piece of news and then reading it.
Group 2: Reading the news' comments and then tapping "like".
Group 3: Adding comments under the news.
Group 4: Switching to another piece of news.
Group 5: Sharing the news to Weibo, Wechat Moments, or any other social Apps.

4   Extraction of the PEMM

The purpose of this section is to extract the sample's PEMM. We designed 5 sets of continuous tasks, each of which included some groups achieved in the above preparation section. Then we calculated the number of the different gestures provided by the App, the corresponding interface elements' types, and analyzed their forms and the feedback forms in the process of completing each continuous task. After that, we mapped the PEMMs of The Paper, ZAKER, and Netease News respectively. The following figures are the ZAKER's PEMM.

By analyzing the PEMMs of The Paper, ZAKER, and Netease News, we can see that a task usually needs more pages to display its content and feedbacks. Therefore, to avoid the sense of separation produced by different pages, we should pay high attention to the interactive effects between two pages' switching. Although the interactive effects are diverse, the feedback form of the same operations follows the same design logic (Figs. 1, 2 and 3).

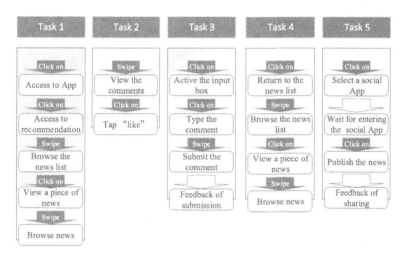

Fig. 1. The ZAKER's PEMM (gestures and functional modules)

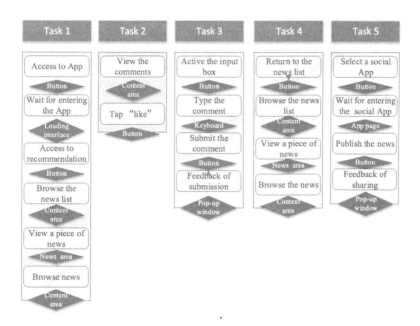

Fig. 2. The ZAKER's PEMM (interface elements and functional modules)

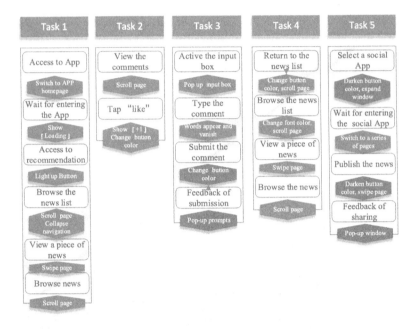

Fig. 3. The ZAKER's PEMM (feedback forms and functional modules)

5 Extraction of the UIMM

Methods of User Interview and Situation Investigation were used to get the raw information about UIMM. First of all, 20 subjects were asked to recall the daily situation about using news Apps. The recalling points included "browsing news", "viewing news", "viewing comments", "adding comments" and "sharing news". Then they were asked to draw out the path of interaction, the corresponding interface elements, the corresponding information feedback, and write down the types of used gestures in completing each task.

Indi Young's method was used to construct the UIMM. The steps were the following:

(1) analyzing the mental information gained from User Interview and Situation Investigation;
(2) picking out the mental information about tasks;
(3) putting tasks with the same attributes together and naming these different task stacks;
(4) putting task stacks with the same attributes together and naming them mental space.

The following figures are the UIMM about news reading (Figs. 4, 5 and 6).

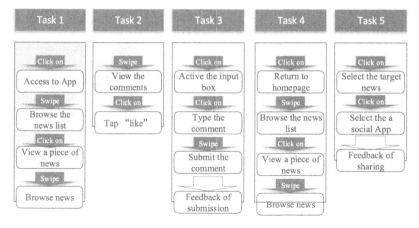

Fig. 4. The UIMM about news reading (gestures and functional modules)

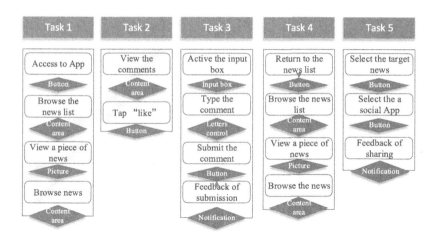

Fig. 5. The UIMM about news reading (interface elements and functional modules)

From the UIMM about news reading, we can see that: (1) the most common gestures are "click on" and "swipe"; (2) the contact area for "click on" is usually interface controls such as the button while the one for "swipe" is often the central content area; (3) subjects do not pay more attention to interaction effects but some basic ones although sometimes they may feel confused and bored by the disordered and chaotic interaction effects.

We compared the PEMM with the UIMM by computing matching degrees of the gesture type, the corresponding interface element's type and form, and the feedback form respectively. The result is seen in Fig. 7, which is the foundation of studying the influencing mechanism of matching degree on Mobile User Experience. In it, the vertical axis is the matching rate between each sample's PEMM and the UIMM, and the horizontal axis is the task type.

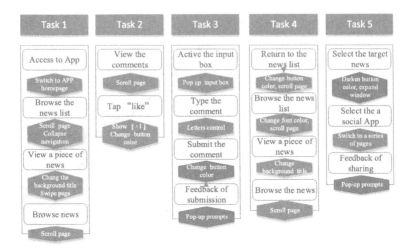

Fig. 6. The UIMM about news reading (feedback forms and functional modules)

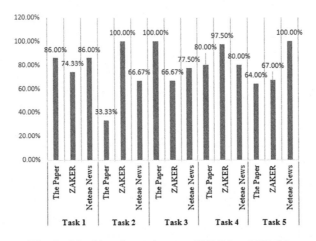

Fig. 7. Matching degree between PEMM and UIMM

6   Experiment

The main purpose of this section is to explore the influencing mechanism of matching degree on Mobile User Experience. The objective performance (Usability Testing) and the subjective perception (USE questionnaire) are both considered in this experiment.

The independent variable is the type of task. It has five levels, which are "browsing news", "viewing news", "viewing comments", "adding comments", and "sharing news" respectively. The control variable is the device platform. Here the Android system is the only operating system in this experiment. The dependent variables are the task's completion rate, the completion time, the efficiency, the error rate, the effectiveness, the ease of use, the learnability, and the satisfaction. The former four are related to Usability Testing, and the latter are related to USE questionnaire.

25 university students aged 18–25 took part in this experiment. 9 of them came from Industrial Design, and the rest of them majored in Mechanical Engineering and Materials Science. All the subjects had the experience of using news Apps everyday.

The data from the experiment were analyzed by SPSS. Some key results are shown in Table 1 and Fig. 8.

Table 1. The standardized results of Usability Testing

App Name	Task	Completion Rate	St.Completion Time	Efficiency	St. Avoiding Error Rate	Total Rate
The Paper	Task 1	67.35 %	48.84 %	19.18 %	98.33 %	58.43 %
	Task 2	59.14 %	49.44 %	9.33 %	92.78 %	52.67 %
	Task 3	72.34 %	50.81 %	52.76 %	97.92 %	68.46 %
	Task 4	62.68 %	50.47 %	16.86 %	90.00 %	55.00 %
	Task 5	39.14 %	54.24 %	14.48 %	73.33 %	45.30 %
ZAKER	Task 1	50.55 %	62.13 %	16.33 %	76.39 %	51.35 %
	Task 2	90.86 %	51.47 %	31.05 %	100.00 %	68.35 %
	Task 3	58.63 %	49.17 %	28.83 %	91.67 %	57.08 %
	Task 4	73.50 %	61.25 %	31.44 %	97.92 %	66.03 %
	Task 5	69.95 %	56.01 %	18.62 %	95.00 %	59.90 %
Netease News	Task 1	67.53 %	53.99 %	23.28 %	98.33 %	60.78 %
	Task 2	67.49 %	67.76 %	13.96 %	97.22 %	61.61 %
	Task 3	65.02 %	41.66 %	35.50 %	93.75 %	58.98 %
	Task 4	71.69 %	36.75 %	17.18 %	90.00 %	53.91 %
	Task 5	82.21 %	51.46 %	35.88 %	94.44 %	66.00 %

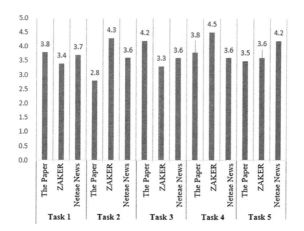

Fig. 8. The result of subjective perception (USE questionnaire)

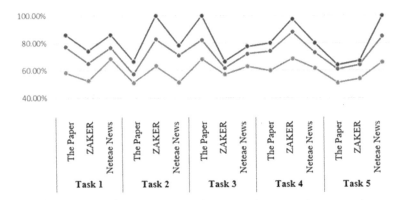

Fig. 9. Comparison of the matching degree with Usability Testing and USE questionnaire

7   Conclusion

By putting the matching degree, the standardized results of the Usability Testing and the USE questionnaire together, seen in Fig. 9, we can see that:

(1) there is a high correlation between the two mental models' matching degree and the user experience. When the matching degree, the consistency, between the two kinds of mental models is high, the user's feeling about the product usability is also high; on the contrary, the user will feel a low product usability and a low user experience;

(2) there is a significant correlation between the two mental models' matching degree and the task type. It is the tasks of "browsing news" and "adding comments", especially the former, that have a higher matching degree between UIMM and PEMM, and there is a lower one in the tasks of "viewing news", "viewing comments" and "sharing news". It shows that there is a bigger difference between users and designers in these three tasks.

Acknowledgement. This paper is supported by the HUST high-level international curriculum projects.

References

1. Craik, K.: The Nature of Explanation. Cambridge University Press, Cambridge (1943)
2. Johnson Laird, P.N.: Mental models: towards a cognitive science of language, inference and consciousness. In: Inference & Consciousness Cognitive Science, pp. 481–500. Harvard University Press (1983)
3. Young, I.: Mental Models: Aligning Design Strategy with Human Behavior. Rosenfeld Media, New York (2008)

4. Miwa, K., Kanzaki, N., Terai, H., Kojima, K., Nakaike, R., Morita, J., Saito, H.: Learning mental models of human cognitive processing by creating cognitive models. In: Conati, C., Heffernan, N., Mitrovic, A., Verdejo, M. (eds.) AIED 2015. LNCS, vol. 9112, pp. 287–296. Springer, Heidelberg (2015)

5. Potosnak, K.: Mental Model: Helping Users Understand Software. IEEE Software, 6(5), 85–86, 88 (1989)

6. Norman, D.A.: The Design of Everyday Things. Doubleday Business, New York (1990)

7. Cooper, A., Reimann, R.M.: About Face 3.0: The Essentials of Interaction Design. Wiley, New York (2007)

8. Sasse, M.A.: Eliciting and Describing Users' Models of Computer Systems. University of Birmingham (1997)

Usability Evaluation of 4-Direction Keys for Ladder Menu Operation

Takeshi Nagami[1]([✉]), Yoshikazu Seki[1], Hidenori Sakai[2],
and Hiroaki Ikeda[3]

[1] National Institute of Advanced Industrial Science and Technology (AIST),
Tsukuba, Japan
{nagami-takeshi,yoshikazu-seki}@aist.go.jp
[2] Ricoh Company, Ltd., Tokyo, Japan
hidenori.sakai@nts.ricoh.co.jp
[3] Chiba University, Chiba, Japan
ikeda@faculty.chiba-u.jp

Abstract. In this research, the usability of three typical menu selection operation patterns using 4-direction keys was evaluated. These patterns are often used to set parameters and call functions in information equipment. In this experiment, the independent variables were the key operation methods, menu depth, number of menu items, and user age range. The dependent variables were task execution time and number of key presses. Sixty-two people participated in the experiment. The results show that the effect of menu depth and number of items varies depending on the operation methods. These results will be used to help establish ISO/IEC 17549-21.

Keywords: Menu operation · 4-direction key · Usability · Standardization

1 Introduction

When using information equipment such as mobile phones or digital cameras, a 4-direction key (as shown in Fig. 1) is usually used to operate the menu selections shown in the display area. However, there are no standards established for these operation methods. Because new equipment now includes sophisticated and complex functionalities, operation methods have become complicated. In this situation, the many kinds of operation methods may confuse users. In addition, it is difficult to learn how to operate such equipment. To address these problems, ISO/IEC 17549-2 [6] was published in May 2015.

This paper experimentally evaluates how differences in menu patterns and 4-direction key operations affect usability. This experiment was carried out to develop the international standard described above. The goal was to define operation method guidelines for selection menus that use a 4-direction key.

Menu operations have often been considered a simple form of information equipment interaction. Even in the 1970 s, it was pointed out that the relative merits of menu design also led to operability problems. There has since been much research on menu layout methods and the systematization of menu items [10, 13]. Some research

© Springer International Publishing Switzerland 2016
M. Kurosu (Ed.): HCI 2016, Part II, LNCS 9732, pp. 330–340, 2016.
DOI: 10.1007/978-3-319-39516-6_32

has investigated the role of menu depth and breadth in information system user interfaces [9, 12]. In addition, factors that affect the movement time and accuracy of menu selection using a mouse have also been investigated [11].

However, as mobile technologies have continued to develop, applications have diversified, and mobile functions have increased. In addition, most people now use mobile devices, and the elderly in particular desire an easy-to-use interface. We examine menu operation using the cross key, which is often implemented in information equipment in today.

Usability is generally represented by terms such as ease of use, user-friendliness, and high learning efficiency. In ISO 9126-1 [7], usability is defined as consisting of Understandability, Learnability, and Operability. ISO 9241-11 [8] defines usability as the "extent to which a product can be used by specified users to achieve specified goals with effectiveness, efficiency, and satisfaction in a specified context of use." Based on these documents, the usability characteristics of the 4-direction key operation methods are listed in Table 1.

Fig. 1. Examples of 4-direction keys

2 Experiment for Usability of Menu Operation

The Information Technology Research and Standardization Center within the Japanese Standard Association (JSA) performed a field survey of navigation methods of off-the-shelf electronic equipment [5]. The survey included the following products: cellular phones, digital cameras, digital video cameras, music players, personal digital assistants (PDAs), game machines, printers, multiple function copiers, televisions, and projectors. It concluded that navigation methods could be classified into six types, as shown in Fig. 2.

- Type 1: The focus of operation moves up or down endlessly by an up-key or down-key, respectively. It moves through a menu of the hierarchy by a right-key or left-key, respectively.
- Type 2: The operation of a right-key or left-key switches the top menu endlessly. The focus of operation moves up or down endlessly by an up-key or down-key, respectively.
- Type 3: The focus of operation moves up or down and stops at the top or bottom of the menu by an up-key or down-key, respectively. It moves among the hierarchy of ladder menus by a right-key or left-key, respectively.

– Type 4: The focus of operation moves up or down and stops at the top or bottom of the menu by an up-key or down-key, respectively. A right-key or left-key are used set parameters, or to enable or disable the selected feature.
– Type 5: Key operation is the same as Type 3.
– Type 6: Key operation is the same as Type 2.

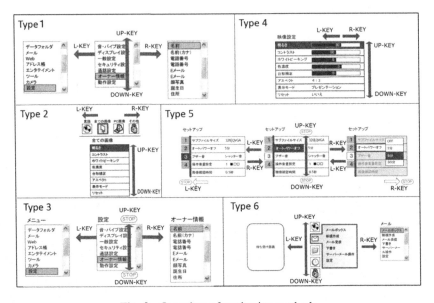

Fig. 2. Overview of navigation methods

In addition, many products were found to use three of the six types.

The purpose of this experiment was to evaluate the usability of the Types 1–3 operation methods described above. The quantitative usability metrics used in this study are listed in Table 1.

Table 1. Characteristics of usability and its metrics

Characteristics	Indices	Metrics
Effectiveness	Clarity of the menu sctucture and key operations	Percentage of correct answers Retry frequency
Efficiency	Operation speed Ease of learning	Number of key presses
Satisfaction	Preference Affinity Tiredness	Impressions Change in task performance time

2.1   Experimental Design

Each participant was given the task of setting up a piece of equipment by selecting menu items, as shown in Fig. 3. The display screen consisted of an issue statement, ladder menu, and 4-direction key. A different scene appeared depending on the factor of the experiment. The factors in this experiment were age range, type of operation method, number of menu items, and depth of menu hierarchy.

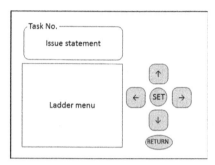 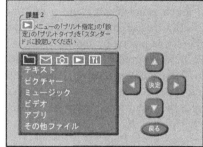

Fig. 3. Design of simulator screen and an example of the task of Type 3

(a) Two age ranges were used: 22–59 years and 60 + years.
(b) Three types of operation methods were selected from the six types listed above: Types 1, 2, and 3.
(c) The number of items in a menu. Six items could be displayed at once on the menu without scrolling. When nine items were displayed, the participant had to scroll the menu, otherwise the target did not appear.
(d) Two levels of number of layers were tested, 3 and 5 layers, including the target item.

    In this experiment, factors b, c, and d were within-subject factors.

2.2   Participants

A total of 62 people participated in this experiment. The sample consisted of 40 men and 22 women. The number of participants for each operation condition of the device and their age ranges are shown in Table 2.

Table 2. The number of participants

Operation tool	Age range(Years)	
	Age22-59	Age60+
Touch Panel	15	15
Mouse	17	15

Thirty of the participants came to a sound-insulated room that was prepared for the experiment. They used a touch panel to operate the menus.

The other 32 participated using their own PC from their home or office over the Internet. They probably operated the menus with a mouse.

2.3 Apparatus

For the experiments in the laboratory, the experimental arrangement comprised a 6-inch touch panel display and a PC. In contrast, the experiments over the Internet comprised a mouse, display monitor, and PC. In addition, the server communicating with them was placed on the Internet.

We built a simulator for the tasks that worked in a Web browser, as shown in Fig. 3. The simulator received a set of stimulation data from the management server and transmitted a log of a participant's operations. When the key operation event occurred, the event was logged in milliseconds.

2.4 Stimulus

The questions and menu items were generated from data based on a survey of products such as digital cameras. Fictitious menus relating to digital cameras, PDAs, and mobile phones were created, as shown in Fig. 4.

―「撮影」メニューの「ISO感度」を「100」に設定してください
(Please select "Camera", select "ISO speed", and set to 100 the ISO speed number.)

―「再生」メニューの「スライドショー」の「設定」の「再生間隔」を「5秒」に設定してください
(Please select "Play", select "Slideshow", select "Setting", select "Interval", set to "5s" the interval time.)

撮影	(Camera)
ムービー	(Movie)
再生	(Play)
画面表示	(Screen info.)
設定	(Setting)

Fig. 4. Examples of questions and menu items

A question sentence was presented that imitated a typical sentence in the operating manual of a piece of equipment. Each sentence was constructed along the order of the menu items until the target was reached. Ten questions for each of the fictional menus were prepared.

The number of levels and menu items were controlled depending on the experimental conditions. However, the top-level menu of each condition has only five items. The length of shortest path to each target was controlled by the almost conditions. A condition of the number of level of menu layer has a case where the length is different (Fig. 5).

To measure user satisfaction, which is one of the characteristics defining usability, a questionnaire was used. A 22-item questionnaire was prepared after reviewing the Software Usability Measurement Inventory [1, 3, 4].

1.	I have been able to quickly understand how to operate the equipment.
2.	I think that there are any useless way in the operating procedure.
3.	I have been able to quickly learn how to operate the equipment.
4.	I think the operations are unified.
5.	I thought the operations were not as hard as expected.
6.	I have the frustration on the behavior of the system.
7.	I was often get lost what to do.
8.	I thought it was easy to understand the operation procedure.
9.	I thought it was easy to find the target item I need.
10.	I thought the menu structures were easy to understand.
11.	I had not been able to know my position during the operation.
12.	I think the operation of the equipment is friendly.
13.	I had been tired while operating.
14.	I became familiar with the operating procedure.
15.	I have confidence in the menu operation of such equipment usually.
16.	I thought my operations were excellent.
17.	I thought the placement of menu and the size of character were clear.
18.	I thought the display of screen was easy to see.
19.	I thought the size of the screen was appropriate.
20.	I had eye fatigue while this experiment.
21.	I left comfortable using the system.
22.	I thought the display speed was appropriate.

Fig. 5. Questionnaire for participants

The questionnaire was created based on some web usability tests, such as SUS. Each question item is classified into four terms of the following.

Q1 to 6: Understandability of the operation system
Q7 to 11: Clarity of the menu structure
Q12 to 16: Familiarity
Q17 to 22: Visibility

2.5 Procedure

Equal numbers of participants used the three navigation methods. Each participant was assigned 30 tasks. The order of the tasks was randomized.

First, participants were to ask practice a task twice. They then performed the actual set of assigned tasks. The time limit for each task was set to 10 m. After all of the tasks were complete, the participants responded to the questionnaire on the screen.

3 Results

Task execution time is the number of seconds taken to reach the goal menu item from the start of the task. Table 3 shows the mean and standard deviation of the task execution time for each condition.

A t-test of these mean values did not show a significant difference ($t(60) = .752$, $p = .45$).

Table 3. Average and standard deviation of task execution time of all tasks

	Operation tool	
	Touch Panel	Mouse
Average(second)	17.63	18.06
SD	13.37	10.08

3.1 Task Execution Time for Each Condition

In the following analysis, results were statistically processed by mixing the output data of the two types of operating device: the touch panel and the PC.

Tables 4 and 5 show the average task execution time for each condition.

Table 4. Average task execution time in 22–59 years

Menu Hierarchies	Menu Items	Types of navigation methods			Average
		Type 1	Type 2	Type 3	
3	6	11.2	11.3	12.2	11.6
	9	10.4	12.3	12.0	11.5
5	6	17.5	20.9	19.1	19.0
	9	14.8	16.6	16.7	16.0
Average		13.3	15.1	14.8	14.3

An ANOVA was used to test the main effects and interactions for significance. Significant main effects were observed for all factors ($p < .01$ for each). There were significant interactions between the age ranges and menu levels ($p < .01$) and between the menu levels and menu items ($p < .01$).

Table 5. Average task execution time in 60 + years

Menu Hierarchies	Menu Items	Types of navgation methods			Average
		Type 1	Type 2	Type 3	
3	6	20.9	22.1	19.4	20.9
	9	20.4	22.8	22.6	21.7
5	6	31.7	34.9	34.2	33.3
	9	26.3	28.7	29.7	27.3
Average		24.5	26.8	26.1	25.6

The main effect of the operation methods, according to a post-hoc test by Tukey's HSD, was the difference between Type 1 and Type 2 ($p < .05$).

In each interaction between the age range and menu levels, as well as the menu levels and menu items, the simple main effects were tested. The difference between age ranges 22–59 and 60 + was greater when the number of menu levels was five. In the interaction of the menu levels and menu items, while the number of menu items was not significant for a menu consisting of three levels, the task execution time of a menu with nine items was significantly shorter than one with six items ($p < .01$) for five levels.

3.2   Number of Key Presses for Each Condition

Tables 6 and 7 show the average number of key presses from start to finish for each task.

Significant main effects were observed for three factors: the type of operation method, age range, and number of menu levels. No main effect was observed for number of menu items. There was a significant interaction between the menu levels and menu items ($p < .01$).

Table 6. Average number of key presses in 22–59 years

| Menu Hierarchies | Menu Items | Types of navigation methods | | | Average |
		Type 1	Type 2	Type 3	
3	6	12.7	11.7	12.6	12.3
	9	13.4	16.1	16.3	15.2
5	6	22.2	23.6	25.2	23.6
	9	20.0	22.5	21.3	21.2
Average		17.0	18.6	18.8	18.1

According to a post-hoc Tukey's HSD multiple comparison, in the main effect of operation methods, there were significant differences between Type 1 and Type 2 ($p < .01$) and Type 1 and Type 3 ($p < .05$).

In the interaction between the menu levels and menu items, a simple main effect was tested. A menu with six items had significantly fewer key presses than one with nine items ($p < .01$) in a menu consisting of three levels. However, in a menu consisting of five levels, a menu with nine items had significantly fewer key presses than one with six items ($p < .01$).

Table 7. Average number of key presses in 60 + years

| Menu Hierarchies | Menu Items | Types of navigation methods | | | Average |
		Type 1	Type 2	Type 3	
3	6	14.3	14.7	13.9	14.3
	9	15.2	18.3	18.3	17.0
5	6	24.8	25.2	27.9	25.8
	9	21.2	23.3	24.4	22.7
Average		18.7	20.4	21.2	19.9

3.3 Retry Frequency

A retry is when a user returns to a previous state when he/she determines that an incorrect key operation has been made. Retry frequency is often used as a metric to assess the clarity of the menu structure and its associated key operations.

Two definitions for a retry were possible in this experiment. One definition of retry is that the operator backtracks through the menu hierarchy. The other definition is the act of returning from too many of up or down operations in the menu. When navigating up or down in a menu that appears on the screen, however, it was not possible to distinguish whether a retry had occurred or the operator was using a particular strategy in the case of an endless scroll. Hence, we examined only the case of returning to the menu hierarchy. Table 8 shows the retry frequency.

Table 8. Retry frequency for each condition

Age ranges	Types of navigation method			Total
	Type 1	Type 2	Type 3	
20-59	27	20	71	118
60+	35	73	79	187
Total	62	93	150	305

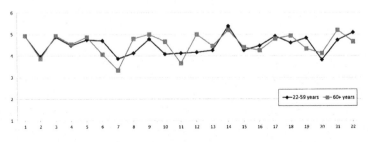

(a) Aggregating by age ranges

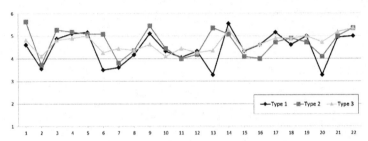

(b) Aggregating by types of navigation method

Fig. 6. Plot of aggregating questionnaire

3.4   Questionnaire

The results of the questionnaire are summarized in Fig. 6. About the questions that is a negative form in Japanese, the value of the answers were inverted. The graphs of the age ranges indicate the same tendencies (Fig. 6(a)), but that of the operation method types indicate some partial differences (Fig. 6(b)). Figure 7 shows question items for which the difference of each category by types of navigation method.

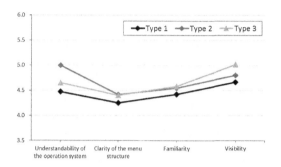

Fig. 7. Difference of each category by types of navigation method

4   Conclusions

Given the task execution time, number of key presses, and retry frequency results, it is appropriate to recommend the operation method of Type 1. Equivalently, in terms of effectiveness and efficiency, Type 1 is the best option. In addition, it is recommended to reduce the number of menu levels. In this study, in the same way as the results of previous studies on the depth and breadth of the menus [9, 10, 12], the number of menu items is less impact on the effectiveness and efficiency. For older users, the menu levels should be made as shallow as possible because there was an interaction between the age range and the menu hierarchies. In the age range condition, even though there is no difference in the number of key presses, the task execution time of 60 + years participants was significantly slower than that of the 22–59 years. However, the degree to which these parameters must be reduced varied depending on the operation method. If the number of items is small, Type 2 is also recommended.

About retry frequency, for the age range 60 +, Type 1 had the smallest. For the age range 22–59, Type 2 had the smallest. At any age ranges, the retry frequency of Type 3 was the largest. In contrast, Type 1 was small. However, Type 2 in age ranges was large difference of the retry frequency. Even though the retry frequency of young user was small, that of the elderly was close to the highest value.

According to the results of questionnaire as shown Fig. 7, Type 1 has the most advantage about the understandability of the operation system. About the Visibility, Type 3 is seemed to be the most advantage.

References

1. Bangor, A., Kortum, P., Miller, J.: Determining what individual SUS scores mean: adding an adjective rating scale. J. Usability Stud. **4**(3), 114–123 (2009)
2. Allen, R.B.: Cognitive factors in the use of menus and trees: An experiment. IEEE J. Sel. Areas Commun. **1**, 333–336 (1983)
3. Frøkjær, E., Hertzum, M., Hornbæk, K.: Measuring usability: Are effectiveness, efficiency, and satisfaction really correlated?. In: Proceedings of the ACM CHI 2000, pp. 345–352 (2000)
4. The de facto industry standard evaluation questionnaire for assessing quality of use of software by end users. http://sumi.ucc.ie/
5. Information Technology Research and Standardization Center (INSTAC), JSA. The standardization of 4-direction key interaction of mobile information devices (2010)
6. ISO/IEC 17549-2: User interface guidelines on menu navigation – Part 2: Navigation with 4-direction device
7. ISO 9126-1:2001: Software engineering – Product quality – Part 1: Quality model
8. ISO 9241-11:1998: Ergonomic requirements for office work with visual display terminals (VDTs) – Part 11: Guidance on usability
9. Kiger, J.I.: The depth/breadth trade-off in the design of menu-driven user interfaces. Int. J. Man Mach. Stud. **20**(2), 201–313 (1984)
10. Norman, K.L.: The Psychology of Menu Selection: Designing Cognitive Control at the Human/Computer Interface. Ablex Publishing Corporation, Norwood (1991)
11. Walker, N., Smelcer, J.B., Nilsen, E.: Optimizing speed and accuracy of menu selection: a comparison of walking and pull-down menus. Int. J. Man Mach. Stud. **35**(6), 871–890 (1991)
12. Sisson, N., Parkinson, S.R., Snowberry, K.: Considerations of menu structure and communication rate for the design of computer menu displays. Int. J. Man Mach. Stud. **25**(5), 479–489 (1986)
13. Teitelbaum, R.C., Granda, R.E.: The effects of positional constancy on searching menus for information. In: Proceedings of the SIGCHI Conference on Human Factors in Computing Systems, CHI 1983, pp. 150–153 (1983)

UniWatch: A Soft Keyboard for Text Entry on SmartWatches Using 3 Keys

Watch User-Interface and User Evaluation

Franck Poirier[1](✉) and Mohammed Belatar[2]

[1] Lab-STICC, Université Bretagne Sud, Campus de Tohannic, 56000 Vannes, France
franck.poirier@univ-ubs.fr
[2] Technology and Telecom, Rue Dayat Aoua, 10090 Rabat, Morocco
mohammed.belatar@gmail.com

Abstract. Smartwatches are a fast-expanding type of interactive device. They are wearable computers that can be dependent or independent of the user's smartphone. At the moment, one of the problems of this kind of devices is that they do not offer a usable means of text entry. In this paper, we will first present the user-interface of our text entry method on smartwatches called UniWatch derived from the former UniGlyph method. The main advantage of UniWatch is to minimize the resources on the screen by using a minimal three-key ambiguous keypad. In this paper, we will detail the screen interface and the gesture commands. Then, we will present the results of the user evaluation of UniWatch.

Keywords: Text input · Soft keyboard · Touchscreen · Evaluation · Connected watch · Smartwatch · Internet of things

1 Introduction

Smartwatches are wrist wearable computers which provide time like traditional watches, but offer other uses. At present, there are two types of smartwatches, the companion smatwatches that are connected via Bluetooth to the smartphone and the standalone smartwatches, which are smartphone-independent. The first type is a kind of accessory that gives access to some functionalities of the smartphone. For example, the user can directly answer or make calls from his/her wrist, receive a message notification, take a snapshot or a short video… The second type is more often a sport watch that includes activity tracker features and usually a GPS unit.

All of these smartwatches are characterized by the presence of a tiny screen, no physical keyboard and few buttons. If it is not so difficult to display notifications on this kind of screens, it is much more difficult for the user to produce information. With the current smartwatches in the market, text entry is impossible or very difficult and troublesome due to their 1 to 2-inch screens.

In fact, the user really does not have any other option than using the vocal assistant built-in application to communicate (S Voice on Android, Siri on IOS). The problem is that voice communication is not always possible or appropriate to the context of user

© Springer International Publishing Switzerland 2016
M. Kurosu (Ed.): HCI 2016, Part II, LNCS 9732, pp. 341–349, 2016.
DOI: 10.1007/978-3-319-39516-6_33

interaction: voice is problematic in noisy environments and raises privacy issues in public spaces [15]. Voice communication is provided mainly because there is currently no effective virtual keyboard on smartwatches.

The lack of usable text entry keyboard is probably a key reason for the current failure of wearable devices like smart glasses (i.e. Google Glass). From our point of view, text entry should be present on all mobile or wearable devices [7]. The mass adoption of smartwatches is strongly conditioned by the possibility to enter short text with a smartwatch. That is why text entry on smartwatch is a major research challenge.

In this paper, we present a text entry method for smartwatches called UniWatch derived from the former method UniGlyph, we detail the user-interface and describe the user evaluation.

2   Related Works

For the last three years, different text input methods for smartwatches have been proposed.

Few text entry methods are on the market for smartwatches, e.g. Fleksy [4], Minuum, Swype [17]. These three methods are based on a full QWERTY keyboard. Keys are so tiny that the finger touch does not hit the only desired key, the entry is disambiguated by lexical predictive algorithms. Predictive technologies are not perfect and are not suitable in typing abbreviations, acronyms, proper nouns... Due to the fat finger problem, it seems that a static QWERTY keyboard is not the right solution for smartwatches.

ZoomBoard [10] is one of the first methods based on a zooming user-interface (ZUI) paradigm. It provides a full QWERTY keyboard. The tiny keys around the finger press are iteratively enlarged, the user refines the finger position in order to point to the desired key, once this key is reached, zooming stops and the key is typed upon pressing.

Dunlop et al. [3] propose to divide the watch screen into seven zones, six big ambiguous keys, three at the top of the screen and three at the bottom and a center zone for the input entry field. OpenAdaptxt [8] is used for entry disambiguation and swipe gestures allow to change modes (alphabetical/numerical, lower/upper case, punctuation...), complete a word or enter a space.

DragKeys [2] is a circular keyboard composed of 8 ambiguous keys arranged around the text cursor. At most five letters are assigned to each key. To enter a letter, a first dragging gesture is made toward the key associated with the desired letter and a second dragging gesture in order to move the letter on the text cursor line.

The analog keyboard project [1] explores direct handwriting on the small touch screen.

Another approach is to use IR proximity sensors to capture gestures performed above the device, for example Gesture Watch [5] and HoverFlow [6]. This approach has the advantage of reducing screen occlusion, but needs specific mechanisms, it does not provide tactile feedback, and is not very discrete.

3   Source of UniWatch

UniWatch is an adaptation for smartwatches of UniGlyph [14]. It is not possible to summarize in this paper our former research in text entry [11–13]. For details, refer to the original articles.

In summary, UniGlyph is based on the structure of Latin characters composed by a specific sequence of primitive shapes (curve, stroke, loop...).

The set of primitive shapes is reduced to only 3 symbols: (1) diagonal stroke, (2) curve and (3) horizontal or vertical line. Each primitive shape is dedicated to one key of the keypad called respectively diagonal-shape key, loop-shape key and straight-shape key (Fig. 1).

Fig. 1. The UniGlyph character set and the associated input keys: (1) diagonal-shape key, (2) loop-shape key, (3) straight-shape key.

Each letter of the English alphabet is represented by only one primitive shape according to the shape of the uppercase letter. In order to recall the coded key, the user needs to follow a very simple rule (Fig. 1):

– if the capital letter contains a diagonal stroke, then click on the diagonal-shape key (1);
– otherwise, if it contains a loop or a curving stroke, then click on the loop-shape key (2);
– otherwise, click on the straight-shape key (3).

As there are many more characters than primitives, each primitive corresponds to a set of letters. The expected word is deduced by a linguistic predictor like for all the ambiguous keyboards (T9®, SureType®, iTap®...).

The UniGlyph keypad contains three shape keys and one command key used to switch the different input modes and to select the expected word.

4   User-Interface of UniWatch

Form Factor Problem. Smartwatches have much smaller touchscreens than PDAs or smartphones. For example, by comparing an Apple Watch (model 1.65'') to a iPhone 6, the screen is 8 times smaller; comparing an Apple Watch (model 1.5'') to a iPhone 6 Plus, the screen is 15 times smaller.

Clearly, the fat finger problem on touch screens becomes a big fat finger problem on smartwatches!

We understand that QWERTY-like keyboard and even reduced, but not-too-reduced keyboards are not well suited to text entry on smartwatches.

According to Hick-Hyman's law, the more the keyboard will be reduced, the more key selection will be fast. According to Fitts' law, the more the keyboard will be reduced, the more keys will be big and the more keypress will be fast.

Our research challenge is to design a strongly reduced keyboard in order to deal with the fat finger problem.

Therefore, it can be argued that an adaptation of UniGlyph that uses only 3 shape keys is a pragmatic response to the problem of text entry on tiny connected objects like smartwatches.

Design Approaches. We have proposed different approaches for entering text on the smartwatch screen with UniWatch [14]. In this paper we consider only the more direct adaptation based on key presses, more precisely button taps on the soft keypad.

Other adaptations based on flick gesture and direct finger drawing have been developed. The evaluation has shown that the keypress approach is preferable because it implies a better feedback (the coded letters are recalled on the keys), it is easier to use (compared to the flick gesture approach), and it is quicker and more reliable (compared to the finger drawing approach) [14].

The UniWatch prototype has been implemented on a Sony Smartwatch.

Screen Layout. As shown on Fig. 2, the keypress approach of UniWatch uses only three keys, the original command-key of UniGlyph is replaced by touch-based gestures for controlling the whole entry process. The three keys are placed on the lower side of the screen. The user interaction is limited to single taps on these keys (3 soft buttons). Due to the size of the keys the risk of error is very low.

Fig. 2. The UniWatch keypad: text entry approach by button tapping

The whole entry window consists of two main zones: at the top, the display area and, at the bottom, the entry area. The display area includes always two lines. Depending of the entry mode, the entry area consists of a 3-key keypad or a 6-key keypad (Fig. 3). Note that the three shape keys occupied the quarter of the screen, the complete entry window with the text line and the prediction line nearly occupies the three quarter of the screen.

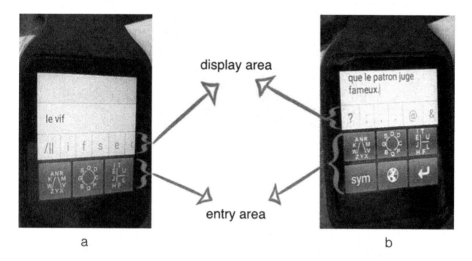

Fig. 3. a- the 3-key keypad, b- the 6-key keypad

The 3-key keypad is the minimum keyboard that contains, on one line, the diagonal-shape key, the loop-shape key and the straight-shape key. It is important to note that each shape key displays the associated letters. The labels 'A', 'K', 'M', 'N', 'R', 'V', 'W', 'X', 'Y', 'Z' are displayed on the diagonal-shape key. The labels 'B', 'C', 'D', 'G', 'O', 'P', 'Q', 'S' are displayed on the loop-shape key. The labels 'E', 'F', 'H', 'I', 'J', 'L', 'U', 'T' are displayed on the straight-shape key. In this way, even if the user doesn't know the UniWatch character map, he/she can easily enter text by reading on the keys. These labels are in fact knowledge in the world [9] that forms a good feedback for the user.

The 6-key keypad contains two lines. The bottom line, from left to right, consists of the key mode, the entry method key and the enter key. The upper line is the same than for the 3-key keypad. The key mode allows switching between the alphabetical mode, the numeric mode and the symbol mode. The entry method key allows switching between the UniWatch method and the built-in entry method. The enter key produces a new line in the text by button tapping.

As with all ambiguous keyboards, e.g. the method proposed by Dunlop [3] each key is ambiguous, a disambiguation engine gives the word prediction. The word prediction list is displayed on the bottom line of the display area (Fig. 4). The word prediction line consists of soft buttons. Each predicted word can be selected by tapping on it. Due to the efficiency of the word prediction algorithm, the desired word is more often placed at the beginning of the prediction line.

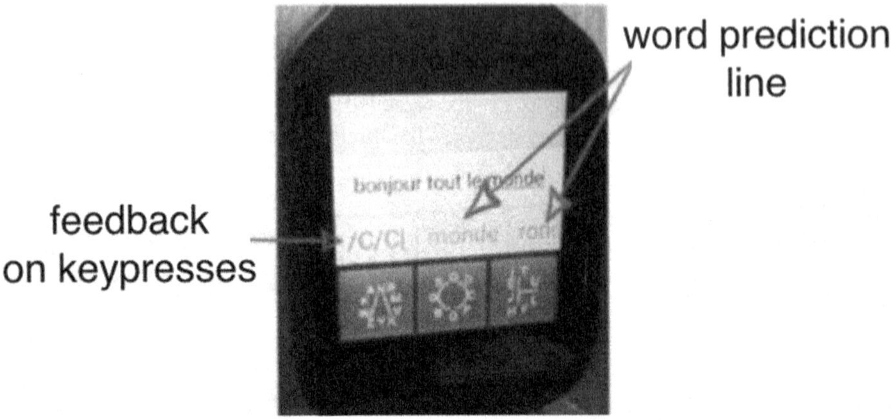

Fig. 4. Detail on the display area

An Example of Text Entry. The sentence *"The quick brown fox jumps over the lazy dog"* (*"le vif renard brun saute par dessus le chien paresseux"* in French) is a panagram or holoalphabetic sentence. It is usually used in text entry research. Consider the word "renard" ("fox" in English), it is entered by pressing successively on the keys '/', 'l', '/', '/', '/', 'C'. Then the prediction line displays the words "verras", "renard", "vivras"... The user taps on the second word to enter "renard" in the text and a space character is automatically entered before the next word.

Figure 4 shows the 3-key keypad and the display area when the user wants to enter the word "monde" ("world" in English). The prediction line begins by the word "monde" and is followed by the word "ronde" ("round" in English).

Gesture Commands. As explained earlier, button taps are used to select a letter or a word. In order to simplify the input interface, the number of buttons has been minimized. All the commands are made by gestures on the tactile screen. Flick gestures are used for a long time [18]. A flick gesture is a particularly fast way for entering a command, the gesture direction is significant but not the amplitude. The flick gestures can be executed from a starting point towards one side of the screen (top, bottom, left or right side).

Table 1 shows the commands performed by flick gestures.

It is important to note that processes that allow to speed up the entry, such as keyboard shortcuts, access keys, hot keys are always appreciated by users. Flick gesture commands are a kind of shortcut that speed up the interaction. They allow to reduce the number of interaction and to increase the pace of interaction. They correspond to one of the 8 Golden Rules expressed by Shneiderman ("Enable Frequent Users to Use Shortcuts") [16] and also one of the eight ISO-Standard 9241-110 Dialogue Principles ("Suitability for Individualization").

Table 1. Flick gesture commands

Gesture	Command
flick right	insert space character
flick down left	insert enter character
small flick left	delete character
flick left	delete word
flick down on 6-key keypad	switch to 3-key keypad
flick up	switch to 6-key keypad
flick down from 3-key keypad	switch between modes

5 User Evaluation

Corpus. The corpus is composed of ten simple non-accentuated French sentences, 23 to 35 characters long. The number of characters is 250 (spaces excluded) and 302 (spaces included). The number of words is 62, the average of letters per word is 4.

This corpus is quite well-balanced of written French. The minimum threshold of occurrences for each letter is 3. It concerns letters 'f', 'g', 'h', 'k', 'w', 'x', 'y' and 'z'. The frequency of the most frequent letter 'e' is 17 % (Table 2).

Table 2. The French sentence set used in the experiment

1.	Il a le nez rouge comme un clown
2.	Le cowboy joue du banjo au saloon
3.	Les voyages forment la jeunesse
4.	Je veux acheter deux kilos de sucre
5.	Il joue de la kora le dimanche
6.	Vous pouvez prendre mon stylo
7.	Tu peux tout faire seul
8.	La fille mange quelques kiwis
9.	Est assez riche qui ne doit rien
10.	Qui paie bien est bien servi

Participants. Five master students (4 men and 1 woman) participated to a primary evaluation of UniWatch.

The principles of UniGlyph have been explained during 5 min. The subjects were seated at a table. The 10-sentence corpus was written on a sheet of paper located on the table. The subjects wore the watch on their wrist. They were allowed to try the method for two minutes before starting the evaluation.

Results. The "input rate" or "typing speed" is measured in words per minute (WPM) or CPS (characters per second). In this experiment, the average input rate is 9.84 WPM (considering that the average word length in French is 5 characters) or 0.82 CPS. The maximum input speed is 13.78 WPM or 1.15 CPS obtained for the sentence

"Les voyages forment la jeunesse". The minimum input speed is 8.09 WPM or 0.67 CPS obtained for the sentence *"Il a le nez rouge comme un clown"*. Note that the minimum speed is obtained on the first sentence of the corpus.

The scanning time in the prediction list in order to select the desired word considerably increases the WPM. That is the case for the selection of the words *"clown"*, or "cowboy". These words are put in the corpus to balance it, but are not very frequent in the real context of short sentences entered on a smartwatch. With more realistic sentences, the effective WPM should be more than 10 WPM. In case of a simple sentence where the desired words are at the beginning of the prediction list (in the first, second or third position), the entry speed should be around 15 WPM.

6   Conclusion

In this paper, we have presented one of the three user-interface approaches of UniWatch. We have chosen the approach based on keypresses because it is the most direct and efficient [14]. We have also presented the primary results of the evaluation. These results are encouraging because they are very close to the results obtained earlier on PDAs or smartphones. We can conclude that UniWatch is nearly also efficient on the very tiny screen of a smartwatch than UniGlyph on the small screen of a personal assistant [12].

In conclusion, we can argue that text entry on smartwatches is not impossible and even not more difficult than on the other small-screen interactive devices.

References

1. The Analog Keyboard Project. Microsoft Research 2014. http://research.microsoft.com/en-us/um/redmond/projects/analogkeyboard
2. Cho, H., Kim, M., Seo, K.: A text technique for wrist-worn watches with tiny touchscreens. In: Proceedings of ACM UIST 2014, pp. 79–80. ACM Press, Honolulu, HI, USA (2014)
3. Dunlop, M., Komninos, A., Durga, N.: Towards high quality text entry on smartwatches. In: Proceedings of ACM CHI 2014, pp. 2365–2370. ACM Press, Totonto, ON, Canada (2014)
4. Fleksy keyboard. www.fleksy.com
5. Kim, J., He, J., Lyons, K., Starner, T.: The Gesture Watch: a wireless contact-free gesture based wrist interface. In: Proceedings of 6th International Semantic Web Conference ISWC 2007, pp. 11–13. Busan, Korea (2007)
6. Kratz, S., Rohs, M.: Hoverflow: exploring around-device interaction with IR distance sensors. In: Proceedings of MobileHCI 2009, pp. 1–4. ACM Press, Bonn, Germany (2009)
7. MacKenzie, S., Tanaka-Ishii, K.: Text Entry Systems: Mobility, Accessibility. Universality. Morgan Kaufmann Publishers, San Francisco (2007)
8. Minuum keyboard. www.minuum.com
9. Montaparti, S., Dona, P., Durga, N., Meo, R.D.: OpenAdaptxt: an open source enabling technology for high quality text entry. In: Proceedings of CHI Workshop on Designing and Evaluating Text Entry. ACM Press (2012)
10. Norman, D.: The Design of Everyday Things. Basic Books. MIT Press, London, New York (1988)

11. Oney, S., Harrison, C., Ogan, A., Wiese, J.: ZoomBoard: a diminutive QWERTY soft keyboard using iterative zooming for ultra-small devices. In: Proceedings of ACM CHI 2013, pp. 2799–2802. ACM Press. Paris, France (2013)

12. Poirier, F.: Glyph: a new stroke-alphabet for stylus-based or key-based text entry. In: Proceedings of HCI International 2005. Springer (2005)

13. Poirier, F., Belatar, M.: UniGlyph: only one keystroke per character on a 4-button minimal keypad for key-based text entry. In: Proceedings of HCI International 2007. Springer (2007)

14. Poirier, F.: Text entry methods for handheld devices or for AAC writing system. In: Proceedings of ACM CHI 2012. ACM Press. Austin, TX, USA (2012)

15. Poirier, F., Belatar, M.: UniWatch - some approaches derived from uniglyph to allow text input on tiny devices such as connected watches. In: Kurosu, M. (ed.) Human-Computer Interaction. LNCS, vol. 9170, pp. 554–562. Springer, Heidelberg (2015)

16. Sawhney, N., Schmandt, C.: Nomadicradio: speechand audio interaction for contextual messaging in nomadic environment. ACM Trans. Comput. Hum. Interact. **7**(3), 353–383 (2000). ACM Press

17. Shneiderman, B., Plaisant, C.: Designing the user interface: Strategies for effective Human-Computer Interaction. Addison Wesley, Boston, MA (2004)

18. Swype keyboard. www.swype.com

19. Venolia, G., Neiberg, F.: T-Cube: a fast, self-disclosing pen-based alphabet. In: Proceedings of the SIGCHI Conference on Human Factors in Computing Systems - CHI 1994, pp. 265–270. ACM Press, Boston, MA, USA (1994)

Multi-platform, Migratory and Distributed Interfaces

An Information Display System with Information Scrapping User Interface Based on Digital Signage Terminals and Mobile Devices for Disaster Situations

Ryosuke Aoki[1]([✉]), Akihiro Miyata[2], Shunichi Seko[2], Ryo Hashimoto[1], Tatsuro Ishida[3], Masahiro Watanabe[1], and Masayuki Ihara[1]

[1] NTT Service Evolution Laboratories, NTT Corporation, Yokosuka, Japan
{aoki.ryosuke,hashimoto.ryo,watanabe.masahiro,
ihara.masayuki}@lab.ntt.co.jp
[2] NTT Resonant, Inc., Tokyo, Japan
{miyata-a,shunichi}@nttr.co.jp
[3] NTT Plala, Inc., Tokyo, Japan
t-ishida@plala.co.jp

Abstract. In the East Japan Earthquake of 2011, a lot of people stranded at a station in a metropolitan city gathered and stayed in front of digital signage terminals displaying disaster information. The situation had the potential to cause a secondary disaster such as crowding accidents. To solve this problem, we propose an information display system with information scrapping user interface based on a digital signage terminal and mobile devices. Users can watch disaster information on the screen of their own mobile device by access to a digital signage terminal through Wi-Fi connection. The information scrapping user interface allows users to save target disaster information on the screen of their own mobile device and meta-information related with the target information by encircling the target information roughly. The main effect of this system is to shorten the time needed to access disaster information and save the desired information in a mobile device. We conduct a field experiment to evaluate the performance of the proposed system. The main effect of the system was confirmed by comparing with noting or taking photos of desired information among disaster information displayed by a digital signage terminal.

Keywords: Disaster · Digital signage · HTML5 · Information scrapping

1 Introduction

We aim to construct an information display system for stranded people, who gather and stay in front of digital signage terminals after disasters happen, to quickly access the disaster information stored in the digital signage terminals by their own mobile device and save their target information with meta-information even if they roughly operate the mobile device in a panic situation. In the East Japan Earthquake of 2011, digital signage terminals at stations displayed disaster information and many stranded people gathered and stayed in front of the digital signage terminals for a long time to get disaster information. This crowd had the potential to cause a secondary disaster such as a

© Springer International Publishing Switzerland 2016
M. Kurosu (Ed.): HCI 2016, Part II, LNCS 9732, pp. 353–363, 2016.
DOI: 10.1007/978-3-319-39516-6_34

stampede. Since digital signage terminals are expected to be key disaster information presentation devices, it is important to solve this problem. Shortening the time needed to find and save disaster information cuts the time they stay together in front of the terminal.

There are various ways for digital signage terminals to present information on the screen. General digital signage terminals display information on the screen in Slideshow view. Recent interactive digital signage terminals display multiple pieces of information on the screen at the same time and details of selected information are presented in response to touch inputs. However, the details shown on the screen will not satisfy all users. Even if the details include user's target information, it is difficult to save the information by camera etc. due to the crowded situation. Due to the East Japan Earthquake of 2011, major centers, where a lot of people gather, have been setting Wi-Fi cells and electricity generators. Therefore, we focus on a system that maximizes the utility of digital signage terminals and mobile devices.

A recent study proposed an information display system that combines a digital signage terminal and mobile devices for a multiuser environment [1]. A user can actively select his/her target information from among multiple pieces of information on the screen of a digital signage terminal by using his/her mobile device to implement pointing input; details of the target information are sent to the user's mobile device for display and screenshot capture. Each user can access his/her own target information directly and watch it on the screen of his/her own mobile device. However, it is difficult for users to perform pointing operations given the extreme crowding expected. Moreover, the screenshot will include not only the desired information but also extraneous information and may not include meta-information related to the desired information such as a title and so on. The meta-information helps the user to remember which screenshot holds which information. The work in [2] allows users to cut their target information from screenshots and add notes by finger action to the target information. However, the finger action isn't suitable for the panic situation likely to develop after a disaster due to the extra time needed to finish writing the information and rough finger action.

Thus, it is important for users to quickly access disaster information stored in a digital signage terminal by their own mobile phone and save the desired information together with meta-information by rough operations in a panic situation. Our contributions include an

Fig. 1. The scene of the field test Left: Conventional system, Right: The proposed system

information display system with an information scrapping user interface suitable for digital signage terminals and mobile devices and the results of a field test, see Fig. 1.

2 Related Work

2.1 Roles and Problems of Digital Signage for Disaster Situations

Digital signage terminals are seen as attractive information display devices in disaster situations. Actually, digital signage terminals displayed disaster information and helped stranded people to obtain disaster information after the East Japan Earthquake of 2011. Since centers such as department stores and stations have installed many digital signage terminals and portable generators recently, digital signage terminals would be used in future disaster situations. However, after a disaster, stranded people tend to panic when a crowd forms around sites that might offer information. The situation has the potential to cause a further disaster and block the street in front the digital signage terminal. In discussions with a company managing digital signage terminals, we found that they were concerned about further injuries and damage. To solve this problem, it is important for stranded people to shorten the time when they find their desired information and save the information to their own mobile device.

General digital signage terminals in the market aren't suitable for situations where multiple users want to obtain information at the same time. Since most centers have established strong Wi-Fi coverage, collaboration between digital signage terminals and mobile devices is feasible in the near future, as was predicted [3, 4]. Therefore, we focus on creating efficient collaboration systems.

2.2 Collaboration Between Digital Signage and Mobile Devices

The main topics when addressing the collaboration of digital signage and mobile devices are operation methods of digital signage terminals using mobile devices for users to access the desired information on the screen of the terminals and information scrapping methods that can download the information to the user's mobile device.

Practical operation methods in the field areas include sending system commands from the mobile device to the digital signage terminal by SMS or voice input and entering digital signage terminal cursor operation commands by touch operations on the screen of the mobile device [1]. Collaboration systems currently in the research stage include an interaction system for NFC devices and digital signage terminals [5], and a flashlight-based pointing interface [6]. Current information scrapping methods are capturing the information displayed by the digital signage terminal by the mobile device's camera or making gestures while holding mobile devices [3, 8].

However, no of these systems are suitable for the situation envisaged, many stranded people attempting to access the same digital signage terminal and save disaster information stored in the terminal to their own mobile device. It is critical that the stranded people be able to rapidly confirm if the terminal holds the desired information and save the information to the mobile device without impeding the other people's access to the terminal. In the envisaged situation, it is preferable that they can watch the information stored in the terminal on the screen of their own mobile device.

2.3   Information Scrapping Methods on the Screen of Mobile Devices

Since disaster information displayed by digital signage terminals includes the information to share and check repeatedly at another location, it is preferable for stranded people to save the information in their own mobile device. However, the saved information isn't useful when they cannot remember which saved information includes what kinds of information. It is difficult to include meta-information on the images captured by screenshot etc., in the case that disaster information isn't watched without screen scrolling. Cutting operations by finger action may have a loss of some information. Especially, operations are rough in a panic situation. Therefore, it is important to save target information with meta-information such as title and so on by the rough operations.

3   Proposed System

From the discussions given in Sect. 2, we focus on a collaboration system based on digital signage terminals and mobile devices to shortening the time to find and save target disaster information stored in the terminals. The system should meet two points.

- To check the disaster information stored in a digital signage terminal quickly
- To scrape and save target disaster information with meta-information in mobile devices by rough finger action

Our proposed information display system satisfies these two conditions. The system has two features.

Feature 1: Disaster information held by a digital signage terminal is displayed on the mobile device through a wireless connection. Figure 2 shows the feature. Users do not have to wait for their desired information to be displayed on the terminal but can actively browse the information on their own mobile device within the range of the wireless connection. This reduces the time taken to find the desired information. Another key merit is eliminating the need to have line of sight to the terminal. They can also move from the digital signage terminal to a safety position due to the connection

Feature 2: When roughly encircling target information with single finger on the mobile device, not only the target information but also meta-information related with the target are scrapped and saved to the mobile device (Fig. 3). In Fig. 3, the image about a location and a part of a text about a way to go to the location are scrapped by finger action and the saved information include the name of the location as meta-information and the full of the image and the text. Thus, the system automatically adds meta-information and save the full of the target information even if finger action is rough. Meta-information helps the user to remember what information the entry includes and why they saved the information. Both are helpful when users access the saved information later.

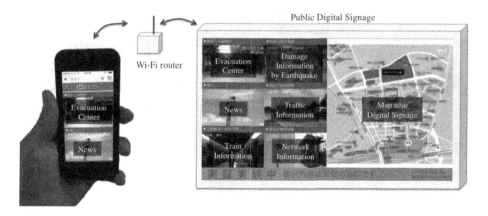

Fig. 2. Proposed information display system

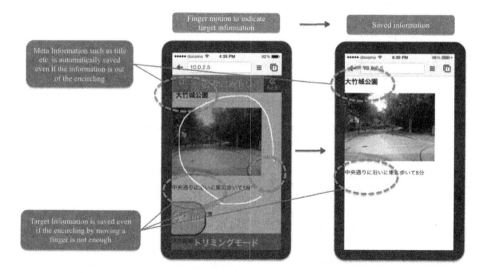

Fig. 3. Information scrapping user interface

Figure 4 shows an example of the flow of this system.

1. To access the digital signage terminal from a mobile device through a wireless connection and display the list of disaster information on the mobile device
2. To select an item of the list and find target information among the details by screen scrolling on the device
3. To trigger the information scrapping user interface and encircle the target information
4. To push a decision key such as OK button

These simple operations reduce the dwell time in front of the digital signage terminal.

Fig. 4. The flow of the proposed system

4   Implementation

4.1   Communication Method

We adopt Wi-Fi as the communication method linking digital signage terminals to mobile devices. Wi-Fi access points are being set in various major centers and Wi-Fi is standard in most smartphones. Users are becoming more familiar with Wi-Fi connections in daily life. Blutooth, which is superior to Wi-Fi in terms of power consumption, is not suitable as not many people are familiar with it. NFC is not suitable since its short communication distance will encourage crowding.

4.2   Web-Based Implementation

The proposed system is a client-server system and instead of native applications of Android or iOS is realized as an HTML5 compliant Web application. This web-based implementation has many merits.

Merit 1: Users can use their favorite web browser without further action. Native applications of Android or iOS would have to be downloaded from the Internet and then installed. However, Internet connections are unreliable in disaster situations and the application servers would become overloaded. It is a burden for users to download and update native applications in advance. Either of HTML5 browsers tends to be preinstalled in current mobile devices.

Merit 2: Users can access information simply by connecting their own mobile device to the Wi-Fi portal of the digital signage terminal, and launching their favorite web browser. Since dense Wi-Fi cells are being created in various major spots, users know that they exist. Familiar operations are useful in panic situations. The Wi-Fi portal redirects to the registered URL, which eliminates the need to input the URL of the terminal.

Merit 3: Meta-information related to the target information selected by users is found easily. Since HTML pages are formed as combinations of elements such as headers, paragraphs, items and so on and the structure of the pages is clear, the system can easily find the meta-information from the elements and the relationship between the elements. Basic HTML texts consist of headers such as (<h1>) and paragraph elements (<p>). If a paragraph element (<p>) is selected by users, the system regards the header immediately above the paragraph element as the meta-information. HTML pages made for disaster relief must be simple so this feature is useful.

Merit 4: The proposed system uses CSS to the display the scrapped and saved information. Since the system save all information including elements, it is easy to adjust layout and character size. To support users in using safety information in disaster situations, readability and viability are important factors.

Merit 5: Cost and resources needed to develop applications are minimized. Since HTML5 is a Web technology standardized by W3C, web-based systems are most suitable for disaster situations since many kinds of mobile devices will try to access the system.

Merit 6: The algorithm to recognize information scrapped by encircling roughly is simple. Elements of HTML5 have attributes such as position, width and height. If more than three points among five points in an element shown in Fig. 5 are within a polygon created by finger action, the system save the selected element.

Fig. 5. Recognition of scrapped information

4.3 Digital Signage Contents

A digital signage terminal that implements our proposal must clearly show that it holds safety information useful to the users. Thus it must have significant physical presence to show its location, and its screen must clearly show the type of information that its holds. The screen of the terminal is divided into multiple frames and each frame holds a different kind of information. An example is shown in Fig. 2 right. The contents are likely to consist of evacuation centers, traffic around the digital signage terminal, train, network, damaged situation, news about the disaster and map of surroundings. Other types of information could be added if found necessary. The digital signage terminal is useful for users who don't have mobile devices and have the devices running out of the battery.

5   Field Experiment

5.1   Purpose

To evaluate the feasibility of the proposed system, we conducted an experiment in front of the digital signage terminal at Shinjuku station, see Fig. 1. This digital signage terminal displayed disaster information after the East Japan Earthquake of 2011 and many people gathered and stayed for a long time in front of the terminal. The terminal's location sees heavy foot traffic every day.

5.2   Experiment Design

A within-subject test was used. The independent variable was Method (MEMO, PHOTO, The proposed system). The dependent variable was time to complete "TASK", which required the subject to find the answers (information) to five queries associated with disaster information and to save the answers by Method. The five queries were derived from the results of a prior investigation and given by the experimenter. One query was "Find the magnitude of this earthquake in the area your parent lives in", see Fig. 6.

Fig. 6. One query

In the case of "MEMO", volunteers searched and noted the answers on the screen of the digital signage terminal that displayed disaster information by Slideshow. In the case of "PHOTO", volunteers searched for and took photos of the answers on the screen of the digital signage terminal that displayed disaster information by Slideshow. Figure 7 left shows an example of disaster information on the screen of the digital signage terminal.

Twenty volunteers per day participated and a total of 100 volunteers participated. Figure 8 shows the rate of their ages. 83 % of the volunteers had experience in using smartphones or tablets. A net research company gathered the volunteers and we asked the company to focus on relatively inexperienced IT users. This is because various kinds of people will need disaster information.

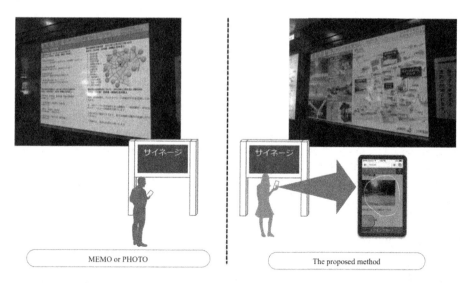

Fig. 7. The screen of the digital signage terminal in the field test Left: Conventional system, Right; The proposed system

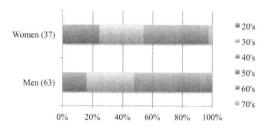

Fig. 8. Ages of volunteers

5.3 Procedure

Twenty volunteers at a time gathered at some distance from the digital signage terminal. Each volunteer was randomly assigned a smartphone (iphone 5 or Android4.x). Volunteers received instruction on how to use the information scrapping user interface of the proposed system for thirty minutes at most. The 20 volunteers were divided into two groups (GA, GB). When GA took the test, GB waited at the center. This is because the number of volunteers in front of the digital signage terminal was limited to ten for safety.

Either of the groups moved the digital signage terminal from the center by about five minutes walking. Since we needed the volunteers to react as in a disaster situation, we conducted a scenario-based experiment. The volunteers heard the following scenario in front of the digital signage terminal.

"You live with your family. You came here by train. You have just had lunch. Suddenly, your own smartphone issues an Earthquake Early Warning. A big earthquake then strikes. You wait at the center until the earthquake stops. This takes a few minutes.

You try to use of your smartphone to get information, but phone and Internet are disconnected. You are worried about the safety of your family and are not familiar with this area. You decide to go the nearest station. You see the digital signage terminal around which a lot of people have gathered. You see that the terminal is displaying disaster information. You go to the digital signage terminal to collect disaster information."

After hearing the scenario, the volunteers received five queries from the experimenter. The experimenter told them "you are in a panic and you try to find the answers one by one". The experimenter instructed them to save the answers by MEMO, PHOTO or the proposed method. When the volunteer finished the task, they told the experimenter their completion. After all volunteers finished, they returned to the center. They rested at the center for thirty minutes. Each group repeated the test three times. METHOD was counterbalanced.

5.4   Result and Discussion

The average completion time of each METHOD (MEMO/PHOTO/The proposed method) was 14.8/12.9/8.3 min, respectively. We performed a within-subject analysis of variance (ANOVA) for Method. Figure 9 shows the results. The proposed method is effective in shortening the time taken to access and save the disaster information.

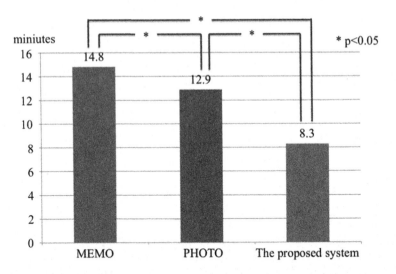

Fig. 9. Proposed information display system

Since the information is shown in Slideshow view, the user has to wait the entire Slideshow if the target information is missed the first time. Every time a new slide is shown, the user has to scan all information on the slide to confirm its contents. In addition, noting on paper takes a long time. Taking photos of a slide takes less time. However, the users disturb each other in their attempt to get a good position. Since the photos are taken in a panic, the photos are sometimes blurry so average speeds are lower. This shows that feature 1 of the proposed system is effective.

77 % of the volunteers answered that the content of scrapped information was adequate. 24 % of the volunteers noticed the meta-information and all of them answered that the meta-information was useful.

6 Conclusion

This paper focuses on the problem of overcrowding in front of digital signage terminals in disaster situations. Our contribution is to propose an information display system with the information scrapping user interface, that links digital signage terminals to mobile devices via wireless links, and report the evaluation of the system in the field test. The field experiment confirmed that the proposed method is very effective in reducing the time users stay in front of a digital signage terminal to collect the desired information and the level of effort needed to store the information in their personal mobile devices.

Acknowledgement. This research is supported by the Ministry of Internal Affairs and Communications, Japan.

References

1. Miyata, A., Seko, S., Aoki, R., Hashimoto, R., Ishida, T., Isezaki, T., Watanabe, M., Ihara, M.: An Information Display System Using a Digital Signage and Mobile Devices for Multiuser Environments. J. Inf. Process. Soc. Jpn. **56**(1), 106–117 (2015). in Japanese
2. ScrapBook: http://www.sony.net/Products/x-Application/eu/x-ScrapBook/index.html
3. Boring, S., et al.: Shoot & copy: phonecam-based information transfer from public displays onto mobile phones. In: Proceedings of the Mobility 2007, pp. 24–31 (2007)
4. Boring, S., et al.: Touch projector: mobile interaction through video. In: Proceedings of the CHI 2010, pp. 2287–2296 (2010)
5. Clinch, S.: Smartphones and pervasive public display. IEEE Pervasive Comput. **12**(1), 92–95 (2013)
6. Davies, N., et al.: Using bluetooth device names to support interaction in smart environments. In: Proceedings of the MobiSys 2009, pp. 151–164 (2009)
7. Davies, N., et al.: Open display networks: a communications medium for the 21st century. IEEE Comput. **45**(5), 58–64 (2012)
8. She, J., et al.: Smart signage: a draggable cyber-physical broadcast/multicast media system. In: Proceedings of the CPSCom 2012, pp. 468–476 (2012)
9. Hardy, R., et al.: Exploring expressive NFC-based mobile phone interaction with large dynamic displays. In: Proceedings of the NFC 2009, pp. 36–41 (2009)
10. Karnik, A., et al.: PiVOT: personalized view-overlays for tabletops. In: Proceedings of the UIST 2012, pp. 271–280 (2012)
11. Lee, J.Y., et al.: Dual interactions between multi-display and smartphone for collaborative design and sharing. In: Proceedings of the VR 2011, pp. 221–222 (2011)
12. Shirazi, A.S., et al.: Flashlight interaction: a study on mobile phone interaction techniques with large displays. In: Proceedings of the MobileHCI 2009, pp. 93:1–93:2 (2009)

Challenges for the Application of Migratory User Interfaces in Industrial Process Visualizations

Lukas Baron[✉] and Annerose Braune[✉]

Institute of Automation, Technische Universität Dresden, Dresden, Germany
{lukas.baron,annerose.braune}@tu-dresden.de

Abstract. The increasing familiarity of users with modern human-machine interaction concepts (e.g. touch gestures) and corresponding devices makes these devices and concepts interesting for industrial applications. However, the *combination* of well-established stationary devices and newer mobile devices may cause negative effects on human operator's workflows if the applications – industrial process visualizations in our case – are not well-designed to conform to the user's expectations. These expectations especially focus on the ability of simultaneously used devices to allow users to collaborate with each other or to change their devices frequently. This motivates the use of migratory user interfaces (MUI) which are able to change devices without losing relevant information, and thus, without interrupting the workflow. Hence, in this paper, we present excerpts of the established concept of MUIs and analyze it with respect to the demands given by the domain of industrial process visualizations. We are able to show that these demands require certain extensions of current MUI techniques, for example, explicit markup telling relevant and non-relevant parts of the UI state apart. Our review of the related work reveals that there is no suitable solution which meets the demands. In order to demonstrate the feasibility of migratory UIs in the industrial domain, we present a case study which focuses on extending already existing user interfaces with the required functionality for migration.

1 Introduction

New human-machine interaction concepts that make use of touch displays, motion sensing, etc. have come to mainstream popularity. This fosters the introduction, e.g. of mobile devices, in industrial applications. In such environments, user interfaces (UI) – process visualizations in our case – currently are designed specifically for a certain set of devices. Each device and its respective UI thereby has its own dedicated purpose which is not intended to change over its lifetime. Examples for such UIs are process visualizations in operator stations or on in-field devices like panel PCs. Mobile devices shall *supplement* such stationary devices in order to allow the process supervision and control to be handled more flexible. For example, a mobile device may allow access to certain process data from any location within the plant in order to conduct maintenance tasks. Such

© Springer International Publishing Switzerland 2016
M. Kurosu (Ed.): HCI 2016, Part II, LNCS 9732, pp. 364–378, 2016.
DOI: 10.1007/978-3-319-39516-6_35

tasks often require multiple users to cooperate with each other while being situated in different locations, e. g., one user is close to the device to maintain and another user keeps observing the process from the operating room. In such a scenario, the UI is expected to support collaborative functionalities. Moreover, users may need or want to change the currently used device during the conduction of a single task, for example, caused by changing their location away from a stationary device. However, doing this could have a negative effect on the user's effectiveness because it takes time to get the UI on the new device to a state from where the interaction – and the conduction of the task – can be continued. Briefly speaking, the user may need to enter data or navigate to the same part of the visualization on the new device.

Instead, such a change of device is supposed to work without interrupting the user's ongoing work – and thus, not reducing his/her effectiveness. By automatically taking into account the recent interaction history with the UI, the time needed to change the device and to proceed interaction can be reduced. Moreover, the same mechanism which allows the smooth change of the device can be used to realize collaborative UIs. This kind of freely transferable UIs – referred to as migratory or nomadic UIs (MUI) [1] – are state of the art in multimedia applications [9], home automation [4], or collaborative education software [8] but not yet in industrial environments.

Migration-related procedures may enable or at least support a more effective handling of tasks in which users may switch from stationary to mobile devices, e. g., to conduct maintenance or commissioning tasks. However, safety, security, and reliability are critical measures of quality for applications in the industrial domain, and thus, for user interfaces as well. Hence, special attention has to be payed to the satisfaction of these demands when realizing migratory UIs for industrial applications.

In this paper, we will briefly introduce the established concept of migratory UIs. Furthermore, the influence of the industrial domain on the functional parameters of MUIs will be discussed in detail. Finally, a case study is presented in order to show the feasibility in accordance with the requirements and to emphasize an industrial use case for migratory UIs.

2   Migratory User Interfaces

Before the industrial requirements for migratory user interfaces can be deduced, we want to introduce the MUI theory. In the first subsection the general characteristics are presented which are common to MUIs. The second section provides an excerpt of properties that allow the classification of migratory applications.

2.1   Functional Aspects

According to [3], an MUI is characterized by a transfer from a source device on which the user started interaction to a known target device on which to proceed immediately. The authors claim that the most important part is to transfer the UI *state* instead of exclusively transferring the static artifacts defining the UI's software implementation. The UI state is constituted by the complete user interaction history prior to the moment of migration, consisting of internally stored properties, the user's and the system's in- and output and called functions including the gained results. The objective of the state transfer is to achieve a *continuous interaction*. If either the target device differs in hard- or software or if its environment changes, usage continuity also requires adaption capabilities.

Aspects of distributed user interfaces (DUI) have to be considered if a UI concerning a specific technical process is split up into parts that are located on multiple devices [1]. For providing usage continuity, a migration can be applied in case of a change of the UI distribution, i. e., users swap devices, including an optional change of the device number or type. A change of distribution does not necessarily include a migration mechanism, though. Of course, such a redistribution implies a transfer of static UI elements to new devices. However, usage continuity relies on the state transfer. Hence, this applies even in scenarios where the UI distribution stays static.

In summary, the steps necessary for migrating a UI can be derived from the following three aspects of MUIs [1]:

1. **Distribution**: transfer of static UI components causing a change of the distribution configuration,
2. **State transfer**[1]: determination and transfer of the UI state which also needs to reflect the change of distribution,
3. **Adaption**[2]: static components of the UI have to be adapted to the changed device, environment, or execution runtime which may also require an adaption of the transferred state.

In [3], the term *migration engine* has been defined which covers the implementation realizing the migration process. Such an engine needs parameters in order to perform a migration, e. g., information about source and target devices, a set of concrete UI elements to migrate, the UI state to consider, the users associated with each device, etc. These migration parameters in combination with the migration engine determine what we call the *migratory behavior* which also includes the actions users have to take in order to provide the parameters. The migratory behavior provides *conformity to expectations* if the provided parameters lead to the intended result. This, however, requires a predictable operation of the migration engine.

2.2   MUI Classification

The (intended) behavior of an MUI can be described by means of 13 identified classifiers [1,3,10]. We will only present some selected ones which are relevant for this paper:

---

[1] In [1], this is referred to as the migratory aspect of a UI.

[2] also referred to as UI plasticity [1].

① **Initialization.** A migration can be triggered *automatically* or *on demand* by users. The trigger might originate from arbitrary devices connected to the UI system. If the triggering device is the migration source, it is called *pushing* – *pulling*, in case it is the target. To each single migration a direction can be assigned which distinguishes the triggering device from its passive counterpart. Thus a migration can be pushed from the triggering device as the source or pulled onto the triggering device as the target. Hybrid modes – pulling and pushing at the same time, e. g., when swapping content between devices – are also possible.

② **Scope.** The transfer of information may include the UI en bloc – *total* – or excerpts thereof – *partial*. In a redistribution scenario, the process may *distribute* the UI from one to many devices, *aggregate* from many to one device, or *mix* it with multiple devices as sources and targets as well.

③ **Adaption Type.** The UI adaption may be realized completely *dynamically* (at runtime), *precomputed* (at design time) by loading a complete *static* UI, or as an intermediate type, for instance, by using templates that are assembled at runtime during the migration procedure.

④ **System Architecture.** The system architecture describes the organization of the migration engine. The engine can either be distributed on each of the UI devices which arrange themselves autonomously – *peer-to-peer* – or concentrated on an additional entity acting as a migration *server*. In the latter case, target and source UIs act as migration *clients*. Furthermore, in such a migration-server and migration-client architectures, *client-based* and *server-based* approaches can be distinguished. This classification describes the entity responsible for determining and obtaining the migration parameters including the required UI state to transfer.

⑤ **Simultaneous Usability.** In multi-user and -device scenarios, many users may use a single device (N-1 relation), one user may use multiple devices (1-N), or many users use many devices (N-M), e. g., in a collaborative task. In the context of migratory and distributed applications, this term also includes the mode of state transfer which can be *continuous* (synchronizing different UIs over time) or *discrete* (transfer the state once, i. e., the state is outdated after the migration has been completed).

3   Industrial Demands

3.1   Software and Engineering Requirements

In order to classify the requirements of industrial process visualizations, we distinguish between a *design phase* and a *runtime* life cycle phase. The latter phase covers the operative period of the UI starting from the point in time when the UI has been connected to the technical process. Thus, this phase also includes timeframes in which the process itself is not functional but the UI is required to work (e. g. during maintenance or commissioning). Prior to this, the design phase covers planning, engineering, implementation, and testing of the UI.

An industrial visualization has to interact with complex and expensive technical systems which poses requirements to its reliability in terms of safety and

security. Likewise, the accountability of the engineering results in specific requirements that need to be considered during the design phase. In particular, the UI's
presentation and (migratory) behavior during runtime has to be predictable. The
characteristics to be provided by UIs (e. g. visually) are specified in standards of
the respective domain, company, or contractee. The functional features depend
on the tasks that a user has to fulfill [6]. Hereby, the standards are amongst
other things concerned with usability aspects which have an influence on presentational and behavioral parameters. Thus, the UI and potential migration
capabilities have to ensure by design that users are not being disturbed, for
example, through unneeded functions and UI elements or unexpected behavior.

3.2   UI Structure and Functionality

Industrial process visualizations usually consist of panels connected via navigation elements. However, primarily they contain elements for the display and
manipulation of certain aspects or parts of the technical process [13]. Such elements are often associated with each other reflecting functional dependencies
of their corresponding components within the process plant. This means that
certain UI elements must not be divided arbitrarily (e. g. during partial migrations) but with respect to the user's task in a way that all needed functionality
is available before and after a migration. Information about such relations are
usually not explicitly available within visualization applications. For example,
some pumps and valves are related to each other due to the pipes that connect
them. But even if both, pipes and devices, are visibly connected in the visualization, the functional dependencies are not identifiable automatically. Such
knowledge is provided only by domain experts, although not necessarily in a
manner which is suitable for an automatic interpretation by machines. In terms
of migration, this has to be considered in order to support the determination of
optimal migration parameters for the users' workflow. If this knowledge is well
formalized, some algorithms determining which elements belong together could
be applied as proposed in [2]. However, the demand of predictable behavior (see
Sect. 3.1) requires means for developers to amend or to override an algorithm's
result by providing information manually. For that purpose, either the algorithm
must be adjustable or its results have to be obtained during the design phase
to be stored in an intermediate data structure that can be edited by the UI
engineer in order to configure migration engines at runtime.

Another peculiarity of a process visualization is its real-time communication
with process data servers or (non-real-time connections to) historical databases
in order to provide a continuously updated process view (for example, visualized
by changing and animating selected UI elements). Such process visualizations
are extended by an authorization mechanism which is an important part of the
security and safety design. It grants or denies read and write access to single
data items with respect to the current UI device, its assigned user, as well as the
user's roles within the company. Typically, there is only one user at a time with
exclusive control rights to (a limited part of) the process – granted by a control

token. During runtime, the tokens might be transferred, but only with mutual consent and granted access rights.

A UI's structural, functional, and perceptual design is strictly bound to its well-defined use case, the intended role of a user, the device, and the environment [14]. Thus, it is common that the same technical process is equipped with multiple individual (and individually designed) UIs. For example, consider the following scenario: An operator located in a control room with a stationary desktop PC wants to migrate some panels of a UI to service personnel in the field in order to give instructions. Both UIs have a completely different use case and thus a different level of detail. The operator's view is limited to the functionality necessary for nominal operations. On the other hand, servicing needs access to all parameters of the faulty device plus eventually further devices that are functionally associated or collocated. However, both UIs would not only differ in the displayed content, there may be organizational or presentational differences, too. That is why a migration engine would need to mediate between different use cases for corresponding UIs by adapting them in case of migration.

3.3 Implications for MUI Properties

As we explained in the previous section, the UIs considered in this contribution always need to communicate with process data servers. By transferring these data to the UI, they obviously become part of its state. Since this functionality can be presumed in any case, we have to separate different parts of the state from each other. In Fig. 1, the state is depicted decomposed into an injected and an internal state.

By *injected*, we refer to all information and process data that are imported exclusively from external providers and, thus, can be reconstructed without any additional information. The *internal* state is only known to the UI itself and may, for instance, be incorporated by internal variables which are created at runtime. Each part of the state can be used for output on the UI's presentational feature. Interactors of course intend to influence the internal state in order to provide user input. Algorithms f implemented within the UI (see Fig. 1) may calculate required information based on the injected and/or the internal state. In terms of state transfer, the injected state *can* be omitted (as it can be recreated on the target device) but in the industrial domain it *must* be omitted due to authorization mechanisms that may be bypassed otherwise. If bypassed, the migration engine may yield access to process data for users who are not supposed to have access. That is why we will concentrate on the internal state only.

Since the division of the state into the internal and the injected parts is usually only implemented implicitly within UIs, we need additional explicit markup that allows the automatic handling of the state transfer. Depending on the current situation, e. g., characterized by a certain task, in which a migration occurs, not the complete internal state is relevant. This results in a further division of the internal state into *relevant* and *non-relevant* parts of which only relevant parts will be migrated. In analogy with the definition of partial migration in Sect. 2.2, this can be considered as a *partial internal state transfer*.

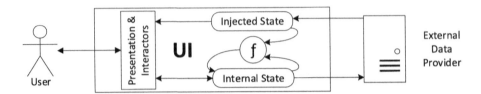

Fig. 1. Decomposition of the internal UI state

Taking the industrial demands for engineering and the UI characteristics into account, it is possible to put further restrictions to the MUI classifiers (cf. Sect. 2.2) without raising claim to completeness:

① **Initialization.** Frequently incoming or outgoing automatic migrations are conflicting with design guidelines (e. g. [12]) because of the likely negative impact on human operator's work. On the other hand, MUIs have the potential to enhance the support of the planning and conducting of maintenance work or to make the human communication more efficient. This might be true even if the migration is initiated manually. If applied, automatic migrations should rely on a set of well-tested rules. User-initiated migrations have the advantage of an easier implementation by omitting the rule evaluation plus a better situational awareness for the current tasks of the user and the respectively needed parts of the UI. This assumes that manual initialization also means that users select which elements to migrate. As an optimum between interfering with the target user's current work and exploiting the situational awareness of the source user, we propose a *migration relaying mechanism* as a hybrid method (cf. Sect. 2.2-①). This means that at first the source user has to notify the target user who may then actively pull the migration, i. e., no migration shall open itself automatically without the target user's request. The other way around, a pull that is initiated by the target user could be realized by asking the respective source user for his/her consent or, even more detailed, for the information he/she is willing to share within the limits given by authorization policies.

By adding a migration server as an *intermediate* location between the source and the target device, migrations are able to cope with interrupted connections. These intermediate locations would then act like chat servers that store migrations temporarily when transferring them from source to target.

In terms of directions of migrations, a pull mechanism (see Sect. 2.2) must prohibit the transfer of private data (such as control token, etc.) if not permitted by access rights of the user associated with the target device. In case of automatic triggering, the same restrictions apply to push mechanisms as well. In certain situations (process failures, etc.), and given the required access rights, a migration push may be required to overrule the above-explained migration relaying mechanism – which was intended not to open unrequested migrations on the target device – i. e., the migration system could be used to support the user in handling urgent situations.

② **Scope.** The access levels of the users also limit the set of migratable elements. If access to the plain/static UI is not restricted but access to process data providers in the background is restricted, total *and* partial migrations can be implemented without considering authorization issues. This will result in visualizations which are not updated completely in case a user has no complete read access. In cases where this poses risks to the process – because an important information is not available or only transferred once, but expected to be updated continuously, and thus, pretending normal operations – total migration is *forbidden*. On the other hand, partial migration, only limited to data that the receiver has access to, should not be safety-critical because the unavailability of required information is not hidden.

③ **Adaption Type.** If a migration requires adaption of the UI, either because of the changed device or incompatible access rights, both the adaption strategy and the result have to be predictable in order to ensure compliance with expectations given by standardization (see Sect. 3.1). It may even be necessary that the result of each migration has to be plannable in advance (during design phase).

In case of adaptions that are completely driven by algorithms at runtime, a set of adjustable formalized rules is needed. The applicability depends on the development costs necessary for the identification of relevant factors of influence and for the runtime gathering of each of the factors. If such rule evaluations are not performing well enough, such adaption mechanisms should not be considered.

Precomputed target UIs should always meet industrial requirements in terms of quality. If designed by domain experts, runtime adaptions are not necessary, but costs more or less depend on the number of precomputed UIs, as each of them has to be developed individually. If this approach is used, the migration engine requires means to identify corresponding elements across these UIs in order to navigate to the migrated elements on the target device. This is realized by creating links from a source element to its counterparts in other UIs.

④ **System Architecture.** The use of process data servers as central entities has already been indicated in Sect. 3.2. Typically, there are multiple tasks that these entities are delegated to, e.g., logging user interaction, alarm acknowledgement, user authorization, etc. The most important requirement when designing additional features like migration functionality is not to interfere with the server's real-time capabilities. This means that potentially expensive functionality (in terms of computation time) should be outsourced to separate instances. Concerning migration, we propose using a migration server and migration client structure in parallel to already existing UI clients and process data servers. Hereby, migration clients integrate with each UI in order to provide access to its state and means for users to control migrations (e.g. in case of user-initiated migrations, parameters like the target device have to be selected).

⑤ **Simultaneous Usability.** The ability to synchronize selected parts of the internal state of different UIs, for example, in a collaborative scenario, possibly results in the best performance regarding continuous usage. Because, once migration and synchronization have been initiated, users are able to swap devices without the need to *re*-initiate state transfers.

Multi-user scenarios may affect safety-critical behavior of a UI if, for example, the state of an input element is accessible by a second person without knowledge of the person who is in control of the process. Synchronizing certain UI elements continuously can be seen as a *hidden* control token transfer or token split onto multiple users which is forbidden in case they are not aware or not allowed to control the process. However, it is not unreasonable to synchronize certain UI aspects: For example, an operators view in a control room could be synchronized with a corresponding view on a field device – limited to non-safety-critical elements or to a read-only mode on the device without the actual control token – in order to achieve a four-eye-control or simply improved means to communicate. Non-safety-critical elements are, for example, navigators (synchronizing the view in focus) or in- and output elements for historical features like trends.

In a single-user and multi-device scenario, a synchronization of safety-critical UI elements is risky if the user assigned to a certain device is not in its physical operating range and thus not able to observe its inaccessibility by other persons. A mechanism for an automatic locking of the respective safety critical function depending on the user's position could be applied in order to prevent harmful interference.

In consequence, a migration feature that enables simultaneous use requires an additional markup of the relevant internal state allowing or disallowing its synchronization, and the direction in which to synchronize, e. g., in a read-only mode on the source or target side.

Although, we discussed only 1-N and N-M scenarios, N-1 relations do not seem to be unrealistic. Such a scenario would require means to quickly and reliably identify and authorize the user triggering a safety-critical action out of all simultaneously acting users.

3.4 Summary

In this section, we discussed the implications on functional aspects of migratory UIs in the industrial domain. In order to enable UI migration, such UIs need to be enhanced with markup (1) concerning functional dependencies between UI elements with respect to the underlying process, (2) telling relevant and non-relevant parts of the UI state apart, and (3) allowing the configuration of the synchronization in multi-user/-device scenarios.

For automatic initializations and runtime adaptions, algorithms are required that evaluate formalized rules. This depends on the availability and reliable gathering of relevant factors of influence. Furthermore, it is important to be able to easily adjust such algorithms in order to ensure predictable behavior.

In case of manual triggering of migrations, user-selected migration parameters, and the use of precomputed UI adaptions, we propose data models containing the three types of markup that we have mentioned plus information about corresponding UI elements across the precomputed UIs (UI links). These data are created during design phase and are used for configuring migration engines at runtime. Hence, they have to be manually amendable.

4   Case Study

4.1   Existing Migration Engines

The analysis of available case studies and respective underlying designs reveals a limited applicability in the industrial domain. Tools for dynamic web migration [7] and TERESA-based applications [2] include a set of tools for runtime analysis of existing UIs in order to compensate missing explicit markup of migration-related information. However, it is not explained whether rules can be easily adjusted in order to amend the algorithm's results. The use of precomputed UIs as described in Sect. 3.3-③ seems not to be supported. MASP is another solution [4] with abilities to plan situations (different distribution scenarios regarding the available devices) in advance. The adaption mechanisms are not clarified, though [11]. The DireWolf framework [8] gives an idea of how to synchronize the state between different UIs but not with respect to the usual functionality of industrial process visualizations (see Sect. 3.2). Most of these approaches neither distinguish between relevant and non-relevant parts of the UI state, as introduced in Sect. 3.3, nor do they allow by design the detailed amending of migratory behavior. In case of using rule based algorithms at runtime, they have not been evaluated for the domain of industrial automation.

4.2   Concepts

The design of our case study ensures compliance to industrial UI standards by using individually engineered and thus precomputed UIs (see Sect. 3.3-③). For the configuration of our migration engine, we designed a data model as proposed in Sect. 3.4 – a *migration model* – covering additional information about the functional dependencies between UI elements, the description of its relevant state, and how to transfer it.

This approach is independent of the concrete UI adaption strategy or tools selected at the design phase which may rely on independently designed UIs for each device or even on an automatic deduction of a specialized UI from a *pre-existing* version (e. g. transformation from desktop to mobile UI).

Figure 2 shows the basic components of our migration engine mainly consisting of an MUI server that relays migrations and synchronizations via connections to available migration-clients. For that, it uses the migration model and an authorization mechanism. Each migration client integrates itself into the UI with a technology-dependent plug-in in order to get access to the state properties (client-based approach). The migration client provides users with controls that are necessary for triggering the migration and defining its respective parameters, such as the migration target.

4.3   Migration Model

Figure 3 shows the concept of our migration model. The migration-relevant part of the internal state is indicated by explicitly tagging migratable elements and

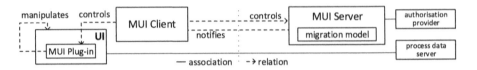

Fig. 2. Plug-in concept for enabling migration in common UI technologies

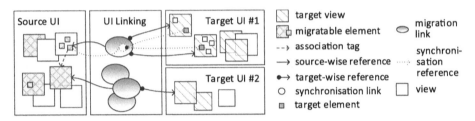

Fig. 3. Migration Model for UI linking and tagging

each of its relevant properties. The elements can be part of the presentational feature and the internal state as well. In addition, elements can be tagged as *associated* in order to reflect functional relations as discussed in Sect. 3.2. By defining such an association, the migration process can be influenced in three different ways: always migrate elements together (deny migration if not possible), migrate together if possible (otherwise allow separate migration of elements), or forbid simultaneous migration. If a UI is intended to act as a migration target, its respective presentations need to be tagged in order to determine distinct migration results. Analogously to the relevant state within the source UI, the target state properties need to be tagged.

The connection, and thus the description of the migration procedure itself, is realized by a set of migration links each telling the migration engine which presentation to display for each migrated element with respect to the concrete UI that is opened on the target device. As a subordinate feature of each migration link, synchronization links refer to state properties of the source UI and to each corresponding target UI property. As a property of a synchronization link, the mode of synchronization can be defined as once/continuous and target-wise/source-wise/bidirectional.

Concerning migration links, synchronization links, and element associations, we presume each property to be either enabled or disabled at runtime in order to be able to provide situational sensitivity for the migration behavior. This could be realized by integrating additional logic evaluating process properties (e. g. the alarm status), the user (as discussed in Sect. 3.3-⑤), the devices (e. g. battery status), or the environment[3]. Thus, there may exist multiple – and thus ambiguous – migration links for the current set of elements to migrate but, for example, pointing to different migration targets or including different synchronization links. Hence, an adaptation mechanism may also change the migration

---

[3] consistent with the context of use as described in [5].

model and thus the migration behavior, for example, by influencing the property of being enabled/disabled of different migration links.

4.4 Results

For the implementation of the migration engine, we decided to concentrate on user-initiated migrations only including the preceding selection of UI elements to migrate and of the migration targets. Possible migration targets are (1) devices that are assigned to the user initiating the migration and (2) other users. If a certain device is selected, the migration is pushed directly to this device. In case a user is selected, the migration will use the hybrid push/pull method as proposed in Sect. 3.3-①. The respective controls can be seen in the upper part of Fig. 4. If a user wants to select elements for migration, a UI overlay gets activated which shows migratable elements with half-transparent boxes in order not to overlap with any important information that might be displayed. The boxes can be clicked (switching to highlighted state – represented by the symbols A1-A3 in Fig. 4) in order to select the respective element. In the example, we selected a pump (cf. symbol A1 in Fig. 4) and a connected valve (A2) as well as the associated control elements (A3) for migration. This could be applicable in a service scenario where controls for a damaged unit (the pump) need to be transferred to a mobile device for in-field repairs as proposed in Sect. 3.2. The other components might be useful for testing after repairs have been completed. A migration can be initiated by hitting the "migrate" button (cf. symbol B in Fig. 4) with an optionally activated continuous synchronization feature (check box "keep synced"). On the target device (see Fig. 5 – left part), the user gets notified by the display of the incoming migration in a message box. After opening the message, the user is able to select an available UI for his target device and for his respective authorization level.

The message box could also be seen as a task-sensitive navigation hub, i. e., it provides special navigation shortcuts to panels that could all be required for a certain task. Normally, the user would have to navigate on arbitrary (not task-specific) paths to these panels. In the example denoted in Fig. 4, the source user could have assigned the task (e. g. to check the devices that belong to the migrated elements) to the target user.

In the example depicted in Fig. 6, a different UI has been opened compared to the migration source. By changing the layout of the UI, we simulated an adapted version for mobile devices.

5   Summary and Conclusions

In this contribution, we presented the fundamental basics of MUIs and discussed constraints and requirements to the UI development in the domain of industrial automation. We continued by discussing consequences for selected MUI properties. Finally, we introduced our case study including a migration model which is intended to work as an intermediate between MUI development on the one hand

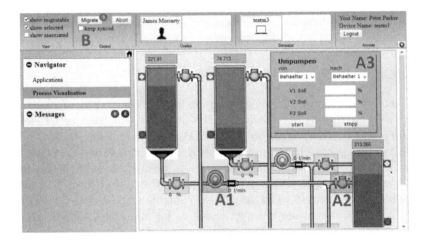

Fig. 4. Migration client with its controls (upper part) and an opened process visualization (right part)

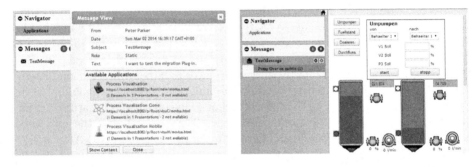

Fig. 5. Incoming migration notification on the target

Fig. 6. Opened target UI (differs from the source UI

and migration engines at runtime on the other hand. Despite the creation of the migration model being still relatively simple if the required domain expertise is available, it becomes difficult to manage in bigger projects and therefore should be supported by appropriate tools. If functional dependencies between UI elements are modeled well enough and thus the selection of elements to migrate becomes easy, we expect conformity of the migration behavior with user expectations. Better support for the user's current task is needed in order to be able to preselect UI elements for migration. Moreover, we intend to design a rule-based system in order to initiate migrations automatically.

By showing our first working prototype, we gave a sound indication for the potential of MUIs in industrial applications. By using a runtime architecture which integrates itself via plug-ins into the UIs, we enabled our migration engine for potential use in common industrial visualization applications. However, this kind of integration with existing visualization technologies requires proper public interfaces which the visualization system used in the case study does provide. However, in case another system shall be used, it yet has to be evaluated if these interfaces are present. Concerning authorization, our solution is based on restrictions to the whole UI instead of to UI parts or to single process data items. In the future, we also want to realize a fine-grained authorization and a token-based mechanism in order to dynamically control access when migrating.

This approach to migratory user interfaces in industrial process visualizations could be valuable in the future. Especially in the context of emerging paradigms which are propagating flexible production processes and logistics, such as *industry 4.0*, where user interfaces with migratory features can be an outstanding supplement to *plug&produce* scenarios, for example.

References

1. Balme, L., Demeure, A., Barralon, N., Calvary, G.: CAMELEON-RT: a software architecture reference model for distributed, migratable, and plastic user interfaces. In: Markopoulos, P., Eggen, B., Aarts, E., Crowley, J.L. (eds.) EUSAI 2004. LNCS, vol. 3295, pp. 291–302. Springer, Heidelberg (2004)
2. Bandelloni, R., Paternò, F.: Flexible interface migration. In: Proceedings of the 9th International Conference on Intelligent User Interfaces. IUI 2004, ACM (2004)
3. Berti, S., Paternó, F., Santoro, C.: A taxonomy for migratory user interfaces. In: Gilroy, S.W., Harrison, M.D. (eds.) DSV-IS 2005. LNCS, vol. 3941, pp. 149–160. Springer, Heidelberg (2006)
4. Blumendorf, M., Roscher, D., Albayrak, S.: Dynamic user interface distribution for flexible multimodal interaction. In: International Conference on Multimodal Interfaces and the Workshop on Machine Learning for Multimodal Interaction. ICMI-MLMI 2010, ACM (2010)
5. Chen, G., Kotz, D., et al.: A survey of context-aware mobile computing research. Technical report, Technical Report TR2000-381, Department of Computer Science, Dartmouth College (2000)
6. DIN EN 9241–110: Ergonomics of human-system interaction - Dialogue principles (2008)
7. Ghiani, G., Paternò, F., Santoro, C.: On-demand cross-device interface components migration. In: Proceedings of the 12th International Conference on Human Computer Interaction with Mobile Devices and Services. MobileHCI 2010, ACM (2010)
8. Kovachev, D., Renzel, D., Nicolaescu, P., Klamma, R.: DireWolf - distributing and migrating user interfaces for widget-based web applications. In: Daniel, F., Dolog, P., Li, Q. (eds.) ICWE 2013. LNCS, vol. 7977, pp. 99–113. Springer, Heidelberg (2013)
9. Lachenal, C., Coutaz, J.: A reference framework for multi-surface interaction. In: Proceedings of the HCI International (2003)
10. Paternò, F., Santoro, C.: A logical framework for multi-device user interfaces. In: Proceedings of the 4th ACM SIGCHI Symposium on Engineering Interactive Computing Systems. EICS 2012, ACM (2012)
11. Paternò, F., Santoro, C., Spano, L.D.: MARIA: a universal, declarative, multiple abstraction-level language for service-oriented applications in ubiquitous environments. ACM Trans. Comput.-Hum. Interact. **16**, 19:1–19:30 (2009)

12. VDI 3814–7: Building automation and control systems - Design of user interfaces (2012)
13. VDI, VDE 3699–3: Process control using display screens - mimics (2014)
14. VDI, VDE 3850–1: Development of usable user interfaces for technical plants - Concepts, principles and fundamental recommendations (2014)

Human-Computer Interfaces
for Sensor/Actuator Networks

Lawrence Henschen[✉] and Julia Lee

Northwestern University, Evanston, IL, USA
henschen@eecs.northwestern.edu, julialee@agep.northwestern.edu

Abstract. In this paper we study the features needed for a generic but robust user interface for monitoring and controlling sensor/actuator networks. The need for such a generic interface will increase as the Internet of Things develops and reaches not only major industries but small enterprises that do not have the resources to develop such systems on their own. We propose a general mark-up language that can be used as the basis for a generic interface for sensor/actuator networks. We present an initial list of features that such an interface should have and then describe a set of tentative mark-ups which, with the use of XSLT and other XML-based technology, could lead to a generic interface that could be used for any sensor/actuator network. Because many sensor/actuator nodes and related devices may not have XML capability, we also address the technical issue of where in the pipeline the appropriate marked-up text should be inserted.

Keywords: Sensor networks · Sensor network interface · Mark-up language

1 Introduction

Sensor networks are becoming increasingly important in modern society. This trend will increase dramatically as the Internet of Things becomes a reality. While much attention has been paid to the underlying technologies, such as general communications and networking, relatively little attention has been devoted to the issue of a generic human-computer interface for sensor/actuator networks in general. There have been some interfaces for sensor/actuator networks described for specific applications, for example [1–3] and others. However, no generic solution that can be used directly as a convenient and comprehensive interface has been put forward. This is an important need that must be met in the future of the Internet of Things because more and more sensor/actuator networks will be used by small-to-medium enterprises that do not have resources to develop the networks and interfaces themselves and yet should not have to buy services from providers. The goal of our research is to develop a generic interface that any enterprise, large or small or even an individual, can download and easily use to describe and then use its own sensor/actuator network. Moreover, the deployment and use of the interface should not require technical expertise in HCI or networking. Ordinary users with no training in HCI or XML or networking should be able to describe, monitor, and control their sensor/actuator networks.

The development of a generic user interface depends on two key aspects - (1) the use of a standardized mark-up language to represent information about the sensors,

M. Kurosu (Ed.): HCI 2016, Part II, LNCS 9732, pp. 379–387, 2016.
DOI: 10.1007/978-3-319-39516-6_36

actuators, network, and the data transmitted and (2) a platform independent system using the mark-up language along with XSLT to extract relevant information and UIML to implement the actual interface. This paper introduces both of those topics and provides an initial list of features that such a generic interface should have.

There are, in fact, two separate interfaces that are needed to make a truly generic system that can be both configured and used by people with limited backgrounds in HCI, XML, computer networks, etc. The first interface would be used when the network was first created or when new nodes, sensors, or actuators were added. Ordinary users should be able to describe in human-oriented terms the nodes, sensors, and actuators in the network, how raw values from the sensors translate into meaningful values to a person monitoring the sensors, what kinds of control is available for the actuators, etc. In Sect. 3.5 we describe an interface for this. The second interface would be used by people monitoring the sensors in the network and issuing commands to the network and the actuators. Sections 3.1–3.4 describe the features we initially propose for this interface. Samples of pages from each of these interfaces are also given in the appropriate sections. Of course, these two types of interfaces can be built into one system with controlled accesses to different functionalities.

In Sect. 2 we mention some related prior work. In Sect. 3 we describe the features that should be present in any generic interface system. In Sect. 4 we describe how a suitable mark-up language could make the implementation of a generic interface system feasible. Finally, in Sect. 5 we make some concluding remarks.

2   Related Work

As noted in the Introduction, there are examples of interfaces made for specific application areas or even specific instances of sensor/actuator networks. In addition to those, there exist some examples of interfaces focusing on narrow aspects of sensor/actuator networks. For example, Representational State Transfer (REST) [4] provides some limited mechanism for accessing sensor/actuator nodes through GET/PUT/POST/DELETE, but this is hardly enough for a robust and useable interface. [5] provides a means of communication through their Binary Web Service, but they say nothing about the actual user interface. Moreover, in their system the interpretation of a command is left to the individual node, which leads one to believe the human user may not have had complete information about the functionalities in individual nodes. We believe the user interface should clearly specify exactly what functions are available in each node and what the consequences are of invoking that functionality. There are also interfaces designed for network structures, such as in [6]. These do not address issues like displaying information from the sensors themselves or allowing a user to control individual actuators in the network. Thus, there is a serious lack of well-designed but generic user interfaces focusing on the monitoring and control of the nodes in a sensor/actuator network.

Some work on standardized mark-up for sensor/actuator networks has been done. For example, SensorML [7] defines the standard for representing sensor nodes and networks as well as individual sensors and actuators. Observation and Measurement [8] defines the standard representation for data. Although these two could form a basis for a generic interface system, important key components are missing that are necessary for a robust, usable, and learnable generic interface for using the sensors and actuators in a network.

We believe HCI issues should be a major driving factor in these standardization efforts. What do the humans sitting at a computer need in order to do what they need to do with the sensors and actuators? Our goal is to lay the foundation for an interface system that can simply be downloaded by anyone and used directly and immediately no matter what the application area or the nature of the sensors and actuators.

3   Features Necessary for Robust Interfaces

As noted in the Introduction, it is essential that the user interface be easy to use by people who know about sensor/actuator networks, or at least know about their own network, and who likely do not know about networking principles or HCI principles. Our own prior work in [9] was aimed at this goal; there we developed a user interface for programming sensor/actuator nodes that could be used by people who did not know how to program in traditional languages like C. The vast majority of sensor/actuator systems will be deployed and used by people who are not computer engineers. The systems they use should not require them to become computer engineers.

Based on our study of hundreds of applications described in the literature and our own experience, we have categorized the problem into the following layers – network layer, node layer, and sensor/actuator layer. The following sections describe features and capabilities that should be present at each of these layers in order to have a generic system that can be used by many different applications. Some special applications might need additional features, of course, but the system we propose based on a standardized mark-up language can easily be extended. What we describe here would be sufficient for most sensor/actuator network interfaces. Section 4, then, describes potential mark-ups that could be used to facilitate the features described here.

3.1   Network Level Display and Control

The primary functionality at this layer is to define and view the set of all nodes in the network. A user should be able to add and delete nodes in the interface. For each node the user should be able to provide a name, a generic description of that node, the internet address of that node, etc. (Section 3.2 describes additional information that should be described in individual nodes. At the network layer the user is concerned with the structure of the network as a whole, not the details inside individual nodes.) A user should be able to specify the layout of the nodes, ranging from a simple two-dimensional grid to a three-dimensional distribution of nodes. Users may leave the node display as a simple grid but should also be able to drag nodes to position them on the display in correspondence to their actual physical distribution.

In addition to basic network structure the user should be able to identify and name groups of nodes and groups of sensors. A simple example of where this might be used is an environmental monitoring system. Users might need to focus on groups of nodes in different sections of a large building (e.g., on each floor of a high-rise).

Alternatively, users might want to view all the temperature information throughout the entire building, temporarily filtering out other sensor data such as humidity or the presence of motion. The forming of such groups transcends individual nodes and should therefore be implemented at the system-view level.

Users should be able to view the network as a whole, zooming out to get a more global picture and zooming in to get a more detailed picture of portions of the network. As the user zooms in, details of individual nodes can begin to be displayed. In addition, a user should be able to click on an individual node and perform all the operations described in the next section. Network layer information should include information such as whether or not the node is still functioning and communicating.

Users should be able to issue network-wide commands. These would include, at a minimum, global reset and synchronize/reset clocks. Commands that cause global data acquisition and processing, as opposed to data acquisition and processing in a single node, would also be useful.

3.2 Node Level Display and Control

A user should be able to select any node in the network and view information about that node. Basic information about the node includes its name and general description, for example "Room 2-229" and "Temperature/Humidity Sensor Node". The user should also be able to see similar information about each sensor and actuator in that node. Each of these should have a name and a general description. For example, an actuator could have name "Window Vent" and general description "Adjust opening of vent by window". This kind of information helps the user understand the purpose and capabilities of the node as a whole.

A user should also be able to instruct the node to perform any action of which it is capable. Basic node-level actions include reset and download new code. Actions relating to individual sensors or actuators are described in the next section.

3.3 Sensor and Actuator Level Display and Control

In addition to name and basic description, each device should have information specific to its operation. Each device should have meta-information about its values or units. For example, a temperature sensor should show its range (e.g., $0o$–$150o$), units (e.g., Fahrenheit degrees), raw value (e.g., 47 out of range 0–255), and calibrated value (e.g., $32o$ F). An actuator should show its range, units, type (digital or analog), and current state (raw value and calibrated value). Additional meta-information could include manufacturer, model, energy consumption, etc. For sensors, the user should be able to see if the data is single-point or aggregated, for example averaged over a certain number of readings or a certain time period. For actuators, the user should be able to control the actuator to the extent possible in the node itself. For a digital actuator that means the user can turn the actuator on or off. For an analog actuator, the user should be able to adjust the output within the actuator's range. We note that values from sensors and the current status of actuators is dynamic information. The user interface should always display the most recent values for these, although users should have the option to view historical values at the user's discretion. Other information, such as names and ranges, is static.

3.4   Sample Scenario

We illustrate the features described in Sects. 3.1–3.3 with a sample scenario from a home monitoring system. Figure 1 shows a network view of the system with one of the nodes selected by the user and expanded for detailed viewing. Note that the information is displayed in terms that a non-technical, ordinary homeowner could easily understand. We will show in the next paragraph how such information is initially entered into the system. Figure 2 shows the display of a particular sensor that has been selected by the user. Now suppose the user decides that the vent needs to be turned on, and assume that the node is able to accept a command to that effect. Figure 3 shows the display in which the user can activate the vent and select the speed of the fan.

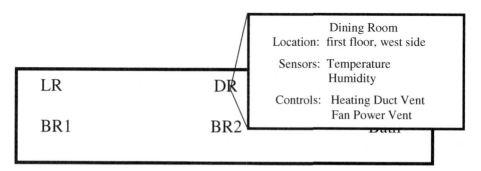

Fig. 1. View of a network with one node expanded

```
                Dining Room Humidity Sensor
    Description:  Shows relative humidity in range
                  10% to 90%.
    Current value:  raw=147   relative humidity=58%
```

Fig. 2. View of one sensor

```
            Dining Room Fan Power Vent Control
    Description:  Controls the window fan that
                  vents air to the outside.
    Current setting:  OFF
    Click a new setting to change:     HIGH
                                       MEDIUM
                                       LOW
                                       OFF
```

Fig. 3. View of one control

3.5　Inserting the Marked-up Text

In Sect. 4 we will describe some of the elements of a suitable mark-up language that could facilitate the implementation of features like the ones described in Sect. 3. Although not directly relevant to HCI, the question of how and where the marked-up text gets inserted into the data stream is important and must be answered in order to make a system like we are advocating possible. Many elements of a sensor network, such as RFID tags and battery operated motes, do not have the computing power to augment their sensor readings with suitable mark-up. There are several possible approaches. In [10], for example, the central system adds the mark-up to raw values that come from anywhere in the network. However, in principle the mark-up could be added at any point along the information path, for example at the lowest possible levels in the network, that is, at the point closest to the actual nodes where the element does have the computing power to annotate the data from sensors or extract command to the actuators from annotated text received from higher up in the network. This could be the node itself or the sink to which that node is connected. In a large system the managers at the central point of the system may not know all the details of the individual parts of the network. For example, in a large factory, the managers in the central office may not know details about the sensors and actuators in one small area of the manufacturing floor. However, the people who deploy and monitor those smallest parts of the network should know what their own local system has and should be able to describe the nodes, sensors, and actuators in their own small area.

Of course, there should be an interface at those points to allow a user to easily provide the descriptions needed. A system like our prior work in programming sensor nodes described in [9] can easily be implemented. In such a system the user will be prompted to enter the information about each node, sensor, and actuator in human terms. For example, the user will be prompted to type in the node name (e.g., "EV1"), the node location (e.g., "2-229 FORD"), and similar information for each sensor and actuator. The system then will automatically generate code for annotating information received from the sensors in the nodes and extracting and reformatting commands from the central system to the actuators in that local network. During operation, that element of the system will receive data from sensors and add the mark-up before transmitting further up the network structure. In the reverse direction, that element will extract commands

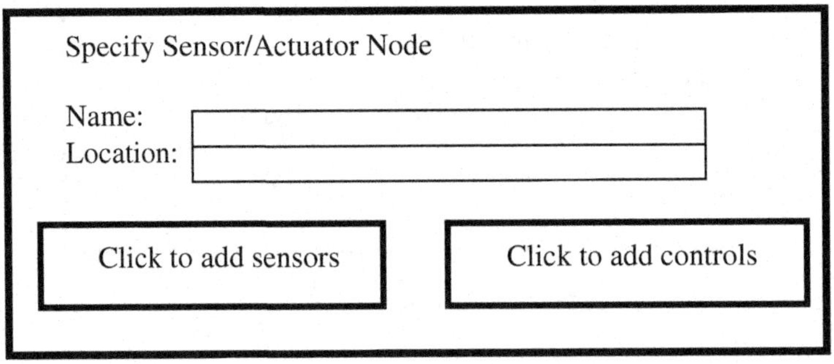

```
Specify Sensor/Actuator Node

Name:     [                        ]
Location: [                        ]

[   Click to add sensors   ]   [   Click to add controls   ]
```

Fig. 4. Dialogue box to specify a node

received in marked-up form from the network and pass the raw commands to nodes underneath. Continuing the example from Sect. 3.4, Figs. 4, 5 and 6 show dialogue boxes in which a user can specify what information to display for the node, the sensor, and the actuator mentioned in that section.

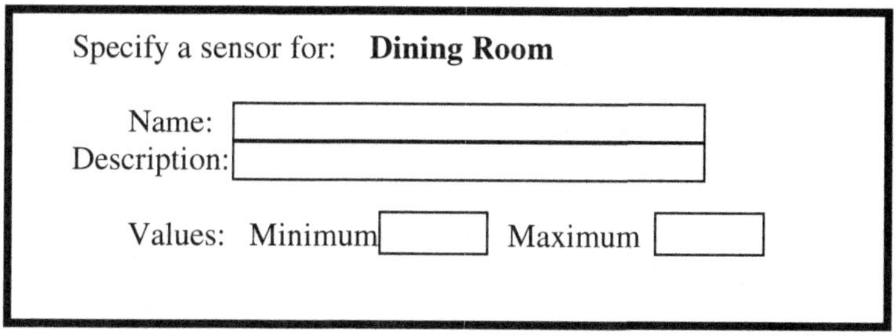

Fig. 5. Dialogue box to specify one sensor

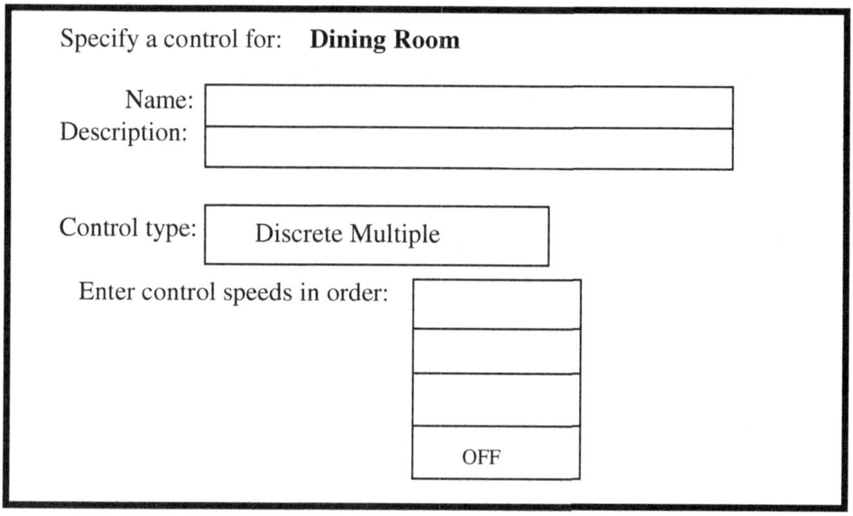

Fig. 6. Dialogue box to specify one control - partially filled in

4 Mark-up Language for Sensor/Actuator Networks

We are developing a mark-up language suitable for the application and features described in Sect. 3. Existing mark-up languages, such as [5, 6], can easily be adapted and augmented. Space precludes a complete presentation, so we illustrate with a few examples to show the general nature of the language.

For the network layer the items of interest are the list of nodes in the network, the display of the network structure, and groups. Marked-up text might look like this.

```
<network  name="sample network">
    <nodelist>
        <node  id="..."     > </node>
            ...
    </nodelist>
    <group  id="GP1"  name="First Floor">
        <groupnode  id="GN1"   nodemember="N3"/>
            ...
    </group>
        ...
    </network>
```

The marked-up text for an individual node might look like the following.

```
<node  id="N1"  name="Room 2-229"    nodeaddress="..."  ... >
    <sensorlist ... >
        <nodesensor  sensor="S1"/>
            ...
    </sensorlist>
    <actuatorlist ... >
        <nodeactuator  actuator="A42"/>
            ...
        </actuatorlist>
```

The string "Room 2-229" is part of what a user would see when he/she selected this node from the network display. The mark-up for an individual device, such as an actuator, might look like the following.

```
<actuator  id="A42"   name="Ventilator control" ... >
    <description>
        This control turns the vent fan motor off or to one of
        three speed levels.
    </description>
    <control  controltype="discrete"  numberoflevels="4">
        <controllevel  level="0"  name="OFF"/>
        <controllevel  level="1"  name="LOW"/>
        <controllevel  level="2"  name="MEDIUM"/>
        <controllevel  level="3"  name="HIGH"/>
    </control>
</actuator>
```

A user viewing this actuator in the interface would see the name and description and would be presented with four choices for control - OFF, LOW, MEDIUM, and HIGH.

As can be seen, the element and attribute names are quite generic, and specific details are relegated to attribute values or element text.

5 Conclusion and Future Work

We have proposed a generic system that would allow users to easily configure the inter-action for sensor/actuator networks. The system consists of two separate interfaces. The first allows a user to describe in human terms the nodes, sensors, and actuators in the system and to provide all the information needed for the second part of the interface system. That second interface allows a user to monitor the sensors and control the actuators in the network also in human terms that the user can easily understand. Many features, such as alarms or trends or history as in [3], can be added on top of the basic system, but these will not require additions to the mark-up language. Similarly, stand-ards, such as the ISO standard form smart grids [11], can be built on top of a system like we have proposed. The availability of a system like we have described will bring the usage of sensor/actuator networks and in the future the Internet of Things within the realm of users who are not trained in HCI but who nevertheless need to monitor and control their networks.

Acknowledgements. This work was supported in part by Northwestern University.

References

1. Kosnik, D., Henschen, L.: A web-enabled data management interface for health monitoring of civil infrastructure. In: Proceedings of the 15th HCII International Conference, vol. 2, pp. 107–116 (2013)
2. Keller, I., Lehmann, A., Franke, M., Schlegel, T.: Towards an interaction concept for efficient control of cyber-physical systems. In: Proceedings of the 14th HCII International Conference, vol. 17, pp. 149–158 (2014)
3. SCADA System for Industrial and Utilities Automation. http://www.scada-system.net
4. REST. https://en.wikipedia.org/wiki/Representational_state_transfer
5. Castellani, A., Bui, N., Casari, P., Rossi, M., Shelby, Z., Zorzi, M.: Architecture and protocols for the internet of things: a case study. In: Eight Annual IEEE International Conference on Pervasive Computing and Communications, pp. 678–683 (2010)
6. SwissEx. http://www.swiss-experiment.ch/index.php/SwissEx:Infrastructure
7. OGC.SensorML. http://www.ogcnetwork.net/SensorML_Spec
8. ISO 19156:2011. Geographic Information – Observation and Measurements. http://www.iso.org/iso/catalogue_detail.htm?csnumber=32574
9. Henschen, L., Lee, J.: A web-based interface for a systems that designs sensor networks. In: Proceedings of the 15th HCII International Conference, vol. 4, pp. 688–697 (2013)
10. Week 5, OpenIoT paper. ISO/IEC 30101:2014. Sensor network and its interfaces for smart grid system: http://www.iso.org/iso/iso_catalogue/catalogue_tc/catalogue_detail.htm?csnumber=53221
11 ISO/IEC 30101:2014. Sensor network and its interfaces for smart grid system: http://www.iso.org/iso/iso_catalogue/catalogue_tc/catalogue_detail.htm?csnumber=53221

Seeing Through Multiple Sensors into Distant Scenes: The Essential Power of Viewpoint Control

Alexander M. Morison[✉], Taylor Murphy, and David D. Woods

The Ohio State University, Columbus, OH, USA
{morison.6,murphy.1018,woods.2}@osu.edu

Abstract. Sensors are being attached to almost every device and vehicle and integrated together to form sensor systems that extend human reach into distant environments. This means human stakeholders have the potential to see into previously inaccessible environments and to take new vantage points and perspectives. However, current designs of these human-sensor systems suffer from basic deficiencies such as an inability to keep pace with activities in the world, the keyhole problem, high re-orienting costs, and the multiple feeds problem. Principled approaches to the development of human-sensor systems are necessary to overcome these challenges. Principles for viewpoint control provide the key to overcome the limitations of current designs.

Keywords: Human-sensor systems · Viewpoint control · Perspective control · Human-robot interaction · Data overload · Keyhole effect · Wide-area surveillance · Sensor systems · Virtual environment · Multiple feeds problem

1 Introduction: Current Human-Sensor Systems

Sensors are sprouting up everywhere. They are being attached to almost every device and vehicle and can be found in many public and private spaces. Often, multiple sensors are integrated together to form sensor systems that extend human reach into distant environments. This means stakeholders have the potential to see into previously inaccessible environments and to take new vantage points and perspectives. All of the data feeds from sensors provide the basis for people to take action, authorize actions by other systems, or delegate authority to increasingly autonomous systems.

Many different types of sensor systems can be found in a wide range of applications like telemedicine, wide-area surveillance, emergency response, and oil exploration. In telemedicine alone several types of sensors systems can be found. Robot's move equipment and material between rooms, allow medical personnel to monitor patients remotely, and act as surgical aids in the case of robotic-assisted surgery. For emergency response, sensors provide the potential for new access to previously inaccessible areas. This inaccessibility can arise from limited physical access, in the case of a collapsed building, or because of danger in the case of a suspicious package. In each of these examples, and all of these domains, stakeholders and sensor systems form human-sensor systems that allow stakeholder's to see and act in environments in which they are not present [1].

© Springer International Publishing Switzerland 2016
M. Kurosu (Ed.): HCI 2016, Part II, LNCS 9732, pp. 388–399, 2016.
DOI: 10.1007/978-3-319-39516-6_37

Despite the advances in sensor technologies, actual deployments of more and more sensors have produced surprising challenges as the scale of data and reach of these systems have grown. One of the challenges is the inability to keep pace with activities in a remote environment, in particular when the sensor system is a network of sensors like in wide-area video surveillance [2]. A second challenge related to pacing is a lack of peripheral awareness, which is where a narrow "keyhole" view makes it impossible for a stakeholder to see what is just beyond their current view [3]. A third challenge is the difficulty shifting viewpoints across sensor feeds to find informative views, called the multiple feeds problem [4]. A fourth challenge for human-sensor systems arises from confounding sensor control with action potential in the design of the sensor platform. This confounding creates the possibility for sensor platforms, like robot's, to get stuck, lost, or bump into things.. At the heart of these observations is a single basic challenge for human-sensor systems using today's technologies. As sensor systems widen our ability to monitor distant environments and the amount of sensor data increases by orders of magnitude, human observers are less able to shift their viewpoint and the viewpoint of the sensor systems to keep pace with interesting activities.

This paper uses basic principles about viewpoint control derived from human perception to explain why the above observation recurs with current technologies. The paper also introduces viewpoint control technology – the basic principles for designing interactions that allow people to shift viewpoint fluently. Fluent viewpoint control is a prerequisite for people to track what is interesting at different scales as the data streams about activities in the world change.

2   Basic Deficiencies in the Design of Current Human-Sensor Systems

There are several important deficiencies with the existing designs of human-sensor systems. The first of these is the inability of these systems to keep pace with activities in the distant environment. The second deficiency is that keyhole effects are everywhere and in many cases sensor systems experience multiple keyholes either from multiple sensors or the poor design of navigation mechanisms – like in the case of large field-of-view sensors described in this section. A related deficiency to the keyhole effect is the limited navigation support that exists for looking across multiple sensor feeds.. And lastly, sensor system designers have confounded viewpoint control and action capability to the point that even simple tasks become complex.

2.1   Inability to Keep Pace with Activities

The pace or tempo of activities and events is a fundamental concept for any human-technology system including human-sensor systems. As a temporal and relational property it is usually absent from the design and analysis of interactive systems. Pace is a difficult concept to include in studies and designs because it captures a dynamic relationship between an environment and an observer(s). Pace depends on both the activities and events in the world, but also the knowledge, experience, and other tasks of the observers. The relationship between these temporal processes is also dynamic, which of these processes leads a change in pacing and which follows depends on context. In the end, an observer's ability to track events must match the tempo of activities and events in the world of interest.

The limited ability of human-sensor systems to keep pace with activities can be illustrated at the scale of a network of multiple sensors. There are several sources of complexity that make tracking activities across multiple sensors difficult within a wide area video surveillance network (Fig. 1A). A few of these sources include different perspectives, overlapping and non-overlapping sensor coverage, and sensor data displays that remove spatial relationships between sensors. The net result is that wide area surveillance systems are most valuable in forensic analysis after events have already occurred. In forensic analysis, observers slow down the flow of sensor data as a work-around to escape from the inherent pacing limitations of the human-sensor system. Current designs impose high cognitive load as the observer must keep a model in their head of the relationships across cameras, the directions the cameras point, the orientation of the activity to be monitored, and the gaps in camera coverage.

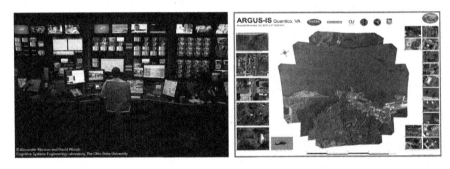

Fig. 1. A. Wide area video surveillance network. B. Image from a large, high resolution field-of-view sensor.

Another trend in the development of human-sensor systems is to create extremely large field-of-view sensors, which is a response to the challenges associated with narrow field-of-view sensors (Fig. 1B). These sensors eliminate the need to control multiple sensors at the same time. However, these sensor feeds are so large that people can only take in a portion of the total field-of-view at any one moment. As a result, people shift their focus sequentially over the available field at a scale that is less than the total available field-of-view. This typically means a person must scale and translate – zoom and pan – a virtual view or open up a series of windows each at an appropriate resolution for the task. Neither of these trends in human-sensor system design help users know where to look or focus next as events occur in the scene of interest.

These examples illustrate some basic findings about viewpoint control in human perception and in human-sensor systems [4, 5]. The process of perceiving is an active sampling process. There is no perfect single viewpoint; rather, the view from any single point of observation simultaneously reveals and obscures properties of the scene of interest so that comprehension requires shifts of viewpoint [4]. The key is supporting the control of this sampling process to track what is "interesting" over time.

2.2 The Keyhole Problem

An old challenge that re-emerges for human-sensor systems is the keyhole effect [6], which has been referred to as the "soda straw effect" for sensors on robotic platforms [7]. For example, navigating a robot through broken terrain is difficult when the robot handler is stuck looking through the 'soda straw' of a single camera. The human handling the robot can easily miss important features of the terrain that are difficult to discern, like landmarks along a path [8]. This is one example of how the keyhole makes robot handlers vulnerable to missing important properties of an environment that are just beyond the boundary of the camera's current field-of-view. Expanding the awareness of the robot handler requires moving the camera's view, but in what way and when? This challenge can be illustrated through real-world examples.

Example: Robotic Response at Fukushima. The robot operators at the 2011 Fukushima Daiichi nuclear power plant disaster experienced a perceptual shortfall when using just the sensors located on the robot. The limits imposed by the keyhole effect and lack of peripheral awareness left them unable to supervise and tele-operate the robots in the damaged environment successfully. But as responsible problem holders, the roboticists and engineers adapted their method of deploying robots [9]. Instead of sending a single robot into the nuclear power plant, robots were deployed in pairs (see Fig. 2). The first robot performed the planned tasks, such as opening doors and turning valves. The second robot of the pair was used to provide a view of the first robot relative to the local environment. This second view provided the first robot handler the necessary context around the first robot to successfully navigate doorways and passageways [10]. The adaptations during the response to the Fukushima nuclear power plant disaster provide a real example where resources were reallocated to provide a necessary viewpoint to overcome perceptual limits in order to complete critical tasks and achieve pressing goals.

Fig. 2. At the Fukushima Daiichi nuclear power plant disaster two robots were used to overcome the keyhole effect with a single robot.

2.3   Multiple Feeds Problem

There are several natural responses to the limited ability to perceive through the sensors on robots. These include adding cameras in the scene of interest, adding cameras to the platform, or to add more platforms in the scene of interest. These workarounds quickly result in a new challenge: how to integrate and navigate these diverse sensor feeds now available to remote observers. Shifting viewpoints to find informative views or view transitions for a particular context can be a challenging activity. Viewpoint control is a skill that people exhibit naturally as they move through and explore scenes (e.g., [11]). Re-establishing a basis for fluent skilled control of viewpoint for human-sensor systems extended over these new scales is an extremely difficult design challenge.

2.4   Confounding Viewpoint Control and Action Capability

The challenge of designing viewpoint control is particularly clear when robotic platforms confound action capability and viewpoint control. This confound occurs for any sensor platform where viewpoint control is dependent on moving the platform through the world. When desired actions of the platform produce unintended viewpoint shifts (or the reverse), operators are forced to balance an extremely difficult trade-off. There are many circumstances where operators may wish to move sensors independent from the action potential. Nearly all existing sensor platform system designs fail to design for independent viewpoint control or coordinated interplay between viewpoint shifts and action capability.

An example of how this confound undermines the fluency and capability of the human-robot system is shown in Fig. 3. In this case, a robot operator is attempting to place a cylinder inside a circular aperture as part of a manipulation task. This robot operator quickly realized that there was a large amount of uncertainty about how to grip the cylinder and when to release the cylinder in the aperture accurately. When gripping the cylinder, it was difficult for the operator to determine whether enough of the cylinder had been grasped so that it would not slip through the gripper and fall to the ground. Then, when attempting to release the cylinder in the aperture, it was difficult to determine whether the cylinder would remain in the aperture, or not, after release. All operators struggled with these two decisions and the relationship between them, meaning the best solution for gripping the cylinder to avoid dropping was the worst solution for gripping the cylinder to make sure it remained in the aperture, and vice versa. The irony of this example is that a child easily completes this exact task by the age of 2. This confound occurs commonly in all types of action capable sensor systems such as ground robots, manipulators, and submersibles.

The confound of viewpoint control with platform action assumes that a change in sensor positions will not negatively influence the positioning of action capability, and vice versa. This assumption is violated when viewpoint and action demands occur simultaneously, as they did in the example above. This design makes the assumption that all viewpoint movements are equally informative; an assumption that is not true usually. In the manipulator test, operators had to make complex manipulator arm movements to try to find valuable viewpoints. This is far from how people re-orient as they

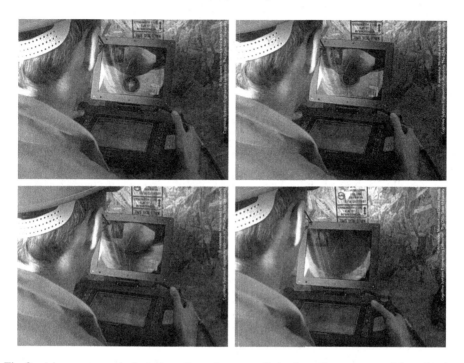

Fig. 3. A human-ground robot attempting to insert a cylinder through an aperture. After releasing the cylinder it tilts back into the gripper, away from the aperture (lower right).

move through a scene. These examples illustrate how current designs of human-sensor systems leave observers to deliberate about properties of the scene via slow, high workload, error prone processes. These weaknesses led designers to attempt to develop an additional layer of external cognitive aids to repair the weaknesses in these deliberative processes. Ironically, the development of human-sensor systems appears to reprise ancient debates about indirect versus direct approaches to explain how human perception works. There is a common theme running through these deficiencies – a lack of viewpoint control that would assist people make comprehensible perspective shifts to track what is informative as events occur and situations change.

3 Perspective Taking Concepts

Human-sensor systems are not designed to help stakeholders shift perspectives, transition across viewpoints, or see what other viewpoints could be taken next. These systems have undermined the skilled perspective shifts that people exhibit naturally as they move through and explore scenes (e.g., [11]). Indeed, a closer examination of sensors systems reveals the ad hoc nature of how these systems are designed. At best, sensors are positioned based on a specific need supporting a single function. At worst, sensors are positioned based on irrelevant factors like mounting space and cabling requirements.

Overcoming the challenges described above requires a principled approach to the design of viewpoint control for human-sensor systems. The works of [1, 12] developed the principles of viewpoint control using findings from visual perception, ecological perception, and the neurobiology of attention as these have been applied to human-technology systems [2, 5, 6].

The first basic principle is that there is no single best view: the view from any point of observation simultaneously reveals and obscures aspects of the scene of interest [13, 14]. As a sensor moves relative to the scene, some properties of that scene, and the objects, people, and activities present, are directly and accurately perceived, while the same perspective shift makes other properties more difficult to perceive accurately [13, 15]. Fundamentally, it is through shifting perspective that observers come to comprehend activities and status of the scene of interest.

The second principle is that getting lost and keyhole effects are diminished or disappear when you can provide two kinds of views effectively in parallel. One view is what can be seen from the current sensor position (its point of observation and its view direction). The second provides the view of a sensor's position and orientation (view direction) relative to the scene. This principle was established by applying results from perception to information system design [6]. The usefulness of the second view increases as the number of sensor viewpoints over which an observer can see and explore increases (see illustrations in [4]). The Fukushima case described earlier is a locally innovative but crude example of providing two views in parallel.

The third principle is that viewpoint control requires both egocentric and exocentric frames-of-reference and a mechanism to transition between these frames-of-reference. An additional constraint on these frames-of-reference is that they are spherical coordinate systems. These coordinate systems provide the foundation for creating comprehensible shifts in perspective – changes in point of observation – and constrain or eliminate poor changes in point of observation.

Fourth, viewpoint control utilizes the principle of center/surround from human perception to break down the keyhole. Center/surround requires a high-resolution central view with a larger (even if lower resolution) surround area. The center specifies the current viewpoint of interest and the surround provides re-orienting cues about where to focus next in the search for interesting structures or activities across the scene of

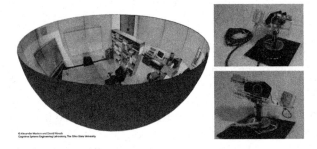

Fig. 4. A panoramic representation created from a narrow field-of-view PTZ camera (left) and two views of a viewpoint control input device or 3-dimensional joystick (right).

interest. This principle has been found to be critical for exploration in virtual environments and underlies the natural organization of the human visual system.

These principles are applied to the design of a wide-area video surveillance system. This system combines center-surround representations of video surveillance feeds, a viewpoint control device that embodies the egocentric and exocentric frames-of-reference, and a virtual three-dimensional environment that acts as the medium where a virtual viewpoint can be navigated over the wide-area sensor network.

4   A Viewpoint Control Demonstration Using a Wide-Area Video Surveillance System

This wide-area video surveillance network system shows how the viewpoint control principles apply to the design of a human-sensor system. This demonstration illustrates how egocentric and exocentric frames-of-reference can be used to control the orientation of a sensor. This example also presents one method for making a smooth transition from an egocentric to an exocentric frame-of-reference. The demonstration also provides an example of how selecting and viewing different sensor feeds can be designed as virtual navigation across sensor views. Lastly, this demonstration establishes how properties of a virtual viewpoint, like virtual distance, can be leveraged to encode sensor network properties like sensor control.

The demonstration is built with three main components, a new viewpoint control device (a 3-dimensional joystick), a panoramic representation built for a pan-tilt-zoom (PTZ) capable video camera, and a 3-dimensional virtual environment. The viewpoint control device and the panoramic representation are shown in Fig. 4. The 3-dimensional virtual environment is shown in Fig. 5. This virtual environment is populated with four video cameras each depicted by a panoramic representation. Since the video camera can only see a narrow field-of-view, the panorama is updated by moving the camera around the scene. The design of the current system balances the update of the panorama with a decay that removes stale data. This update can be seen in the panoramic representation in the lower left area of Fig. 5, where the top half of the panorama is updated, but the bottom half appears decayed. The panoramic representation in the 3-dimensional virtual

Fig. 5. A 3-dimensional virtual environment populated with four panoramic representations created by PTZ cameras.

environment allows an operator to look at current time, but also the recent past. This illustrates a new way of addressing the issue of pacing previously described.

The updating of each panoramic representation is an automatic behavior of the PTZ camera. When an operator needs to track an activity or event of interest, looking at a physical location in the distant environment involves aligning the 3-dimensional joystick, the 3-dimensional virtual viewpoint, and the orientation of the PTZ camera. This alignment is shown in Fig. 6 with the controller in an egocentric configuration. The virtual viewpoint is shown on the left at the center of the panoramic representation, as if at the position of the PTZ camera. The configuration of the joystick and the orientation of the joystick viewpoint are shown on the right of the figure. The relationship between the center of the controller (the white dot annotated as the point-of-observation) and the view direction block to the lower right (the white dot below the point-of-observation) define an egocentric frame-of-reference. The movement of the controller to the left or right creates a similar change in the orientation of the virtual environment viewpoint and the orientation of the PTZ camera.

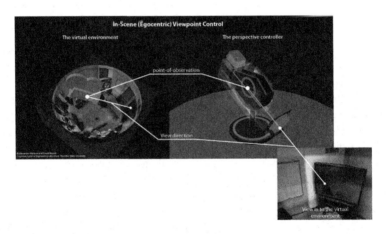

Fig. 6. The egocentric relationship between a virtual camera in a virtual environment with a panoramic sensor representation (left) and the viewpoint input control device (right).

The controller can also be configured to represent an exocentric frame-of-reference as shown in Fig. 7. The exocentric frame-of-reference is created by reversing the orientation of the view direction block (upper left of the controller) relative to the center point of the controller. In the virtual environment, the left panel of Fig. 7, the virtual viewpoint is outside of the panoramic representation. At the same time, the virtual view and camera view align to show a similar PTZ camera view as in the egocentric configuration. This exocentric viewpoint provides a wider virtual viewable field than the PTZ camera, which is an example of the fourth principle. In the current demonstration, the PTZ camera is directly controllable in the exocentric configuration, but control depends on the distance between the virtual viewpoint and the panoramic representation.

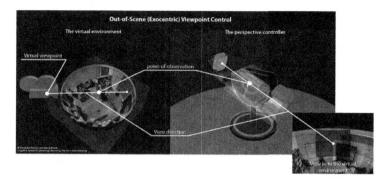

Fig. 7. The exocentric relationship between a virtual camera in a virtual environment with a panoramic sensor representation (left) and the viewpoint input device control device (right).

In both exocentric and egocentric configurations of the controller the distance between the view direction block and the center of the controller can be increased or decreased to create movement of the virtual viewpoint towards or away from the virtual point-of-observation. This ability to move the virtual viewpoint through the 3-dimensional virtual environment provides a unique opportunity for sensor selection.

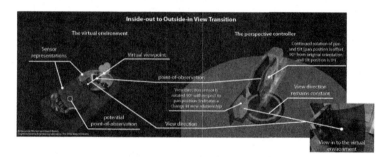

Fig. 8. The transition from an egocentric to an exocentric relationship between a virtual camera in a virtual environment with a panoramic sensor representation (left) and the viewpoint input control device (right).

In the exocentric frame-of-reference the distance of the virtual viewpoint from the sensor panoramic representation can be used to define sensor operator control. A sensor operator must be able to select or de-select a camera for control. Often selection of a camera implies de-selection of the currently controlled camera. In this demonstration, the virtual viewpoint distance to a sensor panoramic representation defines PTZ camera control. One option is to encode the virtual distance as a discrete, binary on-off threshold. The camera is selected if the distance between the virtual viewpoint and the panoramic representation is less than the binary threshold. Otherwise, the camera is not selected. An alternative encoding is to use distance as a continuous dimension. The closer the virtual viewpoint is to the panoramic representation the more frequently the PTZ camera samples from the desired view direction.

The remaining component of the two frames-of-reference is the mechanism for transitioning between referent frames. A snapshot of the 3-dimensional joystick's smooth transition between referent frames is shown in Fig. 8. In this snapshot the transition between the view direction block position and orientation are rotated half way between the positions in the egocentric and exocentric configurations. This transition maintains the virtual view direction while changing the configuration of the 3-dimensional joystick.

5   Conclusion

Human-sensor systems are growing in number and kind. But, despite the benefits of these systems, there are several important deficiencies with existing designs. These deficiencies include the inability to keep pace, the keyhole effect, the multiple feeds problem, and the confounding of viewpoint control and action potential. Four principles for successful viewpoint control were introduced. These principles include the need for a moving point-of-observation, to provide two views in parallel, the use of egocentric and exocentric frames-of-reference, and the design of center-surround relationships. These were demonstrated using a wide-area video surveillance network prototype system. The key components of the demonstration were described including egocentric and exocentric viewpoint control, navigation, and sensor control selection. In short, this paper argues that viewpoint control is present in all existing human-sensor systems, but it is either ad-hoc or happenstance. In order to make coherent progress on the described deficiencies of these systems, fundamental advances in human-sensor system design are necessary. The viewpoint control model and demonstration are the beginning of a principled approach to viewpoint control for human-sensor system design.

References

1. Morison, A.M.: Perspective control: technology to solve the multiple feeds problem in sensor systems. The Ohio State University (2010)
2. Woods, D.D., Sarter, N.B.: Capturing the dynamics of attention control from individual to distributed systems. Theor. Issues Ergon. **11**, 7–28 (2010)
3. Voshell, M., Woods, D.: Breaking the keyhole in human–robot coordination: method and evaluation. In: Proceedings of the Human Factors and Ergonomics Society 49th Annual Meeting (2005)
4. Morison, A., Woods, D., Murphy, T.: Human-robot interaction as extending human perception to new scales. In: Hoffman, R., Hancock, P., Parasuraman, R., Szalma, J., Scerbo, M. (eds.) The Cambridge Handbook of Applied Perception Research, 2nd edn, pp. 848–868. Cambridge University Press, Cambridge (2015)
5. Woods, D.D., Patterson, E.S., Roth, E.M.: Can we ever escape from data overload? A cognitive systems diagnosis. Cogn. Technol. Work **4**, 22–36 (2002). doi:10.1007/s101110200002
6. Woods, D.D.: Visual momentum: a concept to improve the cognitive coupling of person and computer. Int. J. Man Mach. Stud. **21**, 229–244 (1984)

7. Casper, J., Murphy, R.R.: Human-robot interactions during the robot-assisted urban search and rescue response at the World Trade Center. IEEE Trans. Syst. Man Cybern. Part B **33**, 367–385 (2003)
8. Hughes, S., Lewis, M.: Robotic camera control for remote exploration. Comput. Hum. Interact. **6**, 511–517 (2004)
9. Woods, D.D., Hollnagel, E.: Joint Cognitive Systems: Patterns in Cognitive Systems Engineering. CRC Press, Boca Raton (2006)
10. Guizzo, E.: Fukushima robot operator writes tell-all blog. In: IEEE Spectrum (2011). http://spectrum.ieee.org/automaton/robotics/industrial-robots/fukushima-robot-operator-diaries
11. Simons, D.J., Wang, R.F.: Perceiving real-world viewpoint changes. Psychol. Sci. **9**, 315–320 (1998)
12. Roesler, A.: A new model for perspective: the role of point of observation in virtual and remote perspective-taking. The Ohio State University (2005)
13. Tittle, J.S., Roesler, A., Woods, D.D.: The remote perception problem. In: Proceedings of the Human Factors and Ergonomics Society Annual Meeting, pp. 260–264 (2002)
14. Morison, A.M., Voshell, M., Roesler, A., Feil, M., Tittle, J., Tinapple, D., Woods, D.D.: Integrating diverse feeds to extend human perception into distant scenes. In: McDermott, E.B.Y.P., Allender, L. (eds.) Advanced Decision Architectures for the Warfighter: Foundation and Technology, pp. 177–200. Alion Science and Technology, Boulder (2009)
15. Breazeal, C., Berlin, M., Brooks, A., Gray, J., Thomaz, A.: Using perspective taking to learn from ambiguous demonstrations. Rob. Auton. Syst. **54**, 385–393 (2006)

From CAVE2™ to Mobile: Adaptation of *Hearts and Minds* Virtual Reality Project Interaction

Arthur Nishimoto[1], Daria Tsoupikova[2(✉)], Scott Rettberg[3], and Roderick Coover[4]

[1] Computer Science, University of Illinois at Chicago, Chicago, IL, USA
anishi2@uic.edu
[2] School of Design, University of Illinois at Chicago, Chicago, IL, USA
datsoupi@gmail.com
[3] University of Bergen, Bergen, Norway
scottrettberg@gmail.com
[4] Temple University, Philadelphia, PA, USA
roderickcoover@gmail.com

Abstract. Hearts and Minds: The Interrogations Project is an interactive performance made for the CAVE2™ [1] large-scale 320-degree panoramic virtual reality environment that describes veterans' testimonies about military interrogations in Iraq during the American counter-insurgency campaign. The project is based on interviews of American soldiers and on their actual testimonies [2]. The project was achieved through technical innovation, cross-disciplinary and international collaboration. It was developed using a novel method for direct output of the Unity-based virtual reality projects into the CAVE2 environment. Other portable versions of the work were developed to reach new audiences across educational, arts and public arenas which include (1) personal computer version navigable using Xbox 360 controller; (2) web-based version available for free download; (3) Oculus Rift immersive virtual reality HMD version; (4) mobile version of the project for Apple iPad (in progress). This paper describes the development and compares the interaction experiences across platforms.

Keywords: Virtual reality · Navigation · Interaction · Immersive environments · 3D user interface · CAVE2™

List of Abbreviations

3D	Three-dimensional
API	Application programming interface
CAVE	CAVE automatic virtual environment
GUI	Graphical user interface
HMD	Head mounted display
VR	Virtual reality
VRE	Virtual reality environment

© Springer International Publishing Switzerland 2016
M. Kurosu (Ed.): HCI 2016, Part II, LNCS 9732, pp. 400–411, 2016.
DOI: 10.1007/978-3-319-39516-6_38

1   Introduction

The use of Virtual Reality (VR) in sciences, healthcare, arts and design is becoming more and more ubiquitous. The development of virtual art has been influenced by advancements of VR technology and media art movements that examined the concepts of interactivity, installation, immersion, interface design, responsiveness and story-telling. The history of virtual art has been defined by pioneering projects such as "World Skin" by Maurice Benayoun (1997), "Osmose" by Charlotte Davies (1995), "The Legible City" by Jeffrey Shaw (1989), "Placeholder" by Brenda Laurel (1994), "Be Now Here" by Michael Naimark (1995) and many other important works [3]. Relying on major technological and artistic achievements, virtual art established new ways of making, viewing and understanding art through immersion, interaction and presentation inside the virtual space. With the advancement of technology, virtual art gradually moved out of research laboratories and scientific centers into galleries, museums and public exhibitions. The Oculus Rift, Leap motion, Google Glass, Kinect, HoloLens, Unity, and other virtual technologies additionally changed the way that contemporary VR art projects are planned and realized.

VR art has however been consistently limited by the fact that there are no cross-platform standards allowing seamless portability of Virtual Reality Environments (VREs) and interfaces between various domains and technologies. Preddy and Nance [4] argued for the need to establish a standardized API that would provide the ability of working on multiple levels of abstraction to support the portability of virtual environment interfaces. The development of the portable versions of the VRE for different technologies requires significant investments of time and resources. In addition, the authors often need to redesign complicated navigation interfaces from scratch and adjust interaction techniques for each platform to reach out particular target audiences.

One of the goals of our project was to create a virtual environment with sufficient interaction complexity to show on several different VR platforms. To enable a more natural and user-friendly way of interacting with the virtual environment in the CAVE2, on the Xbox controller system running on personal computer, using the

Fig. 1. Presentation of the project using the Xbox controller at Litteraturhuset Oslo, Norway

web-based Unity3D web player and on mobile device (iPad), we have adapted project's interactive interface to employ different interaction techniques. The efficacies of these techniques and interfaces were evaluated with participants during the several exhibitions of this project using informal qualitative methods (informal qualitative interviews and direct observations) [5, 6] (Fig. 1).

This is an ongoing project at the Electronic Visualization Lab (EVL) in Chicago that is being achieved through technical innovation, and cross-disciplinary international collaboration between artists, scientists, and researchers from five different universities. *Hearts and Minds: The Interrogations Project* was developed using a novel method for direct output of Unity-based virtual reality projects into the CAVE2 environment. The project premiered as the first virtual performance utilizing the Unity game engine in the CAVE2 environment. We are currently releasing the mobile version made for personal interaction on the iPad to enhance the project's accessibility for educational use.

2   Development and Technology

2.1   Project Concept

Hearts and Minds addresses a complex contemporary problem: as American soldiers are returning from the wars in Iraq and Afghanistan, it is becoming increasingly apparent that some of them participated in interrogation practices and acts of abusive violence with detainees for which they were not properly trained or psychologically prepared. The mental health impact of deployment during these wars is still being researched, as many veterans are at risk for developing chronic PTSD. At this point, American soldiers and citizens are left with many unresolved questions about the moral calculus of using torture as an interrogation strategy in American military operations. The project raises awareness of these issues and provides a platform for discussion of military interrogation methods and their effects on detainees, soldiers, and society.

2.2   VRE Architecture

The structure of the project consists of nine Virtual Reality Environments (VREs) linked together. The temple panorama, which is the entry point to the project, is positioned in the center. As the audience enters this space, they become acquainted with the four soldier characters who will be the focus of work, through monologues describing their reasons for enlisting in the military. Four open doors allow participants to peak into domestic environments connected to this central panorama: children room, kitchen, living room and the backyard. Participants see the rooms from a first-person perspective. Each connected room contains four interactive objects, the memory triggers, which serve as portals to the linked panorama environments. Users can click the objects using virtual laser pointer to transport themselves into a surreal panorama connected to it, which is intended to represent a subconscious space of interiority, and to provide the audience with a sense of intimate communication with the voices they will hear. The room fades out and participants hear short monologues about the solders' wartime experiences. Once the story is complete, the war panorama fades out and users are transported back into the room. Once all four objects in that room are explored, the viewer is teleported back to the central temple panorama and the door to that room is closed. Once all four rooms are fully explored, the user is returned to the temple scene, which fades out to red accompanied by a heartbeat sound.

2.3   CAVE2

This project was developed at the Electronic Visualization Laboratory (EVL) at the University of Illinois at Chicago, the birthplace of the CAVE2. The CAVE2 is powered by a 37-node high-performance computer cluster connected to high-speed networks to enable users to better cope with information-intensive tasks. It is approximately 24 feet in diameter and 8 feet tall and consists of 72 near-seamless passive stereo off-axis-optimized 3D LCD panels, a 36-node high-performance computer cluster plus a master node, a 20-speaker surround audio system, a 14-camera optical tracking system, and a 100-Gigabit/second connection to the outside world [1]. The CAVE2 provides participants with the ability to see three-dimensional objects at a resolution matching the human visual acuity, explore the environment, and hear surrounding spatial sounds around them, similar to how they hear in real life.

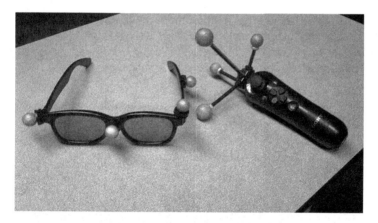

Fig. 2. CAVE2 input devices; the head and the wand controllers with retro-reflective markers for Vicon infrared optical tracking system.

CAVE2 uses a Vicon infrared optical tracking system to track two objects, the wand and the head tracker (Fig. 2). Each object consists of a unique arrangement of retro-reflective markers. These markers allow the tracking system to determine the position and orientation of the object within CAVE2. The head tracker mounted on the participants' tracking glasses is used to calculate the viewpoint according to the participants' body and head movements in CAVE2 allowing for an immersive virtual reality experience. Objects within the virtual space will be drawn at 1:1 scale and displayed based on the position of the tracked user.

The wand enables hand motion interaction in the immersive VRE, and also has buttons and analog controls for user input. Pointing and pressing a button on the wand can be used for grabbing virtual objects or specifying a direction to navigate toward. CAVE2 uses the Omicron Input Abstraction Library [7] to combine mocap and controller data into a single 'wand' event. The project scene is continuously updated according to the orientation and position of the navigator's head, and the virtual laser pointer is moved in accordance with the participant's actual hand movements. When a participant moves inside the CAVE, rotates his or her head or pushes a button on the wand, the computer system controlling these devices will receive the input signals and provide feedback accordingly to achieve a seamless interaction experience.

2.4   Development Platform

The VRE was developed using the Unity game development platform based on C# scripting language (Unity Technologies Inc., CA), that is typically used by video game developers (Fig. 3). 3D objects, spaces, textures, and materials were developed in Maya (Autodesk Inc., CA), which supports all stages of the 3D modeling, including surface creation and manipulation, texturing, lighting and export to Unity. We used freely available 3D models of the utilitarian objects and interiors from royalty-free websites, in which we modified, triangulated and collaged the geometry, reassigned new textures and materials in order to make the scene more realistic. We imported the objects, environments, textures, and animations from Maya into Unity to design our VRE. Animations and special effects were also incorporated into the scene by using advanced Unity techniques in order to further encourage engagement.

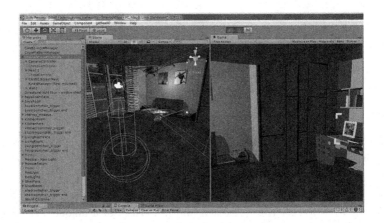

Fig. 3. Development of the VRE in Unity; the CAVE simulator.

One of the goals of our project was to create a convincing environment with sufficient immersion to focus the participant's sense of presence throughout the narrative. The engaging graphics and diverse special effects were employed to enhance immersion in the environment to facilitate involvement. We used a variety of special effects and advanced Unity features to recreate unique atmospheric and geospatial characteristics in the war landscape such as sandstorms, desert grass, smoke, trees, and fires with accompanying visuals and sounds. We added special effects simulating smoke in the living room fireplace and the connected panorama. The smoke particle is configured to the desired settings and the emitter is positioned at the center of the log stack.

The voice recordings performed by professional actors were integrated with interactive media elements and panoramic photographic backgrounds to bring story elements together into an interactive 3D environment. The visual, auditory and narrative elements were brought together using Unity. We used real-time shadows and powerful lighting effects to enhance the illusion.

The getReal3D plugin for Unity developed by Mechdyne Corporation was used to run Unity across the CAVE2 cluster [8]. Scripts from the getReal3D plugin handle the user-centered perspective and synchronize 37 instances of Unity across the cluster creating a seamless 320-degree environment across CAVE2. This includes user inputs, moving objects, anything that uses a random function, and physics collision detection. The getReal3D plugin handles most synchronizations automatically.

User interaction was scripted using the Omicron [7] input abstraction library developed by EVL. Omicron also provides tools to simulate the CAVE2 interaction and display environment for development (Fig. 3). The OmicronManager script handles connection with an Omicron input server, parses events and then broadcast those events to registered Omicron clients (OmicronEventClient.cs). The Omicron Manager also works with the CAVE2Manager to help simplify event handling for head and wand inputs. The CAVE2Manager also provides some basic keyboard emulation of tracking and wand inputs for development systems. Both OmicronManager and CAVE2Manager are packaged into the CAVE2-Manager prefab for easy integration into a CAVE2 Unity project.

3 Interaction

3.1 Interaction Inside the CAVE2

The methods of interaction between the user and the CAVE have been studied by different researcher groups [9, 10]. Several studies described evaluation processes and frameworks to assess the effectiveness of VE interactive technologies [11–13]. Research has shown that navigation in sparsely populated VREs leaves users disoriented without landmarks [14]. Guidelines of VE design and navigation encourage providing orientation and landmark cues [14, 15]. The superiority of pointing and ray-casting techniques for many interactive tasks has been described in the experimental study of interactive devices used performance times as a dependent variable [12]. It has been shown that simple walking can significantly improve the engagement and immersion in the CAVE-based applications and potentially enhance the sense of presence in VRE [16].

CAVE-based applications typically use direct manipulation and navigation, which are considered the core styles of interaction inside the CAVE [14, 17, 18]. Ben Schneiderman described direct manipulation as an interaction style that allows the user to use the use graphical representations to interact with the operating system [19]. The user can select an object and then an action to be performed on that object. A continuous visual representation of virtual objects and related actions as well as immediate feedback are found to be the main characteristics of direct manipulation [20], which are especially important in the CAVE environment.

In order to navigate through our environment in the CAVE2, a participant needs to point the wand to move toward a specific direction and press a button to activate the transition into one of the soldier's stories. The fly mode has been disabled to ensure close proximity of the user to the interactive objects. We also implemented collision control to prevent navigating beyond the project visuals and getting lost in infinite virtual space.

Fig. 4. Interaction in the CAVE2. The performer walks to one of the invisible interactive colliders holding a chair.

CAVE2 provides a large walking space (20 feet) for interaction in comparison to other CAVEs and VR environments. Our project takes advantage of this larger stage and merges the performance elements with the navigation style of interaction. In our CAVE2 performance the performer had to walk to one of two steel folding chairs situated in the physical environment and turn his head facing the direction of the desired entry in order to enter each room (Fig. 4). The chair was positioned in the first collision area prior to the beginning of the performance. In order to enter the second room, the performer had to physically move the chair from one interactive area to a second interactive area inside the CAVE2. The use of a foldable metal chair was inspired by the narrative describing the memory of one of the solders who participated in the interrogation of the detainee exploiting a metal chair.

Fig. 5. Direct manipulation interaction in the CAVE2. By pushing a button on the Wand, the performer can point the virtual laser pointer and click on the watering can trigger object.

Direct manipulation was used to interact with trigger objects in each room. By pushing a specific button on the wand, the performer could point the virtual laser pointer and click on the trigger objects in the room (Fig. 5). The C# code example of wand pointing and triggering an object on multiple platforms is shown in Fig. 6. All input and event processing is done on the master node which then sends the final event trigger across the cluster.

3.2   The Computer Version

In the standalone computer version of the project, navigation is performed using typical first-person shooter interaction using an Xbox controller, which replaces the wand. Instead of physically navigating through the CAVE2 space, movement is controlled by the joystick (Fig. 7). Looking around using the second analog stick can be substituted using the Oculus Rift headset. Pointing on the objects and clicking on the triggers using the Xbox controller was very similar to interacting with the objects using Wand in the CAVE2. We added a target image to simplify the selection of objects using a laser pointer, and decided to discard the direction of the navigator's point of view (the angle) as a required parameter to enter the room.

The performance navigation in which a performer could use his physical position and orientation in the virtual environment by walking to interactive zones was impossible to adapt for the flat screen computer version. Consequently, the performance navigation was converted into a first-person interaction in which the participant had to navigate to each interactive entry using the joystick mode on the controller.

```
public class WandPointer : OmicronWandUpdater {
    ...
    void Update() {
        // Shoot a ray from the wand
        Ray ray = new Ray(transform.position, transform.TransformDirection(Vector3.forward));
        RaycastHit hit;

        // Get the first collider that was hit by the ray
        wandHit = Physics.Raycast(ray, out hit, 100, wandLayerMask);
        if (wandHit) { // The wand is pointed at a collider
            // Send a message to the hit object telling it that the wand is hovering over it
            hit.collider.gameObject.SendMessage("OnWandOver", SendMessageOptions.DontRequireReceiver);

            // If the laser button has just been pressed, tell the hit object
            if (CAVE2Manager.GetButtonDown(wandID,CAVE2Manager.Button.Button3)) {
                hit.collider.gameObject.SendMessage("OnWandButtonDown", laserButton, SendMessageOptions.DontRequireReceiver);
            }
        }
    }
    ...
}

public class TriggerScript : MonoBehaviour {
    ...
    void OnWandButtonDown(CAVE2Manager.Button button)
    {
        if( !triggered && panoramaHider.nextPanorama == -1 )
        {
#if USING_GETREAL3D
            // used to sync trigger across cluster
            // #if define used for cross platform purposes (getReal3D is a Windows only library)
            getReal3D.RpcManager.call("TriggerMemoryEvent");
#else
            // used for non-CAVE cases
            TriggerMemoryEvent ();
#endif
        }
    }
    ...
}
```

Fig. 6. C# code example of Wand pointing and triggering an object on multiple platforms.

3.3 The Web-Based Version

In the web-based version of the project, the navigation was adapted to be used with a game controller or set of standard navigation keys typically used for the web-based games (A/D – rotate left/right. W – Move forward. S – Move backward. R – Menu. Mouse– Point on the objects. Click - Trigger objects). The participant had to navigate to each interactive entry point using navigation keys. The user explores the VRE using the keyboard to move and the mouse for direct manipulation to point and click on objects.

3.4 Mobile Version

For the mobile version of the project, we optimized all the media of elements to achieve decent frame-rate performance. 3D spatial sound effects were converted to 2 channel stereo. The textures were optimized from 4 K resolution in the CAVE version to 1K resolution. Collision triggers were enlarged to ensure smooth collision detection and faster interaction. The navigation interaction was converted to use touch interface of the iPad. The user has to swipe the environment left and right to turn in the desired direction and move forward or backward by swiping up or down. The user can also rotate the camera by tilting the iPad up or down. Instead of wand or controller buttons, the iPad utilized double tap to click on the objects and single tap to activate laser pointer.

Fig. 7. Interaction with the VR environment running on the personal computer using the Xbox 360 controller. By manipulation a joystick on the controller, the participant can navigate and explore the virtual environment.

4 Discussion

We assessed the responses of participants and navigators to the interaction with VRE during project performances, exhibitions, panels and Q&A sessions following the events and demonstrations of the CAVE2, computer and web-based versions of the project. Participants were asked about any difficulties they experienced while navigating through the environment and problems encountered during the interaction. Overall, participant's responses were largely positive regarding the environment, as well as the interactions performed. We also received positive feedback from the performers and the audience about accuracy and time required to learn a navigation system controls. The majority of participants described the project as immersive and provocative, and expressed an interest in exploring the project in more depth and on different platforms.

Acknowledgments. The authors wish to thank Electronic Visualization Lab (EVL) at the University of Illinois at Chicago, the UIC School of Design, Temple University, the Electronic Literature Organization, and the Norwegian Research Council. Thanks to Lance Long for research engineering support, to Mark Partridge for sound design, voice artists Richard Garella, Jeffrey Cousar, Laurel Katz, Darin Dunston, production assistant Mark Baratta and performance artist Mark Jeffrey. Dr. Jeffrey Murer of St. Andrews University, Scotland also contributed as a consultant on the project. The project is based on interviews of American soldiers conducted by political scientist, Dr. John Tsukayama. Special thanks to all visitors who participated in the exhibitions and discussions.

References

1. Febretti, A., Nishimoto, A., Thigpen, T., Talandis, J., Long, L., Pirtle, J.D., Peterka, T., Verlo, A., Brown, M., Plepys, D., Sandin, D., Renambot, L., Johnson, A., Leigh, J.: CAVE2: a hybrid reality environment for immersive simulation and information analysis. In: Proceedings of SPIE 8649, The Engineering Reality of Virtual Reality 2013, p. 864903 (2013)
2. Tsukayama, J.: By any means necessary: an interpretive phenomenological analysis study of post 9/11 American abusive violence in Iraq. Ph.D. dissertation, University of St Andrews, St Andrews, UK (2014)
3. Grau, O.: Virtual Art, From Illusion to Immersion. Leonardo Book Series. MIT Press, Cambridge (2004)
4. Preddy, S.M. Nance, R.E.: Key requirements for CAVE simulations. In: Proceedings of the 34th Conference on Winter Simulation: Exploring New Frontiers, San Diego, pp. 127–135 (2002)
5. Tsoupikova, D., Coover, R., Rettberg, S., Nishimoto, A.: Hearts and minds: the interrogations project. In: Proceedings of the IEEE VIS Arts Program (VISAP), Paris, France (2014)
6. Tsoupikova, D., Rettberg, S., Coover, R., Nishimoto, A.: The battle for hearts and minds: interrogation and torture in the age of war. In: Proceedings of SIGGRAPH 2015 ACM SIGGRAPH 2015 Posters, article no. 12. ACM, New York (2015)
7. Omicron. http://github.com/uic-evl/omicron. Accessed 8 Feb 2016
8. Mechdyne Corporation, getReal3D. http://www.mechdyne.com/getreal3d.aspx. Accessed 8 Feb 2016
9. Sutcliffe, A., Gault, B., Fernando, T., Tan, K.: Investigating interaction in CAVE virtual environments. ACM Trans. Comput. Hum. Interact. **13**(2), 235–267 (2006)
10. Muhanna, M.: Virtual reality and the CAVE: taxonomy, interaction challenges and research directions. J. King Saud Univ. Comput. Inf. Sci. **27**(3), 344–361 (2015)
11. Sutcliffe, A.G., Kaur, K.D.: Evaluating the usability of virtual reality user interfaces. Behav. Inf. Technol. **19**(6), 415–426 (2000)
12. Bowman, D.A., Johnson, D.B., Hodges, L.F.: Testbed evaluation of virtual environments interaction techniques. In: Proceedings of Virtual Reality Software Technology (VRST) 1999, pp. 26–33. ACM Press, New York (1999)
13. Poupyrev, I., Ichikawa, T.: Manipulating objects in virtual worlds: categorization and empirical evaluation of interaction techniques. J. Vis. Lang. Comput. **10**(1), 19–35 (1999)
14. Darken, R.P., Sibert, J.L.: Wayfinding strategies and behaviors in large virtual worlds. In: Tauber, M., Bellotti, V., Jeffries, R., MaCkinlay, J.D., Nielsen, J. (eds.) Human Factors in Computing Systems CHI 1996 Conference Proceedings (Vancouver BC), pp. 142–149. ACM Press, New York (1996)
15. Vinson, N.G.: Design guidelines for landmarks to support navigation in virtual environments. In: Human Factors in Computing Systems CHI 1999 Conference Proceedings, Pittsburgh PA (1999)
16. Usoh M., Arthur K., Whitton MC., Bastos R., Steed A., Slater M., et al. Walking > walking-in-place > flying, in virtual environments. In: Proceedings of the 26th Annual Conference on Computer-Graphics and Interactive Techniques, pp. 359–364. ACM Press, Addison-Wesley Publishing Co. (1999)
17. Hauber, J., Billinghurst, M., Regenbrecht, H.: Tangible teleconferencing. In: Masoodian, M., Jones, S., Rogers, B. (eds.) APCHI 2004. LNCS, vol. 3101, pp. 143–152. Springer, Heidelberg (2004)

18. Bourdot, P., Touraine D.: Polyvalent display framework to control virtual navigations by 6DOF tracking. In: Proceedings of the IEEE Virtual Reality 2002 (VR 2002), pp. 277–278, 24–28 Mar 2002
19. Schneiderman, B.: Direct manipulation: a step beyond programming languages. IEEE Comput. **16**(8), 57–69 (1983)
20. Schneiderman, B., Plaisant, C., Cohen, M., Jacobs, S.: Designing the User Interface: Strategies for Effective Human-Computer Interaction, 5th edn. Addison Wesley, Boston (2009)

Dynamic-Interaction UI/UX Design for the AREIS

Hye Sun Park[✉], Ho Won Kim, and Chang Joon Park

Computer Graphics Research Section,
ETRI - Electronics and Telecommunications Research Institute, Daejeon, Korea
hspark78@etri.re.kr

Abstract. This paper introduces the dynamic interaction UI/UX design of the AREIS (augmented realistic experience information system) used for intelligent and convenient shopping. The proposed system provides a virtual fitting service that enables a user to try on outfits on the screen without actually wear it. The system uses a 3D avatar model which moves following after the user's movement without ruining the user's physical features such as height and waist measurement. In this paper, we design a dynamic-interaction between user and system for an intuitive and familiar interface development. For this, the proposed system firstly observes a user's behavior, next the system recognizes user's meaningful action. Thereafter, the system estimates intend of the user using a proposed interaction model. Through user-study, the proposed interaction-design enhances an understanding of user's both intention and inclination, also improves the usability including ease-of-use. The system demonstrates the benefit of providing user-adaptive information through the proposed dynamic UI/UX design.

Keywords: Dynamic interaction · AR (augmented reality) · AREIS (augmented realistic experience information system) · Virtual clothing fitting service · 3D avatar model · Interaction model · Interaction-design · User-adaptive information · User-study

1 Introduction

With advances in three-dimensional (3D) content and user interface (UI) technologies, the number of information services with which users can experience virtual 3D objects and scenes are constantly growing [1–3]. In this paper, we refer to this type of services as the realistic experience service. To successfully provide realistic experience to users, the service should be well designed in terms of high user satisfaction, ease of use, and good. Therefore, it is important to apply user-centered UI/UX design principles when developing realistic experience services [4, 5]. Among such realistic experience services, we apply a virtual fitting service as shown in Fig. 1. This service is enable to check size and style by using the intelligent mirror looks like wearing real clothes.

The proposed dynamic interaction refers to interactions that require the efforts of a system for the human, this concept is the beyond the concept of human-centered interaction, in this paper. In the dialogue between human and human, it should realize smooth communication, under the following consideration; both situation and the state of the partner. Likewise, if the information system that supports a number of activities of the

© Springer International Publishing Switzerland 2016
M. Kurosu (Ed.): HCI 2016, Part II, LNCS 9732, pp. 412–418, 2016.
DOI: 10.1007/978-3-319-39516-6_39

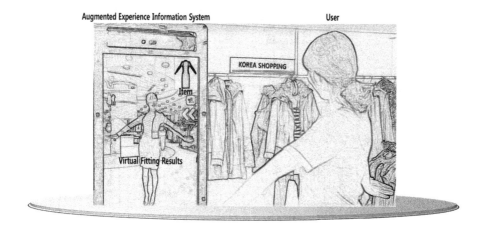

Fig. 1. An example of the AREIS applied to shopping

person, also can estimate the user-conditions such as the thought and the situation then it will be more interaction better fit the needs of the user [1–3]. Therefore, out of the conventional command-response model, the dynamic inter-action model, which provides an appropriate and effective information to the user, by inducing the user's interest, and estimating the psychological state of the user, is required.

This paper proposes an intelligent system with focus on these proactive interaction. In particular, a lot of UI/UX researches based on a visual cue has recently been conducted [4–12]. In this paper, it presents a way not only provide more friendly but also enhance user's interest for UI/UX using the visual cue for an augmented reality experience service. Thus, this paper presents an intelligent information system both which induces the user's interest based on a visual cue, which is suitable on an augmented reality experience service, and which provides into intuitive UI/UX [13–17].

2 The Proposed System: AREIS

The proposed AREIS consists of four stages: user information processing module, experience item processing module, interactive UI processing module, and experience contents service module. The I/O flowchart of the proposed system is presented in Fig. 2. Once a user starts controlling, the system continuously observes, recognizes meaningful actions among user's behaviors and estimates user's intention. Simultaneously, the system is displaying virtual fitting results through mirror-type kiosk, the fitting results show dressed like a real effect in accordance with the user's point of view.

2.1 User Information Processing Module

This module generates a user avatar matching the measured user's body, and tracks the user's motion using Kinect sensor data, webcam data and calibration data. In addition, this module extracts the user features such as gender, age, body and style.

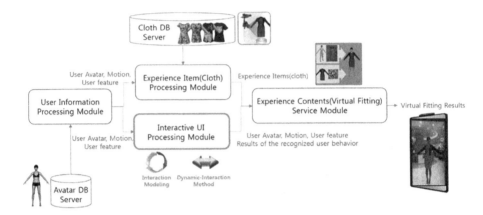

Fig. 2. The I/O flowchart of the AREIS

2.2 Experience Item Processing Module

This module creates 3D geometry data based on the sensor and calibration data, and generates digital experience items with the 3D geometry acquired. Here, the digital experience items mean objects that you can experience 3D content such as clothes, bags.

2.3 Interactive UI Processing Module

With this module as a core module, we propose to interaction modeling based a dynamic-interaction method. To interface interactively, this module observes user's behavior, recognizes user's action, and estimates user's intention. This module has the following advantages:

- This module is adaptively providing users into intelligent and convenient information with a dynamic interaction method. This method performs at the same time both reactive interaction and proactive interaction, between the user and the system. Through this function, users can interact with the system in an easier and more convenient way.
- This module increases both the user's interest and understanding of the system operation, by providing service information relevant to the user's experience level. For instance, the module could estimate the user's level of understanding and interest in the serviced information, and provide customized service to each user based on this information.

This module helps users to easily control the system using interactive gestures that are defined using gesture classification and clustering technology based on user study.

2.4 Experience Contents Service Module

This module presents visual content on the screen including the user's avatar and the experience item, according to the measured user's body, motion, and recognized gestures. This module also visualizes the dynamic UI/UX design based on the user characteristics, and they are displayed on a mirror type display.

3 Dynamic-Interaction UI/UX Design

To develop an intuitive and familiar interface, we design a dynamic-interaction between user and system. In this paper, we propose an idea of interaction modeling, which can be represented by the following scheme:

$$Interaction\ Modeling = Observation \oplus Recognition \oplus Estimation, \tag{1}$$

where $\oplus$ implies dynamic interactions among the functional modules. That is, we define an intelligent information system with observation, recognition, and estimation capabilities and regard these three functions as fundamental submodules to realize dynamic interactions between the user and the system.

By integrating observation, recognition, and estimation, various dynamic information flows are formed. In our model, reasoning implies the function which dynamically controls such flows of information. With the proposed interaction modeling, the system provides information to identify the user's actions and intentions. At this time, the system adaptively performs reactive or proactive interaction based on user's reaction of the provided information. Figure 3 shows the proposed dynamic-interaction between human and information system.

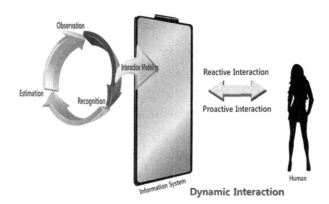

Fig. 3. Dynamic-interaction between human and information system

3.1 AR Based 3D-Experience Service

To implement the proposed intuitive and familiar interface with the dynamic-interaction model, the proposed AREIS performs proactive interactions of the 3 types;

1. In order to attract customers for shopping, the proposed system observes both position and direction of the customer's face, using the extracted user information from

images captured by Kinect and DSLR sensors. Thereafter, the system induces the customer to the system based on a visual cue approach.

2. To measure the customer's body size, the system induces the customer to the measuring position based on a visual cue approach.
3. To control the system using the customer's hand, the system induces the customer's hand to the button on the display based on a visual cue approach.

To increase the effectiveness of the more visual guidance, we were used UI-agent in these three proactive interactions. Figure 4 shows these three proactive interactions. For the experiments, we was implemented using character in game system by one application[1]. For shopping not games, this technology can be incorporated into a suitable UI-agent according to the mood of the shopping center in the shopping center.

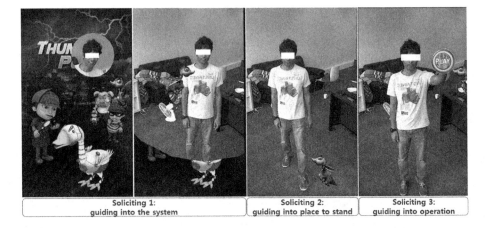

| Soliciting 1: guiding into the system | Soliciting 2: guiding into place to stand | Soliciting 3: guiding into operation |

Fig. 4. Proactive interactions of the 3 types using UI agent based on visual affordance

3.2 Experimental Environment and Analysis Results

For the AREIS, the hardware system setup is formed to provide virtual mirror style visualization. The proposed system consists of a 70-inch full HD display combined with the mirror (mirror reflection: 83 %, the panel transmission: 33 %). The screen shows the graphics generated by a desktop PC (personal computer) running software developed for the AR based 3D-experience service. The test bed is equipped with three imaging sensors: a web cam, a DSLR and a Microsoft Kinect depth sensing camera. The Microsoft Kinect sensor is the main imaging device that is used for tracking users' motion and gesture recognition. While the Kinect sensor also has a RGB color camera, the resolution of the video stream has low quality to fit in a portrait oriented screen. To use higher resolution image as a video background on the screen, the web cam and DSLR can be

---

[1] We deeply appreciate Dr. Gun Lee and Prof. Mark Billinghurst also all participants in HIT(human interface technology) Lab., University of Canterbury, New Zealand. Some of this study was developed in collaboration with HIT LAB.

optionally used with proper calibration between the imaging sensors. We planned to develop the proposed system on the PC platform running Microsoft Windows 7 operating system, using the Unity 3D v4.5 game engine. The main visualization software is developed as a Unity 3D project, while its integration with the gesture interaction module is held through developing a plug-in for Unity. The plug-in is developed using Visual Studio C++ 2010 with Microsoft Kinect SDK v1.7. As of the depth sensing camera, we use Kinect for Windows (v1) which provides 1080×1920 resolutions of RGB image stream, as well as 640×480 resolutions of depth image stream.

Using an user-study, user the results of the satisfaction analysis based on user's expressions and subjective questionnaire ware as follows; the proposed dynamic interaction model enhances an understanding of user's both intention and inclination, also improves the usability including ease-of-use.

4 Conclusions

This paper describes the idea and goal of interaction between human and intelligent information system for a realistic experience service. The overall results show that the proposed user interface concept of using software UI agents as visual affordance cues for gesture interaction with large screen displays is feasible, and it could be applied to public information displays that need to more engage with potential users. The results from the user study suggest using UI agents as visual guides for gesture based interfaces could be beneficial to emotional side of the user experience, yet needs careful consideration of the type of application and the design of the virtual character used as a UI agent.

Acknowledgment. This work was supported by Institute for Information & communications Technology Promotion (IITP) grant funded by the Korea government (MSIP) (No. I5501-15-1016, Instant 3D object based Join & Joy content technology supporting simultaneous participation of users in remote places and enabling realistic experience).

References

1. Park, H.S., et al.: Gaze mirroring-based intelligent information system for making user's latent interest. J. Intell. Inf. Syst. **16**(3), 37–54 (2010)
2. Jacobs, T.J.: On unconscious communications and covert enactments: some reflections on their role in the analytic situation. Psychoanal. Inq. **21**, 4–23 (2001)
3. Hirayama, T., et al.: Estimates of user interest using timing structures between proactive content-display updates and eye movements. IEICE Trans. Inf. Syst. **E93-D**(6), 1470–1478 (2010)
4. Hartson, R.: Cognitive, physical, sensory, and functional affordances in interaction design. Behav. Inf. Technol. **22**(5) 315–339 (2003)
5. Webb, A., et al.: Choreographic buttons: promoting social interaction through human movement and clear affordances. In: Proceedings of the 14th Annual ACM international conference on Multimedia, pp. 451–460 (2006)

6. Sodhi, R., et al.: LightGuide: projected visualizations for hand movement guidance. In: Proceedings of the SIGCHI Conference on Human Factors in Computing Systems, pp. 179–188. ACM, New York (2012)

7. White, S., et al.: Visual hints for tangible gestures in augmented reality. In: Proceedings of the 6th IEEE and ACM International Symposium on Mixed and Augmented Reality, vol. 14. IEEE Computer Society, Washington, DC (2007). doi:10.1109/ISMAR.2007.4538824

8. Anderson, F., et al.: YouMove: enhancing movement training with an augmented reality mirror. In: Proceedings of the 26th Annual ACM Symposium on User Interface Software and Technology, pp. 311–320. ACM, New York

9. Laurel, B.: Interface agents: metaphor with characters (chap. 12). In: Friedman, B. (ed.) Human Values and the Design of Computer Technology, pp. 207–219 (1990)

10. Lieberman, H., Selker, T.: Agents for the user interface. In: Handbook of Agent Technology (2003)

11. Maes, P.: Artificial life meets entertainment: lifelike autonomous agents. Commun. ACM **38**(11), 108–114 (1995)

12. Lester, J.C., et al.: The persona effect: affective impact of animated pedagogical agents. In: Proceedings of the ACM SIGCHI Conference on Human Factors in Computing Systems, pp. 359–366 (1997)

13. Anderson, F., et al.: YouMove: enhancing movement training with an augmented reality mirror. In: ACM User Interface Software and Technology (UIST), pp. 8–11 (2013)

14. Lee, G.A., et al.: User defined gestures for augmented virtual mirrors: a guessability study. In: Proceedings of the 33rd Annual ACM Conference Extended Abstracts on Human Factors in Computing Systems (CHI EA 2015), pp. 959–964 (2015)

15. Piumsomboon, T., Clark, A., Billinghurst, M., Cockburn, A.: User-defined gestures for augmented reality. In: Kotzé, P., Marsden, G., Lindgaard, G., Wesson, J., Winckler, M. (eds.) INTERACT 2013, Part II. LNCS, vol. 8118, pp. 282–299. Springer, Heidelberg (2013)

16. Matsuyama, T.: Cooperative distributed vision: dynamic integration of visual perception, action, and communication. In: Förstner, W., Buhmann, J.M., Faber, A., Faber, P. (eds.) Mustererkennung 1999. Informatik aktuell, pp. 138–151. Springer, Heidelberg (1999). ISBN 978-3-642-60243-6

17. Park, H.S., et al.: In-Vehicle AR-HUD System to Provide Driving-Safety Information. J. ETRI **35**(6), 1038–1047 (2013)

Development of Multiple Device Collaboration System Using Built-in Camera Image

Kazuki Tada[✉] and Jiro Tanaka

University of Tsukuba, Tsukuba, Japan
{kazuki,jiro}@iplab.cs.tsukuba.ac.jp

Abstract. In this paper, we introduce a multi-device collaboration system using the image obtained from the built-in camera. Users can use applications that utilize multiple devices in cooperation without needing special devices such as a touch panel sensor. Our system enables accurate position tracking of a smartphone any screen by obtaining an image from the device's front camera to recognize the device and measure the device's position by template matching [1]. In many multi-device collaboration approaches, it was necessary to overlap the screens. However, our proposed method is capable of multi-device collaboration without overlapping the screens of the devices, and it can be applied using a wide range of off-screens. We implemented some of the applications using this technique. In addition, we showed the usefulness of this approach by evaluation experiments.

Keywords: Multiple device · Image processing · Image recognition · Smartphone · Template matching

1 Introduction

Recently, due to the spread of smartphones and tablet devices, people have come to possess multiple devices. Multi-device collaboration systems permit users to connect many different devices and share the content among them. Such systems are beneficial in improving work efficiency.

Various techniques that recognize different devices collaborating with each other have been proposed. For example, Yatani et al. and Kamo et al. proposed methods to recognize other devices by capturing mobile devices equipped with a marker or infrared LED by room camera [1,2]. Furthermore, a method of overlaying the mobile devices with a conductive material on the touch screen device has been proposed [3]. In this method, since the touch point occurs on the touch screen, the positional relationship between collaborating devices can be determined.

However, in these techniques, special tools (e.g. a touch screen and infrared LED) are required for the multi-device collaboration. In this study, we have implemented a new multi-device collaboration method using a differential image obtained from the device's built-in camera. This approach uses only cameras mounted on the device to determine the positional relationship between multiple devices and implement various cooperative operations.

© Springer International Publishing Switzerland 2016
M. Kurosu (Ed.): HCI 2016, Part II, LNCS 9732, pp. 419–427, 2016.
DOI: 10.1007/978-3-319-39516-6_40

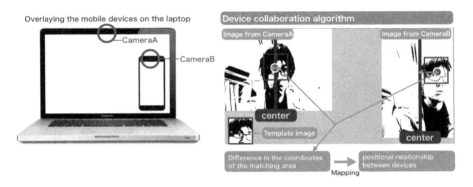

Fig. 1. Structure of device collaboration with built-in camera

2   Related Work

2.1   Multi-device Collaboration with Special Devices or Sensors

Multi-device collaboration methods have been proposed for a long time, many of which have used a sensor. Yatani et al. and Kamo et al. proposed methods to recognize other devices by capturing mobile devices equipped with a marker or infrared LED by room camera [1,2].

Swindells et al. [4] explored a device collaboration system using a digital pen. Cuypers et al. [5] proposed a method to determine the position of a mobile phone by detecting the flashlight that is mounted on it.

Liu et al. and Xu et al. have proposed a system to recognize the position information of the devices by using an acceleration sensor or magnetic sensor mounted on a smartphone and comparing the sensor value between the devices [6,7].

In these techniques, special tools (e.g. an acceleration sensor, magnetic sensor, and infrared LED) are required for multi-device collaboration. Moreover, these techniques cannot determine the position of the collaborating devices.

2.2   Multi-device Collaboration with Touch Screen

For the collaboration of the smartphone and surface, there are many proposed methods that utilize the characteristics of the touch screen. Hahne et al. [3] proposed a method of overlaying the mobile devices with a conductive material on the touch screen device. In this method, since the touch point occurs on the touch screen, the positional relationship between collaborating devices can be determined.

Strohmeier and Yasumoto et al. explored interaction scenarios based on touch events between devices [8,9]. They use the capacitive screen of a tablet computer to track the position of the phones touching it by using 'hand down' capacitance. This method was used by Chan et al. [10] for detecting tangible objects on displays.

2.3 Multi-device Collaboration with Device's Camera

Several multi-device collaboration methods using a camera have been proposed. Chan et al., Cuypers et al., and Rohs et al. proposed a method for device collaboration by reading a special pattern projected onto the display by the phone's camera [11–13].

THAW [14] is a method to overlap the mobile device to the computer screen. By analyzing the information obtained from the back camera of the mobile device, we can determine the positional relationship between collaborating devices. With a multi-device collaboration method using a camera, there is no need to attach extra equipment, such as additional sensors, to the smartphone.

However, it is necessary to project a special pattern on one of the displays or overlap the devices. In contrast, our proposed method is capable of collaboration without overlapping the screens of the devices, and it can be applied using a wide range of off-screens.

3 System Design

Our method uses an image obtained from the device's built-in camera to recognize the device and measure the device's position by template matching. For example, the collaboration between a personal computer and a smartphone is shown in Fig. 1 (left side). In this case, images of the same target are obtained with each of the cameras. A template is dynamically created to form part of the image of one camera. Next, our system tries to match this template image with images from the other camera. From the difference in the coordinates of the matching area, it calculates the positional relationship between the devices, as shown in Fig. 1 (right side).

3.1 System Flow

In this section, the operation of the system in this method will be described using a case where a user is linking a smartphone and laptop computer.

When an application that implements the proposed method is started on each device, the front camera becomes active to take the image. The image taken is sent to the server after the normalization and the binarization processing of the brightness. The server creates a template from the image transmitted from each device and attempts to match the image sent from the other devices. If the threshold of the match exceeds a prescribed value, it is determined that these two devices are in the coordination state (overlapping state), and calculates the difference between the matching position. Thereafter, the smartphone receives a signal from the server side. Then, the user performs calibration to adjust the relative position of the devices. Calibration is completed by performing a tap when the combined smartphone is in the lower right and upper left laptop. We show the system flow in Fig. 2.

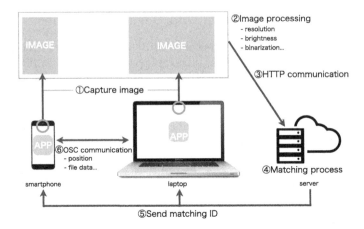

Fig. 2. System flow

4   Implementation

For the implementation, we used an iPhone 5 and 13-inch Macbook Air. The software was developed using C++ (with openFrameworks). For data communications between devices, we used HTTP for image processing for template matching and OSC (open sound control) for send device coordinates. In addition, we used the SSD (sum of squared difference) method as the template matching algorithm.

Hereinafter, by using images obtained from two cameras, we describe the methods to calculate the positional relationship between devices.

4.1   Normalization of Resolution

To correctly understand the positional relationship between the images taken from multiple devices, the resolution of each camera has to be constant (Fig. 3(a)). The adjustment of the resolution will be processed in accordance with the smallest side.

4.2   Normalization of Brightness

To correct the brightness of each camera, the normalized process luminance value has to be determined (Fig. 3(b)). The normalization is calculated based on the maximum brightness of the image obtained from a plurality of cameras. Furthermore, it is subjected to gamma correction, thereby suppressing the variation in brightness.

4.3   Binarization

To facilitate the template matching, the image obtained from the camera is binarized. The binarization uses the single manual threshold method and can adjust the threshold value to suit the environment in which the coordination is manually performed (Fig. 3(c)).

4.4 Making Template Image Dynamically

To generate the template image used for template matching, part of the video from one camera is extracted (Fig. 3(d)). The template image that shows the center of the object moving to the camera is automatically selected. For example, when the user is coordinating a laptop and smartphone, it is often the face of the person sitting in front of the laptop that is templated.

4.5 Matching Template Image with Other Images

Based on the template image generated using the previous technique, template matching of the image obtained from each camera is performed. When the matching is performed, the positional relationship between devices is calculated using the difference in the matching area coordinates of the image obtained from the camera (Fig. 1 left-side). The positional relationship is calculated by using the values of the calibration to be performed before collaboration and correction.

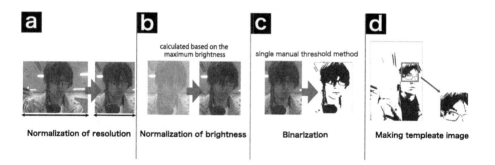

Fig. 3. Image processing algorithm

5 Applications

5.1 Translation Application

Figure 4 (left side) shows an example of using the translation application. When holding the smartphone over an English word on the computer screen, the translation appears on the smartphone. By using our method, without any special devices in addition to the collaborating devices, it is possible to implement these applications. By using such an application method, in addition to the translation application, it is also possible to make applications for, e.g. browsing for more detailed information.

5.2 Sub Display

Figure 4 (right side) shows an operational example of a screen sharing application using device collaboration with our method. In this application, it is possible to move the window on the screen of the personal computer to the smartphone. With conventional methods, the smartphone has to be superimposed on the screen of the personal computer. By using our method, without reducing the display area by covering the screen of the personal computer, it is easily possible to use another device as an extended display.

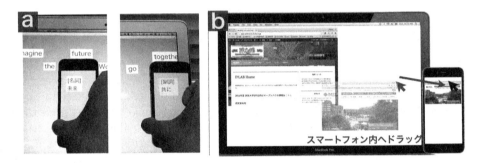

Fig. 4. (a) Example of translation (English to Japanese) application, (b) Example of screen sharing application.

6   Experiment

We implemented the techniques described in the previous section and performed experiments in the two environments (laptop-smartphone and tablet-smartphone).

6.1 Experiment Outline

We measured the recognition speed of the device and the deviation of the detected position. The devices used in the experiments are shown in Table 1. During this experiment, the brightness of the room was about 160 lux. In the experiments, the distance between the smartphone and laptop screen was set to zero.

Table 1. Device list

Device name	Width	Height
Macbook Air (13 in.)	325 mm	227 mm
iPhone 5	58.6 mm	123.8 mm
Iconia tab A500-10S	260 mm	177 mm

Table 2. Result of average recognition speed

	Macbook air	Iconia tab A500-10S
iPhone 5	0.5 s	0.6 s

Table 3. Result of average deviation of detected position

	Macbook air	Iconia tab A500-10S
iPhone 5	18.1 mm (90.5 px) and 14.6 mm (73 px)	10.4 mm (62.4 px) and 8.2 mm (49.2 px)

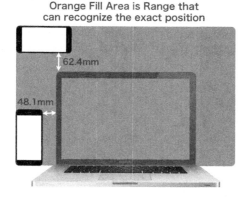

Fig. 5. Available range to measure device's exact position

Tables 2 and 3 show a summary of the combination of the devices and the measurement results. The experimental results revealed that it is possible to accurately perform collaboration, as shown in the next section.

In addition, our method can be used with a wide off-screen range, as shown in Fig. 5. When the device is within this range, it is possible to accurately measure the device's position (measurement error < 25 mm).

6.2   Considerations

The results of the experiment show that the tracking speed was at a practical level. However, the accuracy of the detected position has become inferior to that of previous studies. We think the cause is fluctuation in the brightness of the outside light. Therefore, we think these external factors should be compensated by the image processing.

This detection error is related to the size of the desktop icons. Therefore, our method can be sufficiently applied to applications requiring a rough location and orientation. For example, sub-display applications, such as those mentioned in Sect. 5.2, can be mentioned.

The most characteristic feature of this approach is that it can also cooperate in the off-screen. Therefore, we need to think of an example application that takes advantage of this feature.

7 Conclusion

In this paper, we showed a multi-device collaboration system using an image obtained from a built-in camera. This method is different from the existing approaches in that it does not require a special device for collaboration. We used the example of collaboration of a personal computer and smartphone and studied the collaboration accuracy. In future work, we are planning to improve the performance so that it can be adapted to big screens, such as table-top devices. Moreover, we are planning to perform a user study of applications using our technique.

References

1. Hiroki, K., Sugimoto, M., Yatani, K., Tamura, K., Hashizume, H.: Toss-it: intuitive information transfer techniques for mobile devices. In: Proceedings of the SIGCHI Conference on Human Factors in Computing Systems, CHI 2005, pp. 1881–1884 (2005)
2. Kamo, H., Tanaka, J.: Interlocked surfaces: a dynamic multi-device collaboration system. In: The 15th International Conference on Human-Computer Interaction, HCII 2013, pp. 317–325 (2013)
3. Elstner, S., Hahne, U., Schild, J., Alexa, M.: Multi-touch focus+context sketch-based interaction. In: Proceedings of the 6th Eurographics Symposiumn Sketch-Based Interfaces and Modeling, SMIB 2009, pp. 77–83 (2009)
4. Dill, J.C., Swindells, C., Inkpen, K.M., Tory, M.: That one there! pointing to establish device identity. In: Proceedings of the 15th Annual ACM symposium on User Interface Software and Technology, UIST 2002, pp. 151–160 (2002)
5. Olwal, A., Lightsense: enabling spatially aware handheld interaction devices. In: Proceedings of the 5th IEEE and ACM International Symposium on Mixed and Augmented Reality, ISMAR 2006, pp. 119–122 (2006)
6. Sun, S.W., Cheng, W.H., Liu, K.W., Lin, I.P., Hsu, X.S.C.: G-spacing: a gyro sensor based relative 3d space positioning scheme. In: Proceeding of ACM SIGGRAPH 2015 Posters, SIGGRAPH 2015, Article No. 35 (2015)
7. Momeni, A., Xu, D., Brockmeyer, E.: Magpad: a near surface augmented reading system for physical paper and smartphone coupling. In: Proceedings of the 28th Annual ACM Symposium on User Interface Software and Technology, UIST 2015, pp. 103–104 (2015)
8. Strohmeier, P.: Displaypointers- seamless cross-device interactions. In: Proceedings of the 12th International Conference on Advances in Computer Entertainment Technology, ACE 2015, pp. 86–93 (2015)
9. Yasumoto, M., Teraoka, T.: Vistouch: dynamic three-dimensional connection between multiple mobile devices. In: Proceedings of the 6th Augmented Human International Conference, AH 2015, pp. 89–92 (2015)

10. Roudaut, A., Chan, L., Muller, S., Baudisch, P.: Capstones and zebrawidgets: sensing stacks of building blocks, dials and sliders on capacitive touch screens. In: Proceedings of the SIGCHI Conference on Human Factors in Computing Systems, CHI 2012, pp. 2189–2192 (2012)
11. Chan, L.W., Wu, H.T., Kao, H.S., Ko, J.C., Lin, H.R., Chen, M.Y., Hsu, J., Hung, Y.P.: Enabling beyond-surface interactions for interactive surface with an invisible projection. In: Proceedings of the 23th Annual ACM Symposium on User Interface Software and Technology, UIST 2010, pp. 263–272 (2010)
12. Vanaken, C., Reeth, F.V., Cuypers, T., Francken, Y., Bekaert, P.: Smartphone localization on interactive surfaces using the built-in camera. In: Proceedings of the IEEE International Workshop on Project-Camera Systems, Procam 2009, pp. 61–68 (2009)
13. Raubal, M., Essl, G., Rohs, M., Schoning, H., Kruger, A.: Map navigation with mobile devices: virtual versus physical movement with and without visual context. In: Proceedings of the 9th International Conference on Multimodal Interfaces, ICMI 2007, pp. 146–153 (2007)
14. Heibeck, E., Maes, P., Leigh, S., Schoessler, P., Ishii, H.: Tangible interaction with see-through augmentation for smartphones on computer screens. In: Proceedings of the 27th Annual ACM Symposium on User Interface Software and Technology, UIST 2014, pp. 55–56 (2014)

Author Index

Printed in the United States
By Bookmasters